WORLD TAPESTRIES

An Anthology of Global Literature

WORLD TAPESTRIES

An Anthology of Global Literature

Globe
Fearon

Upper Saddle River,
New Jersey

ESL Consultant: Jacqueline Kiraithe-Córdova, Ph.D.,
    Coordinator of Spanish and TESOL Areas
    Department of Foreign Languages and Literatures
    California State University at Fullerton

Student Reviewers: Special thanks to the students of Martha Jewell's English class at
    Bowsher High School, Toledo, Ohio for their valuable comments on the selections
    in this anthology.

Director of Editorial and Marketing, Secondary Supplementary: Nancy Surridge

Project Editor: Amy Jolin

Editors: Karen Bernhaut, Lynn Kloss, Carol Schneider

Editorial Support: Stephanie Cahill, Keisha Carter, Ann Clarkson, Elena Petron

Editorial Assistants: Brian Hawkes, Kathleen Kennedy

Editorial Development: McCormick Associates, Forest Hills, New York

Market Manager: Rhonda Anderson

Production Director: Kurt Scherwatzky

Art Direction: Joan Jacobus

Production Editor: Rosann Bar

Manufacturing Buyer: Tara Felitto

Electronic Page Production Supervisor: José López

Interior Design and Electronic Page Production: Paradigm Design, New York

Art Insert: Joan Jacobus

Photo Research: Jenifer Hixon

Production Assistant: Heather Roake

Cover: BB&K Design Inc.

Cover Illustration: John Jinks

Printed in the United States of America
  5 6 7 8 9 10   04 03 02 01

ISBN: 0-8359-1813-0

B62

"Bouki Rents a Horse" is from *The Piece of Fire and Other Haitian Tales*. Copyright © 1964
by Harold Courlander. Reprinted by permission of the Estate of Harold Courlander.

The reviewers and contributors on this page gave their advice and expertise throughout the development of this program. We are very grateful for their input.

CONSULTANTS

TEACHER REVIEWERS

CONTENTS

CHAPTER 2 MIDDLE EAST 79

UNIT 2 Asia, Australia, and the Pacific Islands   114

CHAPTER 3 EAST ASIA   118

UNIT
4 The Americas   **304**

CHAPTER 8 LATIN AMERICA   **308**

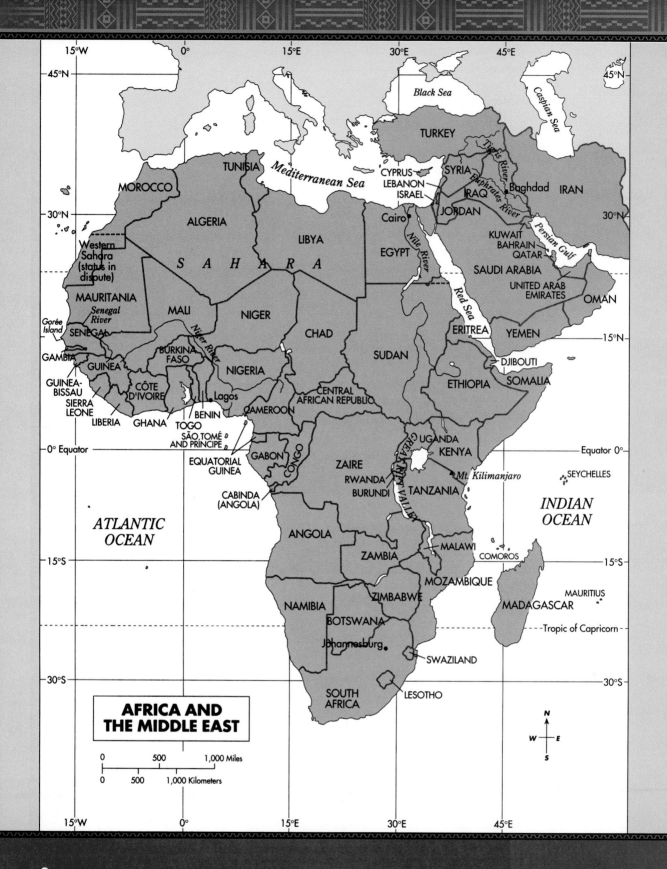

AFRICA AND THE MIDDLE EAST

45°N

15°W 0° 15°E 30°E 45°E

Black Sea

Caspian Sea

TURKEY

Mediterranean Sea

CYPRUS
LEBANON
ISRAEL

SYRIA
Tigris River
Euphrates River
Baghdad
IRAN

IRAQ

TUNISIA

MOROCCO

30°N

JORDAN

Cairo

ALGERIA

LIBYA

EGYPT

KUWAIT
BAHRAIN
QATAR

Persian Gulf

Western
Sahara
(status in
dispute)

S A H A R A

SAUDI ARABIA

UNITED ARAB
EMIRATES

OMAN

MAURITANIA

Senegal
River

MALI

NIGER

Red Sea

ERITREA

YEMEN

15°N

Gorée
Island

SENEGAL

Niger River

CHAD

SUDAN

DJIBOUTI

GAMBIA

BURKINA
FASO

SOMALIA

GUINEA

NIGERIA

GUINEA-
BISSAU

CÔTE
D'IVOIRE

Lagos

ETHIOPIA

SIERRA
LEONE

CENTRAL
AFRICAN REPUBLIC

LIBERIA

GHANA

TOGO

BENIN

CAMEROON

SÃO TOMÉ
AND PRÍNCIPE

UGANDA

KENYA

0° Equator

Equator 0°

EQUATORIAL
GUINEA

GABON

CONGO

ZAIRE

RWANDA

Mt. Kilimanjaro

SEYCHELLES

BURUNDI

CABINDA
(ANGOLA)

TANZANIA

INDIAN
OCEAN

ATLANTIC
OCEAN

ANGOLA

MALAWI

COMOROS

15°S

ZAMBIA

MAURITIUS

MOZAMBIQUE

NAMIBIA

ZIMBABWE

MADAGASCAR

BOTSWANA

Tropic of Capricorn

Johannesburg

SWAZILAND

30°S

SOUTH
AFRICA

LESOTHO

N
W E
S

15°W 0° 15°E 30°E 45°E

0   500   1,000 Miles
0   500   1,000 Kilometers

UNIT 1

Africa and the Middle East

This island between the Tigris in the East and the Euphrates in the West is a marketplace for the world. All the ships that come up the Tigris from [Persia] and beyond will go up and anchor here; wares brought on ships down the Tigris from [cities in the North] and along the Euphrates from . . . Syria and the border marshes, Egypt and North Africa, will be brought and unloaded here. It will be the highway [to India]. Praise be to God who preserved it for me and caused all those who came before me to neglect it. By God, I shall build it. . . . It will surely be the most flourishing city in the world.

Thus, the tiny village of Baghdad was established as the new capital of present-day Iraq by Arab caliph (or king) Al-Mansur in the 8th century A.D.

Al-Mansur was not actually the first to "discover" this region. In fact, the area between the Tigris and Euphrates rivers had been settled many centuries before by the world's first civilization. It is called the Fertile Crescent and was the home of a people called the Sumerians between 4000 and 3500 B.C.

The two regions presented in this unit—Africa and the Middle East—are bound by historical, geographic and cultural ties. Both regions are the homes of human history's "firsts." Many scientists believe that the first homo sapiens appeared on the continent of Africa. Scientists also believe that humanity's first cities and settled civilization appeared in the Tigris-Euphrates Valley in the Middle East.

Africa's great river, the Nile, provided the climate, navigation, and rich soil that would support one of the world's great civilizations: ancient Egypt. The earliest Egyptians, who appeared about 5000 B.C., had formed a budding empire by 3100 B.C. Within 600 years—the blink of an eye, historically speaking—Egypt developed a highly structured society with an intricate religion, a bureaucratic government, and a far-reaching trading empire.

In western Africa, several early civilizations established vast trade routes over the Sahara. This trade brought them enormous wealth. One of those civilizations was Mali. You will read more about Mali in this unit.

Five centuries later, the Ashanti emerged as a regional power in present-day Ghana. United in the late 1600s by strong leaders, the Ashanti developed a powerful, well-trained army which it used to conquer surrounding territories. Each conquest yielded great numbers of prisoners. The Ashanti then sold these prisoners to European slave traders who were eager to supply the slave markets in the Americas. Using gold from the sale of their African prisoners of war, the Ashanti pur-

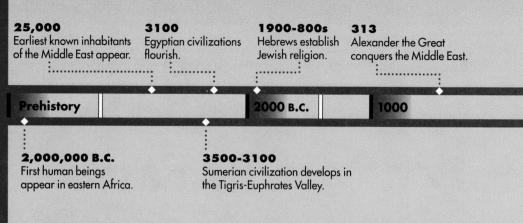

Time Line

Literature titles are placed on the time line to reflect the historical time or event that relates to the selections, not to reflect the publication dates of the selections.

25,000 Earliest known inhabitants of the Middle East appear.

3100 Egyptian civilizations flourish.

1900-800s Hebrews establish Jewish religion.

313 Alexander the Great conquers the Middle East.

Prehistory

2000 B.C.

1000

2,000,000 B.C. First human beings appear in eastern Africa.

3500-3100 Sumerian civilization develops in the Tigris-Euphrates Valley.

chased more guns. These sophisticated weapons quickly helped them wage even greater conquests. The Ashanti were only one of many tribes who sold prisoners to the slave traders. Furthermore, slave traders often attacked and captured peaceful tribes and sold them for high profit.

Soon greed for conquest and gold brought European travelers to Africa. By the late 1800s, European nations had "staked out" claims and established colonies in Africa.

Colonialism was profitable for the Europeans who found valuable natural resources that they exported for their own use at home. However, the resources were acquired at the expense of the Africans, as described by a colonialist of Yorubaland to a British Consul in 1899:

> [The colonialist's] method of procedure was to arrive in canoes at a village, the inhabitants of which invariably bolted on their arrival; the soldiers were then landed, and commenced looting, taking all the chickens, grain, etc., out of the houses; after this they attacked the natives until able to seize their women; these women were kept as hostages until the Chief of the district brought in the required... kilogrammes of rubber.

By 1885, Great Britain, Belgium, France, Italy, Germany, Portugal, and Spain had taken control of the countries of Africa.

During the last three decades of the 20th century, African countries demanded their independence. Some demands were peaceful; others were not. Today, all African nations have gained independence from the European colonialists. However, colonialism has left racial divisions in many nations. When Zimbabwe gained independence from Great Britain, writer Romain Gary made the following demand:

> National independence, I wouldn't settle for that only. That's an old, old trick, and it doesn't work any more. . . . No, my friend, that's not enough for me. I want more. I'm asking them for more. I'm asking them to become human at last, and I shan't settle for less.

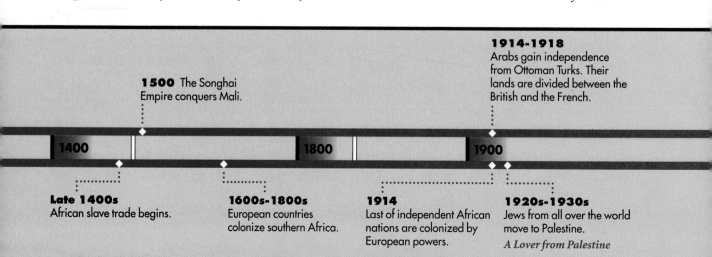

1914-1918 Arabs gain independence from Ottoman Turks. Their lands are divided between the British and the French.

1500 The Songhai Empire conquers Mali.

1400

1800

1900

Late 1400s African slave trade begins.

1600s-1800s European countries colonize southern Africa.

1914 Last of independent African nations are colonized by European powers.

1920s-1930s Jews from all over the world move to Palestine.

A Lover from Palestine

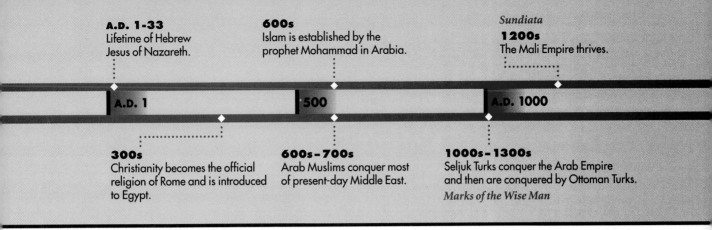

European control has left a legacy of economic and social problems that continue to impact our world, as you will learn in this unit.

The Middle East

This unit will also explore the cultural impact of the Islamic religion, which ties the nations of the Middle East together.

Home of the world's first civilizations, the Middle East is also the sacred birthplace of three of the world's major religions. Judaism was the first religion based on the belief in one God. It was founded by the nomadic Hebrews over 4000 years ago. During Roman rule, Christianity began in Israel. In the 600s, the religion of Islam was founded by a prophet named Mohammad who lived in the city of Mecca on the Arabian Peninsula. From Mecca, a religious army of Arab Moslems (people of the Islamic religion) conquered what are now Egypt, Iran, Iraq, Israel, Jordan, Syria, and Lebanon.

For centuries after its founding, Islam experienced a period of greatness. The Arabic language, religion, and culture flourished throughout the countries of the Middle East.

Today, the major religion of the Middle East continues to be Islam. Yet, the region remains a sacred place for Christians, Jews, and Muslims.

Just as in Africa, though, European nations had an economic and political impact on Middle Eastern countries. Following World War I, the British and the French took over the Arab territories. A British mandate established a Jewish homeland in the region of Palestine. After Britian withdrew in 1948, the State of Israel was proclaimed. Arabs protested bitterly. Hostility and violence over this issue continue to break out between Arabs and Jews in the 20th century. This hostility makes the Middle East one of the world's continuing "hot spots."

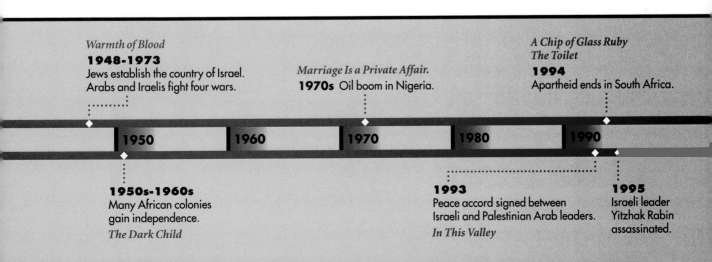

1 Africa

The traditions of literature in Africa began with storytelling, which was passed on orally from parent to child. So effective was the oral tradition that, as in all cultures, it has never completely given way to a written literature. In this chapter, you will read three selections that were passed on orally for centuries.

You will also read some poetry by two 20th century poets who are part of the literary movement in Africa called *Negritude*. Negritude means "African literary nationalism." The poems celebrate the beauty of Africa and African people.

This chapter presents two selections from South Africa and a third from Nigeria which all discuss the racial, political, and personal conflict that has resulted from European colonialism. As you read in the unit opener, colonialism has left vast racial divisions in many African nations.

Some of the literature in this chapter reflects the reconstruction that has occurred as each nation has gained independence. You will read the last chapter of an autobiography in which the author breaks with his traditional family to study in France. He hopes to return to Nigeria to help his people.

The final selection is from Egypt. It is a fantastical story in which the ancient Egyptian civilization plays an important role. You will read stories in Unit 4 with similar magical elements.

As you read the African literature selections of this unit, think about how diversity and the struggle for equality influence all of us.

Sculpture has played an important role in African cultures throughout history. Africans have created sculptures for ceremonial as well as decorative purposes.

from *Sundiata: An Epic of Old Mali*

Reading the Epic in a Cultural Context

To this day in the villages of the Western Sudan, magical legends of Sundiata Keita are told when villagers gather for traditional storytelling. Sundiata, a 13th-century West African leader, established the empire of Mali in 1240. After winning a great battle at Kirina, he consolidated the 12 small kingdoms that, at that time, formed Mali. During the 20 years of his reign, Sundiata began the expansion that would extend Mali rule from the Atlantic coast to—and including—Timbuktu.

The traditional legendary epic tells that Sundiata succeeded because of his vigor, strength, and skill. Undoubtedly that is true, say contemporary African historians. However, the experts point out, Sundiata was also a skillful politician who could "play a crowd." He convinced the citizens that he was a powerful man of magic and enchantment.

The historical legend of Sundiata is one of more than a quarter million African myths, legends, and folktales. Little distinction is made between myths, legends, and history because oral traditions play such a strong, vigorous part in the literary culture. An African audience would regard this legend, then, as a true historical narrative. In oral tradition, such historical legends are quite different from folktales, which are known to be fiction.

Historical legends and myths have always been—and still quite often are—performed by a master griot (GREE-oh), or storyteller. Storytelling is one of the fine arts in Africa. It is so highly regarded and appreciated that some culture groups designate it a profession. Historically, in pre-colonial Africa, griots played a very important role in many cultures, for they were "speaking documents," historians who worked from memory alone. Since there were no written historical records, the griots memorized the customs, traditions, constitutions, and other governing principles of the kings. They also occupied the "chair of history" in a village or kingdom. They performed the highly honored task of memorizing and retelling the songs, stories, proverbs, and histories. To become counsellors to kings and first in the art of historical storytelling, young griots spent many years touring the kingdom's villages and listening to the teachings of the master griots.

Focusing on the Selection

As you read, be aware of the several purposes of the selection. How does the griot establish his own reputation as a master storyteller? What is the griot's aim in performing the Sundiata? How does he characterize Sundiata the hero? What parts of the tale might be based on legend? What parts of the tale might be based on history?

from *Sundiata: An Epic of Old Mali*

edited by *D. T. Niane*
translated by *G. D. Pickett*

The Words of the Griot Mamadou Kouyaté

I am a griot.[1] It is I, Djeli Mamadou Kouyaté, son of Bintou Kouyaté and Djeli Kedian Kouyaté, master in the art of eloquence.[2] Since time immemorial[3] the Kouyatés have been in the service of the Keita princes of Mali; we are vessels of speech, we are the repositories[4] which harbour secrets many centuries old. The art of eloquence has no secrets for us; without us the names of kings would vanish into oblivion,[5] we are the memory of mankind; by the spoken word we bring to life the deeds and exploits of kings for younger generations.

I derive my knowledge from my father Djeli Kedian, who also got it from his father; history holds no mystery for us; we teach to the vulgar[6] just as much as we want to teach them, for it is we who keep the keys to the twelve doors of Mali.

I know the list of all the sovereigns[7] who succeeded to the throne of Mali. I know how the black people divided into tribes, for my father bequeathed[8]

---

[1] **griot** (GREE-oh) *n.* African oral historian
[2] **eloquence** (EHL-uh-kwuhns) *n.* fluent, expressive, and persuasive speaking
[3] **immemorial** (ihm-uh-MAWR-ee-uhl) *adj.* reaching beyond the limits of memory or recorded history
[4] **repositories** (rih-PAHZ-ih-tor-eez) *n. pl.* vessels
[5] **oblivion** (uh-BLIHV-ee-uhn) *n.* the condition of being completely forgotten
[6] **vulgar** (VUL-guhr) *n.* the common people
[7] **sovereigns** (SAWV-er-ihns) *n. pl.* kings
[8] **bequeathed** (bih-KWEETHD) *v.* passed on or handed down

to me all his learning; I know why such and such is called Kamara, another Keita, and yet another Sibibé or Traoré; every name has a meaning, a secret import.[9]

I teach kings the history of their ancestors so that the lives of the ancients might serve them as an example, for the world is old, but the future springs from the past.

My word is pure and free of all untruth; it is the word of my father; it is the word of my father's father. I will give you my father's words just as I received them; royal griots do not know what lying is. When a quarrel breaks out between tribes it is we who settle the difference, for we are the depositories of oaths which the ancestors swore.

Listen to my word, you who want to know; by my mouth you will learn the history of Mali.

By my mouth you will get to know the story of the ancestor of great Mali, the story of him who, by his exploits, surpassed even Alexander the Great;[10] he who, from the East, shed his rays upon all the countries of the West.

Listen to the story of the son of the Buffalo, the son of the Lion. I am going to tell you of Maghan Sundiata, of Mari-Djata, of Sogolon Djata, of Naré Maghan Djata; the man of many names against whom sorcery could avail nothing.

The Characters

Maghan Kon Fatta, (Also **Naré Maghan**) King of Mali and father of Sundiata

Sogolon Kedjou, the buffalo woman, wife of Maghan Kon Fatta and mother of Sundiata

Sogolon Djata, (also **Mari-Djata**) or Sundiata

Kolonkan, daughter of Maghan Kon Fatta and Sogolon, and sister of Sundiata

Sassouma Bérété, the king's first wife

Dankaran Touman, son of Maghan Kon Fatta and Sassouma Bérété

Balla Fasséké, son of Knankouman Doua, Sundiata's griot

Farakourou, the master smith

Manding Bory, son of Maghan Kon Fatta and Namandje

Gnankouman Doua, Maghan Kon Fatta's griot

---

[9] **import** (IHM-pawrt) *n.* meaning or importance

[10] **Alexander the Great** king of Macedonia from 336–323 B.C.; conqueror of Greek city-states and of the Persian empire from Asia Minor and Egypt to India

Childhood

God has his mysteries which none can fathom. You, perhaps, will be a king. You can do nothing about it. You, on the other hand, will be unlucky, but you can do nothing about that either. Each man finds his way already marked out for him and he can change nothing of it.

Sogolon's son had a slow and difficult childhood. At the age of three he still crawled along on all-fours while children of the same age were already walking. He had nothing of the great beauty of his father Naré Maghan. He had a head so big that he seemed unable to support it; he also had large eyes which would open wide whenever anyone entered his mother's house. He was taciturn[11] and used to spend the whole day just sitting in the middle of the house. Whenever his mother went out he would crawl on all fours to rummage about in the calabashes[12] in search of food, for he was very greedy.

Malicious[13] tongues began to blab. What three-year-old has not yet taken his first steps? What three-year-old is not the despair of his parents through his whims and shifts of mood? What three-year-old is not the joy of his circle through his backwardness in talking? Sogolon Djata (for it was thus that they called him, prefixing his mother's name to his), Sogolon Djata, then, was very different from others of his own age. He spoke little and his severe face never relaxed into a smile. You would have thought that he was already thinking, and what amused children of his age bored him. Often Sogolon would make some of them come to him to keep him company. These children were already walking and she hoped that Djata, seeing his companions walking, would be tempted to do likewise. But nothing came of it. Besides, Sogolon Djata would brain the poor little things with his already strong arms and none of them would come near him any more.

The king's first wife was the first to rejoice at Sogolon Djata's infirmity.[14] Her own son, Dankaran Touman, was already eleven. He was a fine and lively boy, who spent the day running about the village with those of his own age. He had even begun his initiation[15] in the bush. The king had had a bow made for him and he used to go behind the town to practise archery with his companions. Sassouma was quite happy and snapped her fingers at Sogolon, whose child was still crawling on the ground. Whenever

---

[11] **taciturn** (TAS-ih-turn) *adj.* almost always silent
[12] **calabashes** (KAL-uh-bash-uhz) *n. pl.* large, gourd-like fruit with a tough shell
[13] **malicious** (muh-LIHSH-uhs) *adj.* spiteful
[14] **infirmity** (ihn-FER-mih-tee) *n.* a disease or disorder that causes bodily weakness
[15] **initiation** (ih-nihsh-ee-AY-shuhn) *n.* a ceremony or ritual with which a new member is admitted

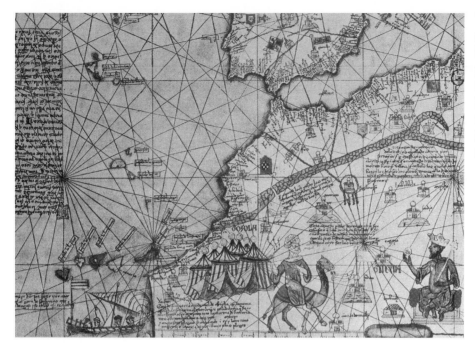

This detail of a map shows Western Africa in 1375. Notice the depiction of Mansa Musa, the King of Mali in the bottom right corner of the map. Musa ruled Mali 100 years after Sundiata.

the latter happened to pass by her house, she would say, "Come, my son, walk, jump, leap about. The jinn didn't promise you anything out of the ordinary, but I prefer a son who walks on his two legs to a lion that crawls on the ground." She spoke thus whenever Sogolon went by her door. The innuendo[16] would go straight home and then she would burst into laughter, that diabolical[17] laughter which a jealous woman knows how to use so well.

Her son's infirmity weighed heavily upon Sogolon Kedjou; she had resorted to all her talent as a sorceress to give strength to her son's legs, but the rarest herbs had been useless. The king himself lost hope.

How impatient man is! Naré Maghan became imperceptibly[18] estranged[19] but Gnankouman Doua never ceased reminding him of the hunter's words.[20] Sogolon became pregnant again. The king hoped for a son, but it was a daughter called Kolonkan. She resembled her mother and had nothing of her father's beauty. The disheartened[21] king debarred[22] Sogolon from his house and she lived in semi-disgrace for a while. Naré Maghan married the daughter of one of his allies, the king of the Kamaras.

---

[16] **innuendo** (ihn-yoo-EHN-doh) *n.* a subtle, often spiteful reference to someone not named

[17] **diabolical** (dy-uh-BAHL-ih-kuhl) *adj.* extremely wicked

[18] **imperceptibly** (ihm-puhr-SEHP-tuh-blee) *adv.* gradually

[19] **estranged** (ih-STRAYNJD) *v.* showing no interest; becoming withdrawn

[20] **hunter's words** the hunter had told Naré Maghan that Sogolon Djata would one day be the king of Mali's greatest empire.

[21] **disheartened** (dihs-HART-uhnd) *adj.* discouraged

[22] **debarred** (dee-BAHRD) *v.* excluded

She was called Namandjé and her beauty was legendary. A year later she brought a boy into the world. When the king consulted soothsayers[23] on the destiny of this son he received the reply that Namandjé's child would be the right hand of some mighty king. The king gave the newly-born the name of Boukari. He was to be called Manding Boukari or Manding Bory later on.

Naré Maghan was very perplexed. Could it be that the stiff-jointed son of Sogolon was the one the hunter soothsayer had foretold?

"The Almighty has his mysteries," Gnankouman Doua would say and, taking up the hunter's words, added, "The silk-cotton tree emerges from a tiny seed."

One day Naré Maghan came along to the house of Nounfaïri, the black-smith seer[24] of Niani. He was an old, blind man. He received the king in the anteroom which served as his workshop. To the king's question he replied, "When the seed germinates[25] growth is not always easy; great trees grow slowly but they plunge their roots deep into the ground."

"But has the seed really germinated?" said the king.

"Of course," replied the blind seer. "Only the growth is not as quick as you would like it; how impatient man is."

This interview and Doua's confidence gave the king some assurance. To the great displeasure of Sassouma Bérété the king restored Sogolon to favour and soon another daughter was born to her. She was given the name of Djamarou.

However, all Niani[26] talked of nothing else but the stiff-legged son of Sogolon. He was now seven and he still crawled to get about. In spite of all the king's affection, Sogolon was in despair. Naré Maghan aged and he felt his time coming to an end. Dankaran Touman, the son of Sassouma Bérété, was now a fine youth.

One day Naré Maghan made Mari Djata come to him and he spoke to the child as one speaks to an adult. "Mari Djata, I am growing old and soon I shall be no more among you, but before death takes me off I am going to give you the present each king gives his successor. In Mali every prince has his own griot. Doua's father was my father's griot, Doua is mine and the son of Doua, Balla Fasséké here, will be your griot. Be insep-arable friends from this day forward. From his mouth you will hear the history of your ancestors, you will learn the art of governing Mali according

---

[23] **soothsayers** (SOOTH-say-uhrz) *n. pl.* people who claim to be able to predict the future
[24] **seer** (seer) *n.* a soothsayer
[25] **germinates** (JER-muh-nayts) *v.* causes to begin to grow; sprouts
[26] **Niani** capital city of Mali

to the principles which our ancestors have bequeathed[27] to us. I have served my term and done my duty too. I have done everything which a king of Mali ought to do. I am handing an enlarged kingdom over to you and I leave you sure allies. May your destiny be accomplished, but never forget that Niani is your capital and Mali the cradle of your ancestors."

The child, as if he had understood the whole meaning of the king's words, beckoned Balla Fasséké to approach. He made room for him on the hide he was sitting on and then said, "Balla, you will be my griot."

"Yes, son of Sogolon, if it pleases God," replied Balla Fasséké.

The king and Doua exchanged glances that radiated[28] confidence.

The Lion's Awakening

A short while after this interview between Naré Maghan and his son, the king died. Sogolon's son was no more than seven years old. The council of elders met in the king's palace. It was no use Doua's defending the king's will which reserved the throne for Mari Djata, for the council took no account of Naré Maghan's wish. With the help of Sassouma Bérété's intrigues, Dankaran Touman was proclaimed king and a regency council[29] was formed in which the queen mother was all-powerful. A short time after, Doua died.

As men have short memories, Sogolon's son was spoken of with nothing but irony[30] and scorn. People had seen one-eyed kings, one-armed kings, and lame kings, but a stiff-legged king had never been heard tell of. No matter how great the destiny promised for Mari Djata might be, the throne could not be given to someone who had no power in his legs; if the jinn loved him, let them begin by giving him the use of his legs. Such were the remarks that Sogolon heard every day. The queen mother, Sassouma Bérété, was the source of all this gossip.

Having become all-powerful, Sassouma Bérété persecuted Sogolon because the late Naré Maghan had preferred her. She banished Sogolon and her son to a back yard of the palace. Mari Djata's mother now occupied an old hut which had served as a lumber-room of Sassouma's.

The wicked queen allowed free passage to all those inquisitive[31] people who wanted to see the child that still crawled at the age of seven. Nearly all the inhabitants of Niani filed into the palace and the poor Sogolon wept to

---

[27] **bequeathed** (bih-KWEETHD) *v.* passed down

[28] **radiated** (RAY-dee-ay-tuhd) *v.* showed

[29] **regency council** a group of people to rule for a child king

[30] **irony** (EYE-ruh-nee) *n.* a wry, mocking way of using words to suggest the opposite of what they literally mean

[31] **inquisitive** (ihn-KWIHZ-ih-tihv) *adj.* curious; prying

see herself thus given over to public ridicule. Mari Djata took on a ferocious look in front of the crowd of sightseers. Sogolon found a little consolation only in the love of her eldest daughter, Kolonkan. She was four and she could walk. She seemed to understand all her mother's miseries and already she helped her with the housework. Sometimes, when Sogolon was attending to the chores, it was she who stayed beside her sister Djamarou, quite small as yet.

Sogolon Kedjou and her children lived on the queen mother's leftovers, but she kept a little garden in the open ground behind the village. It was there that she passed her brightest moments looking after her onions and gnougous.[32] One day she happened to be short of condiments[33] and went to the queen mother to beg a little baobab[34] leaf.

"Look you," said the malicious Sassouma, "I have a calabash full. Help yourself, you poor woman. As for me, my son knew how to walk at seven and it was he who went and picked these baobab leaves. Take them then, since your son is unequal to mine." Then she laughed derisively[35] with that fierce laughter which cuts through your flesh and penetrates right to the bone.

Sogolon Kedjou was dumbfounded. She had never imagined that hate could be so strong in a human being. With a lump in her throat she left Sassouma's. Outside her hut Mari Djata, sitting on his useless legs, was blandly[36] eating out of a calabash. Unable to contain herself any longer, Sogolon burst into sobs and seizing a piece of wood, hit her son.

"Oh son of misfortune, will you never walk? Through your fault I have just suffered the greatest affront[37] of my life! What have I done, God, for you to punish me in this way?"

Mari Djata seized the piece of wood and, looking at his mother, said, "Mother, what's the matter?"

"Shut up, nothing can ever wash me clean of this insult."

"But what then?"

"Sassouma has just humiliated[38] me over a matter of a baobab leaf. At your age her own son could walk and used to bring his mother baobab leaves."

"Cheer up, Mother, cheer up."

"No. It's too much. I can't."

"Very well then, I am going to walk today," said Mari Djata. "Go and tell my father's smiths to make me the heaviest possible iron rod. Mother, do

---

[32] **gnougous** (guh-NOO-goos) a food plant

[33] **condiments** (KON-duh-muhnts) *n. pl.* sauces or spices used as seasonings for food

[34] **baobab** (BAY-oh-bab) *n.* an African tree with a thick trunk and large, hard-shelled, hanging fruit

[35] **derisively** (dih-REYE-sihv-lee) *adv.* mockingly; with ridicule

[36] **blandly** (BLAND-lee) *adv.* pleasantly; gently

[37] **affront** (uh-FRUNT) *n.* insult

[38] **humiliated** (hyoo-MIHL-ee-ayt-ihd) *v.* disgraced

you want just the leaves of the baobab or would you rather I brought you the whole tree?"

"Ah, my son, to wipe out this insult I want the tree and its roots at my feet outside my hut."

Balla Fasséké, who was present, ran to the master smith, Farakourou, to order an iron rod.

Sogolon had sat down in front of her hut. She was weeping softly and holding her head between her two hands. Mari Djata went calmly back to his calabash of rice and began eating again as if nothing had happened. From time to time he looked up discreetly[39] at his mother who was murmuring in a low voice, "I want the whole tree, in front of my hut, the whole tree."

All of a sudden a voice burst into laughter behind the hut. It was the wicked Sassouma telling one of her serving women about the scene of humiliation and she was laughing loudly so that Sogolon could hear. Sogolon fled into the hut and hid her face under the blankets so as not to have before her eyes this heedless boy, who was more preoccupied[40] with eating than with anything else. With her head buried in the bed-clothes Sogolon wept and her body shook violently. Her daughter, Sogolon Djamarou, had come and sat down beside her and she said, "Mother, Mother, don't cry. Why are you crying?"

Mari Djata had finished eating and, dragging himself along on his legs, he came and sat under the wall of the hut for the sun was scorching. What was he thinking about? He alone knew.

The royal forges[41] were situated outside the walls and over a hundred smiths worked there. The bows, spears, arrows and shields of Niani's warriors came from there. When Balla Fasséké came to order the iron rod, Farakourou said to him, "The great day has arrived then?"

"Yes. Today is a day like any other, but it will see what no other day has seen."

The master of the forge, Farakourou, was the son of the old Nounfaïri. Everybody wondered what this bar was destined to be used for. Farakourou called six of his apprentices[42] and told them to carry the iron bar to Sogolon's house.

When the smiths put the gigantic iron bar down in front of the hut the noise was so frightening that Sogolon, who was lying down, jumped up with a start. Then Balla Fasséké, son of Gnankouman Doua, spoke.

---

[39] **discreetly** (di-SKREET-lee) *adv.* modestly; shyly

[40] **preoccupied** (pree-AWK-yoo-peyed) *v.* absorbed

[41] **forges** (FOR-jihs) *n. pl.* furnaces for heating metal

[42] **apprentices** (uh-PREHN-tihs-ehz) *n. pl.* persons who are learning a trade or craft

"Here is the great day, Mari Djata. I am speaking to you, Maghan, son of Sogolon. The waters of the Niger[43] can efface[44] the stain from the body, but they cannot wipe out an insult. Arise, young lion, roar, and may the bush know that from henceforth it has a master."

The apprentice smiths were still there, Sogolon had come out and everyone was watching Mari Djata. He crept on all-fours and came to the iron bar. Supporting himself on his knees and one hand, with the other hand he picked up the iron bar without any effort and stood it up vertically. Now he was resting on nothing but his knees and held the bar with both his hands. A deathly silence had gripped all those present. Sogolon Djata closed his eyes, held tight, the muscles in his arms tensed. With a violent jerk he threw his weight on to it and his knees left the ground. Sogolon Kedjou was all eyes and watched her son's legs which were trembling as though from an electric shock. Djata was sweating and the sweat ran from his brow. In a great effort he straightened up and was on his feet at one go—but the great bar of iron was twisted and had taken the form of a bow!

Then Balla Fasséké sang out the "Hymn to the Bow," striking up with his powerful voice:

"Take your bow, Simbon,
Take your bow and let us go.
Take your bow, Sogolon Djata."

When Sogolon saw her son standing she stood dumb for a moment, then suddenly she sang these words of thanks to God who had given her son the use of his legs:

"Oh day, what a beautiful day,
Oh day, day of joy;
Allah Almighty, you never created a finer day.
So my son is going to walk!"

Standing in the position of a soldier at ease, Sogolon Djata, supported by his enormous rod, was sweating great beads of sweat. Balla Fasséké's song had alerted the whole palace and people came running from all over to see what had happened, and each stood bewildered before Sogolon's son. The queen mother had rushed there and when she saw Mari Djata standing up she trembled from head to foot. After recovering his breath Sogolon's son dropped the bar and the crowd stood to one side. His first steps were those of a giant. Balla Fasséké fell into step and pointing his finger at Djata, he cried:

---

[43] **Niger** (NEYE-juhr) *n.* a river in Africa, flowing through Mali, Niger, and Nigeria into the Atlantic

[44] **efface** (ih-FAYS) *v.* remove by rubbing out; erase

"Room, room, make room!
The lion has walked;
Hide antelopes,
Get out of his way."

Behind Niani there was a young baobab tree and it was there that the children of the town came to pick leaves for their mothers. With all his might the son of Sogolon tore up the tree and put it on his shoulders and went back to his mother. He threw the tree in front of the hut and said, "Mother, here are some baobab leaves for you. From henceforth it will be outside your hut that the women of Niani will come to stock up."

Sogolon Djata walked. From that day forward the queen mother had no more peace of mind. But what can one do against destiny? Nothing. Man, under the influence of certain illusions,[45] thinks he can alter the course which God has mapped out, but everything he does falls into a higher order which he barely understands. That is why Sassouma's efforts were vain against Sogolon's son, everything she did lay in the child's destiny. Scorned the day before and the object of public ridicule, now Sogolon's son was as popular as he had been despised. The multitude loves and fears strength. All Niani talked of nothing but Djata; the mothers urged their sons to become hunting companions of Djata and to share his games, as if they wanted their offspring to profit from the nascent[46] glory of the buffalo-woman's son. The words of Doua on the name-giving day came back to men's minds and Sogolon was now surrounded with much respect; in conversation people were fond of contrasting Sogolon's modesty with the pride and malice of Sassouma Bérété. It was because the former had been an exemplary[47] wife and mother that God had granted strength to her son's legs for, it was said, the more a wife loves and respects her husband and the more she suffers for her child, the more valorous[48] will the child be one day. Each is the child of his mother; the child is worth no more than the mother is worth. It was not astonishing that the king Dankaran Touman was so colorless, for his mother had never shown the slightest respect to her husband and never, in the presence of the late king, did she show that humility which every wife should show before her husband. People recalled her scenes of jealousy and the spiteful remarks she circulated about her co-wife and her child. And people would conclude gravely, "Nobody knows God's mystery. The snake has no legs yet it is as swift as any other animal that has four."

---

[45] **illusions** (ih-LOO-zhuhnz) *n. pl.* mistaken notions or beliefs
[46] **nascent** (NAS-uhnt) *adj.* having recently come into existence
[47] **exemplary** (ihg-ZEHM-pluh-ree) *adj.* model; commendable
[48] **valorous** (VAL-uhr-uhs) *adj.* courageous; bold

POSTREADING

Critical Thinking

1. Why does most of the selection dwell on Sundiata's inability to walk as a child and the effects of that inability on those around him?

2. What attitudes and qualities does the story put forth as desirable?

3. What historical legends exist in your culture that mix legend and history about a leader or leaders from the past? What events in the leader's life are recounted? For what purpose is that particular event recounted? What characteristics does the leader display?

Writing Your Response to "Sundiata"

What aspect of the selection do you find most interesting or satisfying? Why does that particular aspect appeal to you? In your journal, identify your choice, and share the reasons for your choice.

Going Back Into the Text: Author's Craft

An **epic** is a long narrative that recalls a great hero's deeds and reflects the values of the society where it began. Most epics are part of an oral tradition and were told from generation to generation through song and recitation before someone wrote them down.

The Sundiata epic is a form of African folklore that, in its original language, is neither prose nor poetry. This unique African form is elaborate. It contains poetry, song, and proverbs. The African epic, like epics from other cultures, usually concerns the heroic exploits of ancestors. It also celebrates those qualities for which the society has a high regard.

As you review the selection, use these questions as guidelines:

1. What proverbs appear in the selection?

2. What poetic language, particularly similes and metaphors, describes the characters?

3. How does the poetic language help to portray Sundiata as "larger than life?"

4. When is it apparent that Sundiata is a powerful man of magic and enchantment?

5. What qualities does Sundiata display that are important to the culture? What other characters portray desirable qualities? What undesirable qualities are portrayed?

6. Although this selection presents only a short portion of the entire Sundiata epic, how do you know that Sundiata will go on to perform deeds of exceptional valor, strength, and skill?

Owner of the Sky: Olorun the Creator

Reading the Story in a Cultural Context

"In the beginning..."

What culture, what civilization—indeed, what human being—is not curious about its roots? Every civilization that has ever formed part of the world's history pattern has carried an explanation of its own origins, as well as the world's. In literary terms, such explanations are often called *creation myths*. In this context, *myth* means a story of unknown authorship.

The particular creation myth you are about to read is from the ancient Yoruba civilization of western Africa. The Yoruba held power from about A.D. 1100 to the late 1500s in what is now Nigeria, establishing several city-states in the region. A city-state consisted of towns, villages, and any surrounding farms and forests. It was ruled by a kinglike leader called an *oba*. Two Yoruba city-states, Ifé and Benin, grew into large, powerful kingdoms before the arrival of the Europeans.

The Yoruba developed a complex, intricate religion. At the center of their beliefs was a supreme god and more than 400 lesser gods. The supreme overlord, who created the universe and everything in it, kept aloof from human beings. He commanded the other gods to complete tasks that required interacting with the human race.

Retelling this myth about "the time before time" is African-American author Virginia Hamilton, winner of many major awards for her writing for young people. Hamilton's work is consistently praised for its poetic precision, for "sentences [polished] with care," and for stories and characters that are developed with imagination and love. Hamilton retold *Owner of the Sky: Olorun the Creator* for one of her own books, a collection of creation stories from around the world. She explained the stories thus: "Narratives . . . called myths. . . are the truth to the people who believe in them and live by them. They give the people guidance and spiritual strength. . . . Myth stories about creation . . . *go back beyond anything that ever was* and begin *before anything has happened. . . .* Let us read and enjoy these stories for their poetic beauty and the wondrous vision of the people who created them."

Focusing on the Selection

As you read "Owner of the Sky: Olorun the Creator," keep in mind that the most important purpose of a creation myth is to explain something. What is Olorun's official title? What is his function? How does he fulfill his function? What other gods does Olorun use to fulfill his purpose?

Owner of the Sky: Olorun the Creator

retold by *Virginia Hamilton*

Olorun was the Owner of the Sky and the Highest Being. He lived in the sky with other spirits. In the beginning, the earth was all watery, just a marshy place, a waste.

Sometimes, Olorun and the other gods came down to play about in the marsh-waste. There were long spiders' webs hanging from the sky. They draped across sweeping spaces like graceful silk bridges.

Yet there was no solid land anywhere. No ground on which to stand. There could be no human beings under the sky until there was a hard place for them to plant their feet.

Olorun, Owner of the Sky and the Highest Being, called the chief of the divine ones to him. This chief was Great God.

Olorun told Great God, "I want you to make some firm ground down below, right away. Here," Olorun went on, "take this."

He gave Great God a shell. There was a small amount of earth in the shell. And there was also a pigeon in there and a hen with five toes.

Great God did as he was told. He went down to the marsh land, sliding down the spider silks. Then he threw the earth out from the shell and spread it about him. He put the pigeon and the hen down on the bit of earth from the shell.

The pigeon and the hen began scratching and scratching the earth with their feet. It didn't take long for them to scratch the soil over the whole marsh-waste. That was how the firm, hard ground came to be.

Great God went back up to the sky. There he found Olorun waiting.

"It is done. I've formed the ground, and it is solid and true," Great God said.

Olorun sent down Chameleon[1] to take a look at the work of Great God.

Now, Chameleon took his time about most things. He walked slowly, and he went down the spider line from the sky carefully. He rolled his big eyes around, looking at everything. And slowly he changed his color from sky blue to earth brown as he walked the land Great God had made.

"Well, the earth is plenty wide," Chameleon told Olorun when he had returned, "but it's not quite dry enough."

"Go again," Olorun commanded. And Chameleon went down from the sky a second time.

He came back to report once more to the Owner of the Sky.

"It is well," Chameleon said. "The earth is wide, and it is dry this time."

"Good," Olorun said. He named the place Ifé, and that meant wide. Ile was brought to stand on Ifé, and Ile meant house. All other houses came from that first one that stood at Ifé. And to this day, the city of Ile-Ifé is the most sacred to Olorun's people.

African sculptures often "tell stories." With its two seated persons, its two lizards and a sphere, this sculpture might tell a variation of *Olorun the Creator*.

It took four days to make the earth. On the fifth day, Great God was to be worshipped as the Maker.

Then Olorun sent Great God back to Ifé to plant trees and to feed humans when they came, and to give them goods. He planted palm trees with palm nuts. The humans would drink their juice. More trees were planted there, and rain was made to fall and water them.

The first people came from heaven. Olorun sent them down to earth to live. Great God made some of the people's parts out of the earth. He molded their bodies and their heads.

Bringing these still figures to life was left to Olorun, Owner of the Sky, the Creator.

---

[1] **Chameleon** (kuh-MEEL-yuhn) *n.* a small lizard that changes color

Great God was jealous of Olorun's work. He wanted to bring life to the earth figures he had made.

"I will watch Olorun to see how he does it," thought Great God.

So he stayed there with the figures and hid amongst them so that he might see the work of Olorun firsthand.

But Olorun knew everything. He knew whenever there were watchers. He saw Great God there where he had hidden. And he put Great God into a very deep sleep.

Great God slept and slept. When he woke up again, all of the people had come to life. He never saw it happen.

So it is that Great God still only makes the bodies and heads of humans, both men and women. He leaves his marks on them, though. And sometimes, the marks show how unhappy Great God is.

POSTREADING

Critical Thinking

1. How does this myth meet its aim to explain the beginning of the world?

2. What do you learn about Yoruba life from the tale?

3. What other creation stories do you know? How are they like or different from this tale?

Writing Your Response to "Owner of the Sky: Olorun the Creator"

In your journal, write your reactions to the story. What aspect of the story struck you most forcibly? Did you appreciate the manner and language in which the tale was told? Why or why not? Did you find any inconsistencies in the story? Did they bother you? Why or why not?

Going Back Into the Text: Author's Craft

Cause and effect occurs when one event makes another event happen. The first event is called the **cause** and the second the **effect**. In fiction, most plots are a series of causes and effects. In myths as well, cause and effect can be used to explain a natural occurrence for which there appears no logical answer. For example, because there was no firm land on earth, Olorun sent Great God down to make some. The first event—no firm land—*causes* Olorun to assign the task of making some to Great God.

As you review the myth, use these questions as guidelines:

1. Why are the two animals necessary?

2. Why was Chameleon sent down?

3. Why is the Yoruba city of Ifé special?

4. Find three other cause-effect relationships in the tale.

PREREADING

The Sea Eats the Land at Home

Song for the Sun that Disappeared Behind the Rainclouds

Reading the Poems in a Cultural Context

The country of Ghana lies in West Africa on the southern coast of the continent's "bulge." The northern part of Ghana lies near the Sahara and is very dry. The southern section, however, is very wet and rainy. This half of Ghana is drenched by warm, humid air masses from the Atlantic Ocean.

Poet Kofi Awoonor grew up in this wet, rainy southern part of Ghana, and he features it often in his work. Awoonor spent his childhood in Keta, "the flood town, with the sea in my ears." (Keta sits on the edge of Ghana's extreme southeastern coast.) The poet describes the countryside around Keta as a "wide land, marshy in places…[as children] We loved the rains when they came down and soaked the red earth…"

In his poems, Awoonor shares the experiences, both happy and sad, of his life in and around the sea-soaked town of Keta. He often brings the events to life by using imagery—sights, sounds, feelings—from the oral poetry that is part of Africa's literary tradition. Such "borrowed" images, Awoonor believes, give his poetry extra depth and feeling and tie his written poetry to the spoken word.

The poem of the Khoi people (formerly called the Hottentot) is an example of a traditional spoken (oral) poem. Just as Awoonor's poem is filled with strong, vivid sights and sounds, so, too, is "Song for the Sun." Each poem presents a clear, focused "picture" of a natural event, as well as the feelings of the people who are affected by the event.

Focusing on the Selections

In both poems, words and phrases that appeal to the senses help a reader re-create the experiences described in the poems. So specific and well chosen is the language that you may feel like you actually "are" in the place, at the event. As you read, use the sensory language to form pictures and images of places, events, and emotions.

The Sea Eats the Land at Home

Kofi Awoonor

At home the sea is in the town,
Running in and out of the cooking places,
Collecting the firewood from the hearths[1]
And sending it back at night;
The sea eats the land at home.
It came one day at the dead of night,
Destroying the cement walls,
And carried away the fowls,
The cooking-pots and the ladles,
The sea eats the land at home.
It is a sad thing to hear the wails,
And the mourning[2] shouts of the women,
Calling on all the gods they worship,
To protect them from the angry sea.
Aku stood outside where her cooking-pot stood,
With her two children shivering from the cold,
Her hands on her breast,
Weeping mournfully.
Her ancestors have neglected her,
Her gods have deserted her.
It was a cold Sunday morning.
The storm was raging.
Goats and fowls were struggling in the water,
The angry water of the cruel sea.
The lap-lapping of the bark water at the shore,
And above the sobs and the deep and low moans,
Was the eternal[3] hum of the living sea.
It has taken away their belongings.
Adena has lost the trinkets which
Were her dowry[4] and her joy,
In the sea that eats the land at home,
Eats the whole land at home.

---

[1] **hearths** (hahrths) *n. pl.* floors of fireplaces
[2] **mourning** (MAWR-nihng) *adj.* grieving over a loss
[3] **eternal** (ih-TER-nuhl) *adj.* seemingly endless, everlasting
[4] **dowry** (DOW-ree) *n.* money or property brought by a bride to her husband

Song for the Sun that Disappeared Behind the Rainclouds

Anonymous
translated by *Ulli Beier*

The fire darkens, the wood turns black.
The flame extinguishes, misfortune upon us.
God sets out in search of the sun.
The rainbow sparkles in his hand,
the bow of the divine hunter.
He has heard the lamentations[1] of his children.
He walks along the milky way,[2] he collects the stars.
With quick arms he piles them into a basket,
piles them up with quick arms
like a woman who collects lizards
and piles them into her pot, piles them up
until the pot overflows with lizards,
until the basket overflows with light.

The spectacular beauty of the varied African landscape is often a subject of literature. Early humans told stories about ordinary acts of nature, such as the rise and set of the sun. This is a photo of a sunset in Botswana, Africa.

---

[1] **lamentations** (lam-uhn-TAY-shuhnz) *n. pl.* expressions of sorrow
[2] **Milky Way** *n.* the galaxy containing the solar system, seen as a wide band of milky light across the night sky

POSTREADING

Critical Thinking

1. How does the sensory language in both poems help you "see" the places and the events that are taking place? experience the emotions? Read some examples that you think give the clearest "pictures."

2. What details do you learn about the culture of small-town life in Ghana?

3. Have you or someone you know ever been "at the mercy" of the rain or the sea? (Maybe you have followed TV or newspaper coverage of hurricanes, monsoons, or other sea storms.) What dangers did the water present? What steps were necessary to protect life and property? Were the protective steps successful? Why or why not? What damage was unavoidable?

Writing Your Response to "The Sea Eats the Land at Home" and "Song for the Sun that Disappeared Behind the Rainclouds"

Both of the storms described in the poems cause deep feelings in the people who experience them. Awoonor speaks of *wails, mourning shouts, sobs,* and *deep and low moans.* The Khoi poem talks of *lamentations* (cries and/or prayers of grief and sadness). In your journal, write about the emotions that you felt most deeply while reading the poems. What emotion—and the event that caused it—was most real for you? Why?

Going Back Into the Text: Author's Craft

Sensory details are words and phrases that help readers imagine the exact events, people, places, things, or ideas a writer describes. Sensory details make a work more real and concrete, letting you actually share the author's entire experience.

Sensory details use concrete nouns, verbs, adjectives, and adverbs that you can immediately appreciate with any or all of your five senses. For example, Awoonor produces a very concrete, specific "picture" of the sea by describing it as "angry," an emotion that often causes destructive or hurtful actions. In the Khoi poem, the sun's disappearance is called a "misfortune," and the poem provides three unhappy events—specific sensory details—caused by the misfortune.

As you review the sensory details in the poems, use these questions as guidelines:

1. What specific, concrete phrases tell you that the events in both poems occur at night?

2. What intense, vivid verbs does Awoonor use to describe the actions of the "angry" sea?

3. What sounds can you "hear"? What do these sounds add to the poem's experience?

4. What vivid verbs in the Khoi poem describe the results of the rainstorm? God's search for stars?

5. In the Khoi poem, God collecting stars is compared to a woman collecting lizards (simile). How are the stars and the lizards alike? How does this very concrete comparison change the feeling of the poem?

The Prebend Gardens/Interior/ All That You Have Given Me, Africa

Reading the Poems in a Cultural Context

As you recall from the unit introduction, Africa and the Middle East were forcibly colonized by European powers between 1870 and 1914. Many native peoples under the colonists wanted freedom for their countries and began independence movements. Among the leaders was Léopold Senghor, a writer who lived in Senegal, what was then French West Africa. Senghor was born in 1906 in a small village on the Atlantic Coast, and he was sent to France to be educated.

In Paris during the 1930s, Senghor met writers from the French Caribbean. As a group, they began to examine the Western values that had been imposed on them. At the same time, they re-evaluated their own cultures. From these studies, Senghor and his friends co-founded Negritude. One aim of the movement was to protest French rule and the French government's attempts to impose their culture on the native peoples in their colonies. Another aim was to find ways for African and European cultures to enrich each other, yet preserve their own traditions.

Many themes in Senghor's poetry reflect the philosophy of this movement. Often, he attacks what he sees as the "soullessness" of Western civilization, a culture "that has died of machines and cannons." In contrast, he celebrates African culture, using rich sensual imagery to recapture the wonder of Africa's past and the heritage of his ancestors. Through his poems, he frequently claims that Africa's is the only world culture to remain in step with the planet's natural and ancient rhythms.

In addition to creating an African identity, Senghor also works to create poetry that holds the beauties of both the French language and his own native language of Serer. He writes in French and uses the rhythms of Serer. The effect is to make his poetry sing and dance.

Leon Maurice Anoma Kanié, author of the third selection, also grew up under French rule. Born in 1920 in Cote d'Ivoire (Ivory Coast), Kanié, too, celebrates his culture and continent in his poetry. His concern with continuing and preserving native African culture led him to collect and publish a book of African legends and tales, *Quand les betes parliant aux hommes (When Animals Spoke to Men)*, in 1974. To this, he added several French fables that he translated into Ivory Coast Creole, a language blended from French and local dialects.

Focusing on the Selections

As you read, keep in mind that both poets are trying to create a feeling of pride and love for African cultures and countries. What words and phrases describe the African countryside? What traditions and heritage are recalled? How do the poets describe their emotions about the French culture that they have been forced to accept?

The Prebend Gardens

Léopold Sédar Senghor

Prebend[1] gardens
You touched my shoulder
As I walked by your green gates,
Indifferent . . .

But today you are my friend
On this October afternoon
—It is night, it is day in the streets and underbrush—
On this October afternoon
Where in my usual daze I can barely hear
Lamenting[2] and searching its way in some lost clearing in me
A muted[3] trumpet.

The old city in this photograph still stands. It is likely that many generations of this young man's family have lived in the city for centuries.

---

[1] **Prebend** (PREE-behnd) *n.* land owned by the Church of England
[2] **lamenting** (luh-MEHNT-ing) *v.* feeling or expressing great sorrow
[3] **muted** (MYOOT-uhd) *adj.* muffled or softer in sound

Interior

Léopold Sédar Senghor

We bathe in an African presence
Of sparkling soft carpets from Timbuktu,[4]
Moorish[5] cushions,
Musky fragrances,
Dark, heavy furniture from Guinea and the Congo,
Mats thick with silence,
Authentic, primitive masks
On the primitive, solid walls.
And, friendly lamp, your tenderness
Softens my obsession[6] with this presence so
Black, brown, and red, Oh! red as African soil.

All That You Have Given Me, Africa

Anoma Kanié
translated by *Kathleen Weaver*

All that you have given me, Africa
Lakes, forests, misted lagoons[7]
All that you have given me,
Music, dances, all night stories around a fire
All that you have etched in my skin

---

[4] **Timbuktu** (tihm-buhk-TOO) *n.* town in West Africa
[5] **Moorish** (MOOR-ihsh) *adj.* of the Moors, especially those Moslem people of northern
   Africa who invaded Spain in the 8th century A.D.
[6] **obsession** (uhb-SEHSH-uhn) *n.* a thought or emotion that occupies the mind continually
[7] **lagoons** (luh-GOONZ) *n. pl.* bodies of water which are bounded by sandbars or coral reefs

Pigments[8] of my ancestors
Indelible[9] in my blood
All that you have given me Africa
Makes me walk
With a step that is like no other
Hip broken under the weight of time,
Feet large with journeys,
All that you have left to me
Even this lassitude[10] bound to my heels,
I bear it with pride on my forehead
My health is no more to be lost
And I go forward
Praising my race which is no better
Or worse than any other.
All that you have given me Africa,
Savannahs[11] gold in the noonday sun
Your beasts that men call wicked,
Your mines, inexplicable[12] treasures
Obsession of a hostile world
Your suffering for lost paradises,
All that, I protect with an unforgiving hand
As far as the clear horizons
So that your heaven-given task
May be safe forever.

---

[8] **pigments** (PIHG-muhnts) *n. pl.* substances that give color to skin
[9] **indelible** (ihn-DEHL-uh-buhl) *adj.* permanent
[10] **lassitude** (LAS-ih-tood) *n.* feeling of exhaustion or weakness
[11] **savannahs** (suh-VAN-uhz) *n. pl.* flat, treeless grasslands of warm regions
[12] **inexplicable** (ihn-EHK-splih-kuh-buhl) *adj.* not capable of being explained

POSTREADING

Critical Thinking

1. In what ways do both Senghor and Kanié celebrate their African identity?

2. What aspects of African culture, present and past, are presented in the poems?

3. What poems, songs, or anthems have poets from your native culture produced? How do they call up a feeling of national pride? What words and phrases do you consider especially effective?

Writing Your Response to "The Prebend Gardens," "Interior," "All That You Have Given Me, Africa"

Senghor and Kanié want readers to respect the cultures and values about which they write. Both are credited with composing poetry of such an "emotional power" that readers are "drawn deep into their worlds." Did this experience happen to you? In your journal, explain which lines of the poems affected you most deeply, and why. Is the wording or intent in any way similar to patriotic poems or songs in your own culture?

Going Back Into the Text: Author's Craft

Authors in many countries have used poetry for political purposes. A common purpose of **nationalism in poetry** is the creation of feelings of national or ethnic pride. For example, African-American poet and songwriter James Weldon Johnson wrote "Lift Every Voice and Sing," often called the African-American national anthem. During the Civil War, Julia Ward Howe wrote new verses entitled "Battle Hymn of the Republic" to an old tune. Jewish-American poet Emma Lazarus wrote the inscription on the Statue of Liberty to raise awareness of the multiethnic character of the United States.

As you review the selections, find effective examples of poetic language that the poets use to:

1. describe physical objects;

2. create positive feelings for African history and traditions;

3. create negative feelings about the "outside" culture, in this case French.

MAKING CULTURAL CONNECTIONS

AFRICA AND THE MIDDLE EAST

Every region of the world has monuments. Monuments can be buildings, works of art, natural features, or historic structures. Think about the monuments in your community or state. They say something about your culture in the same way that the monuments in the photos on these pages tell about the cultures to which they belong. Use the photos on these pages to find clues to the cultures of this unit.

The Nile River has long been important to the people of Egypt. The Nile was the main source of water for the ancient Egyptians. In addition, the yearly floods of the Nile provided the Egyptians with fertile land to farm. Even today, the Nile is an important water source for Egypt.

Goree Island was established by the French in the 1700s. This port was the last stop made by slave ships before they made the long trek across the Atlantic Ocean with their cargo of African prisoners.

The Wailing Wall in Jerusalem formed the western wall of the courtyard of the Jews' holy temple during biblical times. Today, the Jews continue to assemble at this wall for services in which Jewish traditions and sufferings are remembered.

LINKING
Literature, History, and Culture

What do the photos on this page and the selections in this unit tell you about the cultures of Africa and the Middle East?

▶ The policy of apartheid in South Africa, like Goree Island, reminds people of the cruelty of prejudice. How are the main characters of "The Toilet" and "A Chip of Glass Ruby" affected by apartheid?

▶ Visitors to Africa and the Middle East see traditional machines next to modern ones. How is this contrast between traditional and modern ideas evident in "Marriage Is a Private Affair" and "The Dark Child"?

▶ At the Wailing Wall, Jews remember the people who have died to preserve their homeland and their culture. The issue of a homeland is also important to Palestinians. Compare the different perspectives on homelands in "In This Valley" and "A Lover from Palestine."

Reading the Story in a Cultural Context

South African author and actress Gcina Mhlope was born in Hammarsdale, a city on the country's eastern coast. As you will read, Mhlope grew up under the system of apartheid. A black South African, Mhlope experienced the injustices of apartheid firsthand. For her, the restrictions and unfairness of apartheid were part of her life. She mentions them, explains them quickly and simply, and then moves on.

Moving—in many directions—characterizes Ms. Mhlope's life, propelling her forward in several careers. As an actress starting out in the early 1980s, Mhlope moved her career forward by touring Britain, Europe, and the United States. By 1988, she had become well known internationally, winning acclaim and awards for her acting. When she returned to South Africa, she moved into the directing field. She served as the resident director for the 1989–90 season of the Market Theater in Johannesburg, where she had begun her acting career.

Her writing career has progressed as steadily as her acting career. Beginning as a journalist, she moved into playwriting, turning out the award-winning play *Have You Seen Zandile?*

She is best known for this work. Her writing talent has also moved her into the fields of poetry and children's stories. She has published collections of both.

Most recently, Mhlope has been "on the move"—in both her careers. As an actress, she is receiving attention for her one-woman performances of stories.

Focusing on the Selection

Mhlope says of her writing and storytelling, "I grew up very attached to books as friends. I started writing poems in Xhosa [an African language]. I started writing in English much later, when I was already in Johannesburg, using a public toilet as my study room."

The following selection is the story of that episode in her life. The story unfolds in an easy-to-follow flow, almost as if she were reminiscing over a cup of coffee with friends. As you read, try to identify Mhlope's emotions. How does she feel about using a public toilet as a private place for writing? What conflicts are apparent between Mhlope and South African laws and social customs? between Mhlope and other members of her family?

The Toilet

—◆◆◆—

Gcina Mhlope

Sometimes I wanted to give up and be a good girl who listened to her elders. Maybe I should have done something like teaching or nursing as my mother wished. People thought these professions were respectable, but I knew I wanted to do something different, though I was not sure what. I thought a lot about acting.... My mother said that it had been a waste of good money educating me because I did not know what to do with the knowledge I had acquired. I'd come to Johannesburg[1] for the December holidays after writing my matric[2] exams, and then stayed on, hoping to find something to do.

My elder sister worked in Orange Grove as a domestic worker,[3] and I stayed with her in her back room. I didn't know anybody in Jo'burg except my sister's friends whom we went to church with. The Methodist church up Fourteenth Avenue was about the only outing we had together. I was very bored and lonely.

On weekdays I was locked in my sister's room so that the Madam wouldn't see me. She was at home most of the time: painting her nails, having tea with her friends, or lying in the sun by the swimming pool. The swimming pool was very close to the room, which is why I had to keep very quiet. My sister felt bad about locking me in there, but she had no alternative.[4] I couldn't even play the radio, so she brought me books, old magazines, and newspapers from the white people. I just read every single thing I came across: *Fair Lady, Woman's Weekly,* anything. But then my sister thought I was reading too much.

---

[1] **Johannesburg** (joh-HAN-ihs-berg) a city in South Africa
[2] **matric** (muh-TRIHK) short for matriculation or entrance exams
[3] **domestic worker** *n.* a servant in a household
[4] **alternative** (awl-TER-nuh-tihv) *n.* choice

"What kind of wife will you make if you can't even make baby clothes, or knit yourself a jersey?[5] I suppose you will marry an educated man like yourself."

We would play cards at night when she knocked off,[6] and listen to the radio, singing along softly with the songs we liked.

Then I got this temporary job in a clothing factory in town. I looked forward to meeting new people, and liked the idea of being out of that room for a change. The factory made clothes for ladies' boutiques.[7]

The whole place was full of machines of all kinds. Some people were sewing, others were ironing with big heavy irons that pressed with a lot of steam. I had to cut all the loose threads that hang after a dress or a jacket is finished. As soon as a number of dresses in a certain style were finished, they would be sent to me and I had to count them, write the number down, and then start with the cutting of the threads. I was fascinated to discover that one person made only sleeves, another the collars, and so on until the last lady put all the pieces together, sewed on buttons, or whatever was necessary to finish.

Most people at the factory spoke Sotho,[8] but they were nice to me—they tried to speak to me in Zulu[9] or Xhosa,[10] and they gave me all kinds of advice on things I didn't know. There was this girl, Gwendolene—she thought I was very stupid—she called me a "bari"[11] because I always sat inside the changing room with something to read when it was time to eat my lunch, instead of going outside to meet guys.

The factory knocked off at four thirty, and then I went to a park near where my sister worked. I waited there till half past six, when I could sneak into the house again without the white people seeing me. I had to leave the house before half past five in the mornings as well. That meant I had to find something to do with the time I had before I could catch the seven-thirty bus to work—about two hours. I would go to a public toilet in the park. For some reason it was never locked, so I would go in and sit on the toilet seat to read some magazine or other until the right time to catch the bus.

---

[5] **jersey** (JER-zee) *n.* a pullover sweater
[6] **knocked off** *v. informal* stopped work
[7] **boutiques** (boo-TEEKS) *n. pl.* small shops that specialize in stylish clothes
[8] **Sotho** (SOH-toh) *n.* a Bantu language of Lesotho in South Africa
[9] **Zulu** (ZOO-loo) *n.* the language spoken by the Bantu people of South Africa
[10] **Xhosa** (KOH-suh) *n.* a Bantu language spoken in Cape Province in South Africa
[11] **bari** (BAR-ee) *n.* fool

The first time I went into this toilet, I was on my way to the bus stop. Usually I went straight to the bus stop outside the OK Bazaars where it was well lit, and I could see. I would wait there, reading, or just looking at the growing number of cars and buses on their way to town. On this day it was raining quite hard, so I thought I would shelter in the toilet until the rain had passed. I knocked first to see if there was anyone inside. As there was no reply, I pushed the door open and went in. It smelled a little—a dryish kind of smell, as if the toilet was not used all that often, but it was quite clean compared to many "Non-European"[12] toilets I knew. The floor was painted red and the walls were cream white. It did not look like it had been painted for a few years. I stood looking around, with the rain coming very hard on the zinc roof. The noise was comforting—to know I had escaped the wet—only a few of the heavy drops had got me. The plastic bag in

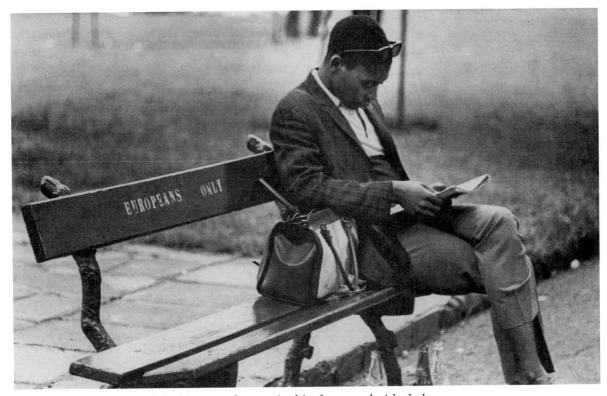

Before Apartheid was abolished in 1994, the man in this photograph risked a large fine and possible imprisonment for the simple act of sitting on a bench marked for "Europeans Only."

[12] **Non-European** *adj.* people not of European ancestry; in this case a reference to toilets reserved for black African people only

which I carried my book and purse and neatly folded pink handkerchief was a little damp, but that was because I had used it to cover my head when I ran to the toilet. I pulled my dress down a little so that it would not get creased when I sat down. The closed lid of the toilet was going to be my seat for many mornings after that.

I was really lucky to have found that toilet, because the winter was very cold. Not that it was any warmer in there, but once I'd closed the door it used to be a little less windy. Also the toilet was very small—the walls were wonderfully close to me—it felt like it was made to fit me alone. I enjoyed that kind of privacy. I did a lot of thinking while I sat on that toilet seat. I did a lot of daydreaming too—many times imagining myself in some big hall doing a really popular play with other young actors. At school, we took set books like *Buzani KuBawo* or *A Man for All Seasons* and made school plays which we toured to the other schools on weekends. I loved it very much. When I was even younger I had done little sketches taken from the Bible and on big days like Good Friday, we acted and sang happily.

I would sit there dreaming. . . .

I was getting bored with the books I was reading—the love stories all sounded the same, and besides that I just lost interest. I started asking myself why I had not written anything since I left school. At least at school I had written some poems, or stories for the school magazine, school competitions and other magazines like *Bona* and *Inkqubela*. Our English teacher was always so encouraging; I remembered the day I showed him my first poem—I was so excited I couldn't concentrate in class for the whole day. I didn't know anything about publishing then, and I didn't ask myself if my stories were good enough. I just enjoyed writing things down when I had the time. So one Friday, after I'd started being that toilet's best customer, I bought myself a notebook in which I was hoping to write something. I didn't use it for quite a while, until one evening.

My sister had taken her usual Thursday afternoon off, and she had delayed somewhere. I came back from work, then waited in the park for the right time to go back into the yard. The white people always had their supper at six thirty and that was the time I used to steal my way in without disturbing them or being seen. My comings and goings had to be secret because they still didn't know I stayed there.

Then I realised that she hadn't come back, and I was scared to go out again, in case something went wrong this time. I decided to sit down in front of my sister's room, where I thought I wouldn't be noticed. I was reading a copy of *Drum Magazine* and hoping that she would come back soon—before the dogs sniffed me out. For the first time I realised how stupid it was for me not to have cut myself a spare key long ago. I kept on hearing noises that sounded like the gate opening. A few times I was sure I had heard her footsteps on the concrete steps leading to the servants' quarters, but it turned out to be something or someone else.

I was trying hard to concentrate on my reading again, when I heard the two dogs playing, chasing each other nearer and nearer to where I was sitting. And then, there they were in front of me, looking as surprised as I was. For a brief moment we stared at each other, then they started to bark at me. I was sure they would tear me to pieces if I moved just one finger, so I sat very still, trying not to look at them, while my heart pounded and my mouth went dry as paper.

They barked even louder when the dogs from next door joined in, glaring at me through the openings in the hedge. Then the Madam's high-pitched voice rang out above the dogs' barking.

"Ireeeeeeeene!" That's my sister's English name, which we never use. I couldn't move or answer the call—the dogs were standing right in front of me, their teeth so threateningly long. When there was no reply, she came to see what was going on.

"Oh, it's you? Hello." She was smiling at me, chewing that gum which never left her mouth, instead of calling the dogs away from me. They had stopped barking, but they hadn't moved—they were still growling at me, waiting for her to tell them what to do.

"Please Madam, the dogs will bite me," I pleaded, not moving my eyes from them.

"No, they won't bite you." Then she spoke to them nicely, "Get away now—go on," and they went off. She was like a doll, her hair almost orange in colour, all curls round her madeup face. Her eyelashes fluttered like a doll's. Her thin lips were bright red like her long nails, and she wore very high-heeled shoes. She was still smiling; I wondered if it didn't hurt after a while. When her friends came for a swim, I could always hear her forever laughing at something or other.

She scared me—I couldn't understand how she could smile like that but not want me to stay in her house.

"When did you come in? We didn't see you."

"I've been here for some time now—my sister isn't here. I'm waiting to talk to her."

"Oh—she's not here?" She was laughing, for no reason that I could see. "I can give her a message—you go on home—I'll tell her that you want to see her."

Once I was outside the gate, I didn't know what to do or where to go. I walked slowly, kicking my heels. The streetlights were so very bright! Like big eyes staring at me. I wondered what the people who saw me thought I was doing, walking around at that time of the night. But then I didn't really care, because there wasn't much I could do about the situation right then.

I was just thinking how things had to go wrong on that day particularly, because my sister and I were not on such good terms. Early that morning, when the alarm had gone for me to wake up, I did not jump to turn it off, so my sister got really angry with me. She had gone on about me always leaving it to ring for too long, as if it was set for her, and not for me. And when I went out to wash, I had left the door open a second too long, and that was enough to earn me another scolding.

Every morning I had to wake up straight away, roll my bedding and put it all under the bed where my sister was sleeping. I was not supposed to put on the light although it was still dark. I'd light a candle, and tiptoe my way out with a soap dish and a toothbrush. My clothes were on a hanger on a nail at the back of the door. I'd take the hanger and close the door as quietly as I could. Everything had to be ready set the night before. A washing basin full of cold water was also ready outside the door, put there because the sound of running water and the loud screech the taps[13] made in the morning could wake the white people and they would wonder what my sister was doing up so early. I'd do my everything and be off the premises[14] by five thirty with my shoes in my bag—I only put them on once I was safely out of the gate. And that gate made such a noise too. Many times I wished I could jump over it and save myself all that sickening careful-careful business!

Thinking about all these things took my mind away from the biting cold of the night and my wet nose, until I saw my sister walking towards me.

"Mholo, what are you doing outside in the street?" she greeted me. I quickly briefed her on what had happened.

"Oh Yehovah![15] You can be so dumb sometimes! What were you doing inside in the first place? You know you should have waited for me so we could walk in together. Then I could say you were visiting or something. Now, you tell me, what am I supposed to say to them if they see you come in again? Hayi!"

She walked angrily towards the gate, with me hesitantly following her. When she opened the gate, she turned to me with an impatient whisper.

"And now why don't you come in, stupid?"

I mumbled my apologies, and followed her in. By some miracle no one seemed to have noticed us, and we quickly munched a snack of cold chicken and boiled potatoes and drank our tea, hardly on speaking terms. I just wanted to howl like a dog. I wished somebody would come and be my

---

[13] **taps** *n. pl.* faucets
[14] **premises** (PREHM-ihs-ehz) *n. pl.* house and yard, property
[15] **Yehovah** (yuh-HOH-vuh) the Hebrew name for God

friend, and tell me that I was not useless, and that my sister did not hate me, and tell me that one day I would have a nice place to live . . . anything. It would have been really great to have someone my own age to talk to.

But also I knew that my sister was worried for me, she was scared of her employers. If they were to find out that I lived with her, they would fire her, and then we would both be walking up and down the streets. My eleven rand[16] wages wasn't going to help us at all. I don't know how long I lay like that, unable to fall asleep, just wishing and wishing with tears running into my ears.

The next morning I woke up long before the alarm went off, but I just lay there feeling tired and depressed. If there was a way out, I would not have gone to work, but there was this other strong feeling or longing inside me. It was some kind of pain that pushed me to do everything at double speed and run to my toilet. I call it my toilet because that is exactly how I felt about it. It was very rare that I ever saw anybody else go in there in the mornings. It was like they all knew I was using it, and they had to lay off or something. When I went there, I didn't really expect to find it occupied.

I felt my spirits really lifting as I put on my shoes outside the gate. I made sure that my notebook was in my bag. In my haste I even forgot my lunchbox, but it didn't matter. I was walking faster and my feet were feeling lighter all the time. Then I noticed that the door had been painted and that a new windowpane had replaced the old broken one. I smiled to myself as I reached the door. Before long I was sitting on that toilet seat writing a poem.

Many more mornings saw me sitting there writing. Sometimes it did not need to be a poem; I wrote anything that came into my head—in the same way I would have done if I'd had a friend to talk to. I remember some days when I felt like I was hiding something from my sister. She did not know about my toilet in the park, and she was not in the least interested in my notebook.

Then one morning I wanted to write a story about what had happened at work the day before; the supervisor screaming at me for not calling her when I'd seen the people who stole two dresses at lunchtime. I had found it really funny. I had to write about it and I just hoped there were enough pages left in my notebook. It all came back to me, and I was smiling when I reached for the door, but it wouldn't open—it was locked!

I think for the first time I accepted that the toilet was not mine after all. . . . Slowly I walked over to a bench nearby, watched the early spring sun come up, and wrote my story anyway.

---

[16] **rand** *n. pl.* a former monetary unit of South Africa

POSTREADING

Critical Thinking

1. What aspects of the public toilet does Gcina Mhlope present? How do these aspects allow her to use the facility as a private place?

2. How does the author portray South African culture? How do you think the narrator feels about her position in society?

3. Have you ever disagreed with friends, family, or your culture group about a "dream" you may have for your future life? How was the disagreement handled?

Writing Your Response to "The Toilet"

In your journal, write about your reactions to the story. Explain how you were affected by Mhlope's wish "to do something different, though I was not sure what." How did you feel about Mhlope's choice for a private place? How does the need "to do something different" or the wish for privacy relate to your own life?

Going Back Into the Text: Author's Craft

Stories are told through the eyes of different people; that is, from different **points of view.** There are two basic points of view: **first-person** and **third-person.** Stories told from third-person point of view are narrated by an observer outside the story. The observer may be *omniscient,* or "all-knowing," describing and commenting on all the characters and actions of the story. The third-person narrator can also tell a story from a single character's point of view.

Stories told from the first-person point of view, such as "The Toilet," are told by one of the characters in his or her own words. When reading a first-person narrative, the reader can be brought close to the narrator and his/her experiences. However, this point of view is limited: the narrator tells his/her own thoughts but cannot tell the thoughts of other characters. Thus, the reader views the actions, events, and other characters only through the eyes of the narrator.

Identifying who the narrator is in a first-person story is important. His or her personal feelings, thoughts, and attitudes affect the way the story is told. As you review Mhlope's first-person narrative of her conflicts as a beginning writer, use these questions as guidelines:

1. How does Mhlope tell about the conflict between herself and other family members? Find several examples from the selection.

2. Do you think Mhlope's thoughts about her sister's feelings and thoughts are accurate? about Madame? Why? What, if any, of these characters' actions support what Mhlope thinks about them?

3. At what point in the story do you feel closest to Mhlope? Why?

PREREADING

A Chip of Glass Ruby

Reading the Story in a Cultural Context

Until 1993, South Africa ruled its citizens by a system called *apartheid* (uh-PAHR-tayt). Instituted in 1948, apartheid allowed South Africa's white minority to remain in power by keeping the black majority completely and totally separate from them. The government enforced strict laws of segregation upon black ethnic groups and set rigid restrictions in every area of their lives as well. In addition, to further control the black majority, the government assigned each of South Africa's ten black ethnic groups to a "homeland." Each group was then forced to move to its new homeland, whether its people wanted to or not.

Blacks and whites were not the only ethnic groups affected by apartheid. The government classified all its citizens into one of four groups: white, black, coloreds, and Asians. Coloreds were descendants of marriages between people of different ethnic groups, usually black, white, and Asian. Asians, who form the smallest ethnic group in South Africa, were mostly from India. The white minority governed the country. No other ethnic group had rights or freedoms equal to the whites. The whites regarded the Asians as little better than the blacks or colored.

Apartheid forms the heart of Nadine Gordimer's writings. In her work, Gordimer, herself a white South African, explores how apartheid affects every area of life and every relationship in South Africa. So forceful and compelling are her stories that, though she has won praise and admiration in the international community, the South African government has banned most of her writings at one time or another.

Gordimer is famous for zeroing in on ordinary individuals who live under apartheid. Her characters try to cope with the system's ugliness in different ways: some ignore it, some confront it, and some work to change it.

In "A Chip of Glass Ruby," Gordimer presents an Indian husband and wife who approach apartheid from two different directions. As the story proceeds, you will see how the two approaches affect the family's relationships. You will also become aware of the inner conflict of one character, as well as the more obvious conflict between a character and South African society.

Focusing on the Selection

Famous for her "keen, observant eye," Gordimer packs her stories with precise, concrete details. As you read, use the details to evaluate the different level of political activism between the two main characters.

A Chip of Glass Ruby

Nadine Gordimer

When the duplicating machine was brought into the house, Bamjee said, "Isn't it enough that you've got the Indians' troubles on your back?" Mrs. Bamjee said, with a smile that showed the gap of a missing tooth but was confident all the same, "What's the difference, Yusuf? We've all got the same troubles."

"Don't tell me that. We don't have to carry passes[1]; let the natives protest against passes on their own, there are millions of them. Let them go ahead with it."

The nine Bamjee and Pahad children were present at this exchange as they were always; in the small house that held them all there was no room for privacy for the discussion of matters they were too young to hear, and so they had never been too young to hear anything. Only their sister and half-sister, Girlie, was missing; she was the eldest, and married. The children looked expectantly, unalarmed and interested, at Bamjee, who had neither left the room nor settled down again to the task of rolling his own cigarettes, which had been interrupted by the arrival of the duplicator.[2] He had looked at the thing that had come hidden in a wash basket and conveyed[3] in a black man's taxi, and the children turned on it too, their black eyes surrounded by thick lashes like those still, open flowers with hairy tentacles that close on whatever touches them.

"A fine thing to have on the table where we eat," was all he said at last. They smelled the machine among them; a smell of cold black grease. He went out, heavily on tiptoe, in his troubled way.

---

[1] **passes** (PAS-uhs) *n.pl.* paperwork required by the South African government for black South Africans only

[2] **duplicator** (DOO-plih-kay-tuhr) *n.* a copy machine

[3] **conveyed** (kuhn-VAYD) *v.* transported

"It's going to go nicely on the sideboard!"[4] Mrs. Bamjee was busy making a place by removing the two pink glass vases filled with plastic carnations and the hand-painted velvet runner[5] with the picture of the Taj Mahal.[6]

After supper she began to run off leaflets on the machine. The family lived in that room—the three other rooms in the house were full of beds—and they were all there. The older children shared a bottle of ink while they did their homework, and the two little ones pushed a couple of empty milk bottles in and out the chair legs. The three-year-old fell asleep and was carted away by one of the girls. They all drifted off to bed eventually; Bamjee himself went before the older children—he was a fruit-and-vegetable hawker[7] and was up at half past four every morning to get to the market by five. "Not long now," said Mrs. Bamjee. The older children looked up and smiled at him. He turned his back on her. She still wore the traditional clothing of a Moslem[8] woman, and her body, which was scraggy and unimportant as a dress on a peg when it was not host to a child, was wrapped in the trailing rags of a cheap sari[9] and her thin black plait[10] was greased. When she was a girl, in the Transvaal[11] town where they lived still, her mother fixed a chip of glass ruby in her nostril; but she had abandoned that adornment as too old-style, even for her, long ago.

Black South Africans used posters like these to free South Africa from the oppression of apartheid. These efforts succeeded in 1994, when apartheid was abolished.

---

[4] **sideboard** *n.* a piece of dining room furniture containing drawers with shelves

[5] **runner** *n.* a long, narrow strip of cloth, as for a table

[6] **Taj Mahal** (tahzh muh-HAHL) *n.* a famous white marble tomb, or mausoleum, in India

[7] **hawker** (HAWK-uhr) *n.* a street peddler

[8] **Moslem** (MAHZ-luhm) *adj.* of the religion of Islam and the teachings of Mohammad

[9] **sari** (SAH-ree) *n.* an outer garment worn by women of India and Pakistan, consisting of a length of cloth wrapped about the waist to form a skirt with one end draped over the head or shoulder

[10] **plait** (playt) *n.* a braid of hair

[11] **Transvaal** (trans-VAHL) *n.* a province of South Africa

A Chip of Glass Ruby ◆ **45**

She was up until long after midnight, turning out leaflets. She did it as if she might have been pounding chillies.

Bamjee did not have to ask what the leaflets were. He had read the papers. All the past week Africans had been destroying their passes and then presenting themselves for arrest. Their leaders were jailed on charges of incitement,[12] campaign offices were raided—someone must be helping the few minor leaders who were left to keep the campaign going without offices or equipment. What was it the leaflets would say—"Don't go to work tomorrow," "Day of Protest," "Burn Your Pass for Freedom"? He didn't want to see.

He was used to coming home and finding his wife sitting at the table deep in discussion with strangers or people whose names were familiar by repute.[13] Some were prominent Indians, like the lawyer, Dr. Abdul Mohammed Khan, or the big businessman, Mr. Moonsamy Patel, and he was flattered, in a suspicious way, to meet them in his house. As he came home from work the next day he met Dr. Khan coming out of the house and Dr. Khan—a highly educated man—said to him, "A wonderful woman." But Bamjee had never caught his wife out in any presumption;[14] she behaved properly, as any Moslem woman should, and once her business with such gentlemen was over would never, for instance, have sat down to eat with them. He found her now back in the kitchen, setting about the preparation of dinner and carrying on a conversation on several different wavelengths[15] with the children. "It's really a shame if you're tired of lentils,[16] Jimmy, because that's what you're getting—Amina, hurry up, get a pot of water going—don't worry, I'll mend that in a minute, just bring the yellow cotton, and there's a needle in the cigarette box on the sideboard."

"Was that Dr. Khan leaving?" said Bamjee.

"Yes, there's going to be a stay-at-home[17] on Monday. Desai's ill, and he's got to get the word around by himself. Bob Jali was up all last night printing leaflets, but he's gone to have a tooth out." She had always treated Bamjee as if it were only a mannerism that made him appear uninterested in politics, the way some woman will persist in interpreting her husband's bad temper as an endearing gruffness hiding boundless good-will, and she talked to him of these things just as she passed on to him neighbours' or family gossip.

[12] **incitement** (ihn-SEYET-muhnt) *n.* act of stirring up

[13] **repute** (rih-PYOOT) *n.* reputation

[14] **presumption** (prih-ZUMP-shuhn) *n.* speech or conduct that is too bold

[15] **wavelengths** *n. pl.* lines of thought or communication

[16] **lentils** (LEHN-tuhlz) *n. pl.* small, flat, beanlike seeds eaten as a vegetable

[17] **stay-at-home** *n.* a strike

"What for do you want to get mixed up with these killings and stonings and I don't know what? Congress should keep out of it. Isn't it enough with the Group Areas?"[18]

She laughed. "Now, Yusuf, you know you don't believe that. Look how you said the same thing when the Group Areas started in Natal.[19] You said we should begin to worry when we get moved out of our own houses here in the Transvaal. And then your mother lost her house in Noorddorp, and there you are; you saw that nobody's safe. Oh, Girlie was here this afternoon, she says Ismail's brother's engaged—that's nice, isn't it? His mother will be pleased; she was worried."

"Why was she worried?" asked Jimmy, who was fifteen, and old enough to patronize[20] his mother.

"Well, she wanted to see him settled. There's a party on Sunday week[21] at Ismail's place—you'd better give me your suit to give to the cleaners tomorrow, Yusuf."

One of the girls presented herself at once. "I'll have nothing to wear, Ma."

Mrs. Bamjee scratched her sallow[22] face. "Perhaps Girlie will lend you her pink[23] eh? Run over to Girlie's place now and say I say will she lend it to you."

The sound of commonplaces often does service as security, and Bamjee, going to sit in the armchair with the shiny armrests that was wedged between the table and the sideboard, lapsed into an unthinking doze that, like all times of dreamlike ordinariness during those weeks, was filled with uneasy jerks and starts back into reality. The next morning, as soon as he got to market, he heard that Dr. Khan had been arrested. But that night Mrs. Bamjee sat up making a new dress for her daughter; the sight disarmed[24] Bamjee, reassured him again, against his will, so that the resentment he had been making ready all day faded into a morose[25] and accusing silence. Heaven knew, of course, who came and went in the house during the day. Twice in that week of riots, raids and arrests, he found black women in the house when he came home; plain ordinary native women in doeks,[26] drinking tea. This was not a thing other Indian women would have in

---

[18] **Group Areas** refers to an act of Congress that enforced racial segregration of neighborhoods
[19] **Natal** (nuh-TAL) *n.* a province of South Africa
[20] **patronize** (PAY-truh-neyez) *v.* "talk down" to, be condescending
[21] **Sunday week** a British expression meaning "a week from Sunday"
[22] **sallow** (SAL-oh) *adj.* having a sickly, yellowish color
[23] **pink** *n.* implies pink dress
[24] **disarmed** (dihs-AHRMD) *v.* removed anger or suspicion from
[25] **morose** (muh-ROHS) *adj.* gloomy
[26] **doeks** (derks) *n. pl.* headscarves

their homes, he thought bitterly; but then his wife was not like other people, in a way he could not put his finger on, except to say what it was not: not scandalous,[27] not punishable, not rebellious. It was, like the attraction that had led him to marry her, Pahad's widow with five children, something he could not see clearly.

When the Special Branch[28] knocked steadily on the door in the small hours of Thursday morning he did not wake up, for his return to consciousness was always set in his mind to half past four, and that was more than an hour away. Mrs. Bamjee got up herself, struggled into Jimmy's raincoat which was hanging over a chair and went to the front door. The clock on the wall—a wedding present when she married Pahad—showed three o'clock when she snapped on the light, and she knew at once who it was on the other side of the door. Although she was not surprised, her hands shook like a very old person's as she undid the locks and the complicated catch on the wire burglarproofing. And then she opened the door and they were there—two coloured policemen in plain clothes. "Zanip Bamjee?"

"Yes."

As they talked, Bamjee woke up in the sudden terror of having overslept. Then he became conscious of men's voices. He heaved himself out of bed in the dark and went to the window, which, like the front door, was covered with a heavy mesh of thick wire against intruders from the dingy lane it looked upon. Bewildered,[29] he appeared in the room, where the policemen were searching through a soapbox of papers beside the duplicating machine. "Yusuf, it's for me," Mrs. Bamjee said.

At once, the snap of a trap, realization came. He stood there in an old shirt before the two policemen, and the woman was going off to prison because of the natives. "There you are!" he shouted, standing away from her. "That's what you've got for it. Didn't I tell you? Didn't I? That's the end of it now. That's the finish. That's what it's come to." She listened with her head at the slightest tilt to one side, as if to ward off a blow, or in compassion.

Jimmy, Pahad's son, appeared at the door with a suitcase; two or three of the girls were behind him. "Here, Ma, you take my green jersey." "I've found your clean blouse." Bamjee had to keep moving out of their way as they helped their mother to make ready. It was like the preparation for one of the family festivals his wife made such a fuss over; wherever he put

---

[27] **scandalous** (SKAN-duhl-uhs) *adj.* shameful, bringing disgrace
[28] **Special Branch** *n.* a certain branch of the police force in South Africa
[29] **bewildered** (bih-WIHL-duhrd) *adj.* confused

himself, they bumped into him. Even the two policemen mumbled, "Excuse me," and pushed past into the rest of the house to continue their search. They took with them a tome[30] that Nehru[31] had written in prison; it had been bought from a persevering[32] travelling salesman and kept, for years, on the mantelpiece. "Oh, don't take that, please," Mrs. Bamjee said suddenly, clinging to the arm of the man who had picked it up.

The man held it away from her.

"What does it matter, Ma?"

It was true that no one in the house had ever read it; but she said, "It's for my children."

"Ma, leave it." Jimmy, who was squat and plump, looked like a merchant advising a client against a roll of silk she had set her heart on. She went into the bedroom and got dressed. When she came out in her old yellow sari with a brown coat over it, the faces of the children were behind her like faces on the platform at a railroad station. They kissed her goodbye. The policemen did not hurry her, but she seemed to be in a hurry just the same.

"What am I going to do?" Bamjee accused them all.

The policemen looked away patiently.

"It'll be all right. Girlie will help. The big children can manage. And Yusuf—" The children crowded in around her; two of the younger ones had awakened and appeared, asking shrill questions.

"Come on," said the policemen.

"I want to speak to my husband." She broke away and came back to him, and the movement of her sari hid them from the rest of the room for a moment. His face hardened in suspicious anticipation against the request to give some message to the next fool who would take up her pamphleteering until he, too, was arrested. "On Sunday," she said. "Take them on Sunday." He did not know what she was talking about. "The engagement party," she whispered, low and urgent. "They shouldn't miss it. Ismail will be offended."

They listened to the car drive away. Jimmy bolted and barred the front door, and then at once opened it again; he put on the raincoat that his mother had taken off. "Going to tell Girlie," he said. The children went back to bed. Their father did not say a word to any of them; their talk, the crying of the younger ones and the argumentative voices of the older, went on in the bedrooms. He found himself alone; he felt the night all around him. And then he happened to meet the clock face and saw with a

---

[30] **tome** (tohm) *n.* a large, heavy book
[31] **Nehru** (NEHR-oo) *n.* statesman and first prime minister of India
[32] **persevering** (per-suh-VEER-ihng) *adj.* not giving up

terrible sense of unfamiliarity that this was not the secret night but an hour he should have recognized: the time he always got up. He pulled on his trousers and his dirty white hawker's coat[33] and wound his grey muffler up to the stubble on his chin and went to work.

The duplicating machine was gone from the sideboard. The policemen had taken it with them, along with the pamphlets and the conference reports and the stack of old newspapers that had collected on top of the wardrobe[34] in the bedroom—not the thick dailies of the white men but the thin, impermanent-looking papers that spoke up, sometimes interrupted by suppression or lack of money, for the rest. It was all gone. When he had married her and moved in with her and her five children, into what had been the Pahad and became the Bamjee house, he had not recognized the humble, harmless and apparently useless routine tasks—the minutes of meetings being written up on the dining-room table at night, the government blue books that were read while the latest baby was suckled, the employment of the fingers of the older children in the fashioning of crinkle-paper Congress rosettes[35]—as activity intended to move mountains. For years and years he had not noticed it, and now it was gone.

The house was quiet. The children kept to their lairs, crowded on the beds with the doors shut. He sat and looked at the sideboard, where the plastic carnations and the mat with the picture of the Taj Mahal were in place. For the first few weeks he never spoke of her. There was the feeling, in the house, that he had wept and raged at her, that boulders of reproach[36] had thundered down upon her absence, and yet he had said not one word. He had not been to inquire where she was; Jimmy and Girlie had gone to Mohammed Ebrahim, the lawyer, and when he found out that their mother had been taken—when she was arrested, at least—to a prison in the next town, they had stood about outside the big prison door for hours while they waited to be told where she had been moved from there. At last they had discovered that she was fifty miles away, in Pretoria.[37] Jimmy asked Bamjee for five shillings to help Girlie pay the train fare to Pretoria, once she had been interviewed by the police and had been given a permit to visit her

---

[33] **hawker's coat** *n.* garb worn by peddlers
[34] **wardrobe** (WAWRD-rohb) *n.* closet or piece of furniture for holding clothes
[35] **crinkle -paper Congress rosettes** *n.pl.* handmade paper flowers worn as a form of protest
[36] **reproach** (rih-PROHCH) *n.* blame
[37] **Pretoria** (prih-TAWR-ee-uh) *n.* administrative capital of the Republic of South Africa

mother; he put three two-shilling pieces on the table for Jimmy to pick up, and the boy, looking at him keenly, did not know whether the extra shilling meant anything, or whether it was merely that Bamjee had no change.

It was only when relations and neighbours came to the house that Bamjee would suddenly begin to talk. He had never been so expansive[38] in his life as he was in the company of these visitors, many of them come on a polite call rather in the nature of a visit of condolence.[39] "Ah, yes, yes, you can see how I am—you see what has been done to me. Nine children, and I am on the cart all day. I get home at seven or eight. What are you to do? What can people like us do?"

"Poor Mrs. Bamjee. Such a kind lady."

"Well, you see for yourself. They walk in here in the middle of the night and leave a houseful of children. I'm out on the cart all day, I've got a living to earn." Standing about in his shirt sleeves, he became quite animated;[40] he would call for the girls to bring fruit drinks for the visitors. When they were gone, it was as if he, who was orthodox[41] if not devout and never drank liquor, had been drunk and abruptly sobered up; he looked dazed and could not have gone over in his mind what he had been saying. And as he cooled, the lump of resentment and wrongedness stopped his throat again.

Bamjee found one of the little boys the centre of a self-important group of championing brothers and sisters in the room one evening, "They've been cruel to Ahmed."

"What has he done?" said the father.

"Nothing! Nothing!" The little girl stood twisting her handkerchief excitedly.

An older one, thin as her mother, took over, silencing the others with a gesture of her skinny hand. "They did it at school today. They made an example of him."

"What is an example?" said Bamjee impatiently.

"The teacher made him come up and stand in front of the whole class, and he told them, 'You see this boy? His mother's in jail because she likes the natives so much. She wants the Indians to be the same as natives.' "

"It's terrible," he said. His hands fell to his sides. "Did she ever think of this?"

---

[38] **expansive** (ihk-SPAN-sihv) *adj.* showing one's feelings freely and openly
[39] **condolence** (kuhn-DOH-luhns) *n.* expression of sympathy
[40] **animated** (AN-uh-may-tihd) *adj.* lively
[41] **orthodox** (OR-thuh-dawx) very religious

"That's why Ma's *there*," said Jimmy, putting aside his comic and emptying out his schoolbooks upon the table. "That's all the kids need to know. Ma's there because things like this happen. Peterson's a coloured teacher, and it's his black blood that's brought him trouble all his life, I suppose. He hates anyone who says everybody's the same because that takes away from him his bit of whiteness that's all he's got. What d'you expect? It's nothing to make too much fuss about."

"Of course, you are fifteen and you know everything," Bamjee mumbled at him.

"I don't say that. But I know Ma, anyway." The boy laughed.

There was a hunger strike among the political prisoners, and Bamjee could not bring himself to ask Girlie if her mother was starving herself too. He would not ask; and yet he saw in the young woman's face the gradual weakening of her mother. When the strike had gone on for nearly a week one of the elder children burst into tears at the table and could not eat. Bamjee pushed his own plate away in rage.

Sometimes he spoke out loud to himself while he was driving the vegetable lorry.[42] "What for?" Again and again: "What for?" She was not a modern woman who cut her hair and wore short skirts. He had married a good plain Moslem woman who bore children and stamped her own chillies. He had a sudden vision of her at the duplicating machine, that night just before she was taken away, and he felt himself maddened, baffled and hopeless. He had become the ghost of a victim, hanging about the scene of a crime whose motive he could not understand and had not had time to learn.

The hunger strike at the prison went into the second week. Alone in the rattling cab of his lorry, he said things that he heard as if spoken by someone else, and his heart burned in fierce agreement with them. "For a crowd of natives who'll smash our shops and kill us in our houses when their time comes." "She will starve herself to death there." "She will die there." "Devils who will burn and kill us." He fell into bed each night like a stone, and dragged himself up in the mornings as a beast of burden[43] is beaten to its feet.

One of these mornings, Girlie appeared very early, while he was wolfing bread and strong tea—alternate sensations of dry solidity and stinging heat—at the kitchen table. Her real name was Fatima, of course, but she had adopted the silly modern name along with the clothes of the young factory girls among whom she worked. She was expecting her first baby in a week

---

[42] **lorry** (LAWR-ee) *n.* British for *truck*
[43] **beast of burden** an animal, such as a donkey, used to carry loads

or two, and her small face, her cut and curled hair and the sooty arches drawn over her eyebrows did not seem to belong to her thrust-out body under a clean smock. She wore mauve[44] lipstick and was smiling her cocky little white girl's smile, foolish and bold, not like an Indian girl's at all.

"What's the matter?" he said.

She smiled again. "Don't you know? I told Bobby he must get me up in time this morning. I wanted to be sure I wouldn't miss you today."

"I don't know what you're talking about."

She came over and put her arm up around his unwilling neck and kissed the grey bristles at the side of his mouth. "Many happy returns! Don't you know it's your birthday?"

"No," he said. "I didn't know, didn't think—" He broke the pause by swiftly picking up the bread and giving his attention desperately to eating and drinking. His mouth was busy, but his eyes looked at her, intensely black. She said nothing, but stood there with him. She would not speak, and at last he said, swallowing a piece of bread that tore at his throat as it went down, "I don't remember these things."

The girl nodded, the Woolworth baubles[45] in her ears swinging. "That's the first thing she told me when I saw her yesterday—don't forget it's Bajie's birthday tomorrow."

He shrugged over it. "It means a lot to children. But that's how she is. Whether it's one of the old cousins or the neighbour's grandmother, she always knows when the birthday is. What importance is my birthday, while she's sitting there in a prison? I don't understand how she can do the things she does when her mind is always full of woman's nonsense at the same time—that's what I don't understand with her."

"Oh, but don't you see?" the girl said. "It's because she doesn't want anybody to be left out. It's because she always remembers; remembers everything—people without somewhere to live, hungry kids, boys who can't get educated—remembers all the time. That's how Ma is."

"Nobody else is like that." It was half a complaint.

"No, nobody else," said his stepdaughter.

She sat herself down at the table, resting her belly. He put his head in his hands. "I'm getting old"—But he was overcome by something much more curious, by an answer. He knew why he had desired her, the ugly widow with five children; he knew what way it was in which she was not like the others; it was there, like the fact of the belly that lay between him and her daughter.

---

[44] **mauve** (mohv) *adj.* a light reddish or grayish purple
[45] **baubles** (BAW-buhlz) *n. pl.* showy pieces of jewelry of little value

POSTREADING

Critical Thinking

1. How does Nadine Gordimer's use of detail help you form a clear picture of both Mr. and Mrs. Bamjee? their thoughts and emotions? Locate and share examples to support your opinion.

2. What aspects of Moslem culture contribute to the conflict between Mrs. and Mr. Bamjee?

3. What opportunities exist in your community or school for political activism for your age group? How are these activities like or different from the political activities in the Bamjee's community? Which activities in your community could you support? not support? Why?

Writing Your Response to "A Chip of Glass Ruby"

Which character do you feel most comfortable with? What ideas, behavior, and thoughts make you sympathetic to or help you understand that character best? In your journal, write about that character, explaining why you can "identify" so closely with the character. If you, or someone in your own life, resembles the character of your choice, be sure to include that fact.

Going Back Into the Text: Author's Craft

Conflict occurs when two forces or characters in a story oppose each other or disagree. Conflict can be *external*, such as the conflict between Mrs. Bamjee's ideas and actions and those of the South African government. Conflict can also be *internal*, occurring when a character faces doubts and arguments within him or herself.

As you review the internal conflicts in the story, use these questions as guidelines:

1. Which character appears to be experiencing the greatest internal conflict? the least? What details helped you make your decision?

2. What conflict does Mrs. Bamjee's chip of glass ruby symbolize? Is this conflict external or internal? What is symbolized by her removal of the chip?

3. What external conflict adds to Mr. Bamjee's inner conflict? Why?

MODEL LESSON

Marriage Is a Private Affair

Responding to Literature

Notice the sidenotes in the margins of "Marriage Is a Private Affair." These notes reflect one student's reading of the story by Chinua Achebe. The student recognizes the strong opposition Okeke has against his son's marriage and his apparent prejudice towards Nnaemeka's wife because she is from outside the Ibo tribe. Compare this student's observations to your own.

Reading the Story in a Cultural Context

During the late 19th century, most of Africa was colonized by European powers. In the scramble to annex territory, the Europeans largely ignored the boundaries between different ethnic groups and cultures.

The territory now known as Nigeria came under the rule of Great Britain. British rule joined the three major cultural groups in Nigeria, the Hausa, the Ibo, and the Yoruba, under a single colonial government.

In 1960, Nigeria gained its independence from Britain. Unfortunately, struggles between the main ethnic groups led to civil war. The Ibo created their own country, Biafra. However, after a bloody conflict in which thousands were killed or starved to death, Biafra was retaken.

The victors, largely made up of the Hausa people, were generous. Few Biafran leaders were executed or jailed, and the Ibo once again held positions in the government of the nation.

During the 1970s, Nigeria grew rich from its great reserves of crude oil. This prosperity drew many people from all over the country to the large urban areas in search of jobs. A young, educated, professional class developed in such cities as Lagos and Port Harcourt. Separated from their traditional, rural way of life, these young people embraced both modern technology and modern attitudes.

Much of Chinua Achebe's writing reflects the problems created by the end of colonial rule and the sudden wealth brought by the oil boom. Born in Nigeria in 1930, Achebe celebrates the positive aspects of his culture without ignoring its problems. In "Marriage Is a Private Affair," Achebe writes about the marriage of a modern urban couple. The story explores the difficulties created when young people from different ethnic backgrounds challenge the beliefs and prejudices of their elders.

Focusing on the Selection

As you read "Marriage Is a Private Affair," think about the conflicts in the story. What understanding of human nature does the author reveal? How does the story reflect the conflict between traditional and modern attitudes in Nigeria?

Marriage Is a Private Affair

▬▬▬◆◆◆▬▬▬

Chinua Achebe

"Have you written to your dad yet?" asked Nene one afternoon as she sat with Nnaemeka in her room at 16 Kasanga Street, Lagos.[1]

"No. I've been thinking about it. I think it's better to tell him when I get home on leave!"

"But why? Your leave is such a long way off yet—six whole weeks. He should be let into our happiness now."

Nnaemeka was silent for a while, and then began very slowly as if he groped for his words: "I wish I were sure it would be happiness to him."

"Of course it must," replied Nene, a little surprised. "Why shouldn't it?"

"You have lived in Lagos all your life, and you know very little about people in remote parts of the country."

"That's what you always say. But I don't believe anybody will be so unlike other people that they will be unhappy when their sons are engaged to marry."

"Yes. They are most unhappy if the engagement is not arranged by them. In our case it's worse—you are not even an Ibo."[2]

This was said so seriously and so bluntly that Nene could not find speech immediately. In the cosmopolitan[3] atmosphere of the city it had always seemed to her something of a joke that a person's tribe could determine whom he married.

> It seems to me that Nnaemeka is already certain that his father will oppose the marriage.

---

[1] **Lagos** (LAY-gahs) *n.* the capital of Nigeria in Africa
[2] **Ibo** (EE-boh) *n.* an African people in Nigeria
[3] **cosmopolitan** (kahz-muh-PAHL-uh-tuhn) *adj.* composed of many people from many parts of the world

At last she said, "You don't really mean that he will object to your marrying me simply on that account? I had always thought you Ibos were kindly-disposed[4] to other people."

"So we are. But when it comes to marriage, well, it's not quite so simple. And this," he added, "is not peculiar to the Ibos. If your father were alive and lived in the heart of Ibibio-land he would be exactly like my father."

"I don't know. But anyway, as your father is so fond of you, I'm sure he will forgive you soon enough. Come on then, be a good boy and send him a nice lovely letter . . ."

"It would not be wise to break the news to him by writing. A letter will bring it upon him with a shock. I'm quite sure about that."

"All right, honey, suit yourself. You know your father."

As Nnaemeka walked home that evening he turned over in his mind different ways of overcoming his father's opposition, especially now that he had gone and found a girl for him. He had thought of showing his letter to Nene but decided on second thought not to, at least for the moment. He read it again when he got home and couldn't help smiling to himself. He remembered Ugoye quite well, an Amazon[5] of a girl who used to beat up all the boys, himself included, on the way to the stream, a complete dunce at school.

I have found a girl who will suit you admirably—Ugoye Nweke, the eldest daughter of our neighbor, Jacob Nweke. She has a proper Christian upbringing. When she stopped schooling some years ago her father (a man of sound judgment) sent her to live in the house of a pastor where she has received all the training a wife could need. Her Sunday School teacher has told me that she reads her Bible very fluently. I hope we shall begin negotiations when you come home in December.

On the second evening of his return from Lagos, Nnaemeka sat with his father under a cassia[6] tree. This was the old man's retreat[7] where he went to read his Bible when the parching December sun had set and a fresh, reviving wind blew on the leaves.

"Father," began Nnaemeka suddenly, "I have come to ask for forgiveness."

> Maybe Nnaemeka does not tell Nene about Ugoye because he does not want to upset her. If I were Nene, I would be upset by the letter and would resent Nnaemeka's father's involvement in his son's marriage plans.

> Nnaemeka's father mentions that Ugoye reads the Bible fluently. He himself reads the Bible during his leisure time. Maybe he is a devout Christian. I wonder if Nene is Christian.

---

[4] **disposed** (dih-SPOHZD) *v.* inclined to act in a certain manner
[5] **Amazon** (AM-uh-zahn) *n.* mythological race of female warriors; a tall, strong female
[6] **cassia** (KASH-uh) *n.* kind of tropical tree
[7] **retreat** (rih-TREET) *n.* a safe, peaceful place

"Forgiveness? For what, my son?" he asked in amazement.

"It's about this marriage question."

"Which marriage question?"

"I can't—we must—I mean it is impossible for me to marry Nweke's daughter."

"Impossible? Why?" asked his father.

"I don't love her."

"Nobody said you did. Why should you?" he asked.

"Marriage today is different . . ."

"Look here, my son," interrupted his father, "nothing is different. What one looks for in a wife are a good character and a Christian background."

Nnaemeka saw there was no hope along the present line of argument.

"Moreover," he said, "I am engaged to marry another girl who has all of Ugoye's good qualities, and who . . ."

Nnaemeka's father feels he knows what is best for his son. He does not seem willing to hear Nnaemeka's carefully framed arguments.

Depending on his tribal or family traditions, this Nigerian may already have chosen a wife for the grandson he holds in his arms.

His father did not believe his ears. "What did you say?" he asked slowly and disconcertingly.[8]

"She is a good Christian," his son went on, "and a teacher in a Girls' School in Lagos."

"Teacher, did you say? If you consider that a qualification for a good wife I should like to point out to you, Emeka, that no Christian woman should teach. St. Paul in his letter to the Corinthians says that women should keep silence." He rose slowly from his seat and paced forwards and backwards. This was his pet subject, and he condemned vehemently[9] those church leaders who encouraged women to teach in their schools. After he had spent his emotion on a long homily[10] he at last came back to his son's engagement, in a seemingly milder tone.

"Whose daughter is she, anyway?"

"She is Nene Atang."

"What!" All the mildness was gone again. "Did you say Neneataga, what does that mean?"

"Nene Atang from Calabar.[11] She is the only girl I can marry." This was a very rash reply and Nnaemeka expected the storm to burst. But it did not. His father merely walked away into his room. This was most unexpected and perplexed Nnaemeka. His father's silence was infinitely more menacing than a flood of threatening speech. That night the old man did not eat.

When he sent for Nnaemeka a day later he applied all possible ways of dissuasion.[12] But the young man's heart was hardened, and his father eventually gave him up as lost.

"I owe it to you, my son, as a duty to show you what is right and what is wrong. Whoever put this idea into your head might as well have cut your throat. It is Satan's work." He waved his son away.

"You will change your mind, Father, when you know Nene."

"I shall never see her," was the reply. From that night the father scarcely spoke to his son. He did not, however, cease hoping that he would realize how serious was the danger he was heading for. Day and night he put him in his prayers.

Nnaemeka, for his own part, was very deeply affected by his father's grief. But he kept hoping that it would pass away. If it had occurred to him

Nene is obviously educated. Perhaps this is important to Nnaemeka, despite the fact that his father objects to it.

The author uses the word "homily" to imply that Nnaemeka's father is preaching at him.

Okeke uses arguments from the Bible in order to justify his rejection of Nnaemeka and Nene. Yet, his behavior does not reflect truly Christian attitudes.

Perhaps Nnaemeka's father's reaction would have been less violent if other Ibo had married outside of the tribe in the past.

---

[8] **disconcertingly** (dihs-kuhn-SERT-ihng-lee) *adv.* in a manner that confuses and disturbs

[9] **vehemently** (VEE-uh-muhnt-lee) *adv.* forcefully; earnestly

[10] **homily** (HAHM-uh-lee) *n.* sermon; sermonlike speech

[11] **Calabar** (KAL-uh-bahr) *n.* port city in Nigeria

[12] **dissuasion** (dih-SWAY-zhun) *n.* advising against

that never in the history of his people had a man married a woman who spoke a different tongue, he might have been less optimistic. "It has never been heard," was the verdict of an old man speaking a few weeks later. In that short sentence he spoke for all of his people. This man had come with others to commiserate[13] with Okeke when news went round about his son's behavior. By that time the son had gone back to Lagos.

"It has never been heard," said the old man again with a sad shake of his head.

"What did Our Lord say?" asked another gentleman. "Sons shall rise against their Fathers; it is there in the Holy Book."

"It is the beginning of the end," said another.

Six months later, Nnaemeka was showing his young wife a short letter from his father:

It amazes me that you could be so unfeeling as to send me your wedding picture. I would have sent it back. But on further thought I decided just to cut off your wife and send it back to you because I have nothing to do with her. How I wish that I had nothing to do with you either.

When Nene read through this letter and looked at the mutilated picture her eyes filled with tears, and she began to sob.

"Don't cry, my darling," said her husband. "He is essentially good-natured and will one day look more kindly on our marriage." But years passed and that one day did not come.

For eight years, Okeke would have nothing to do with his son, Nnaemeka. Only three times (when Nnaemeka asked to come home and spend his leave) did he write to him.

"I can't have you in my house," he replied on one occasion. "It can be of no interest to me where or how you spend your leave—or your life, for that matter."

The prejudice against Nnaemeka's marriage was not confined to his little village. In Lagos, especially among his people who worked there, it showed itself in a different way. Their women, when they met at their village meeting, were not hostile to Nene. Rather, they paid her such excessive deference[14] as to make her feel she was not one of them. But as time went on, Nene gradually broke through some of this prejudice and even began

---

[13] **commiserate** (kuh-MIHZ-uh-rayt) *v.* sympathize
[14] **deference** (DEHF-uhr-uhns) *n.* courteous respect

to make friends among them. Slowly and grudgingly they began to admit that she kept her home much better than most of them.

The story eventually got to the little village in the heart of the Ibo country that Nnaemeka and his young wife were a most happy couple. But his father was one of the few people in the village who knew nothing about this. He always displayed so much temper whenever his son's name was mentioned that everyone avoided it in his presence. By a tremendous effort of will he had succeeded in pushing his son to the back of his mind. The strain had nearly killed him but he had persevered,[15] and won.

Then one day he received a letter from Nene, and in spite of himself he began to glance through it perfunctorily[16] until all of a sudden the expression on his face changed and he began to read more carefully.

> . . . *Our two sons, from the day they learnt that they have a grandfather, have insisted on being taken to him. I find it impossible to tell them that you will not see them. I implore[17] you to allow Nnaemeka to bring them home for a short time during his leave next month. I shall remain here in Lagos . . .*

The old man at once felt the resolution he had built up over so many years falling in. He was telling himself that he must not give in. He tried to steel[18] his heart against all emotional appeals. It was a reenactment of that other struggle. He leaned against a window and looked out. The sky was overcast with heavy black clouds and a high wind began to blow filling the air with dust and dry leaves. It was one of those rare occasions when even Nature takes a hand in a human fight. Very soon it began to rain, the first rain in the year. It came down in large sharp drops and was accompanied by the lightning and thunder which mark a change of season. Okeke was trying hard not to think of his two grandsons. But he knew he was now fighting a losing battle. He tried to hum a favorite hymn but the pattering of large rain drops on the roof broke up the tune. His mind immediately returned to the children. How could he shut his door against them? By a curious mental process he imagined them standing, sad and forsaken, under the harsh angry weather—shut out from his house.

That night he hardly slept, from remorse[19]—and a vague fear that he might die without making it up to them.

I think Okeke deserves the misery he experiences. He has brought it upon himself by acting out of prejudice.

The storm marks a change of season. Perhaps the season of forgiveness is near.

Even nature will not allow Okeke to find comfort in his religion while acting in such a manner. The rain drowns out his hymn.

---

[15] **persevered** (puhr-suh-VEERD) *v.* continued; kept trying

[16] **perfunctorily** (puhr-FUNGK-tuh-ruh-lee) *adv.* in an uninterested manner

[17] **implore** (ihm-PLAWR) *v.* ask urgently; beg

[18] **steel** (steel) *v.* harden

[19] **remorse** (rih-MAWRS) *n.* bitter regret or guilt

POSTREADING

Critical Thinking

1. How does Chinua Achebe reveal his attitude toward Okeke's behavior?

2. What aspects of Nigerian culture contribute to the conflict between Nnaemeka and his father?

3. Have you ever been in conflict with someone because of your traditions or beliefs? How was the conflict resolved?

Writing Your Response to "Marriage Is a Private Affair"

In your journal, write about your reactions to the story. What part of the story was most meaningful to you? How did it relate to your own life?

Going Back Into the Text: Author's Craft

A **conflict** is a struggle between opposing forces. The struggle may be internal, within the character's mind. The struggle may also be external. There are many forms of external conflict. For example, the struggle may take place between characters or between a character and a natural force (such as a storm).

As you review the conflicts in the story, use these questions as guidelines:

1. What internal conflicts do the characters in this story experience?

2. What traditions and beliefs create the external conflicts in the story?

3. How are the conflicts eventually resolved?

PREREADING

from *The Dark Child*

Reading the Story in a Cultural Context

Camara Laye belongs to the "second generation" of French African writers. He began his career in the years following World War II. The earlier generation of writers, led by Léopold Senghor and Anoma Kanié, had established a "national [African] voice." These writers were still very active in writing to protest French rule and promote independence. Thus, Laye and his contemporaries felt that they could take other subjects for their work. The first subject Laye chose was his own life.

Had he wished, Laye could have begun his autobiography with an account of his ancestors. They were Sudanese who were part of the kingdoms united by Sundiata Keita to establish the Mali Empire. Laye chose instead to present a warm, memorable "slice of life" in the traditional town of Kouroussa, French Guinea (present day Guinea.) Titled *The Dark Child*, the novel brought him almost instant international fame. It was described as "poetic," "romantic," and "idyllic" and received compliments for its simple language, its graceful charm, and the aura of dignity and sincerity with which Laye presented his family. He wrote the book in his twenties while he was studying engineering in Paris, during the early 1950s.

Although that book was a favorite with international readers, literary experts generally agree that Laye's most important work is *The Radiance of the King* (*Le Regarde du Roi*), a novel about a white man's search for personal salvation in the mysterious atmosphere of the West African jungle. Published in 1953, critics consider the novel one of the most imaginative ever produced by an African writer.

In his third novel, *A Dream of Africa*, Laye turned to political protest. His native country of Guinea gained its independence from France in 1958. The country's new, independent government had seized control of the economy and created a socialist state. Throughout the 1960s and early 1970s, the government severely punished any opposition and imprisoned many of its critics. Laye was forced to flee to neighboring Senegal in 1965 because he disagreed with the new government's policies. He wrote his third novel while he was in exile. This novel attacks the harsh methods of Guinea's ruling party at that time.

Focusing on the Selection

As you read the following excerpt from *The Dark Child*, keep in mind that Laye has written his memoir in such a way as to make it as easy as possible for readers to relate to one kind of traditional family life. What do you learn about his mother's place and power in a traditional family? How does Laye's father feel about his son's desire for "nontraditional" knowledge? How does the frequent dialogue prepare the reader for upcoming events?

from *The Dark Child*

◆◆◆

Camara Laye

When I returned to Kouroussa with my proficiency certificate in my pocket and feeling, I must confess, a little swollen with success, I was greeted with open arms, with the same eagerness and affection that had awaited me at the end of every school year. This time I had a fresh sense of pride. On the road from the station to our concession[1] there had been the most enthusiastic demonstrations of welcome, and they had all sprung from the same love and friendship. But while my parents embraced m e—my mother was probably rejoicing more over my return than over the diploma—my mind was uneasy, especially so far as she was concerned.

Before I had left Conakry the director of the school had sent for me and asked me if I would like to go to France to finish my studies. I had blithely[2] answered yes, but I had said it without having consulted my parents, without having consulted my mother. My uncles in Conakry had told me that it was a unique opportunity and that I didn't deserve to live if I turned it down. What would my parents say? Especially my mother? I did not feel at all comfortable. I waited until the first ecstatic[3] greetings were over and then announced loudly, as if the news would be a source of delight to everyone:

"And that's not all: the director wants to send me to France!"

"To France?" my mother said.

I saw her face stiffen.

---

[1] **concession** (kuhn-SEHSH-uhn) *n.* a business which is allowed to operate in a certain place
[2] **blithely** (BLEYETH-lee) *adv.* in a carefree manner; cheerfully
[3] **ecstatic** (ehk-STAT-ihk) *adj.* showing great joy

"Yes. I'm to be given a scholarship. It won't cost us anything."

"As if the cost mattered! So you're going to leave us again."

"Well, I'm not sure."

I could see that what I had been afraid of had happened. I had been too hasty in saying yes to the director.

"You're not going!" she said.

"No. But it wouldn't be for more than a year."

"A year?" said my father. "A year? That's not so very long."

"What?" my mother broke in sharply. "A year isn't so very long? For the last four years our son has been with us only on holidays, and you stand there and say a year is not so very long?"

"Well . . ." my father began.

"No, no! He's not going. That's that!"

"All right," my father said. "We won't speak of it again. This is the day of his return, his day of success. Let us rejoice. We'll talk about the other matter later."

We said no more, for people were beginning to crowd into the concession, eager to celebrate my arrival.

Late that night when everyone was in bed I went and sat beside my father under the veranda[4] of his hut. The director had told me he had to have my father's formal consent before he could do anything, and that it should reach him with as little delay as possible.

"Father," I said, "when the director asked me if I would like to go to France I said yes."

"Ah! You've already accepted."

"I couldn't help saying yes. I didn't think what I was saying at the time, or what you and my mother would think."

"Do you really want to go?"

"Yes. Uncle Mamadou says it's a unique opportunity."

"You could have gone to Dakar. Your uncle went to Dakar."

"It wouldn't be the same thing."

"No, it wouldn't. But how are we going to break the news to your mother?"

"Then you agree I should go?"

"Yes. . . . Yes, I'm willing. For your sake. For your own good."

---

[4] **veranda** (vuh-RAN-duh) *n.* a roofed porch

And he was silent a while.

"It's something I've often thought about," he said. "I've thought about it night and day. I knew quite well that eventually you would leave us. I knew it the very first time you set foot in school. I watched you studying with such eagerness, such passionate eagerness! . . . Yes, since that day I have known how it would be. And gradually I resigned myself to it."

"Father!"

"Each one follows his own destiny, my son. Men can not change what is decreed.[5] Your uncles too have had an education. As for me—but I've already told you; remember what I said when you went away to Conakry—I hadn't the opportunities they had, let alone yours. This opportunity is within your reach. You must seize it. You've already seized one, seize this one too, make sure of it. There are still so many things to be done in our land. . . . Yes, I want you to go to France. I want that now, just as much as you do. Soon we'll be needing men like you here. . . . May you not be gone too long!"

Many "traditional" Africans travel to Europe for education. This student is reading medical textbooks written in English.

---

[5] **decreed** (dih-KREED) *v.* ordered by (divine) law

We sat under the veranda for a long time without saying anything, looking out into the night. Then suddenly my father said in a broken voice:

"Promise me that you will come back."

"I will come back."

"Those distant lands . . ." he whispered slowly.

He left the phrase unfinished and continued to stare into the darkness. I could see him by the light of the storm lantern, staring as if at a fixed point and frowning as if he were dissatisfied at what he saw.

"What are you looking at?" I asked.

"Take care never to deceive anyone," he said. "Be upright in thought and deed. And God will be with you."

Then he made what seemed a gesture of despair and turned his eyes away from the darkness.

The next day I wrote the director that my father had given his permission. I kept it a secret from everyone but Kouyaté. Then I began a tour of the district. I had been given a pass and took the train wherever I wanted. I visited the nearby towns. I went to Kankan, our holy city. When I returned my father showed me the letter the director had sent him. It confirmed my departure and named the French school where I was to study. It was at Argenteuil.

"Do you know where Argenteuil is?" he asked.

"No. I'll go and have a look."

I looked it up in my dictionary and saw that it was only a few miles from Paris.

"It's near Paris," I said.

And I began to dream about Paris. I had heard about Paris for so long! Then my thoughts returned abruptly to my mother.

"Have you told her yet?" I asked.

"No. We'll go together."

"You wouldn't like to tell her yourself?"

"By myself? No, my son. Believe me, even if we both go we'll be outnumbered."

We went to look for her. We found her crushing millet[6] for the evening meal. My father stood watching the pestle[7] falling in the mortar.[8] He scarcely knew where to begin. The decision he had had to make would hurt my

---

[6] **millet** (MIHL-iht) *n.* white seeds of a grassy plant, used as a food grain

[7] **pestle** (PEHS-tuhl) *n.* a tool with a heavy rounded end, used for crushing or mashing substances

[8] **mortar** (MAWR-tuhr) *n.* a bowl in which substances are ground with a pestle

mother, and his own heart was heavy. He stood there watching the pestle and saying nothing. I dared not lift my eyes. But she was not long in guessing what was up. She had only to look at us to understand everything or almost everything.

"What do you want?" she asked. "Can't you see I'm busy?"

And she began pounding faster and faster.

"Don't go so fast," my father said. "You'll wear yourself out."

"Are you teaching me how to pound millet?" she asked.

Then all of a sudden she went on angrily: "If it's about the boy's going to France you can save your breath. He's not going!"

"That's just it," said my father. "You don't know what you're talking about. You don't realize what such an opportunity means to him."

"I don't want to know."

Suddenly she dropped the pestle and took a few steps toward us.

"Am I never to have peace? Yesterday it was the school in Conakry; today it's the school in France; tomorrow . . . what will it be tomorrow? Every day there's some mad scheme to take my son away from me! . . . Have you already forgotten how sick he was in Conakry? But that's not enough for you. Now you want to send him to France! Are you crazy? Or do you want to drive me out of my mind? I'll certainly end up raving mad. . . . And as for you," she cried, turning to me, "you are nothing but an ungrateful son. Any excuse is good enough for you to run away from your mother. But this time it won't be as *you* want. You'll stay right here. Your place is here. . . . What *are* they thinking about at the school? Do they imagine I'm going to live my whole life apart from my son? Die with him far away? Have they no mothers, those people? They can't have. They wouldn't have gone so far away from home if they had."

She lifted up her eyes to the sky and addressed the heavens:

"He's been away from me so many years already! And now they want to take him away to their own land! . . ."

Then she lowered her gaze and looked at my father again:

"Would you let them do that? Have you no heart?"

"Woman! Woman! Don't you know it's for his own good?"

"His own good? The best thing for him is to stay here with us. Hasn't he learned enough already?"

"Mother," I began.

But she turned on me violently:

"You be quiet! You're still just a little boy, a nobody. What do you want to go so far away for? Do you have any idea how people live out there? . . . No, you don't know anything about it. And tell me this, who's going to look after you? Who's going to mend your clothes? Who'll cook for you?"

"Come, come," said my father. "Be reasonable. The white men don't die of hunger."

"So you haven't noticed, you poor crazy thing, you haven't even noticed that they don't eat the way we do. The child will fall sick; that's what will happen. And then what will I do? What will become of me? Oh! I had a son once, but now I have none!"

I went up to her and took her in my arms.

"Get away from me!" she shouted. "You're no son of mine!"

But she did not push me away. She was weeping and she held me close.

"You won't leave me alone, will you? Tell me you won't leave me all alone."

But now she knew that I would go away and that she could not stop me, that nothing could stop me. Perhaps she had known from the first. Yes, she must have guessed that this was a matter where there were wheels within wheels. They had taken me from the school in Kouroussa to Conakry and finally to France. All the time she had been talking and fighting against them she must have been watching the wheels going round and round: first this wheel, then that, and then a third a greater wheel, then still more many more, perhaps, which no one could see. And how could they be stopped? We could only watch them turning and turning, the wheels of destiny turning and turning. My destiny was to go away from home. And my mother began to turn her anger on those who, she thought, were taking me away from her. But by now her anger was futile: "Those people are never satisfied. They want to have everything. As soon as they set eyes on something they want it for themselves."

"You shouldn't malign⁹ them," I replied.

"No," she said bitterly. "I shall not malign them."

Finally her anger and her rage were spent. She laid her head on my shoulder and wept loudly. My father had crept away. I held her close, I dried her tears, I said . . . what did I say to her? Everything and anything that came into my head but nothing of any importance. I don't think she understood a word. All she was aware of was the sound of my voice. That was enough. Her sobs gradually became quieter and less frequent. . . .

---

⁹ **malign** (muh-LEYEN) *v.* speak evil of

That was how my departure was arranged. And so one day I took a plane for France. Oh! it was a terrible parting! I do not like to think of it. I can still hear my mother wailing. I can still see my father, unable to hide his tears. I can still see my sisters, my brothers. . . . No, I do not like to remember that parting. It was as if I were being torn apart.

In Conakry the director told me that the plane would land at Orly.

"From Orly," he said, "you will be taken to Paris, to the Gare des Invalides. There you will take the *métro* to the Gare Saint-Lazare, and then the train to Argenteuil."

He unfolded a map of the Paris *métro* and showed me my route underground. But the map meant nothing to me. The very idea of the métro was extremely vague.

"Are you sure you understand?"

"Yes."

But I did not quite understand everything.

"Take the map with you."

I slipped it into my pocket. He looked at me.

"You're not overdressed."

I was wearing white cotton trousers, a sleeveless sports shirt open at the throat, sandals, and white socks.

"You'll have to dress warmer over there. This time of year it's already beginning to get colder."

I left for the airport with Marie and my uncles. Marie was going with me as far as Dakar where she was to continue her education. Marie. . . . I got into the plane with her. I was crying. We were all crying. Then the propeller began to turn. In the distance my uncles were waving to us for the last time. The earth, the land of Guinea, began to drop rapidly away. . . .

"Are you glad to be going?" Marie asked me when the plane was nearing Dakar.

"I don't know. I don't think so."

And when we landed she asked me: "Will you be coming back?"

Her face was wet with tears.

"Yes," I said. "Yes . . ."

I nodded yes again as I fell back in my seat, for I did not want anyone to see my tears. Surely I would be coming back! I sat a long while without moving, my arms tightly folded to stifle the sobs that wracked me. . . .

Later on I felt something hard when I put my hand in my pocket. It was the map of the *métro*. . . .

POSTREADING

Critical Thinking

1. What conflicts among the characters are revealed through dialogues between Laye and his mother? Laye and his father? his mother and father?

2. What aspects of traditional family life do you learn about through the dialogue?

3. What could a listener learn about you and a friend by listening to your conversation?

Writing Your Response to "The Dark Child"

In your journal, write about a thought, idea, or feeling that you had as you read the conversations in the selection. What was it in the dialogue that caused your reaction? How did the dialogue relate to your life or the life of someone you know?

Going Back Into the Text: Author's Craft

Dialogue is a conversation between characters. Authors can use dialogue to give background information, reveal character and character relationships, or advance the story's action, or plot. The selection's opening dialogue does all three things.

1. **Give background information.** Through the conversation, the reader learns that the main character has received a scholarship to attend school in France and that he has not lived at home for four years.

2. **Reveal character and character relationships.** Dialogue between the mother and father reveals that they disagree about the necessity and the effects of the main character's time away from home. The mother appears, at this first meeting, to be possessive and controlling. The father seems eager to avoid confrontation.

3. **Advance the story's action, or *plot*.** The opening dialogue is part of the story's exposition. The exposition gives information necessary to understanding the situation. It sets up the story and moves it along. From the conversation, you immediately learn of a long-standing family conflict and that the conflict will be at the center of the story.

Dialogue also physically moves the story from one event to the next. The ending lines of the opening dialogue are the father's agreement to forget the matter of the son's scholarship for the moment and to "rejoice." The conversation stops and friends begin arriving to welcome the son home.

As you review the selection's dialogue, use these questions as guidelines:

1. What conversations are part of the plot's rising action, the events that build the reader's expectation of a confrontation?

2. What conversation produces the selection's crisis, the confrontation between the son and father and the mother?

3. When does the conversation indicate that the crisis has ended and that the mother has accepted the son's leaving?

PREREADING

The Chair Carrier

Reading the Story in a Cultural Context

Egyptian writer Yusuf Idris says that he is a writer who never repeats himself. As one of Egypt's major literary figures, he has produced a wide range of plays, novels, and short stories. These works reflect Idris's many interests.

Idris first became famous as one of Egypt's foremost short story writers, a position he continues to hold. When he began his writing career, Idris felt that the kind of short story most popular at the time was sentimental and had no connection to real life. So he decided to take the Egyptian short story in a new and different direction. He filled his short stories with real Egyptian people in real Egyptian settings: poor Egyptian peasants going about their daily routines in the slums of Cairo or in the poor villages along the Nile.

In many of his short stories, Idris also decided that he would not have a plot. In other words, his characters wouldn't follow a sequence of actions or events that solved a problem or conflict. In his stories, nothing really "happens." Instead, Idris presents his characters and lets them share their lives with the reader for as long as their story lasts. Thus, Idris polishes and perfects his characters so that each "shines" with visible qualities and traits. He then places his characters in settings and serves up perfect little pictures of certain persons at certain times.

To "introduce" his characters, Idris often uses a narrator, an "I" who happens to meet and interact with the character. This narrator is like a video camera that focuses on a person in the street and talks with him or her for a short while. Like a camera, too, Idris presents only the "outside" of his characters. He doesn't get "inside" them to find out what makes them act or think the way they do or to learn about the problems that can trouble them.

Focusing on the Selection

As you read, notice what feelings and expectations of his own the narrator tells you. How does the narrator immediately get your attention? What feelings does the narrator have about the chair carrier? How does the narrator hope to help the chair carrier? Is his hope realized or not? How do the narrator's feelings about the chair carrier change?

The Chair Carrier

◆◆◆

Yusuf Idris

You can believe it or not, but excuse me for saying that your opinion is of no concern at all to me. It's enough for me that I saw him, met him, talked to him and observed the chair with my own eyes. Thus I considered that I had been witness to a miracle. But even more miraculous—indeed more disastrous—was that neither the man, the chair, nor the incident caused a single passer-by in Opera Square, in Gumhouriyya Street, or in Cairo[1]—or maybe in the whole wide world—to come to a stop at that moment.

It was a vast chair. Looking at it you'd think it had come from some other world, or that it had been constructed for some festival, such a colossal chair, as though it were an institution all on its own, its seat immense and softly covered with leopard skin and silken cushions. Once you'd seen it your great dream was to sit in it, be it just the once, just for a moment. A moving chair, it moved forward with stately gait as though it were in some religious procession. You'd think it was moving of its own accord. In awe and amazement you almost prostrated[2] yourself before it in worship and offered up sacrifices to it.

Eventually, however, I made out, between the four massive legs that ended in glistening gilded hooves, a fifth leg. It was skinny and looked strange amidst all that bulk and splendour; it was, though, no leg but a thin, gaunt human being upon whose body the sweat had formed runnels[3] and rivulets and had caused woods and groves of hair to sprout. Believe me, by all that's holy, I'm neither lying nor exaggerating, simply relating, be it ever

---

[1] **Cairo** (KEYE-roh) *n.* the capital of Egypt and the largest city in Africa
[2] **prostrated** (PRAS-trayt-ihd) *v.* knelt or laid face down in submission
[3] **runnels** (RUN-uhlz) *n. pl.* streamlets

so inadequately, what I saw. How was it that such a thin, frail man was carrying a chair like this one, a chair that weighed at least a ton, and maybe several? That was the proposition that was presented to one's mind—it was like some conjuring trick. But you had only to look longer and more closely to find that there was no deception, that the man really was carrying the chair all on his own and moving along with it.

What was even more extraordinary and more weird, something that was truly alarming, was that none of the passers-by in Opera Square, in Gumhouriyya Street or maybe in the whole of Cairo, was at all astonished or treated the matter as if it was anything untoward,[4] but rather as something quite normal and unremarkable, as if the chair were as light as a butterfly and was being carried around by a young lad. I looked at the people and at the chair and at the man, thinking that I would spot the raising of an eyebrow, or lips sucked back in alarm, or hear a cry of amazement, but there was absolutely no reaction.

I began to feel that the whole thing was too ghastly to contemplate any longer. At this very moment the man with his burden was no more than a step or two away from me and I was able to see his good-natured face, despite its many wrinkles. Even so it was impossible to determine his age. I then saw something more about him: he was naked except for a stout waistband from which hung, in front and behind, a covering made of sailcloth. Yet you would surely have to come to a stop, conscious that your mind had, like an empty room, begun to set off echoes telling you that, dressed as he was, he was a stranger not only to Cairo but to our whole era. You had the sensation of having seen his like in books about history or archaeology.[5] And so I was surprised

Cairo is an ancient city and a center of commerce. One is likely to see horse-drawn wagons and automobiles traveling on the same streets.

---

[4] **untoward** (uhn-TAWRD) *adj.* improper
[5] **archaeology** (awr-kee-AHL-uh-jee) *n.* the scientific study of the remains of the people, customs, and life of ancient times

by the smile he gave, the kind of meek smile a beggar gives, and by a voice that mouthed words:

"May God have mercy on your parents, my son. You wouldn't have seen Uncle Ptah Ra'?"

Was he speaking hieroglyphics[6] pronounced as Arabic, or Arabic pronounced as hieroglyphics? Could the man be an ancient Egyptian? I rounded on[7] him:

"Listen here—don't start telling me you're an ancient Egyptian?"

"And are there ancient and modern? I'm simply an Egyptian."

"And what's this chair?"

"It's what I'm carrying. Why do you think I'm going around looking for Uncle Ptah Ra'? It's so that he may order me to put it down just as he ordered me to carry it. I'm done in."

"You've been carrying it for long?"

"For a very long time, you can't imagine."

"A year?"

"What do you mean by a year, my son? Tell anyone who asks—a year and then a few thousand."

"Thousand what?"

"Years."

"From the time of the Pyramids,[8] for example?"

"From before that. From the time of the Nile."[9]

"What do you mean: from the time of the Nile?"

"From the time when the Nile wasn't called the Nile, and they moved the capital from the mountain to the river bank, Uncle Ptah brought me along and said 'Porter, take it up.' I took it up and ever since I've been wandering all over the place looking for him to tell me to put it down, but from that day to this I've not found him."

All ability or inclination to feel astonishment had completely ended for me. Anyone capable of carrying a chair of such dimensions and weight for a single moment could equally have been carrying it for thousands of years. There was no occasion for surprise or protest; all that was required was a question:

"And suppose you don't find Uncle Ptah Ra', are you going to go on carrying it around?"

---

[6] **hieroglyphics** (heye-uhr-uh-GLIHF-ihks) *n. pl.* a system of writing, used in ancient Egypt, in which symbols or pictures represent words or sounds

[7] **rounded on** turned against; attacked

[8] **Pyramids** (PIHR-uh-mihdz) *n. pl.* massive monuments found especially in Egypt, each having rectangular bases and four triangular faces

[9] **Nile** (neyel) *n.* the longest river in Africa

"What else shall I do? I'm carrying it and it's been deposited in trust with me. I was ordered to carry it, so how can I put it down without being ordered to?"

Perhaps it was anger that made me say: "Put it down. Aren't you fed up, man? Aren't you tired? Throw it away, break it up, burn it. Chairs are made to carry people, not for people to carry them."

"I can't. Do you think I'm carrying it for fun? I'm carrying it because that's the way I earn my living."

"So what? Seeing that it's wearing you out and breaking your back, you should throw it down—you should have done so ages ago."

"That's how you look at things because you're safely out of it; you're not carrying it, so you don't care. I'm carrying it and it's been deposited in trust with me, so I'm responsible for it."

"Until when, for God's sake?"

"Till the order comes from Ptah Ra'."

"He couldn't be more dead."

"Then from his successor, his deputy, from one of his descendants, from anyone with a token of authorization from him."

"All right then, I'm ordering you right now to put it down."

"Your order will be obeyed—and thank you for your kindness—but are you related to him?"

"Unfortunately not."

"Do you have a token of authorization from him?"

"No, I don't."

"Then allow me to be on my way."

He had begun to move off, but I shouted out to him to stop, for I had noticed something that looked like an announcement or sign fixed to the front of the chair. In actual fact it was a piece of gazelle-hide[10] with ancient writing on it, looking as though it was from the earliest copies of the Revealed Books.[11] It was with difficulty that I read:

O chair carrier,
You have carried enough
And the time has come for you to be carried in a chair.
This great chair,
The like of which has not been made,
Is for you alone.
Carry it

---

[10] **gazelle** (guh-ZEHL) *n.* a slender, swift-running horned antelope of Africa
[11] **Revealed Books** ancient sacred writings

And take it to your home.
Put it in the place of honour
And seat yourself upon it your whole life long.
And when you die
It shall belong to your sons.

"This, Mr. Chair Carrier, is the order of Ptah Ra', an order that is precise and was issued at the same moment in which he ordered you to carry the chair. It is sealed with his signature and cartouche[12]."

All this I told him with great joy, a joy that exploded as from someone who had been almost stifled. Ever since I had seen the chair and known the story I had felt as though it were I who was carrying it and had done so for thousands of years; it was as though it were my back that was being broken, and as though the joy that now came to me were my own joy at being released at long last.

The man listened to me with head lowered, without a tremor of emotion; just waited with head lowered for me to finish, and no sooner had I done so that he raised his head. I had been expecting a joy similar to my own, even an expression of delight, but I found no reaction.

"The order's written right there above your head—written ages ago."

"But I don't know how to read."

"But I've just read it out to you."

"I'll believe it only if there's a token of authorization. Have you such a token?"

When I made no reply he muttered angrily as he turned away:

"All I get from you people is obstruction. Man, it's a heavy load and the day's scarcely long enough for making just the one round."

I stood watching him. The chair had started to move at its slow, steady pace, making one think that it moved by itself. Once again the man had become its thin fifth leg, capable on its own of setting it in motion.

I stood watching him as he moved away, panting and groaning and with the sweat pouring off him.

I stood there at a loss, asking myself whether I shouldn't catch him up and kill him and thus give vent to my exasperation. Should I rush forward and topple the chair forcibly from his shoulders and make him take a rest? Or should I content myself with the sensation of enraged irritation I had for him? Or should I calm down and feel sorry for him?

Or should I blame myself for not knowing what the token of authorization was?

---

[12] **cartouche** (kar-TOOSH) *n.* a scroll-like ornament

POSTREADING

Critical Thinking

1. How does Yusuf Idris set the reader up for the story's ironic ending? Give examples from the selection that build an expectation that the chair carrier will be relieved of his heavy burden.

2. What details about the lives of Egyptian peasants do you learn about as you read?

3. How do the narrator's feelings about the chair carrier change from the story's beginning to the end? Does the narrator succeed in making you share his feelings? Why?

Writing Your Response to "The Chair Carrier"

Have you ever been involved in an ironic situation? Have you ever met or had dealings with someone like the chair carrier? In your journal, relate the situation and your feelings. How did the ironic situation finally resolve itself?

Going Back Into the Text: Author's Craft

Irony is a contrast between what is expected to happen and what actually happens, or what is said and what is really meant. Irony may be used for comic or surprising effects in a play, story, essay, or nonfiction.

Irony of situation is the basis for many TV and movie comedies. It occurs when what a person *expects* to happen is far different from what actually does happen.

Verbal irony happens when a person's actual words or thoughts are the opposite of their real meaning.

As you review the irony in the selection, use these questions as guidelines:

1. The author begins the story with a verbally ironic comment: "... your opinion is of no concern to me." What he really means is that the reader/listener's opinion is *very* important: that's why he's telling the story. Can you find other instances of ironic comments in the selection?

2. What irony of situation occurs? Explain the effect that it has on the listener; that is, are you amused or surprised? Why?

3. Does the story's ending satisfy you? Why?

Reviewing the Region

1. Choose two authors of selections in this chapter. Discuss their attitudes toward their culture. Give examples from the selection.

2. What are the various ways authors can show their feelings about their country? Choose a poem and a story from this chapter and discuss this question as it applies to the selections you have chosen.

3. Choose a character with whom you identify from one of the selections in this chapter. Have you had to confront problems similar to those dealt with by this character? Explain.

2 Middle East

Literature of the Middle East is not that of a single people or even a group of related nations. The Moslem religion has contributed much to Middle Eastern literary traditions. However, not all the writers in its long history have been Moslems. Cultural groups such as Persians, Turks, Europeans, Jews, and northern and central African peoples have contributed to the Middle Eastern literary traditions.

The earliest form of writing to become an enduring part of the Arabic literary tradition was poetry. This chapter begins with a part of one of the oldest Arabic poems called *The Masnavi*.

Writers of traditional Arabic poetry and prose gained their reputation as the most learned among the learned. Yet with the European influence in the region, the old traditions began to change. Arabic literature during the 20th century has been shaped by Western literary forms such as fiction, the novel, and the short story. By the end of World War II, Arabic literature had shown the influence of many different voices and a broad range of subjects. Arabs began to look to their own daily lives for literary material. From Turkey and Kuwait, you will read short stories whose main characters are everyday working-class people. You might be surprised at how familiar their experiences seem.

The Arab-Israeli conflict of the past 50 years has had an impact on the literature of the Middle East. Two poems in this chapter reflect the conflicts as they were felt by Arabs in Israel.

You will then read three poems by the famous Israeli poet Yehuda Amichai. Think carefully about why the emotions in all five of these poems are similar.

This chapter ends with a humorous short story from contemporary Israel. The author pokes fun at the high society airs of today's Middle East.

As you read, think about how the political and religious conflicts and the daily lives of the people of the Middle East are both unique to the region and familiar to us.

This terra-cotta relief of a man and woman was crafted over 4000 years ago. It comes from an ancient civilization in the Tigris-Euphrates Valley.

The Marks of the Wise Man, of the Half Wise, and of the Fool

Reading the Poem in a Cultural Context

Persian poet Jalal al-Din al-Rumi was respected and admired for both his spiritual teachings and his poetry. Born in the central Asian city of Balkh, Rumi moved to Anatolia (now Turkey) with his family when he was ten. His father, a religious teacher, continued his profession in Konya, the capital of Anatolia, and on his death in 1231, Rumi took over his position.

At that time, many Moslems felt that the ruling classes led worldly and immoral lives. These Moslems called for people to return to strict Islam teachings. These teachings encouraged the fear of God. They also reminded people of the shortness of life in this world and warned them to prepare for Judgment Day. Rumi agreed with such beliefs. Filled with an overwhelming love for God, he founded his own brotherhood. This sect, called Sufism, is a branch of Islam. Members of this sect were called "whirling dervishes" because they twirled or spun as they meditated. Rumi himself performed a whirling dance whenever he meditated. He taught that such dancing enhanced meditation, brought enlightenment and wisdom, and could lead to direct communication with Allah.

Sufism had a tremendous influence, not only in the Arab world, but eventually in other countries as well. Its influence was due in part to the poetry Rumi wrote at the suggestion of his students. His most famous work is the *Masnavi*, a long poem that contains his teachings and beliefs. The *Masnavi* provided guidance for his students, as well as future generations, to attain wisdom. He composed his verses as he meditated, at any time and in any place. Once Rumi had finished a poem, he rarely reworked or revised it; most of his poetry retains the fresh, vibrant quality of having "just been thought of."

The *Masnavi* is considered one of the most important works of Islamic mysticism. It has been translated into many languages and read and analyzed by many religious and literary scholars. Many contemporary Moslems continue to seek guidance from it on the path to wisdom.

Focusing on the Selection

As you read "The Marks of the Wise Man, of the Half Wise, and of the Fool," keep in mind that because Rumi's purpose was to teach, his poetry is filled with emotion and images taken from the daily life of the times. How does Rumi describe the qualities of the wise man? How is the fool recognizable? the half-wise man?

The Marks of the Wise Man, of the Half Wise, and of the Fool

Rumi
translated by *E. H. Whinfield*

The wise man is he who possesses a torch of his own;
He is the guide and leader of the caravan.[1]
That leader is his own director and light;
That illuminated one follows his own lead.
He is his own protector; do ye[2] also seek protection
From that light whereon his soul is nurtured.
The second, he, namely, who is half wise,
Knows the wise man to be the light of his eyes.
He clings to the wise man like a blind man to his guide,
So as to become possessed of the wise man's sight.
But the fool, who has no particle of wisdom,
Has no wisdom of his own, and quits the wise man.
He knows nothing of the way, great or small,
And is ashamed to follow the footsteps of the guide.
He wanders into the boundless desert,
Sometimes halting and despairing, sometimes running.

This illustration is titled "Solon and His Students." It was drawn during the Seljuk Dynasty that ruled Turkey 200 years before Rumi was born.

---

[1] **caravan** (KAR-uh-van) *n.* a group of people traveling together for safety
[2] **ye** (yee) *pron.* old-world term for *you*

He has no lamp wherewith to light himself on his way,
Nor half a lamp which might recognize and seek light.
He lacks wisdom, so as to boast of being alive,
And also half wisdom, so as to assume to be dead.
That half wise one became as one utterly dead
In order to rise up out of his degradation.[3]
If you lack perfect wisdom, make yourself as dead
Under the shadow of the wise, whose words give life.
The fool is neither alive so as to companion with 'Isa,[4]
Nor yet dead so as to feel the power of 'Isa's breath.
His blind soul wanders in every direction,
And at last makes a spring, but springs not upward.

---

[3] **degradation** (dehg-ruh-DAY-shuhn) *n.* low status; shame
[4] **'Isa** (EYE-suh) *n.* Jesus, considered by Moslems to be an important prophet

POSTREADING

Critical Thinking

1. How does Rumi describe each kind of man?

2. What are the cultural values that Rumi's work reflect?

3. How could you apply his message to your life?

Writing Your Response to "The Marks of the Wise Man"

In your journal, write your response to Rumi's teachings. Do you agree with the qualities and duties that Rumi assigns to each kind of man? Would you be able to follow his guidelines? Would you want to? Why?

Going Back Into the Text: Author's Craft

Didactic poetry and literature teaches factual information or moral lessons. Didactic literature is an important part of many religions. This literature teaches its lessons through simple stories, short tales, or fables.

Didactic literature defines a culture's values and establishes rules and standards of behavior. It often teaches through *aphorisms,* or short pointed statements, such as: see no evil, hear no evil, speak no evil. A didactic story contains or ends with a *moral,* a rule about right and wrong conduct.

As you review the teachings in the poem, use these questions as guidelines:

1. With what does Rumi compare the wisdom of the wise man?

2. What is the wisdom that the half-wise man possesses?

3. What are the duties of the wise man?

4. How can the half-wise man and the fool gain wisdom?

The House
on the Border

Reading the Story in a Cultural Context

Aziz Nesin is one of the most popular contemporary Turkish writers. He is often labeled "humorist and humanitarian" as well as "writer." Nesin was jailed many times in his life because of his disagreement with Turkey's government. Since the government would not allow him to publish under his own name, Nesin has written under more than two hundred false names.

Nesin's work as a writer has never been easy or financially rewarding. However, his stories show a sense of humor that is rooted in a sense of life's absurdity and its injustice. Many of Nesin's characters, caught in strange circumstances, laugh and give a sort of shrug that says, "Oh, well, what's a person to do?" This acceptance creates a mood that Islamic book reviewers have called a total surrender to *kismet*, the Moslem belief in fate.

Nesin's storytelling comes from two primary sources: popular Islamic literature and the street theaters of his childhood. His sense of life's basic silliness and unfairness comes from Islamic traditions. The street plays and folklore taught him "nonsense" formulas and how to make patterns of repeated conversations.

Some literary techniques that Nesin uses are the result of needing to outwit the censors. For example, his writing is often in the form of a folktale. He might locate a story in unreal settings, or he might not describe a setting at all. He gives very few details about his characters. This kind of creativity allows Nesin to continue producing the kind of books and plays he wants to, rather than the official and "safe" literature that is accepted by his government.

One of Nesin's favorite themes is an innocent victim or scapegoat caught in a world ruled by dishonest people and fools. Perhaps his childhood in an orphanage, his prison sentences, and his years in poverty contribute to this theme. Yet they also contribute to a feeling of kinship with the masses of common people in his country.

Focusing on the Selection

Nesin says that in his stories he addresses himself to the common yearnings, longings, and frustrations that all human beings share. As you read the selection, be aware of the characters' emotions and what causes them. What do the main characters want? What causes the neighbors' visit? What is the reaction of the police in both precincts to the man's predicament? How realistic is the situation in which the new homeowners find themselves?

The House on the Border

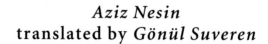

Aziz Nesin
translated by *Gönül Suveren*

We had moved into the house the day before. It was a nice place. That morning when I walked out, our next-door neighbor, an old man, was watching the street with avid curiosity and called us from his window.

"You shouldn't have rented that place," he cackled.

I stared at him coldly.

"Is this a new way of greeting neighbors?" I growled. "What do you mean we shouldn't have moved in there?"

He was not fazed.[1]

"Thieves break into that house often," he announced with relish. "It's my neighborly duty to warn you."

As if the thieves couldn't break into his house too! Why should robbers favor only ours?

Rather annoyed, I entered the grocery store at the corner to buy cigarettes.

"There are such characters around," I mumbled.

"What's the matter?" asked the grocer.

"Some old goat told me that thieves usually rob the house we just moved into," I complained.

The grocer nodded. "Well, the old goat was right. You shouldn't have rented that house. It's robbed frequently."

I was furious. Without answering him, I walked out of the store. The whole day was ruined, naturally. I fumed till evening. That night a couple

---

[1] **fazed** (fayzd) *v.* bothered; worried

from our block visited us. They were nice people. We talked about this and that till midnight. When they were about to leave, the husband turned and looked at us strangely.

"It's a beautiful house," he said, "but thieves never leave it alone."

Since they were already out of the house, I couldn't ask him: "Why is this house supposed to be irresistible to thieves? Why shouldn't they honor your home too?"

Seeing my ferocious scowl, my wife started to laugh.

"Dearest," she said, "don't you understand? God knows, they have thousands of tricks for scaring tenants away. This must be the newest one. They will drive us out, and, since the rent is low, they will either move in themselves or bring in one of their relatives."

It was possible. But I couldn't sleep a wink that night. It was as if I had a date with the thief. I waited for him breathlessly, whispering to myself: "He will be here any moment."

I must have dozed off. I jumped up at a slight noise and grabbed the gun I had hidden under my pillow.

"Don't move or I'll shoot," I yelled into the darkness.

As I already said, we had moved in the day before. Now, confronted with a nocturnal[2] visitor, I forgot where the light switch was. Groping in the dark, I got entangled in every conceivable object and bumped into the walls in search of a switch. As if this was not enough, some darned thing coiled around my shapely ankles, and with a resounding crash, I found myself on the floor. "The dirty—," I muttered under my breath. "He tripped me." Unfortunately, during my solo flight to the floor, the gun had fallen from my hand and bounced away.

The darkness was suddenly filled with a horrible laughter: "Heh! Heh! Heh!"

"Are we shooting a domestic horror movie?" I shouted. "If you are a man, show your face, you . . . you villain!"

"I suppose you were looking for the switch," a voice said in the darkness. "It's amazing how all the new tenants make the same mistake."

"Do you know what I'm going to do to you?"

"No," said the man in the darkness. "I don't know. Now, may I turn on the lights and help you?"

---

[2] **nocturnal** (nahk-TER-nuhl) *adj.* nighttime

I heard the click of the switch, and the room was flooded with light. Apparently, when I had crashed down, I had rolled under the table. As for my wife, she was securely lodged under the bed.

There in the middle of the room stood a man larger than life—twice my size, I mean.

I knew that if I emerged from my hiding place, I couldn't scare him. I decided he wouldn't be able to size me up if I stayed there.

Imitating a basso profundo[3] to the best of my ability, "Who are you?" I asked. It was a deep-chested growl.

"I'm the thief," he answered calmly.

"Oh, yeah?" I said. "If you think I'm a fool, you're mistaken. You're not a thief. You're trying to scare us away and move in here. Look at me, look closely. Do I look like an idiot?"

He didn't answer my question. "You'll see whether I'm a thief or not," he said instead.

You'd have thought it was his own father's house. He started to rummage through the drawers, picking out what items he fancied and talking to us all the while. I have to admit that he was quite friendly.

"So you turned this into a bedroom. . . . The family before you used it as a study. The ones before them too . . ."

"Now look," I said. "You're robbing me. I'll report you to the police."

Without stopping, "Please do," he replied. "Go to the precinct. And don't forget to give them my best regards."

"But you'll run away while I'm gone."

"I won't."

"You will! You will clean up the whole house and steal away." It was a dilemma. "I have an idea," I said. "First I'll tie you up, then I'll go to the police."

"Help!" shrieked my wife suddenly.

Were all the neighbors waiting on our doorstep, I wonder? As if on cue, they stampeded into the house, chattering excitedly. But did they look at us or offer sympathy? No. They were full of curiosity and in good spirits.

"Another robbery," they said.

"What, again?"

"Who is it this time?"

"Let's see."

---

[3] **basso profundo** *n.* a deep, heavy voice, as that of a male singer

Some of them were downright friendly with the thief. They even asked him how he was, while he calmly went on packing our things.

"Help!" I croaked. "Help! I must bind him up. I'll go to the precinct."

One of the neighbors shook his head.

"It won't do you any good," he said. "But I never stop people from doing what they want. . . . Go ahead."

What kind of a neighborhood was this anyway?

Suddenly emboldened, my wife brought me the clothesline. The thief didn't resist while I tied him up securely. We carried him into another room and locked the door.

We ran to the police. My wife considered herself the spokesperson of the family and told the story to the chief. He asked for our address.

"Aha," said the chief. "That house."

"Yes," I answered, "that house."

"We have nothing to do with that house," he informed us. "It's not in our jurisdiction."[4]

"What are we going to do now? Did we tie that poor fellow up for nothing?"

"If you lived in the house next door, we could have done something," the chief said. Then, as if addressing a couple of morons, he added, "You would have been in our jurisdiction."

"That house was not vacant," my wife explained patiently. "So we moved into this one."

We learned that our house was right on the border between areas under the jurisdiction of two precincts.

"The other precinct should look into the matter," said the chief.

The other precinct was quite far away. By the time we reached it, the sun was already high in the sky. We told our story again, and again they asked our address.

"That house," said one of the cops.

"That house," I said.

"If you lived next door, we would have done something. Your house is not within our jurisdiction."

"Poor man," murmured my wife. "We tied him up."

"Tell me," I cried out impatiently. "Tell me one thing. Under whose jurisdiction are we? Who is supposed to look after us?"

---

[4] **jurisdiction** (joor-ihs-DIHK-shuhn) *n.* range of authority

"The state gendarmerie,"[5] said the cop. "Your house is under their jurisdiction. The police have nothing to do with it."

We left the cops.

"Let's go home first," suggested my wife. "I'm worried about the thief. He might die, you know."

She was right, of course. What if the thief should die of hunger? Or heart failure? After all, he was trussed up like a chicken. What if the ropes would impede the circulation of his blood? What if . . .

We went home. The thief was where we had left him.

"How are you?" I asked anxiously.

"Fine, fine," he answered. "But I'm hungry."

My wife ran to the kitchen. Alas, we had spinach, but—would you believe it—it was the only dish the thief detested. My wife dashed to the butcher, bought some steaks, and fed the thief.

This time we went to the gendarmerie. After listening to our story, the commandant asked for our address.

"Aha," he said. "That house."

Apparently, we had rented a famous place.

The commandant shook his head. "This is not a case for the gendarmerie. You should call the police."

"Now look," I cried. "We went to the police. They sent us here. Now you say we must call the cops. Is this a runaround? Isn't there anybody to look into the case?"

The commandant pulled out a map.

"I hope you know how to read a map," he said. "Here, it gives the height. See? One hundred and forty feet. This is the water tower—116 feet—and here is the hill. Now, this area is under the jurisdiction of the gendarmerie. If your house were built further up, say about two yards toward the northwest, you would have been in our area."

"All this for two lousy yards," I said. "Do something, man! What would happen if you helped us now?"

The commandant pursed his lips. "What would happen?" he repeated. Then he nodded his head sagely. "Only we know what would happen. . . . Only we know." Again he put his finger on a spot on the map. "Look, this is your house. Right on the line that separates our area from the police's. See? Of course, a part of your garden is under our jurisdiction. But the robbery didn't take place there, did it?"

---

[5] **gendarmerie** (jahn-DAHRM-uh-ree) *n.* police force

The Gray House was painted by Marc Chagall during the 20th century. Most of his life was spent in France; yet paintings such as this depict the Russian town where he was born.

There was nothing we could do but go to the police again.

"Let's first see how the thief is doing," my wife suggested. "God help us if something should happen to him."

So we went home.

I almost clasped the thief to my bosom. "How are you?" I panted.

"Water! Quick!" he cried out. "I'm thirsty!"

After drinking the water, he looked at us sternly.

"Listen," he said. "Don't say that I didn't warn you. You have no right to hold me here. You are restricting the freedom of a citizen. I have a good mind to sue you."

"But what can we do?" I cried. "We don't know who is supposed to look after us. Apparently, we are in the middle of nowhere. Why they built this house right on the border line is beyond me."

"Didn't I tell you? . . . Now, let me go. Otherwise I'll drag you through the courts for restricting my freedom."

"Give me time," I begged. "Give me till tonight. I want to go to the police again."

"By all means," he replied affably.[6] "Go and see anyone you wish. But it's futile.[7] I've been aware of the situation for a long time now. They have to decide whether to include your house in one of the areas or change the borders. Till then . . ."

Again we went to the precinct. This time the chief brought out a map too.

"Look," he sighed, "this area is under the jurisdiction of the gendarmerie. Your garden and a small part of the house are within their area. Only a fraction of the house is under our jurisdiction."

"The bedroom is in your area," I pointed out. "And the robbery took place there."

He looked at me owlishly. "Quite. First this must be definitely established. Then there is another problem: the thief didn't fly in through the window, did he? He crossed the garden and then entered your house. Right? And the garden is under the jurisdiction of the gendarmerie. Yours is not a new problem. It is already under discussion. First they have to reach a decision; then they have to inform us of their decision concerning the area your house is supposed to be in. Then we can act accordingly."

We returned home. Our elderly next-door neighbor was at the window, as usual.

"So they broke into the house again," he cackled.

"Yes," I nodded.

"No one stays there long," he said cheerfully. "That's why the rent is low. Neither the owner nor the tenants could live there. The owner decided to pull down the house and rebuild it two yards further up. But then he found you fools—I mean he found you and rented the place."

His wife was looking at us sadly. "It's not your fault," she informed us. "It's the owner's. When they build a house they think of water, gas, electricity, and the view. But do they think of the jurisdiction? No! What sort of a fool would build a house right on the border?"

I couldn't answer that question even if I wanted to.

Since we had paid the whole year's rent in advance, to move away was out of the question. So we went home and untied the thief. Then we settled down comfortably in the study and discussed the world situation for a while. The thief dined with us that evening.

"So long," he said after the meal. "I'll be back tonight."

---

[6] **affably** (AF-eh-blee) *adv.* in a friendly manner
[7] **futile** (FYOO-tihl) *adj.* useless

Now we have five or six resident thieves. All our neighbors are familiar with them. We collaborate[8] with the thieves too. That is to say, we help them to defend our home against other, unfriendly thieves, who are, after all, strangers to us.

I don't know what will happen eventually. Either all eight of us, my wife and I and the six thieves, will spend the remainder of the year here, or they will include the house in one of the areas, thus enabling me to complain to the authorities. But we are now used to our friends, the thieves. And to report them would be rather embarrassing—after all, they share the household expenses now.

---

[8] **collaborate** (kuh-LAB-uh-rayt) *v.* cooperate; work together

POSTREADING

Critical Thinking

1. How does Aziz Nesin reveal his feelings about each character through actions or conversation?

2. What aspects of local government increase the frustration of the main character?

3. Have you ever been caught "in the middle" of an argument or struggled with local political "red tape?" How did you solve your problem?

Writing Your Response to "The House on the Border"

Remember that Nesin writes to "the common yearnings, longings and frustrations that all human beings share." In your journal, tell whether or not Nesin achieved his aim with you. Use a scene from the story to support your opinion, explaining how the story did or did not relate to your life.

Going Back Into the Text: Author's Craft

Literary satire is writing that ridicules or calls forth in the reader feelings of amusement, contempt, or scorn. These feelings are directed at the weaknesses and wrongdoings of individuals, groups, institutions, or humanity in general. Satire aims to change behavior, whether the behavior is simply silly and thoughtless or carefully planned and destructive.

Satire can be gentle and humorous or fierce and scornful. Satirists can use many techniques to show human weakness or destructive behavior—humor, absurdity, exaggeration, sarcasm, irony. As you review the selection's satire, use these questions as guidelines:

1. What characters does the author seem to be satirizing?

2. What part do attitudes and beliefs play in this satire?

3. How does the ironic ending contribute to the satire?

MAKING THEMATIC CONNECTIONS

Reflections of the Past

All literature has its beginnings in folktales, or traditional stories that have been handed down from generation to generation. Through word of mouth as well as the written word, the tradition of storytelling helps define a culture's ideals, values, and goals while it entertains the listener.

Folktales have been created by many different cultures and can take many different forms. Some traditional tales in this book, such as "Savitri" and "Sundiata," show char-acters overcoming a problem through cleverness, wisdom, and goodness.

Some folktales attempt to explain how events in nature came to be. These stories are called creation myths or legends. The selection from the *Popol Vuh*, which is the bible of the Mayan people, not only tells of the creation of man, but of the origins of the rich and the poor. The myth from Yoruba in this unit, "Owner of the Sky: Olorun the Creator" explains human suffering as the result of con-

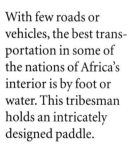

With few roads or vehicles, the best transportation in some of the nations of Africa's interior is by foot or water. This tribesman holds an intricately designed paddle.

flict between the gods. In the Australian folktale "Tangaroa, Maker of All Things," God makes everything on the earth from pieces of himself. You'll read about the legend of the creation of New Zealand in "Maui and the Great Fish."

You'll also read two fables. The poem "The Marks of the Wise Man, of the Half Wise, and of the Fool" describes the differences among all three types of men. The story

"The Nightingale's Three Bits of Advice" tells a humorous tale of what happens when a man doesn't heed some wise counsel.

Through these folktales, we learn about the storytellers' culture, values, and beliefs. By entertaining their listeners and readers with colorful characters and humorous adventures, storytellers make sure that their audiences learn the lesson that is taught in each tale.

ACTIVITY

As you have read, folktales often attempt to explain how the world was created, why events occur in nature, or how people overcome problems in their lives. Unlike modern writings, folktales were fequently created and changed by many people, often over many generations. They are a group effort.

In this activity, you will work with a group to create your own folktale. Remember that in folktales, any character can talk or act in any way you wish to illustrate your point. Your aim is to tell a tale that will teach your listeners a lesson.

1. Form a group of four to five students.

2. Decide among yourselves what story you will tell or what lesson you will teach. You might explain why the sun rises in the morning or tell a tale about someone who has achieved a goal through kindness to others. Your characters can be people, animals, plants, or objects.

3. Decide on a time and place for your folktale. It could be set in the past or present, at a certain time of year, or even at a certain time of day or night. The place can be real or imagined.

4. Sketch out your folktale. Everyone in the group should add to the story.

5. Each group member should write his or her own version of the story. Group members should take turns reading their folktales aloud.

6. Use elements of each member's folktale to construct a group folktale. Each group should then read its folktale aloud to the class.

PREREADING

4 + 1 = 1

Reading the Story in a Cultural Context

Ismail Fahd Ismail is one of the best-known writers on the Arabian peninsula. He lives in Kuwait, the small oil-rich country on the peninsula's eastern coast that was the focus of the Persian Gulf War in early 1991. Although Ismail worked in film and theater, he earned his reputation with his short stories and novels. These works have been well-received on the Arab literary scene.

The most striking characteristic of Ismail's work is its variety of subject and theme. In his novels and short stories, he has explored many issues that are relevant in Middle Eastern culture. He has written on such issues as the Arab-Israeli conflict, terrorism, and Egyptian history. His writings also reflect his analysis of Iraqi and Kuwaiti societies. Often, his main characters are "running away" from their present situations, not in a physical sense but in a mental sense. Often they are looking for ways to change their lives. Sometimes they change in ways that are accepted by their society. Sometimes they do not.

His writing style and use of language are qualities for which he has received much attention. He avoids long narrative passages and generally provides few descriptions of setting, characters, or emotion. Most of his prose features short sentences, often in the form of exclamations or brief dialogue. Indeed, Ismail uses dialogue, between characters as well as within a character, to convey information that other writers might describe in paragraphs. Not only can he present setting and character through dialogue, but he can also accurately and effectively convey mood.

In "4+1=1," Ismail writes about a group of workers who act together to save a fellow worker. In a sense, they "act as one," which is the meaning of the title. The story could take place anywhere but it is set in Kuwait, where the power and wealth of the country are concentrated in the hands of the ruling family. Ordinary people like the workers in the story have few rights. Therefore, the kindness of the workers is all the more remarkable.

Focusing on the Selection

As you read "4 + 1 = 1," be aware that some of the dialogue is *external*, among the workers. However, much of the dialogue is *internal*, within the central character's mind. Pay close attention to the "extra" information the dialogue presents. Where does this story take place? What are the people like who are in charge? How do the workers feel about each other?

4 + 1 = 1

Ismail Fahd Ismail
translated by
Roger Allen and Christopher Tingley

The noise from the machines was overpowering; if you needed to talk to the man working alongside you, you had to shout at the top of your voice. The few workers manipulated the machines with swift, disciplined movements. The cleaner was sweeping the floor with a long-handled broom, his head bowed as he concentrated totally on his job, unaware of anything that was happening round him. But when he was just underneath the fan, he stopped for a moment and leaned on the broom, smiling as he let the breeze from the whirling fan cool him.

"I'll have this corridor finished in a few minutes," he thought. He took out a handkerchief. One of the workers squeezed past between him and one of the machines, and he moved slightly, without saying a word to the man. He mopped the sweat from his face.

"Only the next corridor left now."

He put the handkerchief back in his pocket.

"There's the director's office too, of course . . ."

He grabbed the broom halfway down the handle and moved back a step to pick up the pile of dust from the floor.

"What on earth's happened?"

A cry of panic almost shot out of his mouth. The broom-handle had crashed into something, the broom was shaking in his hand. There was a muffled sound amid the din of the machines.

"Why didn't I look behind me?"

Pieces of broken glass all over the floor.

"I'm an idiot!"

Electrical contact. A flashing spark.

"We'll all be burned to a crisp!"

The shock of it all paralyzed his senses.

"What have I done?"

Puffs of smoke. Power failure.

"Now what's happening?"

The machines begin to slow down.

"Are they going to stop?"

They stopped.

"It was the broom-handle! It . . ."

All-pervasive[1] silence, except for the fan which started to slow down too.

"What's happened?" asked one of the workers in alarm, from behind the row of machines.

All the workers came over to the spot where there was broken glass on the floor.

"Who broke the regulator?" one of them asked in disbelief.

". . ."

The workers exchanged glances; then they all stared at the cleaner. He turned as white as a sheet, his lips quivering.

"I don't know how . . . how it . . ." he mumbled.

"You broke it?"

All he could do was blink.

This painting by Rudolf Bisinger is called *The Gas Plant*. Imagine a setting like this as you read 4+1=1.

---

[1] **pervasive** (per-VAY-sihv) *adj.* penetrating

"You're the one who caused all this . . ."

The worker said no more. Several seconds of silence.

"I wasn't paying attention," the cleaner muttered.

"Do you realize how much that regulator costs?" one of them asked.

". . ."

"You'll have to work for the factory owner for ten years to pay it off!" commented another worker.

Now the oldest worker spoke, in the tone of a man who was used to supervising production. "The thing that's really important," he said, "is that the machine's going to stay idle until the regulator's repaired!"

"What are we going to do then?" the fourth worker asked in dismay.

The cleaner looked at them all in despair.

"If only that stupid broom-handle hadn't . . ." he thought.

The oldest worker took a look at his watch. "The factory owner's going to be here in half an hour!" he said.

"You'll have to pay for it," said another worker, pointing at the cleaner with a bit of a grin on his face.

The cleaner didn't say a word. He felt he could almost hear the factory owner's footsteps. Then his voice. "Why aren't the machines working? Come here, cleaner!"

He was brought back to reality by the worker who'd asked what they were going to do. "What are we going to do now?" he asked again. There was a serious edge to his voice, and something of an imperative quality as well.

The four workers looked at one another again.

"That's right. What *are* we going to do?"

"We're supposed to . . ."

The second worker tried to take it further. "We have to . . ."

The cleaner moved his weight from one leg to the other, thinking of the factory owner.

There was a tense silence.

"Perhaps I could reconnect the current to the machines," said the oldest worker.

No one said a word.

"We must hurry!"

He headed over to a large iron fuse-box that was attached to the far wall.

"Get me some wire," he called out. The order wasn't directed at anyone in particular. One of the workers hurried over to a side door. The oldest worker spoke again.

"Unplug the broken machine!"

Once again the order wasn't given to anyone in particular, and the two other workers collided as they rushed to carry it out. The cleaner stood there stupefied, the broom feeling heavy in his hand.

The electricity was restored and the machines began to work, slowly at first, then faster and faster. After a few seconds they were working at regular speed.

The cleaner looked at the broken machine. Its very silence rose, ever more loudly, as he imagined the factory owner shouting: "Who was it? Come here, you!" A shudder went through him. "You'll have to work for ten years before . . ."

The fan started going round again, slowly at first, then picking up speed until, like the machines, it was back to normal.

He looked around him. The factory owner hadn't arrived yet. One of the workers came over to him.

"What are you standing there for?" he shouted at the top of his voice.

The machines were making such a noise that his shouting was almost inaudible.[2] But he went on even so. "Finish your job!"

The worker's face seemed to swim before his eyes.

"I . . . I . . ."

He lost his grip on the broom and it fell to the floor. He hurriedly bent over and picked it up, and the worker moved away. The broom seemed reluctant to slip across the floor.

"My hand's trembling!" he thought.

He could feel a moist warmth in his eyes.

"Why am I going to pieces . . . ?"

"This blasted dust! Why doesn't it pile up properly?"

"My whole body's shaking!"

Sweat was pouring down his face.

"If only I'd looked behind me!"

He stopped working and took out his handkerchief.

"The broom-handle doesn't need to be as long as that!"

Maybe he took a long time wiping the sweat off his face. He felt a hand placed on his shoulder and he turned round. The worker who'd shouted at him a short while before was now giving him an encouraging smile. Then the smile vanished. "What are you hanging about round here for?" he shouted.

" . . ."

He looked at the broken machine, but the worker pushed him away with a friendly shove.

"It wasn't you who broke the machine," he shouted into the cleaner's ear.

---

[2] **inaudible** (ihn-AW-duh-buhl) *adj.* impossible to be heard

POSTREADING

Critical Thinking

1. What kind of person is the main character? Give examples from the dialogue to support your answer.

2. What do you learn about the feelings of the workers? about the people in charge of the building? What might this information tell you about the government and/or society in which these workers live?

3. What other stories do you know in which you learn about setting, character, and mood through dialogue? How do you feel about using dialogue this way? Would you prefer that a writer gave information through descriptions? Why?

Writing Your Response to "4 + 1 = 1"

In your journal, write about your reaction to the story. With what part of the story could you best identify? Why? Have you ever been part of a situation like the one in the story? What circumstances caused the situation? How was the situation resolved?

Going Back Into the Text: Author's Craft

A **dialogue** is a conversation. Most often, a dialogue takes place between two or more people in a story, but as you can see from this selection, a dialogue can take place within a character's mind. A writer can use dialogue as well as thoughts to reveal a character's personality, values, and beliefs about him-or herself and the other characters.

As you review the dialogue, look for examples that demonstrate the following:

1. the first concerns of the workers when the fan breaks

2. how the first worker shows compassion for the cleaner's predicament

3. how the compassion spreads from one worker to another

4. who the last is to demonstrate compassion. What does he say or do?

PREREADING

A Lover from Palestine/
Warmth of Blood

Reading the Poems in a Cultural Context

Recall from the unit introduction that the Israelis and the Arabs have been at war over the division of the historic region of Palestine. From the Arab viewpoint, the U.N.'s decision to split Palestine deprived the Arabs who lived there of a homeland. Suddenly, their country ceased to exist. They felt anger and despair. They saw no reason they should be forced to give up their homeland.

For Arab poets Mahmud Darwish and Ali al-Sharqawi, the senses of loss and longing form the heart of their work. Darwish, a Palestinian living in Israel, has been imprisoned often by Israeli authorities for his forceful plea that Palestine be returned to the Arabs. Palestine fills his poetry, both as a destroyed land and as a future state. Using his country as a centerpiece allows him to maintain his identity and to help other Palestinians remember who they are and where they came from.

His attachment to his lost land is so essential that Darwish combines people and things to present a symbolic "double view." For example,

he may talk about his beloved, and his beloved will be not only a woman, but also a symbol for the lost country of Palestine. Sometimes he may present three or four concepts on top of one another. In this way, Darwish can offer a completely blended poem about homeland, love, nature, and freedom all at the same time.

The desire for freedom and a homeland is also a central theme of Ali al-Sharqawi's poetry. A Bahraini by birth, he is one of the many Arabs who support the Palestinians' claim to the land Israel occupies. In his poems, as in Darwish's, Palestine is a sad and wounded country. Al-Sharqawi then pleads for justice or freedom for his people.

Focusing on the Selections

As you read both poems, think about the backgrounds as well as the aims of the poets. Whom does the "you" symbolize? How does Darwish describe his homeland? How does he describe his own feelings? How does al-Sharqawi keep warm in his cold prison cell? What emotions do the two poets rouse?

A Lover from Palestine

Mahmud Darwish

I saw you yesterday at the harbor,
Leaving without a people, without supplies,
I ran toward you like an orphan.

I saw you in mountains of thorns—
A shepherd without sheep,
Chased in the wilderness.
You were my garden,
Now I am a stranger in my own house.

I saw you by the cave,
Hanging out your orphans' garments.
I saw you wandering in the streets,
In the songs of orphanhood and misery.

You are Palestinian in looks,
Palestinian in name, dreams, and voice,
Palestinian in birth and death,
Palestinian in my childhood memories.
Take me under your eyes,
Restore to me my color,
The light of my heart,
The salt of my bread,
The taste of my homeland.

While the Middle East is known primarily for its political strife, it is also a region of great beauty. This painting called *Landscape* by Ludwig Blum captures that beauty.

Warmth of Blood

Ali al-Sharqawi
translated by *Lena Jayyusi* and
Naomi Shihab Nye

You said:
>   Prison cells are cold
>   I shall send you a woollen garment
>   Wrap yourself up
I said:
>   The chill is warmed
>   by songs of comrades,
>   memories of love rising
>   in the branches of embrace.
And it is warm
>   when you appear in my dreams.
Your longing voice, a stoked and radiant fire . . .
I wrap myself in your words like an ember that says:
>   Freedom.
I clasp my vision, reined in by the mind
curb my flowing sorrow.
Do not send me a woollen garment.
>   only
>   come to me
>   with the dream.

POSTREADING

Critical Thinking

1. How does Darwish make his emotions obvious? al-Sharqawi?

2. What do you learn about the Palestinian political situation from the poems?

3. Compare two similes or metaphors from the poems. What comparison is being made? Which comparison speaks more effectively to you?

Writing Your Response to "A Lover from Palestine" and "Warmth of Blood"

What idea, thought, or feeling in the poems is related most closely to you? the loss of someone or something you love? the warmth and security of a friendship? In your journal, explain what part of the poems spoke most pointedly to a personal situation. Also note which part of the poems might have had no meaning for you because it had no relation to your experience.

Going Back Into the Text: Author's Craft

To help readers better understand ideas and feelings, writers often use **figurative language**. Figurative language is phrases or sentences that go beyond the literal meaning of its words. A figurative expression often contains a comparison of two things that are not alike. By using such imaginative comparisons, writers add color to their works and often expand the reader's understanding.

The most common figures of speech are **similes** and **metaphors**. A *simile* compares two things using the words "like" or "as": The baby's cry was as shrill as a train's whistle. A *metaphor* implies a comparison: His eyes were small, cold pieces of coal, black and hard.

As you review the poems, use these questions as guidelines:

1. What comparisons do the poets make using similes? metaphors?

2. How do the similes and metaphors expand your understanding of the poets' ideas or feelings?

3. Which figure of speech do you think best conveys the feeling of loss and longing? Think of another simile or metaphor that either poet could use.

PREREADING

In This Valley/Once a Great Love/ Late in Life

Reading the Poems in a Cultural Context

Yehuda Amichai is a voice for Israel and for the Israeli view of the Arab-Israeli conflict. Amichai suffers the anguish of the conflict over Palestine, as do the two Arab poets whose work you have just read. You can see that the lives and emotions of both Arabs and Iraelis are shadowed by constant warfare.

Born in Germany, Amichai emigrated with his parents to Palestine in 1936. He participated in the war that created the state of Israel, as well as most of the other major Arab-Israeli confrontations. His adult life has been lived in the midst of continuous violence and hostility. He himself claims to have been formed "half by the cruelties of war."

War, love, and loss haunt Amichai's poetry. His verses often describe landscapes where every view presents a reminder of war, or tell about the loss of someone or something destroyed by the war. His poetry also deals with love and loss of love.

Amichai believes deeply that to be alive means to remember whomever or whatever one has loved and lost. "What I will never see again I must love forever" is his first rule.

The thoughts and emotions that Amichai focuses on are complex; yet his poems are concise, clearly expressed, and to the point. The poet writes in a conversational tone, using only essential words and images.

The energy and creativity in Amichai's poetry appears in the form of figurative language. He fills his poems with sensory detail, similes, and metaphors. He often uses exaggeration to show the intensity of his emotion. Some of the figurative language is so unusual that the reader must pause to think about it.

Focusing on the Selections

As you read Amichai's poetry, think about how he portrays his homeland, as well as the emotions of love and sorrow. What picture does he present of Israel? What emotions about love do you think Amichai evokes most clearly? most consistently?

In This Valley

Yehuda Amichai

In this valley which many waters
carved out in endless years
so that the light breeze may now
pass through it to cool my forehead,
I think about you. From the hills I hear
voices of men and machines wrecking and building.

And there are loves which cannot
be moved to another site.
They must die at their place and in their time
like an old clumsy piece of furniture
that's destroyed together with
the house in which it stands.

But this valley is a hope
of starting afresh without having to die first,
of loving without forgetting the other love,
of being like the breeze
that passes through it now
without being destined for it.

Dancing Lesson by Raphael Soyer. Dancing together requires cooperation. Each partner knows what to expect of the other. Is it possible for relationships between people, families, or nations to cooperate as if they were dancing?

Once a Great Love

Yehuda Amichai

Once a great love cut my life in two.
The first part goes on twisting
at some other place like a snake cut in two.

The passing years have calmed me
and brought healing to my heart and rest to my eyes.

And I'm like someone standing in
the Judean[1] desert, looking at a sign:
"Sea Level."
He cannot see the sea, but he knows.

Thus I remember your face everywhere
at your "face level."

Late in Life

Yehuda Amichai

Late in life I came to you
filtered through many doors
reduced by stairs
till almost nothing remained of me.

You are such a surprised woman
living with half courage,
a wild woman wearing spectacles —[2]
those elegant reins of your eyes.

---

[1] **Judean** (joo-DEE-uhn) *adj.* ancient region in southern Palestine
[2] **spectacles** (SPEHK-tuh-kuhlz) *pl. n.* eyeglasses

"Things like to get lost and be
found again by others. Only
human beings love to find themselves,"
you said.

After that you broke your whole face
into two equal profiles: one
for the far distance, the other for me —
as a souvenir. And then you went.

POSTREADING

Critical Thinking

1. What kinds of love does Amichai talk about? Give examples from his poems to support your answer.

2. How do Amichai's poems show that he has lived a great part of his life under the conditions of war?

3. What other poems or songs do you know that deal with love? How are they like or different from Amichai's? Which of Amichai's images appeal to you most strongly? Why?

Writing Your Response to "In This Valley," "Once a Great Love," and "Late in Life"

In your journal, tell which poem you responded to most strongly and explain why. Which of Amichai's figurative phrases or sentences could describe your feelings? Why? Compose a phrase or sentence that uses figurative language to describe your feelings about someone or something you love.

Going Back Into the Text: Author's Craft

As you have already learned, figurative language includes sensory details, similes, and metaphors. Figurative language also includes **hyperbole**, the use of exaggeration for effect. For example, lovers often claim to "give their hearts away," but the reader knows that this is not possible. A writer uses hyperbole to let the reader know how deep his/her feelings are about an emotion or event.

As you review Amichai's poems about different kinds of love, use these questions as guidelines:

1. Identify at least one sensory detail, one simile, and one metaphor.

2. Give examples of some of Amichai's hyperbole. Explain what kinds of emotion he expresses.

3. Which figure of speech do you think Amichai uses most effectively? Why?

PREREADING

You Can't Fool Menashe

Reading the Story in a Cultural Context

Yehuda Amachai is considered Israel's national poet; Ephraim Kishon is considered Israel's national humorist. One reviewer claimed, "Only a man who loves his country greatly can be as funny as Mr. Kishon is about life in Israel today; and . . . as deft at poking fun at their foibles."

Kishon was born in Budapest, Hungary, in 1924. He was one of the hundreds of thousands of Jews who fled to Israel after its founding in 1948. In Israel he worked on a *kibbutz* (a farming commune) as a plumber, electrician, groom, and bathroom cleaner. Meanwhile, he sharpened his skills as a writer and learned Hebrew. In 1953, he began his long and successful writing career with a daily newspaper column. In his column Kishon used satire to poke fun at the manners, behavior, and politics of his fellow countrymen and -women.

Since then, he has authored more than 50 books and written and produced hit plays for Israeli theaters. He has made films that have won many awards, including two Golden Globes and an Oscar nomination for the Best Foreign Picture. His stories have been translated, without losing any of their humor, into languages as different as Japanese, Korean, Esperanto, Braille, and Icelandic.

Kishon is a constant observer of the people around him, from the smallest detail of their dress to the least twitch of an eye or cheek muscle that indicates the presence of a laugh. No matter where he is or what he is doing, he is always the dedicated writer observing the human drama. His observations let him create situations and characters—especially characters—whom readers in every country can recognize and enjoy.

Focusing on the Selection

As you read "You Can't Fool Menashe," think about the characters in the story. What kind of person is Menashe? How do you get to know Menashe? How do the other characters feel about Menashe? What kind of people are the other characters?

You Can't Fool Menashe

◆ ■ ◆

Ephraim Kishon

One of those wet evenings we were again sitting, Ervinke and I, at our café command post, watching the flotsam and jetsam[1] flowing between the tables. Suddenly the writer Tola'at Shani plowed his way toward us and started biting his nails.

"I'm terribly nervous," he confessed. "Right now the Repertory Committee is deciding the fate of my play."

We sympathized with him. If they rejected the play, all was lost. On the other hand, if they accepted it the possibility of its reaching the stage by mistake need not be ruled out altogether. We tried to calm the poet, but he was tense to distraction, and from time to time broke into hysterical giggles and threatened to emigrate.[2]

Then something strange happened. A tall, lean man who passed our table and greeted Ervinke with a light wave of his hand stopped in front of Tola'at Shani, raised his head, his nostrils trembling, his face contorted with a superhuman effort. This lasted for a fraction of a second, then the man relaxed, raised a languid[3] finger and threw an icy "Hi!" at Tola'at Shani. Then his noble figure was swallowed up in the thick smoke blanketing the café.

"Sorry, Tola'at Shani," Ervinke said sadly. "The Repertory Committee has rejected your play. Unanimously, I'm afraid."

The poet shuddered and gripped the edge of the table.

"But . . . how do you . . . know?"

"From the successometer," Ervinke said, motioning in the general direction of the tall man. "Menashe never errs."

---

[1] **flotsam and jetsam** *n.* odds and ends
[2] **emigrate** (EHM-ih-grayt) *v.* leave a native country to settle in another
[3] **languid** (LANG-gwihd) *adj.* weak; drooping

"Menashe is a genius at societymanship," Ervinke explained. "He always sticks to successful people and shuns them like the plague once their star begins to fade. As far as I am concerned, Menashe is a perfect one-man Gallup poll.[4] From the way he greets me I know with dead certainty what my social standing is at any given moment."

Suddenly I also remembered. Of course! Only a few years ago the man never failed to slap me on the back whenever he passed our table. Once, if I remember rightly, it was after the State Department had invited me to the U.S. No, come to think of it, it was the day before the invitation came through. He actually sat down and inquired about my health.

"Menashe is a born barometer," Ervinke continued. "His nervous system resembles a sensitive radar network. He registers the slightest social tremors, any wisp of success, any achievement, any intimation of failure—and treats his acquaintances accordingly. Whoever gets a loud and hearty 'Shalom'[5] from him can be quite certain that he is on top at the moment. Those with checkered careers get a cursory[6] wave of the finger and sometimes, when an artist gets a particularly murderous review in the press, or someone

A café lined street, typical of West Jerusalem.

goes bankrupt, Menashe gives him a subsonic[7] hello which hardly registers even on the most sensitive listening devices.

"And the most fantastic part of it is," Ervinke went on, "the successometer does not necessarily react only to current status. He is liable to hug a writer who has only recently been crucified[8] on the pages of the literary supplements because his electronic brain has already sensed a future box-office success, or a prize in the offing, or a legacy[9]. He has an uncanny ability to make snap decisions on the success coefficient[10] of the person he is meeting. See what I mean?"

---

[4] **Gallup poll** *n.* a public opinion survey
[5] **Shalom** (shah-LOHM) *n.* a Hebrew word meaning "peace"
[6] **cursory** (KER-suh-ree) *adj.* hasty
[7] **subsonic** (suhb-SAW-nihk) *adj.* inaudible
[8] **crucified** (KROO-suh-feyed) *v.* destroyed by criticism
[9] **legacy** (EHG-ih-see) *n.* an inheritance
[10] **coefficient** (coh-ih-FIHSH-uhnt) *n.* factor or level

"No."

"I'll give you an example," said Ervinke. "The moment Menashe caught sight of Tola'at Shani, the little wheels in his brain started spinning. 'A poet of uncertain employment,' the transistors flashed. 'I'll give him the standard No. 8 greeting—"How are you, boy?"—medium volume, and what's more, since the critic Birnbaum mentioned his collected poems two days ago, I'll slow down as I pass his table.' On the other hand, since Kunstatter the Great has not invited Tola'at Shani to his table for the past two weeks (and besides the writer's son has a bad cold), Menashe drops the too cordial 'boy.' However, it is well known that Mrs. Tola'at Shani has a rich uncle in Brooklyn, so Menashe turns on a fairly friendly grin and lifts three fingers during the 'How are you.' That was the successometer's reckoning, but at the last moment Menashe registered a supersensory message concerning the Repertory Committee's decision to reject the play. This automatically canceled the friendly grin, the 'How are you' was replaced by a nine-below-zero 'Hi' and even that with only one finger raised to barely hip height.

"From that I knew," Ervinke continued, "that the play had been rejected unanimously. Had there been *any* votes in favor, Menashe would have raised two fingers shoulder-high."

As Ervinke finished his lecture, the theater manager came towards us.

"Disaster!" he informed Tola'at Shani. "They all voted against the play."

At midnight, after we had dragged Tola'at Shani's ghost into a taxi, Menashe appeared in the café doorway and made a beeline[11] for Ervinke. He pinched my friend's cheek and said in a clear voice, grinning broadly, "Say, where have you been these last few days?"

The broad grin lasted for one—two—three—four whole seconds! Ervinke grew deathly pale, ran to the nearest lottery stand and checked the list of winners. Then he broke into cheers. He had won 4,000 shekels.[12]

"Only one thing I don't understand," Ervinke mused after he had calmed down somewhat. "Why did Menashe not kiss me? Above three thousand shekels he always kisses. Hopp!" He slapped his forehead. "I forgot—I owe sixteen hundred shekels!"

As we left, I gave Menashe a particularly cheerful "Good night." He looked through me at the night horizon as if I simply were not there.

What's the matter? What's . . . the matter . . . ?

---

[11] **beeline** *n.* the fastest and most direct course
[12] **shekels** (SHEHK-uhlz) *n. pl.* ancient Hebrew coins; a unit of money in Israel

POSTREADING

Critical Thinking

1. What does Kishon reveal about his characters through their actions and conversations?

2. What aspect of his culture do you think Kishon is satirizing? Why?

3. Measuring and gaining social success vary from culture to culture. How are your culture's views about such success different from or the same as those satirized in the story?

Writing Your Response to "You Can't Fool Menashe"

In your journal, describe the scene, character, or dialogue that seemed funniest to you as you read the selection. What particularly "tickled your funny bone?" Did it remind you of someone you know?

Going Back Into the Text: Author's Craft

Strong **characterization** is one of the most important qualities of literature. When we read stories, we find out what happens to people and why they act as they do. A story's character can help us understand ourselves, and "give us a clue" as to why we did or did not act in the same way in a similar situation. Some writers have created truly great characters. These characters show a variety of human responses to hopes, cares, and confusions that we all face.

To characterize the people in a story, to reveal how and why they act as they do, authors use a number of methods. Writers may directly describe or explain a character and his or her actions. Writers may also let their characters reveal themselves through their actions, speech, or thoughts. Authors can also reveal characters through the reactions of others.

As you review the characterization in the selection, use these questions as guidelines:

1. Which of the methods listed above does Kishon use to reveal Menashe's personality?

2. How are the other characters revealed?

3. How is Menashe like the other characters? How is he different?

4. Which characters do you think are the most effective? Do you think that the method of characterization made them so? Why?

Reviewing the Region

1. Select two of the authors represented in this chapter. Compare their views of conditions in their countries. Use examples from their works to support your statements.

2. Authors often exaggerate in order to make a statement about people or about society. Choose a selection from the chapter and show how the author uses exaggeration for this purpose.

3. Which selection in this chapter taught you a lesson that you can apply to your own life? Explain.

FOCUSING THE UNIT

COOPERATIVE/COLLABORATIVE LEARNING

With a small group of classmates, hold a news conference on recent events in Africa and the Middle East. Each member of the group should select one important event in the region and explain its impact on the area, on the United States, and on the world. Below is part of a sample news conference that one group of students used. It can be a starting point for your news conference.

Student 1: Welcome to the 6:00 news. Tonight we have three late-breaking stories about important events in Africa and the Middle East. These major social and political movements impact not only their area, but also the world at large. Stay tuned!

Student 2: In 1995, after extensive negotiations, an Israeli-PLO agreement expanded Palestinian self-rule in the West Bank. The recent elections in Israel, however, have placed the historic agreement in jeopardy.

How will the new prime minister and his cabinet respond to the Palestinians? What effect will the change in power have on the rest of the world?

Student 3: Americans in favor of Israel's reclaiming the West Bank are responding with increased economic support to Israel. Others, in contrast, are urging Israeli leaders to embrace the late prime minister Yitzhak Rabin's call for peace and reconciliation with Israel's Arab neighbors.

Writing Process

Literature does many things: it persuades, describes, explains, and entertains. Review the journal entries you made for this unit. Choose two or more selections that you particularly liked.

Imagine yourself in a scene from one of these stories. From what you know about Africa or the Middle East, how would the scene look? Write a descriptive essay in which you describe this scene using sensory images and details.

If you wish, you can incorporate some of the characters from the story as well. Refer to the Student Handbook at the back of the book for help with the writing process. Use the model essays as a guideline.

Problem Solving

Drastic social change can present serious problems for the people of many cultures. The clash between the old and the new can make people feel lost. What problems resulted from social change in Africa and the Middle East?

Choose one or more of the selections included in Unit 1 and analyze how the characters deal with social change. What problems do they see as a result of "progress?" How would they solve these problems? In a brief play, song, essay, or speech, express your ideas about the problems and some possible solutions. You can work on your own, with a classmate, or in a small group.

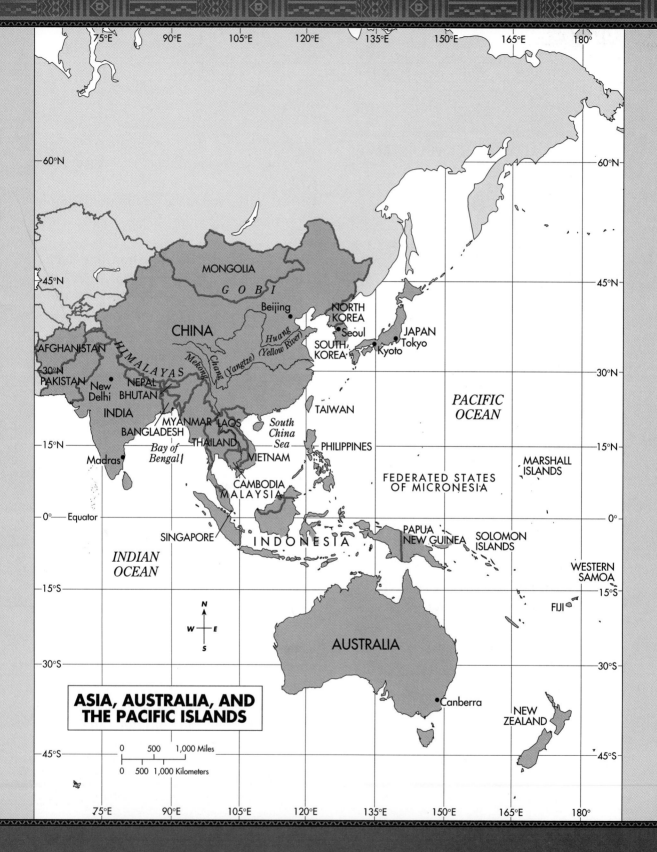

ASIA, AUSTRALIA, AND THE PACIFIC ISLANDS

0   500   1,000 Miles

0   500   1,000 Kilometers

MONGOLIA

G O B I

CHINA

Beijing

Huang (Yellow River)

HIMALAYAS

Mekong

Chang (Yangtze)

AFGHANISTAN

PAKISTAN

New Delhi

NEPAL

BHUTAN

INDIA

MYANMAR

BANGLADESH

LAOS

Bay of Bengal

THAILAND

Madras

South China Sea

VIETNAM

CAMBODIA

MALAYSIA

SINGAPORE

INDONESIA

NORTH KOREA

Seoul

SOUTH KOREA

Kyoto

JAPAN

Tokyo

TAIWAN

PHILIPPINES

PACIFIC OCEAN

MARSHALL ISLANDS

FEDERATED STATES OF MICRONESIA

PAPUA NEW GUINEA

SOLOMON ISLANDS

WESTERN SAMOA

FIJI

INDIAN OCEAN

Equator

N
W   E
S

AUSTRALIA

Canberra

NEW ZEALAND

75°E 90°E 105°E 120°E 135°E 150°E 165°E 180°

60°N

45°N

30°N

15°N

0°

15°S

30°S

45°S

UNIT 2

Asia, Australia, and the Pacific Islands

Since our Empire owns the world, there is no country on this or other sides of the seas which does not submit to us. . . . You, Japan, are our Eastern frontier, and for generations you have performed tributary duties. The longer the time, the more respectful you have become.

These words were written by a member of the Ming Dynasty in 1436 to the shogun (or military governor) of Japan in recognition of Japan's special service to China. As you can see, the Chinese emperors believed that their empire was the center of the world. Indeed, until the 1500s, Asia was more advanced than Europe in its cultural and technological development. Early Asians founded complex cities, set up governments, and established trade routes. They also developed writing systems and created great works of literature. China had no need for products from Europe even in 1793, when the emperor Ch'ien Lung sent a letter to King George III of England in reponse to England's request for increased trade.

I do not forget the lonely remoteness of your island, cut off from the world by intervening wastes of sea. . . . [But] our Celestial Empire possesses all things in abundance. We have no need for barbarian products.

The emperor's letter clearly shows how China viewed itself as self-sufficient and as superior to all other countries.

China was ruled by powerful dynasties for much of its history. As one ruling family lost power, another fought to take its place. This transfer of power occurred many times in Chinese history.

The history of China is also a history of invasions. Tribes from the northern steppes, or plains, often moved south toward China looking for better pastures for their herds. About 215 B.C. the Chinese began building a Great Wall along the northern border to keep out these invaders. Later, the Mongols, under the leadership of Genghis Khan, overran large parts of China. The Mongol conquest of China was complete by 1279.

For most of its history, China was the center of civilization in East Asia. The Chinese used such inventions as the compass, gunpowder, and silk cloth. However, during times of political upheaval in China, refugees fled to Korea. These Chinese refugees brought with them their ideas, customs, and Buddhist religion.

The Koreans, in turn, sent missionaries to Japan. With the missionaries came Buddhism and Chinese customs and ideas. Ultimately, the Japanese adapted the Chinese system of writing, government, and religion to their own language and culture.

India There were other early civilizations in Asia. India's civilization is as old as China's. In India's long history, many different groups have ruled the country.

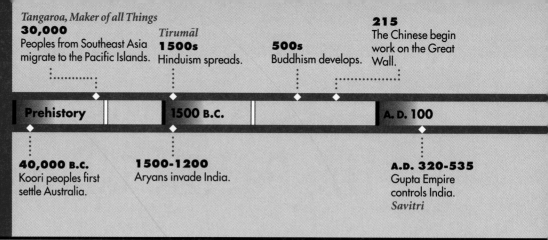

Time Line

Literature titles are placed on the time line to reflect the historical time or event that relates to the selection, not to reflect the publication dates of the selections.

Tangaroa, Maker of all Things
30,000
Peoples from Southeast Asia migrate to the Pacific Islands.

Tirumāl
1500s
Hinduism spreads.

500s
Buddhism develops.

215
The Chinese begin work on the Great Wall.

Prehistory | 1500 B.C. | A. D. 100

40,000 B.C.
Koori peoples first settle Australia.

1500-1200
Aryans invade India.

A.D. 320-535
Gupta Empire controls India.
Savitri

During the Gupta Empire (A.D. 320-535), India enjoyed an era of greatness. Scientists, philosophers, and artisans flourished. It was during the rule of the Gupta Empire that the Europeans began trading spices and textiles with the East, a relationship that would have an enormous impact on India.

When Gupta rule declined in the A.D. 500s, the trading stopped. In the 1400s, Europeans once again looked eastward. The nations of Europe set up trading posts and established colonies in Asia. By the late 1800s, India had become a colony of Great Britain. The British took advantage of the cheap native labor and excercised their power as a ruling class. An official in 1775 described the extravagance in India as follows:

> A councillor never appears in the street with a train of less than 20 [Indian servants], nor walks from one room to another in his house unless preceded by four silver staves. [rods, a symbol of authority]

By the end of World War II, the people of India demanded self-rule. Their leader, Mohandas Gandi, had gained such a following that the independence movement was too strong to be ignored. In 1947, Britain ended its colonial rule of India.

Japan For centuries, Europeans and Americans knew very little about Japan. Japanese rulers strictly controlled contact with foreign people and their ideas. This changed dramatically in 1853, when U.S. Admiral Perry sailed to Japan with a fleet of warships to demand trade. After the first unsuccessful request, Perry promised to return, and a decree was issued by Japan's shogun that read in part:

> We are without a navy, and our coasts are undefended. Meanwhile, the Americans will be back next year. Our policy shall be to evade any definite answer to their request, while at the same time keeping a peaceful demeanor. It may be they will . . . use violence. For that we must be prepared, lest the country suffer disgrace.

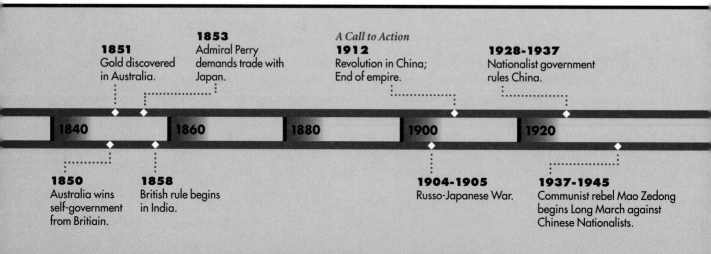

1851
Gold discovered in Australia.

1853
Admiral Perry demands trade with Japan.

A Call to Action
1912
Revolution in China; End of empire.

1928-1937
Nationalist government rules China.

1840 | 1860 | 1880 | 1900 | 1920

1850
Australia wins self-government from Britiain.

1858
British rule begins in India.

1904-1905
Russo-Japanese War.

1937-1945
Communist rebel Mao Zedong begins Long March against Chinese Nationalists.

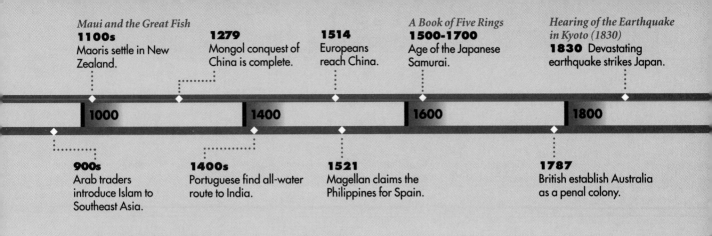

Maui and the Great Fish
1100s
Maoris settle in New Zealand.

1279 Mongol conquest of China is complete.

1514 Europeans reach China.

A Book of Five Rings
1500-1700 Age of the Japanese Samurai.

Hearing of the Earthquake in Kyoto (1830)
1830 Devastating earthquake strikes Japan.

1000   **1400**   **1600**   **1800**

900s Arab traders introduce Islam to Southeast Asia.

1400s Portuguese find all-water route to India.

1521 Magellan claims the Philippines for Spain.

1787 British establish Australia as a penal colony.

At Perry's visit the following year, Japanese rulers decided that they were no match for Perry's cannons. They signed a treaty giving the United States the right to trade with Japan. Within 15 years, the Japanese had turned their attention to the West. By 1900 Japan had become a modern industrial nation.

Australia and the Pacific

Australia, New Zealand, and the Pacific Islands have a history that is quite different from those of their neighbors to the north. Australia was first settled by immigrants, called Kooris, from southeast Asia about 40,000 years ago. Isolated from the rest of the world, these nomadic peoples developed their own language and customs. In spite of many differences, the Kooris are united by their religious bond with nature.

New Zealand was settled a mere 800 years ago by the Maoris. These seafaring people also came from southeast Asia. Unlike the Australian Kooris, the Maoris were farmers whose lives were centered around village life.

The Kooris of Australia and the Maoris of New Zealand came into contact with Europeans in the 1700s and 1800s, when the British arrived to colonize these islands. Britian first used Australia as a place of exile for criminals. Then, when gold was discovered in 1851, many prospectors rushed to the island continent. As European contact in the Pacific increased, many nations realized that the islands offered harbors for supplying trading ships and raw materials for European industries. Even the United States took possession of islands that could serve as safe harbors on the way to Asia.

Today, the countries of Asia and the Pacific remain diverse. There are many different forms of government. Some nations are highly developed, while others are just developing modern economies. You will read more about the modern history of this region in the chapters of this unit.

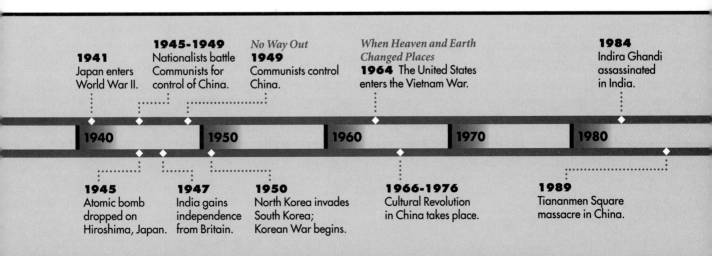

1941 Japan enters World War II.

1945-1949 Nationalists battle Communists for control of China.

No Way Out
1949 Communists control China.

When Heaven and Earth Changed Places
1964 The United States enters the Vietnam War.

1984 Indira Ghandi assassinated in India.

1940   **1950**   **1960**   **1970**   **1980**

1945 Atomic bomb dropped on Hiroshima, Japan.

1947 India gains independence from Britain.

1950 North Korea invades South Korea; Korean War begins.

1966-1976 Cultural Revolution in China takes place.

1989 Tiananmen Square massacre in China.

CHAPTER

3 East Asia

East Asia has a long and distinguished literary tradition. The ancient writers explored Confucian principles and ideals. However, the common people preferred legends and folktales that supported Buddhist beliefs about fate or taught moral lessons. In this chapter, you will find one such lesson in a folktale from the 10th century.

As trade and travel increased during the late 1800s, Western literary forms began to influence Chinese writers. In 1911, China's emperor was overthrown by revolutionaries. Turmoil continued, and by 1949, a Communist government had taken power. Chinese writers began to stress new themes, such as the dignity of the common people. Plots told of workers' victories over evil or extraordinary efforts made by peasants.

China's communist government used such literature to demonstrate the ideal Chinese citizen and to glorify the values of the state. You will read two selections by authors who opposed China's government during these times. The first is by a female protester who was beheaded for writing poems like the ones you will read. The second selection is part of an autobiography by one of the many people sent to labor camps for opposition to the state.

Like China, Korea and Japan have an ancient tradition of poetry. The ability of the samurai, who were Japanese warriors, to write elegant poetry was as important as their skill with the sword. In this chapter, you will read a Japanese poem as well as an excerpt from a handbook for samurai warriors. The advice for living that is

This 19th century Japanese painting depicts a river scene. Japan is an island with many waterways. This two-hulled boat is an early version of today's catamaran which has been used by the islanders of the South Pacific for centuries.

described in this handbook is followed by business people even today.

Literature in Japan changed a great deal after atomic bombs destroyed two cities at the end of World War II. The destruction inspired writers of science fiction, who created such monsters as Godzilla and Rodan. This unit features a science fiction story about a more modern "monster"—garbage.

As you read this chapter, try to contrast the values in the ancient stories to the values expressed in the selections from this century.

from *A Book of Five Rings*

Reading the Essay in a Cultural Context

In Japan, Miyamoto Musashi is known as "Kensei," which means "Sword Saint." Born in 1584, Miyamoto belonged to the samurai, or warrior, class. During his lifetime he became a legend for his fighting prowess.

At the time of Miyamoto's birth, Japan was recovering from more than four centuries of internal fighting among different lords. One of the military rulers, called the Shogun, grew to have great power. Under the Shogun, people lived in a rigid class structure.

The highest class was the daymio, which included lords and senior government officials. The daymio hired warriors, and foot soldiers called samurai. With the rise of one powerful Shogun, the civil wars in Japan ended and many samurai were out of work. These warriors roamed the country and became known as "ronin." They devoted their lives to teaching military arts, particularly the art of kendo.

Kendo is the Way of the Sword. In Japan, kendo is considered to be one of the most important studies. It is a moral teaching as well as a military art. A person who trains in kendo must practice endlessly, learn to be levelheaded in the face of peril, and live by a code of honor. Kendo is also about strategy in combat.

By the time he was 16, Miyamoto had become a ronin, traveling through the countryside and learning the Way of the Sword. Although he was successful in all his encounters, Miyamoto remained humble and single-minded. He later wrote that he didn't understand strategy until he was about 50 years old.

In 1643, Miyamoto retired to live alone in a cave. There he wrote a book of advice addressed to a pupil named Teruo Nobuyuki. This book, called *Go Rin No Sho (A Book of Five Rings)*, tells the lessons Miyamoto learned during his life. It is about single combat, and he called it "a guide for men who want to learn about strategy." Today, Miyamoto's guide is read by most Japanese business leaders.

The excerpt you are about to read begins with a discussion of weapons. Miyamoto wants his pupil to understand the unique advantages of each of the weapons he might use in battle.

The next topic for Miyamoto is timing. Timing is extremely important in battle—and in life. As Miyamoto says, "There is timing in everything." You will notice in this section that he provides a list of nine principles that his pupil must learn in order to master timing in strategy. These principles are the basis for understanding Miyamoto's teaching.

Focusing on the Selection

As you read the selection from *A Book of Five Rings*, think about the author's message. In what ways can Miyamoto's teaching apply to everyone's life? In what ways does Miyamoto's book reflect the culture of Japan?

from *A Book of Five Rings*

■▲▲▲▲▲▲▲▲▲▲▲▲ ◈◆◈ ▲▲▲▲▲▲▲▲▲▲▲▲■

Miyamoto Musashi

The Benefit of Weapons in Strategy

There is a time and a place for use of weapons.

The best use of the companion sword is in a confined space, or when you are engaged closely with an opponent. The long sword can be used effectively in all situations.

The halberd[1] is inferior to the spear on the battlefield. With the spear you can take the initiative; the halberd is defensive. In the hands of one or two men of equal ability, the spear gives a little extra strength. Spear and halberd both have their uses, but neither is very beneficial in confined spaces. They cannot be used for taking a prisoner. They are essentially weapons for the field.

Anyway, if you learn "indoor" techniques,[2] you will think narrowly and forget the true Way.[3] Thus you will have difficulty in actual encounters.

The bow is tactically[4] strong at the commencement[5] of battle, especially battles on a moor,[6] as it is possible to shoot quickly from among the spearmen. However, it is unsatisfactory in sieges,[7] or when the enemy is more than forty yards away. For this reason there are nowadays few traditional schools of archery.[8] There is little use nowadays for this kind of skill.

---

[1] **halberd** (HAL-buhrd) *n.* a weapon with a long curved blade, used by women to defend their homes

[2] **"indoor" techniques** studies practiced indoors with a great deal of formality and rituals

[3] **Way** the Way of strategy

[4] **tactically** (TAK-tihk-lee) *adv.* wisely planned

[5] **commencement** (kuh-MEHNS-muhnt) *n.* a beginning; start

[6] **moor** (mawr) *n.* a broad stretch of open land, often with swampy areas and patches of low shrubs

[7] **sieges** (SEEJ-ihz) *n. pl.* blockades of towns or fortresses by armies

[8] **archery** (AHR-chuh-ree) *n.* the skill of shooting with a bow and arrow

From inside fortifications, the gun has no equal among weapons. It is the supreme weapon on the field before the ranks clash, but once swords are crossed the gun becomes useless.

One of the virtues of the bow is that you can see the arrows in flight and correct your aim accordingly, whereas gunshot cannot be seen. You must appreciate the importance of this.

Just as a horse must have endurance and no defects, so it is with weapons. Horses should walk strongly, and swords and companion swords should cut strongly. Spears and halberds must stand up to heavy use: bows and guns must be sturdy. Weapons should be hardy rather than decorative.

You should not have a favourite weapon. To become over-familiar with one weapon is as much a fault as not knowing it sufficiently well. You should not copy others, but use weapons which you can handle properly. It is bad for commanders and troopers to have likes and dislikes. These are things you must learn thoroughly.

Japanese ink drawing of Samurai warrior in armor with his lance, his short sword, and his long sword. Samurai warriors and their strict code have been a part of Japanese culture for centuries.

Timing in Strategy

There is timing in everything. Timing in strategy cannot be mastered without a great deal of practice.

Timing is important in dancing and pipe or string music, for they are in rhythm only if timing is good. Timing and rhythm are also involved in the military arts, shooting bows and guns, and riding horses. In all skills and abilities there is timing.

There is also timing in the Void.[9]

There is timing in the whole life of the warrior, in his thriving and declining, in his harmony and discord. Similarly, there is timing in the Way of the merchant, in the rise and fall of capital. All things entail rising and falling timing. You must be able to discern[10] this. In strategy there are various timing considerations. From the outset you must know the applicable timing and the inapplicable timing, and from among the large and small things and the fast and slow timings find the relevant timing, first seeing the distance timing and the background timing. This is the main thing in strategy. It is especially important to know the background timing, otherwise your strategy will become uncertain.

---

[9] **Void** (void) *n.* one of the five elements of Buddhism that makes up the cosmos; Nothingness, a Buddhist term for the illusionary nature of worldly things

[10] **discern** (dih-SERN) *v.* to understand clearly

You win in battles with the timing in the Void born of the timing of cunning by knowing the enemies' timing, and thus using a timing which the enemy does not expect.

All the five books are chiefly concerned with timing. You must train sufficiently to appreciate all this.

If you practise day and night in the above Ichi[11] school strategy, your spirit will naturally broaden. Thus is large scale strategy and the strategy of hand to hand combat propagated[12] in the world. This is recorded for the first time in the five books of Ground, Water, Fire, Tradition (Wind), and Void. This is the Way for men who want to learn my strategy:

1. Do not think dishonestly.

2. The Way is in training.

3. Become acquainted with every art.

4. Know the Ways of all professions.

5. Distinguish between gain and loss in worldly matters.

6. Develop intuitive[13] judgement and understanding for everything.

7. Perceive those things which cannot be seen.

8. Pay attention even to trifles.[14]

9. Do nothing which is of no use.

It is important to start by setting these broad principles in your heart, and train in the Way of strategy. If you do not look at things on a large scale it will be difficult for you to master strategy. If you learn and attain this strategy you will never lose even to twenty or thirty enemies. More than anything to start with you must set your heart on strategy and earnestly stick to the Way. You will come to be able to actually beat men in fights, and to be able to win with your eye. Also by training you will be able to freely control your own body, conquer men with your body, and with sufficient training you will be able to beat ten men with your spirit. When you have reached this point, will it not mean that you are invincible?[15]

---

[11] **Ichi** (EE-chee) *n.* a martial arts system

[12] **propagated** (PRAHP-uh-gayt-uhd) *v.* made known or accepted

[13] **intuitive** (ihn-TOO-ih-tihv) *adj.* based on instinct

[14] **trifles** (TREYE-fuhlz) *n. pl.* things of slight importance

[15] **invincible** (ihn-VIHN-suh-buhl) *adj.* too strong or powerful to be defeated

Moreover, in large scale strategy the superior man will manage many subordinates[16] dextrously,[17] bear himself correctly, govern the country and foster[18] the people, thus preserving the ruler's discipline. If there is a Way involving the spirit of not being defeated, to help oneself and gain honour, it is the Way of strategy.

The second year of Shoho (1645), the fifth month, the twelfth day.

Teruo Magonojo   SHINMEN MUSASHI

---

[16] **subordinates** (suh-BAWR-duhn-ihts) *n. pl.* persons of a lower rank
[17] **dextrously** (DEHK-struhs-lee) *adv.* skillfully
[18] **foster** (FAHS-tuhr) *v.* care for

POSTREADING

Critical Thinking

1. How would you describe Miyamoto's attitude to his advice?

2. How have contemporary Japanese applied Miyamoto's advice on strategy to business and government?

3. With which of the nine principles listed by Miyamoto do you agree? Why? Which ones would you not practice? Why?

Writing Your Response to "A Book of Five Rings"

In your journal, respond to the advice on timing in strategy that Miyamoto offers. Write about an example of such timing that you can relate to your own life. For example, how could timing be important in your strategies for studying? for making friends?

Going Back Into the Text: Author's Craft

A Book of Five Rings is an example of **didactic** writing. In other words, it is an expository book that is intended to teach or instruct. As you know, Miyamoto addressed this book to a pupil and referred to it as a guide.

As you review the teachings in Miyamoto's book, use these questions as guidelines:

1. How does the author make sure his points are clear?

2. On what traditions and beliefs does the author base his teachings?

3. In what ways does the author state that his advice can be applied?

PREREADING

Till the Candle Blew Out

Reading the Story in a Cultural Context

Many writers with international reputations return to their roots and cultural heritage for inspiration. The writer Kim Yong Ik is a good example. He was born in Korea in 1920 and attended college first in Japan and later in the United States. He taught English literature both in America and at Korea University in Seoul. He also taught creative writing courses at several American universities.

Although many of Kim Yong Ik's stories have been published in American magazines, collected in books by American publishers, and received American awards, much of his work is set in small communities of farmers in Korea.

The story you are about to read comes from a book of Kim Yong Ik's stories called *Love in Winter*. This story, titled "Till the Candle Blew Out," takes place in a little village near the sea. It is a portrait of a simple existence in which the characters live close to nature and in tune with the seasons. It includes many fascinating details of life in a Korean village and illustrates the way that people in a small community look out for one another.

"Till the Candle Blew Out" is also a story about relationships and how they affect the way people think and act. In any good story, the characters must have motivation for the things that they say and do. A motive is any feeling, desire, or idea that causes someone to act in a certain way. Sometimes the motive is easily determined. In other instances, the reader must analyze the character's speech, thoughts, and actions to pinpoint his or her motive.

The young boys in this story, Life-Stone and Sunny-Tiger, are very good friends, but they are fiercely competitive. Although they play together every day and sit together in school, they also fight constantly. As season follows season, the boys continue to try to outdo one another. By the end of the story, however, events cause the boys to change their thinking, and their actions as well.

Focusing on the Selection

As you read "Till the Candle Blew Out," think about why Life-Stone and Sunny-Tiger act the way they do. Ask yourself what causes such competition between them. What happens to change the way the boys behave?

Till the Candle Blew Out

from *Love in Winter*
Kim Yong Ik

In the village near the fishing dock, among the tall silvery poplar trees, Life-Stone and I, Sunny-Tiger, grew up. His home had a flimsy thatched[1] roof. On the shore above the rolling water, three huts away from his, stood my tile-roofed home.

Unlike Life-Stone, who longed for a tile-roofed house, I hated my tile-roofed abode[2] and wished I might live in one with a thatched roof and a pumpkin-flower vine growing over the doorway. Especially did I wish this after we had had a fight with each other. For when the village women would hear Life-Stone yelling such an unhappy cry after I had beaten him in a tussle, they would always think I was to blame.

To Life-Stone, my life in a tile-roofed home meant happy times and prosperity;[3] it meant white rice instead of barley; snapper fish instead of sardines; ginseng herb tea with honey instead of the juice of mugwort[4] in case of sickness; tennis shoes instead of straw sandals; and an oil-paper umbrella instead of one on a patched frame with burlap sacks. All the things which I had better than his he believed caused me to win in a fight, for I was physically stronger.

Sometimes when I had caught a glimpse of a "grandpa" frog and had tried to get it to give to Gentle-Flute, the fatherless daughter of a hunch-back, he would claim that he had seen it first and therefore it was his. When I had given it to her and he had seen her gentle smile which brought

---

[1] **thatched** (thacht) *adj.* made of plant stalks, such as straw or reeds
[2] **abode** (uh-BOHD) *n.* a home
[3] **prosperity** (prah-SPEHR-ih-tee) *n.* economic success
[4] **mugwort** (MUG-wuhrt) *n.* an herb plant

tenderness in her eyes and charming dimples in her cheeks, he would yell loudly, as tears as large as beans fell down his face.

Once after I had found and given her an abalone[5] shell, and he had started to shout, I had forced him down with many blows, and I called out, "You toothless, crying rat!" Later, with his left hand full of mud, he had stood near my bamboo fence waiting for me to come out, and with a tearful voice cried, "Someday, Sunny-Tiger, you big rat, when my home is tile-roofed, you will see!"

Along the shore and in the paths, we played together each day until the time came for us to enter the Little School, where the teacher placed Life-Stone and me at the same desk. His left-hand writing and using the abacus[6] gave me some inconvenience and vice versa,[7] for I wrote with my right hand. Across the desk, we drew a line, with a piece of white chalk. This meant each was not to cross, but often his elbow and mine over the line caused a worse argument than if we had had no line.

Nevertheless, he could draw wonderful pictures with his left hand, usually of a blue mountain and a narrow winding path leading down to a tile-roofed house at the bottom of the paper.

I tried hard to draw pictures, especially of a thatched-roof hut with a pumpkin flower blooming beside it and an orange sunset on the horizon. Above this, I would place the Korean peninsula, looking like a purple rabbit floating on a cloud.

When the teacher with horn-rimmed glasses came around and stopped at our desk, he would show both pictures to the class, then say, "Sunny-Tiger, you did not put forth any effort on your picture," and the class would giggle. Seeing Life-Stone's picture, the little boys and girls exclaimed, "Even the devil would be surprised at that picture!" Observing Gentle-Flute's entranced[8] look as she stared at his picture, her pencil in her mouth, I blushed at my poor one, while Life-Stone hung his head and turned lobster red, feeling himself the center of attention.

However, the music class was my chance, and I would wait for that class. When I had sung one of my favorites, "The Moon Over the Old Thatched House," the class would remain very quiet for a few minutes after the song. Next, Life-Stone would sing, but the teacher would interrupt to ask, "Are you reading or singing?" He would then do his best, making his face

---

[5] **abalone** (ab-uh-LOH-nee) *n.* a soft-bodied sea animal whose shell has a brightly colored lining

[6] **abacus** (AB-uh-kuhs) *n.* a device for counting and computing consisting of parallel rods with sliding beads

[7] **vice versa** (VEYE-suh VER-suh) the other way round

[8] **entranced** (ehn-TRANST) *adj.* dreamy

all red-pepper color with the veins prominent in his neck. Then the class would giggle so much that he could not even finish but would have to sit down. In shame he would wipe the tears with his dirty sleeve, leaving grimy marks around his eyes.

To Gentle-Flute I would often give a pencil; then Life-Stone would cut down a bamboo stem, attach it to his short pencil to make it seem longer than mine, then give it to Gentle-Flute.

Sometimes I exchanged my lunch with her—my lunch of rice, without any barley, and spinach sprinkled with sesame powder, for her two or three fist-sized sweet potatoes, which she brought in a tiny handkerchief of hemp cloth. After school, Life-Stone would take her to the shore in front of his hut to catch shrimps. To a little string he would tie a bubbling crab and dangle it over the shallow pool to tease the shrimp out. As soon as one would show its legs, Life-Stone would quickly seize it. All the time he would be laughing, showing his two front teeth missing, while he fed the shrimp one by one to the hunchback's little daughter.

If I went through the alley down between the huts to the shore, he would stand in my path, his legs spread apart and his arms fully extended, and exclaim, "Sunny-Tiger, beyond this, all is mine!" I really thought the shore all belonged to him since his thatched hut was there. I would stand far back, yet as near as I dared, to watch him dive, then come back up with his doggie paddle stroke as he put on a show for Gentle-Flute.

When the beacon was lighted over the water, he would read aloud the same lesson over and over again, so loud that Gentle-Flute in her hut could hear him. His mother, too, coming down from the village could hear him, and being quite satisfied that he was studying his lessons, she would give him more food for being a studious [9] boy. She had never believed in silent study, since there was no way for her to tell whether her son was studying or not. Once my mother, nearby in a neighbor's garden, said, "Life-Stone reads aloud so clearly. Why don't you read aloud sometime? His reading sounds so good." Then when I would read aloud, I could hear his voice become louder than before.

Once when Gentle-Flute was sick, I took some honey from my home, boiled it with garlic water, and gave it to her. After she drank it, I covered her all up with a blanket, even her head, until she perspired.

When my mother found out that I had stolen the honey, she spanked me, saying, "I do not give you half the spankings Life-Stone gets, yet you deserve more."

---

[9] **studious** (STOO-dee-uhs) *adj.* devoted to study

Once my uncle took me to Pusan[10] and bought me "squeaking shoes," the name the villagers give to Western-style shoes of leather. All the class gathered round to admire the sound they made when I walked into the school room, wearing them for the first time.

Immediately Life-Stone wanted a pair like mine, so to make his rubber shoes wear out faster, he bit holes in them on the sides and told his mother that the dog had chewed them. His mother found out that he had made the holes, so with a poplar twig she chased him, crying, around the hut. However, when his father came back just before Harvest Day, he took his son to the next town and bought the "squeaking shoes" for him also. At school, in front of Gentle-Flute, he and I lined up to see which shoes had the most shine and the most squeak; and always his seemed to have more shine than mine. When his mother would send him on an errand, he would go out and spit on a rock in front of his door, saying, "Before that spit dries up, I will come back." Then he would dash down the path along the grassy road, often skipping along, carrying his shoes in his hands, so they would not be worn out too soon.

When winter came, we always had a kite-flying contest. I bought my kite and string, but Life-Stone always made his. He had an aunt who sometimes gave him money when he visited her. Usually he spent it later for cotton candy or rice candy sprinkled with sesame powder. One kite season, when he wanted some money to buy paper, he went to see his aunt. After he had stayed awhile, he got up and went to the door, saying "Good-by." As his aunt did not offer him money, he came back in and again bade her farewell. This he did for the third time, when his aunt, pretending she did not know what he wanted, said, "Come again!" At that he grew angry and boldly told her why he had come. Laughing, she gave him some coins.

Having bought the paper, he drew on it a dragon with big eyes, using a soybean sauce bowl turned upside down to trace the circles that were the eyes. Cutting bamboo pieces, he attached them to the paper. For string he unwound an old fish net which he had found on the shore. When finished, his kite was more beautiful, more arched, and better for flying than mine.

The school had warm Western-style overcoats for sale, and my father purchased one for me of black cloth with two rows of metal buttons down the front. When I wore it to school, I put Gentle-Flute's small hand in one of my pockets, for she looked so cold.

After this, Life-Stone nagged his mother to give him money for an overcoat. When she refused, he used his dirty trick of seeming not to eat

---

[10] **Pusan** (POO-sahn) a port city in South Korea

all day. Really he sneaked into the kitchen when his mother had gone out and ate cooked barley. Next morning when his mother insisted on his eating, again he would not. At last she cut a twig of poplar to whip him with, and Life-Stone yelled very loud but would not shed a tear. When she whipped him more desperately, he prayed, "Oh! Father, come home and help your little boy!" At that she burst into tears, dropped her twig, and later bought him an overcoat like mine, except that his was a bit too large.

Again Life-Stone came to school with his usual smile and along the road bowed very politely to elderly people, something he had not done before. When he met my father, he bowed more deeply and gracefully than he had ever done. On a picnic day in the Second Moon,[11] when we had all taken off our heavy clothing and put on lighter spring garments, Life-Stone still came in his overcoat.

At the picnic, feeling so proud, he began to brag how his mother could make the best pickled vegetables—of turnips, pears, peppers, garlic, and juice of vegetable boiled.

Then he told us all to eat some of it. He gave Gentle-Flute a large portion, then all of us ate so heartily that soon it was all gone. Sadly he said, "Next time, I am going to tell my mother not to make it so good, for you, bottomless stomachs, eat too much!"

That year, we expected a golden harvest, seeing the thickly budding rice stems. Farmers looking at the paddy fields,[12] said, "I feel full in the stomach, just looking at those rice plants." But one morning, I awoke to hear women crying. I got up and slowly went out the door into the path. Soon out came Life-Stone and Gentle-Flute, looking too frightened even to seem awake.

The storm of that one night had made the village roofless; both tile and thatch roofs were blown away. The tall poplar trees had smashed down on the frail huts which in turn had fallen against other houses. All lay in a twisted mass. Farmers were looking in dismay[13] at rice fields which had been so prosperous-looking only yesterday, but now buds and flowers had blown away, leaving only the shortest stubble in the paddy fields. Women wept more than they would have done at the death of a dear relative. We all cried and sobbed together, we children hardly realizing what it all meant, but feeling most hopeless with our elders.

---

[11] **Second Moon** a month in spring
[12] **paddy fields** *n. pl.* wet lands on which rice is grown
[13] **dismay** (dihs-MAY) *n.* sudden loss of confidence

Soon everyone was busy, taking out of the rubble the rice, the barley, the clothing, or whatever could be found, to spread it in the sun to dry. For the day had dawned bright, a gentle wind was blowing, and the roar of the sea was faint as if there had never been a typhoon[14] in this sad land.

Ten days later we learned that the hunchback and her daughter were leaving suddenly that evening on the night boat. Accustomed to gathering the rice left in the fields after the harvest, the hunchback despaired[15] of life for herself and little girl. Since the crop had been entirely lost, life would be too hard, and she was taking Gentle-Flute to relatives in a remote city. Gentle-Flute would be even now rolling up their few possessions and clothing into bundles.

In the afternoon, Life-Stone and I bicycled hard to the next village along the winding path, the one sitting on the frame between the handle bars while the other pedaled, then changing position. In the village, Life-Stone sold his overcoat for a hundred won.[16] Now he was very happy, because he sold his coat for so good a price. He said, "She needs fifty for her passage on the boat and I can give her a hundred. That makes me so happy."

It was a starry night, cool and clear. I came down to the docks wearing my overcoat. The sea wind and impending[17] farewell made us all chilly and goose-pimpled. Life-Stone and I carried the bundles of the poor hunch-back and her daughter down to the small boat in which we would paddle out to the coast-line ship. When well out into the water, I held up our candle-lighted lantern to signal the passing ship. It approached, saw

The title of this 17th century Korean painting is *Concert on a Boat*.

---

[14] **typhoon** (teye-FOON) *n.* a severe tropical hurricane occurring in the western Pacific
[15] **despaired** (dih-SPAIRD) *v.* lost all hope
[16] **won** (wawn) *n.* Korean monetary unit
[17] **impending** (ihm-PEHND-ihng) *adj.* likely to happen soon

our signal, and gave two shrill whistles. I took off my overcoat, and Life-Stone put in the pocket very carefully the money tightly wrapped. Then I put the coat on Gentle-Flute, and Life-Stone put her arms in the sleeves.

We lifted their few bundles up to the sailors on deck, then watched the two go up the ladder the sailors let down for them.

The ship gave out a two-toned whistle as though it had already waited too long for the hunchback and her daughter. The phosphorescent[18] waves moved in; our boat began to rock. I couldn't steady my hand, and the candle blew out.

Since then, we have not fought with each other.

---

[18] **phosphorescent** (fahs-fuhr-REHS-uhnt) *adj.* glowing

POSTREADING

Critical Thinking

1. After reading this story, how would you say that Kim Yong Ik feels about his homeland?

2. What are some of the cultural values that this story suggests?

3. Have you ever competed with a friend? How did this affect your relationship?

Writing Your Response to "Till the Candle Blew Out"

In your journal, write about your response to this short story. What lesson do you think the story teaches? Do you agree or disagree with it? Why?

Going Back Into the Text: Author's Craft

The **motivation** in a story is the key to why a character behaves in a certain way. Desires, experiences, feelings—even the wishes of others—can affect a character's motivation. As a reader, look for clues that will help you clarify the motivation.

As you analyze why the characters in this story act the way they do, use these questions as guidelines.

1. What do you think causes the boys to act the way they do in the beginning of the story?

2. What motivates the boys at the end of the story?

3. Why do you think Life-Stone's mother stops whipping him at the mention of his father?

PREREADING

The Ch'i-lin Purse

Reading the Story in a Cultural Context

For many people, some of the best childhood memories are the stories they heard at home. These rich beginnings might include family stories, books read aloud, or traditional tales told by one generation to another.

For Linda Fang, who spent her childhood in Shanghai, China, the greatest treat was listening to her mother tell stories. Her mother would first read the stories aloud from a book; then she would retell them from memory. Linda Fang says of her mother, "She was such a wonderful storyteller that all the characters in the book—heroes, villains, emperors, high officials, beautiful maidens, and handsome young men, as well as simple, honest folk—came to life."

Not surprisingly, Linda Fang became a professional storyteller when she grew up. She now lives in Washington, D.C., and helped found the Washington Storytellers' Theatre there.

A favorite story told by Linda Fang's mother was "The Ch'i-lin Purse." The author writes that this story "touched me deeply and has stayed with me ever since." Years later, Linda Fang decided to share this story with a larger audience. The title of the story became the title of her first book, *The Ch'i-lin Purse: A Collection of Ancient Chinese Stories.*

"The Ch'i-lin Purse" comes from a Peking opera called *So-lin-nang.* Many of the stories told in the Peking opera are based on traditional texts and scripts from ancient times. *So-lin-nang* is set in the time of the Sung Dynasty (A.D. 960–1279).

In "The Ch'i-lin Purse," two brides on the way to their weddings meet by chance. A spontaneous act of kindness by one of the young women has lasting effects on both couples.

Focusing on the Selection

As you read the story of "The Ch'i-lin Purse," focus on the character of Hsiang-ling. What is she like in the beginning of the tale? How does she change? What causes this change?

The Ch'i-lin Purse

◆◆◆

retold by *Linda Fang*

It is said that many years ago in China, in a small town called Teng-chou,[1] there lived a wealthy widow, Mrs. Hsüeh.[2] She had only one daughter, Hsüeh Hsiang-ling.[3] Hsiang-ling was beautiful and intelligent, and her mother loved her dearly. But since everything Hsiang-ling wanted was given to her, she became rather spoiled.

When Hsiang-ling was sixteen years old, her mother decided that it was time for her to marry. Through a matchmaker,[4] Hsiang-ling was engaged to a young man from a wealthy family in a neighboring town.

Mrs. Hsüeh wanted to prepare a dowry[5] for Hsiang-ling that no girl in town could match. But Hsiang-ling was hard to please. Almost everything her mother bought for her was returned or exchanged at least two or three times.

When the dowry was finally complete, Mrs. Hsüeh decided to add one more item to it. It was the Ch'i-lin Purse,[6] a red satin bag embroidered on both sides with a *ch'i-lin*, a legendary animal from ancient times. The *ch'i-lin* had scales all over its body and a single horn on its head. In the old Chinese tradition, the *ch'i-lin* is the symbol of a promising male offspring. Mrs. Hsüeh wanted to give Hsiang-ling the purse because she hoped that her daughter would give birth to a talented son.

---

[1] **Teng-chou** (DEHNG-joh) *n.* the name of a town
[2] **Hsüeh** (SHOO-ay) *n.* a family name
[3] **Hsüeh Hsiang-ling** (SHOO-ay SHEE-ahng-lihng) *n.* a woman's name
[4] **matchmaker** *n.* someone who arranges marriages
[5] **dowry** (DOW-ree) *n.* the property that a woman brings to her husband at their marriage
[6] **Ch'i-lin Purse** (CHEE-lihn pers)

When the purse Mrs. Hsüeh had ordered was ready, a family servant brought it home. But Hsiang-ling was not satisfied at all. "I don't like the pattern, take it back!" she said.

The servant returned to the store and ordered another. But when it was brought home, Hsiang-ling merely glanced at it and said, "The colors of the *ch'i-lin* are too dark, take it back!"

The servant went to place another order, but the new purse still did not please her. This time the servant broke down in tears.

"I won't go back again, young mistress. The people in the store laugh at me. They say I am hard to please. This is not true. You are the one who is hard to please. If you don't want this purse, I am going to leave you and work for someone else."

Although Hsiang-ling was spoiled, she was not a mean-spirited person. She somehow began to feel sorry for the old man, who had been with her family for more than forty years. So she looked at the purse and said, "All right, I will have this one. You may go and pay for it." The servant went back to the store, paid for the purse, and gave it to Mrs. Hsüeh.

Hsiang-ling's wedding fell on the eighteenth day of the sixth month according to the lunar calendar. It was the day Hsiang-ling had longed for since her engagement. She was very excited and yet a bit sad, because she knew she was leaving her mother and the home she had lived in for sixteen years.

Hsiang-ling wore a red silk dress and a red silk veil over her head. As she sat in her *hua-chiao*, a sedan chair draped with red satin, and waited to be carried to her new home, her mother came to present her with the Ch'i-lin Purse.

"My dear child," she said as she lifted up the satin curtain in front, "this is your *ta-hsi-jin-tzu*,[7] your big, happy day. I am delighted to see you get married even though I will miss you terribly. Here is the Ch'i-lin Purse. I have put some wonderful things in it. But don't open it now. Wait until you are in your new home, and you will feel that I am with you."

Hsiang-ling was hardly listening. She was thinking about the wedding and wondering about her husband-to-be, whom she had never met. She took the purse and laid it on her lap. A few minutes later, four footmen came. Picking up the *hua-chiao,* they placed it on their shoulders, and the wedding procession began.

---

[7] **ta-hsi-jin-tzu** (tuh-shee-JIHN-soo) *n.* wedding

As the procession reached the road, it started to rain. Soon it was pouring so heavily that the footmen could not see well enough to continue. The wedding procession came to a halt, and the *hua-chiao* was carried into a pavilion that stood alongside the road.

There was another *hua-chiao* in the pavilion. It was shabby, with holes in the drapes. Hsiang-ling could hear a girl sobbing inside. This annoyed her, because she believed that a person crying on her wedding day could bring bad luck. So she told her maid to go and find out what was wrong.

"The bride is very sad," the maid said when she returned. "She is poor and has nothing to take to her new home."

Hsiang-ling couldn't help feeling sorry for the girl. Then her eyes fell on the Ch'i-lin Purse in her lap. She realized that she was lucky to have so many things, while this girl had nothing. Since she wasn't carrying any money with her, she handed the Ch'i-lin Purse to her maid. "Give this to the girl, but don't mention my name."

So the girl went over and gave the purse to the other bride. The girl stopped crying at once. Hsiang-ling had given away her mother's wedding gift without even finding out what was inside.

A few minutes later, the rain stopped, the footmen picked up Hsiang-ling's *hua-chiao*, and the procession continued on its way. In an hour, Hsiang-ling arrived at her new home. She was happily married that evening, and to her delight she found her husband to be a wonderful and handsome young man. In a year's time, when she became the mother of a little boy, she felt she was the happiest woman in the world.

But six years later, there came a terrible flood. Hsiang-ling and her family lost their home and everything they owned. When they were fleeing their town, Hsiang-ling became separated from her husband and young son in the crowds of other townspeople. After searching for them in vain, Hsiang-ling followed a group of people to another town called Lai-chou. She had given up hope that she would ever see her husband and child again.

As Hsiang-ling sat, exhausted and alone, at the side of the road leading to Lai-chou, a woman came up to her and said, "You must be hungry. Don't you know that a li[8] down the road there is a food-distribution shack? Yüan-wai Lu[9] has opened it to help the flood victims. Talk to his butler. I am sure you can get something to eat there."

---

[8] **li** (lee) *n.* Chinese unit of distance, equal to about 1/3 mile
[9] **Yüan-wai Lu** (yoo-AHN-wee LOO) *n.* a man's name

Hsiang-ling thanked the woman, followed her directions, and found the place. A long line of people with bowls in their hands were waiting to get a ration of porridge. Hsiang-ling had never done such a thing in her life. As she stood in line holding a bowl and waiting her turn, she felt distraught enough to cry, but she forced herself to hold back the tears.

Finally, when it was her turn, Yüan-wai Lu's butler scooped the last portion of porridge into her bowl and said to the rest of the people in line, "Sorry, no more porridge left. Come back early tomorrow."

The person behind Hsiang-ling began to sob. Hsiang-ling turned around and saw a woman who reminded her of her mother, except that she was much older. Without a word, she emptied her porridge into the woman's bowl and walked away.

The butler was surprised at what Hsiang-ling had done. Just as she had made her way back to the road, he caught up with her and said, "Young lady, I don't understand. Why did you give away your porridge—are you not hungry?"

"I am hungry," said Hsiang-ling, "but I am young and I can stand hunger a bit longer."

"You are very unselfish," said the man. "I would like to help you. My master, Yüan-wai Lu, is looking for someone to take care of his little boy. If you are interested, I would be happy to recommend you."

Hsiang-ling gratefully accepted his offer and was brought to the house where Yüan-wai Lu and his wife lived.

Yüan-wai Lu, a man in his early thirties, was impressed with Hsiang-ling's graceful bearing, and he agreed to hire her. "My wife's health is very delicate and she seldom leaves her room. Your job is to take care of our son. You may play with him anywhere in the garden, but there is one place you must never go. That is the Pearl Hall, the house that stands by itself on the east side of the garden. It is a sacred place, and if you ever go in there, you will be dismissed immediately."

So Hsiang-ling began her life as a governess. The little boy in her care was very spoiled. Whenever he wanted anything, he wanted it right away, and if he didn't get it, he would cry and cry until he got it. Hsiang-ling was saddened by his behavior; it reminded her of how spoiled she had been as a child.

One day, Hsiang-ling and the little boy were in the garden. Suddenly, the ball they were playing with disappeared through the window of the Pearl Hall. The boy began to wail. "I want my ball. I want my ball! Go and get my ball!"

"Young Master, I cannot go into the Pearl Hall," said Hsiang-ling. "Your father doesn't allow it. I will be dismissed if I do."

But the little boy only cried louder, and finally Hsiang-ling decided that she had no choice. She walked over to the east side of the garden and looked around. No one was in sight. She quickly walked up the steps that led to the Pearl Hall and again made sure that no one was watching. Then she opened the door and stepped in.

She found herself standing in front of an altar, where two candles and some incense sticks were burning. But in the place where people usually put the wooden name-tablets of their ancestors was the Ch'i-lin Purse! Instantly she recalled the events of her wedding day and how happy she had been. She thought of her wonderful husband and her own son and how much she missed them. She had had everything then, and now she had nothing! Hsiang-ling burst into tears.

Suddenly, she felt a hand on her shoulder. When she turned around she found herself face-to-face with Mrs. Lu, her mistress, and a young maid.

"What are you doing here?" Mrs. Lu asked angrily.

"Young Master told me to come here and pick up his ball," Hsiang-ling replied.

"Then why were you weeping at the altar?"

"Because I saw the purse that once belonged to me."

Mrs. Lu looked startled. "Where are you from?" she asked, as she took the purse from the altar and sat down on a chair that leaned against a long table. There was a tremble in her voice.

"I am from Teng-chou."

"Bring her a stool," said Mrs. Lu, motioning to her maid. Not wanting to wait on another servant, the maid grudgingly brought a stool and put it to Mrs. Lu's right. "You may sit down," said Mrs. Lu. Somewhat confused, Hsiang-ling sat down.

"What was your maiden name?"

"Hsüeh Hsiang-ling."

"When were you married?"

"On the eighteenth day of the sixth moon, six years ago."

"Bring her a chair and put it to my left," Mrs. Lu ordered her maid. Hsiang-ling was told to move to the chair. She was surprised to see herself treated as a guest of honor.

"Tell me how you lost the purse," said Mrs. Lu.

"It was a gift from my mother. My wedding procession was stopped on the road because of a storm, and my *hua-chiao* was carried into a pavilion. There was another *hua-chiao* in it, and the bride was crying."

"Move her chair to the middle and move mine to the right side," ordered Mrs. Lu. The chairs were switched, and once again Hsiang-ling was told to sit down. She was astonished to find herself sitting in the middle seat—the place of the highest honor.

This painting is part of a larger work called *Ladies with Fans* by Chou Fang. The artist created it around A.D. 800. Notice the traditional Chinese gowns the women are wearing. *Metropolitan Museum of Art*

"Please continue," said Mrs. Lu.

"I gave the bride my purse. I never saw it again, and I have no idea how it got here."

Mrs. Lu dropped to her knees in front of Hsiang-ling and cried, "You are my benefactor![10] All these years I have been praying here for your well-being. When I got to my new home, I opened the purse and found it full of valuables, including this." She opened the purse and took out a piece of jade. "My husband and I were able to pawn it for a large amount of money. Using the money, we started a business and have now become very wealthy. So I reclaimed the jade and have kept it in the purse since. We also built the Pearl Hall to house the purse and to honor you.

---

[10] **benefactor** (BEHN-uh-fak-tuhr) *n.* a person who gives financial or other aid to another

"I knew that you lived in the Teng-chou area, so when I heard about the flood I prayed day and night in that direction, begging Buddha[11] to protect you from harm. I was hoping that one day I would find you and show you my gratitude. And here you are, taking care of my son! I know what we must do. We shall divide our property and give you half of it. That will make us all very happy."

Hsiang-ling was speechless as Mrs. Lu placed the purse in her hands. That same day, Yüan-wai Lu sent out servants in all directions to look for Hsiang-ling's husband and son. Soon they were found, in a village not far from Teng-chou.

A great friendship developed between the two families. Later, when Hsiang-ling told people the story about her purse, she would always end the tale by saying, "If you have a chance to do something good, be sure to do it. Happiness will come back to you."

---

[11] **Buddha** (BOO-duh) *n.* the title of Siddhartha Gautama, the Indian philosopher and founder of the religion Buddhism

POSTREADING

Critical Thinking

1. Why did Linda Fang want to retell the story of "The Ch'i-lin Purse"?

2. How is the *ch'i-lin* tradition an example of the values of Chinese culture?

3. Have you ever done a spontaneous act of kindness for someone? What prompted your action?

Writing Your Response to "The Ch'i-lin Purse"

In your journal, record your thoughts about Hsiang-ling's saying, "If you have a chance to do something good, be sure to do it. Happiness will come back to you." Explain whether you agree with this philosophy or follow a different one. What are the words that you live by?

Going Back Into the Text: Author's Craft

Many traditional tales have a **moral**, or instructive message. Often in these stories a character acts in a moral way at some cost to him or herself. However, the right behavior is rewarded in the end and the lesson of the story is made clear.

As you explore the moral aspect of this story, use these questions as guidelines:

1. How does the servant cause Hsiang-ling to consider the feelings of someone else?

2. What causes Hsiang-ling to give away the Ch'i-lin Purse?

3. How is Hsiang-ling rewarded for giving away her porridge? for giving away the purse?

PREREADING

Hearing of the Earthquake in Kyoto (1830)

Reading the Poem in a Cultural Context

A strong earthquake is one of nature's most devastating disasters. As you probably know, earthquakes occur more often in some areas than others. In fact, most of the world's earthquakes occur in two large belts. More than three-fourths of earthquakes take place in the belt known as the circum-Pacific belt, or the Ring of Fire. Japan lies in the middle of this belt. Through the centuries, many major earthquakes have caused enormous destruction to this island country.

In the poem you are about to read describes an earthquake that struck the city of Kyoto on Honshu Island in 1830. At that time, Kyoto was Japan's capital and the home of its emperor. Buddhist temples and Shinto shrines housed many of its cultural treasures. Buildings such as the Imperial Palace and the Temple of the Golden Pavilion made the city spectacular and unique.

In the poem "Hearing of the Earthquake in Kyoto (1830)," a Japanese poet records his personal reaction to news of an earthquake

"terrible beyond recall." The poet is Rai Sanyō (1780–1832), well-known for his outstanding verse and prose.

Sanyō was a student of Chinese literature and philosophy. He began writing in Chinese when he was 12 and at the age of 19, he became the student of a famous scholar. Not many years after that, he began to write a history of his native Japan in the Chinese language. When he was 43, Sanyō bought a house in Kyoto. He built a small cottage in the garden where he continued to work.

In addition to the various Japanese histories that he wrote in prose, Rai Sanyō wrote many poems inspired by events or people of the time. The poem you are about to read is a striking example of an event caused by nature.

Focusing on the Selection

Read "Hearing of the Earthquake in Kyoto (1830)" all the way through to capture a sense of its message. Then read it again and ask yourself who is speaking in this poem. From whose point of view is the poem told?

Hearing of the Earthquake in Kyoto (1830)

Rai Sanyō

By post news from the capital, terrible beyond recall:
"This month, the second day, earthquakes from dusk to dawn.
Seven days and nights the tremors, until the earth must sunder.[1]
We beseech[2] in tears the sky.
Of ten houses nine destroyed;
Families cower[3] in the streets as roof tiles shower down. . . ."
Of my home no word.
Dumbly I scratch my head and gaze
East toward my home on the Kamo[4] banks:
The youngest clinging to my frail wife,
They flee to the river sands,
Fearful for the abandoned house,
While stone embankments topple,
Laying the willow roots bare.
Through deep tides to distant flats[5]
Which way escape?
The eldest boy wades the stream,
The youngest on his nurse's back.

Japanese artist Ando Hiroshige made this woodprint in 1857 as part of a series called *Squall at the Large Bridge Ohashi.*

---

[1] **sunder** (SUN-duhr) *v.* separate; split
[2] **beseech** (bih-SEECH) *v.* ask earnestly
[3] **cower** (KOW-uhr) *v.* crouch or draw back
[4] **Kamo** (KAH-moh) *n.* name of a river
[5] **flats** *n. pl.* areas of level, low-lying ground

From the nest upturned though the eggs be spared,
The mother sickens with care, bearing alone a family's burden.
How can I face you again?
I speed this letter back,
And wait an answer that may never come.
Your death or life unknown,
In this chaos[6] whom shall I entreat?[7]
When dread fate crushes the multitudes,[8]
How can I ask of him or her? . . .
I watch the clouds hurrying north.
Dragons of the sea-rain howl as,
Trembling in dark fear,
I beat out the bars of this long dirge.[9]

---

[6] **chaos** (KAY-ahs) *n.* great disorder or confusion
[7] **entreat** (ehn-TREET) *v.* beg
[8] **multitudes** (MUL-tih-toodz) *n. pl.* large crowds of people; the masses
[9] **dirge** (derj) *n.* funeral song

POSTREADING

Critical Thinking

1. Why do you think Sanyō chronicles the earthquake in his poem?

2. Why is this poem still relevant to life in Japan?

3. Have you ever felt so badly about someone else's misfortune that you didn't know what to say or do? How did you handle the situation?

Writing Your Response to "Hearing of the Earthquake in Kyoto (1830)"

In your journal, write about your response to the poem. What emotions does the poem arouse in you? In what ways do you share the speaker's grief?

Going Back Into the Text: Author's Craft

The **point of view** of a piece of literature is the perspective from which it is told. In the first person point of view, the narrator is the teller of the story and uses the pronouns *I* or *me*. If the work is told in the third person, the pronouns *he*, *she*, or *they* are used.

As you reread this poem to determine the point of view, use these questions as guidelines:

1. Who is speaking in the poem? How do you know?

2. To whom is the poem addressed? How do you know?

3. How might the poem be different if someone in Kyoto were telling it?

A Call to Action/To the Tune "The River Is Red"

Reading the Poems in a Cultural Context

The subjects of poems are as diverse as the poets who write them. While many poems comment on romance, the seasons, or other aspects of nature, still other poems present a message about society. The two poems that you are about to read contain messages about the political state of China at the beginning of the 20th century.

These poems are written by a woman named Ch'iu Chin. She was born in 1879 in China. At that time China was ruled by the Ch'ing (Manchu) dynasty. In 1894–95, China fought a war with Japan. As a result of the war, China grew weak, and European nations began setting up colonies and expanding trade. However, many Chinese people opposed the spread of Western influences in their country. They began to organize secret societies to plan a revolution against the dynasty.

While still in her twenties, Ch'iu Chin went to Japan to study. There, she joined a revolutionary party led by Sun Yat-sen. Soon, she became a leader in this organization. In 1906, Ch'iu Chin returned to China, where she taught school and founded a newspaper for women in Shanghai. The school where Ch'iu Chin taught was also the secret headquarters for the revolutionary army. However, in 1907 Ch'iu Chin was arrested by the Manchu government. Her poems were banned, and she was beheaded for her political ideas. Five years later, in 1912, Sun Yat-sen led his revolutionaries to overthrow the Manchu regime and established a republican government in China.

Ch'iu Chin's poetry reflects her strong feelings about the wrongs of the past and the conflicts that China faced. Although she did not live to experience "the perfume of freedom," her political courage and passionate beliefs live on in her poems.

Focusing on the Selections

As you read "A Call to Action" and "To the Tune 'The River Is Red,'" look for clues to the poet's purpose. Of what threats does she warn? What abuses does she mention? For what action does she call?

A Call to Action

Ch'iu Chin
translated by Kenneth Rexroth and Ling Chung

Without warning their nest
Has become dangerous to the swallows.
Our homeland, grown old, suffers
Under heavy burdens—
From the East the constant threat of invasion,
From the West, threats of devious plotting.
Scholars, throw away your brushes!
Secluded women, take up arms!
Only heroes can save us this time.
Together we can hold back
The flooding waves.

Note the tiny feet of Madam Wu Ting Fang, wife of a Chinese Premier. Until recently, extremely small feet were considered a mark of great beauty in China. Wealthy Chinese women would bind their feet from childhood to keep them small. Women with feet like Madam Wu Ting Fang were in great pain when they walked.

To the Tune "The River Is Red"

Ch'iu Chin
translated by *Kenneth Rexroth* **and** *Ling Chung*

How many wise men and heroes
Have survived the dust and dirt of the world?
How many beautiful women have been heroines?[1]
There were the novel and famous women generals
Ch'in Liang-yü and Shen Yün-yin.[2]
Though tears stained their dresses
Their hearts were full of blood.
The wild strokes of their swords
Whistled like dragons and sobbed with pain.

The perfume of freedom burns my mind
With grief for my country.
When will we ever be cleansed?
Comrades, I say to you,
Spare no effort, struggle unceasingly,
That at last peace may come to our people.
And jewelled dresses and deformed feet
Will be abandoned.
And one day, all under heaven
Will see beautiful free women,
Blooming like fields of flowers,
And bearing brilliant and noble human beings.

---

[1] **heroines** (HEHR-oh-ihnz) *n. pl.* female heroes
[2] **Ch'in Liang-yü** (chihn LEE-ahng-yoo) . . . **Shen Yü-yin** (shehn YOO-ahn-yihn)
n. women's names

POSTREADING

Critical Thinking

1. Why do you think Ch'iu Chin chose poetry as a way of spreading a political message?

2. What do these poems tell you about women in Chinese society about 100 years ago?

3. Ch'iu Chin felt very strongly about China's future. What causes do you care about? How do you express your feelings about them?

Writing Your Response to "A Call to Action" and "To the Tune 'The River Is Red'"

In your journal, record your reactions to these poems. What phrases or lines in the poems do you think are the most effective? Why?

Going Back Into the Text: Author's Craft

When you are reading literature, it is important to decide what the **author's purpose** is. Why did the author write this story or poem? What does he or she want the reader to understand?

As you read these poems, use the following questions to help you identify the author's purpose:

1. In "A Call to Action," with what metaphor does the poet begin to alert readers to the problems she sees?

2. What commands does Ch'iu Chin give in her poems?

3. Why do you think the poet compares women's lives in the past to the future in "To the Tune 'The River Is Red'?"

MODEL LESSON

No Way Out

Responding to Literature

Notice the sidenotes in the margins of "No Way Out." These notes reflect one student's reading of the story by Harry Wu. The student recognizes the extreme power and injustice of the Communist party in China and the author's determination to oppose the party's wishes, despite the great risks involved. Compare this student's observations to your own.

Reading the Autobiography in a Cultural Context

After World War II, the Communists, led by Mao Zedong, took over China. The new Communist government seized control of most industries and farms. To promote economic recovery, Mao set up a Five-Year Plan in 1953. In 1958, he launched a second plan known as the Great Leap Forward. The objective of this plan was to speed the development of the country dramatically.

At about the same time, Harry Wu, a geology student at a university in Beijing, began to make plans too. His goal was to escape the repression of the Communist government by leaving China.

Neither the Great Leap Forward nor Wu's attempt to escape was successful. Instead, China's economy was shattered, people suffered extreme shortages of food and other necessities, and the government became even more radical. In 1960, a day after his graduation, Harry Wu was arrested. His crime: criticizing the Communist party. There was no trial.

For the next 19 years, Harry Wu was a political prisoner in China's "reform-through-labor" system. During these years, he survived the harsh conditions of twelve different labor camps, factories, farms, and mines. He suffered torture, brutalization, and near-starvation. At one camp, he was even isolated in a concrete cell the size of a coffin.

When he was finally released, Harry Wu became an outspoken critic of inhumane conditions. He moved to the United States, settled in California, and started a new life. He has given lectures, appeared on national news programs, and testified before Congress on China's forced labor camps, or gulags.

In 1995, Harry Wu published an autobiography called *Bitter Winds: A Memoir of My Years in China's Gulag*. Through the vivid details of his story, the world was reminded of how hard it is to break the human spirit. The selection you are about to read is from a chapter titled "No Way Out."

Focusing on the Selection

As you read the selection from Harry Wu's autobiography, ask yourself why this story is important. Why is the personal account of one person meaningful for so many others?

No Way Out

◆◆◆

Harry Wu

This is an excerpt from an autobiography, which is a work of nonfiction. This means that the events the author is describing actually occurred.

The more I thought about the nature of the communist system, the more I saw a great wall rising in front of me. During my months of fieldwork in the Shandong countryside, I had watched peasants digging furrows several feet deep to plant their crops, spurred on by zealous[1] cadres,[2] some of whom sought advancement, some of whom believed that such methods would greatly increase the yield. Among the villagers some seemed to believe it possible suddenly to begin producing 10,000 *jin* of wheat rather than 500, on one *mou* of land, but most went along because they dared not oppose the Party's current line. This ill-fated attempt to increase agricultural production was just one of the follies of the Great Leap Forward, a movement that Chairman Mao had initiated early in 1958 in the deluded conviction that he could bring modernization to China in fifteen years. Instead he brought famine and economic collapse.

The Party to which he is referring must be the Communist party. I wonder what happened to people who opposed the Party's wishes.

That autumn I was only twenty-one. I was energetic, ambitious, and technically skilled, but I could see no role for myself in my country's future, since everyone had to support the industrial and agricultural policies of the Great Leap Forward. To object that steel could not be produced by melting down farming tools and cooking implements in the "backyard furnaces" being constructed in the villages, factories, and schools was to oppose the revolution. As the antirightist movement had demonstrated, anyone who questioned the leadership of Chairman Mao was cast out and punished. I found China's situation tragic. The communist system had become totally irrational and self-defeating, yet it resisted and punished any effort to bring about change.

It sounds as if Chairman Mao's government had a very limited vision. Mao wanted to modernize China without realistic plans and without considering the advice of critics.

---

[1] **zealous** (ZEHL-uhs) *adj.* fanatically devoted
[2] **cadres** (KAD-reez) *n. pl.* small groups of dedicated people

Human rights activist Harry Wu meets the press after being released from detainment by Chinese officials who accused him of spying. September 5, 1995.

With all the rashness and overconfidence of youth, I decided that my only hope was to flee my country and leave it to its terrible fate. I guessed that other students who had been labeled as rightists would have reached similar conclusions, and I began subtly[3] to inquire. By late 1958 I had found three who shared my determination to leave, all of whom I believed I could trust. We met furtively,[4] hastily, knowing that we would be arrested, maybe killed, if our escape plans became known. We recognized the risks we faced, but we all agreed that remaining in our present circumstances was intolerable.

Harry Wu is taking a very big risk. The title of this narrative is "No Way Out." This tells me that Wu's attempt to escape will probably fail.

---

[3] **subtly** (SUH-tuh-lee) *adv.* quietly
[4] **furtively** (FUHR-tihv-lee) *adv.* secretly

We devised a series of coded hand gestures so that we could communicate without detection. Our prearranged meeting spot was a particular tree on the campus; our appointed time was ten o'clock at night, just when the students returned from the classrooms and the library to prepare for bed. When one of us signaled by rubbing his nose during the day, the others knew to slip away to the tree that evening, usually to receive a brief message or pass on a map.

Step by step in the spring of 1959 we laid our plans. Everyone knew that the Hong Kong border, which had served as the principal escape route out of China in the early 1950s, had been closed down through vigorous surveillance.[5] Our best chance was to use our skills at cross-country navigation and our expertise with compasses and maps to try and disappear across the remote mountains between China and Burma. We searched through the Geology Institute's library to find detailed regional maps of the terrain we would cross, along with charts intended for use by field geologists and surveying teams. Some we copied, some we ripped from books as we researched the best route across the rugged mountains of Yunnan province far to the southwest of Beijing.

In the midst of these preparations, we all were sent out in late July 1959 for a third field assignment, this time a two-month project to collect information for our senior theses. Everyone had a different destination. I would go to the Beijing Engineering Geology Bureau in the nearby Western Hills to assist the engineers in devising a plan to supply underground water to China's first nuclear power plant, soon to be constructed near Zhoukoudian with financial aid from the Soviet Union. I would first research how many wells were needed and how deep they should be sunk, then try to determine the best method of evaluating the quality and chemical composition of the water.

Before the four in our group left the campus for our separate projects, we agreed on a timetable for our escape. We expected to return to Beijing just before the National Day holiday on October 1, at which time we would request leave to return home and visit our families. In fact, we would meet in the Beijing train station and purchase tickets for the three-day journey to Kunming, the capital of Yunnan province. We planned to sit in separate cars on the same train, then regroup at the station after our arrival. By then we had done all we could to assure a successful escape. We had carefully

Wu is fortunate that he and his fellow rightists are geology students. This gives them an excuse to study regional maps of the land they wish to cross.

If he were a resident of one of the villages he is studying, Wu would probably not be able to consider such an escape plan.

Will their families be under suspicion or punished if the group tries to escape?

[5] **surveillance** (suhr-VAYL-ehns) *n.* the act of watching or supervising closely

chosen our route and had even managed to steal a number of blank letters of introduction, the kind used by geologists in the field to obtain rice, shelter, and other necessities from local village cadres. There was nothing left except to swear that if caught, we would never, even under torture, reveal our plan or the identity of the other participants.

Once again I enjoyed being away from the political tensions of the campus, and I found my research project challenging. But late one afternoon when I was playing basketball after work with the Bureau engineers, I noticed Wang, one of my group, standing outside the fence rubbing his nose to signal that he needed to talk. It was several weeks too early for him to return to Beijing, and I could not imagine what would bring him to the Bureau to look for me. Unable to interrupt the game, I rubbed my nose to signal that I would talk later. After dark I sneaked outside the gate. In rapid whispers Wang explained his predicament.[6] He had fallen in love with an assistant engineer at the Hubei Geology Bureau in Wuhan, but her Party branch leader had discovered her relationship with a rightist. Her work unit had criticized her for associating with a counterrevolutionary,[7] but still she continued to see him. When the relationship was exposed a second time, she faced a serious struggle meeting at which Wang knew her fellow workers would accuse and threaten her for lying to the Party and disobeying its instructions.

Seeing no way to avoid involvement and not wanting to disrupt our escape plans for October 1, Wang had decided to use the 300 yuan[8] advanced to him for expenses at the start of his field assignment and flee to Beijing to find me. He urged me to leave with him and contribute my advance money to buy train tickets to Yunnan for the two of us the next day. I listened to his plan but decided the risk was too great now that he was a fugitive from his work unit and sought by the Public Security Bureau. Moreover, we had no way to include our other two comrades. I urged Wang to turn himself in to the Geology Institute authorities, hand over the state's money, admit his mistake, write a self-criticism, and ask for forgiveness. Becoming involved with a local woman and taking public funds to flee from the supervision of the masses were serious political errors for a rightist, but perhaps not actual crimes, I told him. We would have to postpone our escape plans, but we would try again. He seemed to agree,

Considering how structured their lives are, Wang's arrival must signal trouble. I doubt he was given permission to visit Wu.

Wang must be pretty desperate. Not only is he risking his own safety, but he may be putting Wu's life in danger too.

---

[6] **predicament** (preh-DIK-uh-mehnt) *n.* problem
[7] **counterrevolutionary** *n.* a person who does not support the reform movement, or revolution
[8] **yuan** *n.* currency in China

and I sneaked him into the engineers' dormitory to sleep that night, assured that he would leave to face the school authorities before dawn the next morning. He was gone when I awoke.

Two weeks later, with my fieldwork completed, I returned somewhat apprehensively[9] to the campus. I learned immediately that Wang had been arrested, but no one would talk about the case. I had no way to find out whether he had revealed our escape plans under interrogation.[10] If he had confessed, I would be arrested next. Abandoning all thought of trying to leave the country, I applied to visit my family for the three-day holiday as if nothing had happened. I could think of no alternative but to board the train to Shanghai and hope that Wang had remained silent.

The day before my expected departure for home, Comrade Ma appeared in my dormitory. "A political meeting has been scheduled at the Bureau just after National Day to evaluate your final thought summary," she announced, her eyes expressionless. "Your permission to travel to Shanghai has been denied."

Thirty engineers waited for me in the Party Committee's meeting room at the Geology Bureau on October 3, 1959. Chief Engineer Ning declared that the meeting had been called to assist me in reforming my thoughts. His words sounded ominous,[11] but I noticed with relief that he did not use the label "counterrevolutionary rightist" when he referred to me. He ordered me to make a report, but I had no idea what he expected me to say. All I could think of was to recite my familiar list of self-accusations—my level of political thought was too low, I had a bourgeois[12] background, I hadn't studied Chairman Mao's works hard enough.

"Have you ever done anything to harm the working people?" Ning demanded.

Avoiding his question, I continued speaking about my many mistakes. To my relief Ning called a break in the meeting, and for a few minutes we sat alone at the table. I had always known him to be a fair and kind man, but I was amazed when he poured me a cup of tea. Party cadres do not extend courtesies to rightists. Ning seemed to wait for me to speak. "We have spent two months working together," I began, "and you know me to be a straightforward person. Please tell me what the problem is."

I wonder if Wang was arrested before or after he turned himself in to the authorities. For that matter, I wonder if he turned himself in at all.

I wonder if they have denied Wu's permission to travel because they know about his previous plans to escape the country.

I don't trust Ning. I think he is trying to gain Wu's trust in order to make him confess to something.

---

[9] **apprehensively** (ap-ree-HEHN-sihv-lee) *adv.* nervously

[10] **interrogation** (ihn-terhr-uh-GAY-shuhn) *n.* intense, often cruel questioning

[11] **ominous** (AH-mihn-uhs) *adj.* scary

[12] **bourgeois** (boor-ZHWAH) *adj.* middle class

Ning drew out a bank withdrawal slip for fifty yuan bearing my signature. Stamped on the top line was the date, September 10, the day after Wang had slept in the dormitory. Ning said that one of the engineers had that morning discovered his account missing fifty yuan. I realized immediately that Wang must have forged my name to withdraw money for his escape and failed somehow in the attempt, but I couldn't reveal those facts to Ning. If I claimed that I knew nothing about the bank account, that the signature was not mine, the authorities would investigate further. If I told the truth and said that Wang had slept in the dormitory the previous night, they would ask what he was doing there. I could see no alternative but to confess my guilt and declare myself a thief.

I felt miserable, but I told Ning that I had taken the money to buy tickets to visit my family. Fortunately I had in my pocket the money my stepmother had just sent me to pay for a ticket home to Shanghai, so I pulled out fifty yuan and asked Ning for forgiveness. He put his hand on my back to comfort me and said that sometimes people make mistakes. Then he left the room, assuring me that he would dismiss the struggle meeting and that I shouldn't worry. A few minutes later he walked me to the gate, shook my hand, and urged me to do nothing again that would jeopardize[13] my future. Never had I met a Party member like this, I thought, as I walked toward the bus stop.

Shaken by Ning's kindness and my own fraudulent[14] response, I walked several miles back to the Geology Institute from the central bus station in Beijing, needing time to consider my next step. I decided the only way to deal with the school authorities, who would demand a report of the struggle meeting, was to confess. That evening I told Kong I had stolen fifty yuan from an engineer at the Bureau. He screamed that I was not only a rightist but a thief, then ordered me confined to the dorm while he went off to report my latest outrage. Knowing that Wang might already have confessed and that the authorities might just be waiting to accumulate evidence before arresting me, I dreaded the possible outcome of my statement. For several weeks I wrote my self-criticism again and again, never satisfying the Party leaders at my school and constantly worried that at any moment I would be picked up by the police....

Wu should worry. It seems like the authorities definitely suspect him of counterrevolutionary activity. I think I would do my best to pretend to be satisfied with the government's activities. It will be harder for Wu to escape if the authorities think that he wants to leave.

---

[13] **jeopardize** (JEHP-uhr-deyez) *v.* risk
[14] **fraudulent** (FRAW-dyoo-lunht) *adj.* fake

On April 27, Kong sought me out in the cafeteria. With graduation nearing he rarely accompanied me anymore, so I grew wary when he asked politely whether I had finished eating and could follow him outside for a talk. The sky was gray with clouds as Kong clasped his hands behind his back and led me slowly around the expanse of hardened mud that served as a playing field. He spoke predictably, almost casually, about the necessity of reforming my thoughts. All the while I watched the overcast sky and wondered about the reason for this idle talk. I feared that the authorities had somehow learned about the escape plans made the previous fall. After an hour Kong looked at his watch. It was almost nine o'clock when he announced that we had to attend a meeting.

Over the past two years I had been summoned often to group criticism sessions. Out of habit I took a seat in the back row of the classroom, hoping that this morning would bring merely a repetition of previous proceedings. Then I looked up. On the blackboard, beneath the colored portrait of Chairman Mao, the chalked characters "Meeting to Criticize Rightist Wu Hongda" stared back at me. My stomach tightened. Then Wang Jian strode to the front of the room. Normally Kong and his fellows from the Youth League branch office chaired these criticism meetings themselves. Some people sat stiffly, while others turned awkwardly to look at me. Wang's opening words broke the silence: "Today we meet to criticize the rightist Wu Hongda." A chorus of allegations[15] sprang from the audience.

"Wu Hongda still refuses to reform himself!"

"He opposes the Party, he must be expelled!"

"Down with Wu Hongda, he must now show us his true face!"

For perhaps twenty minutes the accusations continued. I stared straight ahead until Wang Jian signaled for me to stand. "According to the request of the masses and with the full authority of the school," he intoned, "I now denounce, separate, and expel the rightist Wu Hongda, who has consistently refused to mold himself into a good socialist student and has chosen to remain an enemy of the revolution."

Precisely at that moment a uniformed Public Security officer appeared at the doorway. "Representing the people's government of Beijing," he declared as he stepped to the front desk, "I sentence the counterrevolutionary rightist Wu Hongda to reeducation through labor." He motioned me forward and pulled a piece of paper from his jacket pocket. My eyes fixed on the blood-red badge beside his lapel. How could this be happening, I wondered.

---

[15] **allegations** (al-uh-GAY-shuhnz) *n. pl.* accusations made without proof

"Sign here," the officer commanded, pointing to the bottom of the form. His hand seemed purposely to cover the body of the document, preventing me from seeing the charges for my arrest.

"I wish to see the accusation against me," I replied, guessing that my year-old plan to escape had been discovered.

"Just sign your name," he repeated.

"It is my right," I asserted, suddenly feeling bold, "to be informed of my crimes."

"The people's government has placed you under arrest," he countered impatiently. "Whether you sign or not doesn't matter."

I knew that signing the warrant meant agreeing with the decision for my arrest, and I tried to stall, hoping that someone in the room would support my request to know the charges against me. Anger and fear rose in my throat. No one spoke. With no other choice, I bent to scrawl my name. I knew that anyone arrested for trying, even just planning, to escape was usually shot.

The officer grabbed my arm to lead me across the playing field toward my dormitory room to collect some clothes and bedding. My cheeks burned in shame when I saw my former teammates practicing for a baseball game. "Please let go of me," I asked. "I won't run away. There's no place for me to run." The officer released his grip. He even seemed to reassure me.

"Don't worry too much. We all have to change our thoughts. Maybe after three months or six, you'll come back and be given a job. Work hard at reforming yourself, and you'll return a new socialist person."

I had a more immediate worry. The only concrete evidence of our escape plans lay in my dormitory room. Under the sheets of newspaper that served as a liner for my desk drawer, I had hidden a map of the Burmese border taken from the library. The school's security personnel would certainly collect all of my belongings after I left. If they found the map, my life would be worthless.

We walked into my building, North Dormitory Number Five, then up three flights of concrete steps to my room. Six double bunks flanked the walls and six desks clustered in the middle, each with two drawers. Leaning against the bunks, two security cadres watched us enter. Their eyes never left me. Fortunately the far corner of my top bunk lay outside their line of sight.

Acting as if frantic to collect my possessions, I slid out my lower drawer and reached over to dump its contents onto my bunk. A bottle of blue ink spilled across the quilt, and I threw up my hands in dismay. I had formulated a plan. "No need to hurry," one of the cadres said. "Take your time." By then I had found the map. I perched on the bunk and twisted my body toward the wall, slipping the folded page into my pocket.

In the United States, a person can't be convicted for a crime without a trial. Wu is not getting a trial. He can't defend himself. He has no civil rights. Wu has not even been told how long he will be in the forced labor camp.

I think that spending time in a forced labor camp will only make Wu more bitter about the people's government.

Jumping down, I told the Public Security officer I had washed a length of cotton cloth and left it hanging in the basement to dry. "Take only what you need for tonight," he ordered. "The rest will be sent later." Ignoring his words, I darted past him into the corridor. I was agile and strong after my years of athletic training, and I flew down the stairs, hearing his footsteps not far behind me. Just inside the door to the basement, I pulled open the heavy furnace door and stuffed the map inside. By the time the angry officer reached my side, I was calmly folding the cloth beside the drying line. My heart pounded, but I said quietly, "You see? I wanted to have it made into trousers, and I was afraid if I left it here, it would disappear."

I finished tying a few belongings inside my quilt, and the angry officer guided me to a waiting school jeep. At the district police station, a duty officer took my fingerprints and removed my keys and watch, my shoelaces and belt, even my library card.

"This can't be happening," I thought to myself again. "There must be some way out."

Outside they motioned me back to the jeep, where I sat alone for perhaps two hours. I thought about trying to escape, but many police walked around inside the Public Security compound. Finally the driver appeared, then a guard leading a second prisoner, who climbed in beside me on the hard rear seat. He looked dirty and disheveled. I felt insulted to be thrust alongside a common criminal, no doubt a vagrant[16] from the countryside picked up for stealing food from a Beijing market during this time of famine. We rode in silence for more than an hour. I could see nothing outside the olive green canvas roof. The screech of brakes signaled our arrival at the Beijuan Detention Center, which I soon learned was a holding facility for prisoners awaiting relocation to the labor camps.

Inside the first gate a sentry inspected the documents of arrest. A ten-foot-high brick wall stretched as far as I could see across the flat, green expanse of the North China plain. I stared at the second gate. When a duty prisoner motioned me forward, I hoisted my bedroll awkwardly to one shoulder, grabbing my beltless pants with my free hand. Then I waited, squatting awkwardly just inside the yard, seemingly forgotten.

---

[16] **vagrant** (VAY-gruhnt) *n.* a person who wanders from place to place

POSTREADING

Critical Thinking

1. Why do you think Harry Wu wrote this autobiography?

2. How does Harry Wu's experience reflect on the conditions of modern-day China?

3. What are some questions that you would like to ask Harry Wu? Why?

Writing Your Response to "No Way Out"

In your journal, record your reactions to this autobiographical account. What part moved you the most? What actions, if any, did this story make you want to take?

Going Back Into the Text: Author's Craft

An **autobiography** is a first-person account of someone's life. It is written from that person's point of view and often reveals insights into the subject's life and times.

As you read this autobiographical selection, use these questions as guidelines:

1. What factual information about China in the late 1950s does this selection include?

2. What does this excerpt reveal about Harry Wu's opinions and feelings?

3. How would you rate the success of China's reform system?

He-y, Come on Ou-t!

Reading the Story in a Cultural Context

Literature has been an important part of Japanese culture for more than one thousand years. In fact, *The Tale of Genji*, written by a Japanese noblewoman, was the world's first novel.

In more recent times, Japanese interest in fantastic tales, ancient legends, and myths, and their reverence for nature have made it easy to add science fiction to their literary tradition. Science fiction is a form of literature that takes place in an alternate present, a recreated past, or an imagined future. These alterations in time or reality are not just fantasy. The changes are based upon scientific facts and technological or sociological changes that the writer observes now.

Japanese science fiction began in the 1870s when writers were exposed to translations of Jules Verne, the famous French science fiction writer. After World War II, science fiction became very popular. This was due, in part, to the fact that many American soldiers discarded science fiction books, which were quickly collected by second-hand book dealers and purchased by avid Japanese readers. Other books were translated. Soon a large audience for home-grown science fiction developed.

Many contemporary Japanese science fiction writers explore the traditional belief that nature and the environment are sacred. Japan has grown into a highly industrialized society. Pollution and overcrowding have become problems. Many Japanese science fiction writers warn of the dangers of ignoring such problems. They recognize that dealing with garbage, nuclear waste, and chemical pollutants can not be put off.

One such author is Shin'ichi Hoshi, the author of "He-y, Come on Ou-t!" Born in 1926, he has published nearly 1,000 short stories and won several awards for his science fiction. Hoshi's writing often concerns dangers in technology and the environment.

In "He-y, Come on Ou-t!" Shin'ichi Hoshi asks readers to think about how choices made today will affect the future. He suggests that quick and easy solutions may have serious repercussions.

Focusing on the Selection

Science fiction stories often make predictions about what the future will be like. The writers want you to think about what might happen if something does not change. As you read "He-y, Come on Ou-t!" be aware of clues or hints that help you predict the ending. You might not guess because there is a surprise ending.

He-y, Come on Ou-t!

Shin'ichi Hoshi
translated by *Stanleigh Jones*

The typhoon had passed and the sky was a gorgeous blue. Even a certain village not far from the city had suffered damage. A little distance from the village and near the mountains, a small shrine[1] had been swept away by a landslide.

"I wonder how long that shrine's been here."

"Well, in any case, it must have been here since an awfully long time ago."

"We've got to rebuild it right away."

While the villagers exchanged views, several more of their number came over.

"It sure was wrecked."

"I think it used to be right here."

"No, looks like it was a little more over there."

Just then one of them raised his voice. "Hey what in the world is this hole?"

Where they had all gathered there was a hole about a meter[2] in diameter. They peered in, but it was so dark nothing could be seen. However, it gave one the feeling that it was so deep it went clear through to the center of the earth.

There was even one person who said, "I wonder if it's a fox's hole."

"Hey-y, come on ou-t!" shouted a young man into the hole. There was no echo from the bottom. Next he picked up a pebble and was about to throw it in.

---

[1] **shrine** (shreyen) *n.* a site or object that is worshiped
[2] **meter** (MEE-tuhr) *n.* a basic unit of length in the metric system, equal to 39.37 inches

"You might bring down a curse on us. Lay off," warned an old man, but the younger one energetically threw the pebble in. As before, however, there was no answering response from the bottom. The villagers cut down some trees, tied them with rope and made a fence which they put around the hole. Then they repaired to the village.

"What do you suppose we ought to do?"

"Shouldn't we build the shrine up just as it was over the hole?"

A day passed with no agreement. The news traveled fast, and a car from the newspaper company rushed over. In no time a scientist came out, and with an all-knowing expression on his face he went over to the hole. Next, a bunch of gawking curiosity seekers showed up; one could also pick out here and there men of shifty glances who appeared to be concessionaires.[3] Concerned that someone might fall into the hole, a policeman from the local substation kept a careful watch.

One newspaper reporter tied a weight to the end of a long cord and lowered it into the hole. A long way down it went. The cord ran out, however, and he tried to pull it out, but it would not come back up. Two or three people helped out, but when they all pulled too hard, the cord parted at the edge of the hole. Another reporter, a camera in hand, who had been watching all of this, quietly untied a stout rope that had been wound around his waist.

The scientist contacted people at his laboratory and had them bring out a high-powered bull horn, with which he was going to check out the echo from the hole's bottom. He tried switching through various sounds, but there was no echo. The scientist was puzzled, but he could not very well give up with everyone watching him so intently. He put the bull horn right up to the hole, turned it to its highest volume, and let it sound continuously for a long time. It was a noise that would have carried several dozen kilometers[4] above ground. But the hole just calmly swallowed up the sound.

In his own mind the scientist was at a loss, but with a look of apparent composure he cut off the sound and, in a manner suggesting that the whole thing had a perfectly plausible[5] explanation, said simply, "Fill it in."

Safer to get rid of something one didn't understand.

The onlookers, disappointed that this was all that was going to happen, prepared to disperse. Just then one of the concessionaires, having broken through the throng and come forward, made a proposal.

---

[3] **concessionaires** (kuhn-sehsh-uh-NAIRZ) *n. pl.* persons who operate businesses in certain places

[4] **kilometers** (KIHL-uh-mee-tuhrz) *n. pl.* units of length equal to 1,000 meters or 0.6214 miles

[5] **plausible** (PLAW-zuh-buhl) *adj.* reasonable

"Let me have that hole. I'll fill it in for you."

"We'd be grateful to you for filling it in," replied the mayor of the village, "but we can't very well give you the hole. We have to build a shrine there."

"If it's a shrine you want, I'll build you a fine one later. Shall I make it with an attached meeting hall?"

Before the mayor could answer, the people of the village all shouted out.

"Really? Well, in that case, we ought to have it closer to the village."

"It's just an old hole. We'll give it to you!"

So it was settled. And the mayor, of course, had no objection.

The concessionaire was true to his promise. It was small, but closer to the village he did build for them a shrine with an attached meeting hall.

About the time the autumn festival was held at the new shrine, the hole-filling company established by the concessionaire hung out its small shingle at a shack near the hole.

The concessionaire had his cohorts[6] mount a loud campaign in the city. "We've got a fabulously deep hole! Scientists say it's at least five thousand meters deep! Perfect for the disposal of such things as waste from nuclear reactors."

Government authorities granted permission. Nuclear power plants fought for contracts. The people of the village were a bit worried about this, but they consented when it was explained that there would be absolutely no aboveground contamination for several thousand years and that they would share in the profits. Into the bargain, very shortly a magnificent road was built from the city to the village.

Trucks rolled in over the road, transporting lead boxes. Above the hole the lids were opened, and the wastes from nuclear reactors tumbled away into the hole.

Some of the most high-tech and crowded cities in the world are in Japan. This photo shows a street in Tokyo. Garbage disposal is critically important to all crowded cities.

---

6 **cohorts** (KOH-hawrts) *n. pl.* associates or companions

From the Foreign Ministry and the Defense Agency boxes of unnecessary classified documents were brought for disposal. Officials who came to supervise the disposal held discussions on golf. The lesser functionaries, as they threw in the papers, chatted about pinball.

The hole showed no signs of filling up. It was awfully deep, thought some; or else it might be very spacious at the bottom. Little by little the hole-filling company expanded its business.

Bodies of animals used in contagious disease experiments at the universities were brought out, and to these were added the unclaimed corpses[7] of vagrants.[8] Better than dumping all of its garbage in the ocean, went the thinking in the city, and plans were made for a long pipe to carry it to the hole.

The hole gave peace of mind to the dwellers of the city. They concentrated solely on producing one thing after another. Everyone disliked thinking about the eventual consequences. People wanted only to work for production companies and sales corporations; they had no interest in becoming junk dealers. But, it was thought, these problems too would gradually be resolved by the hole.

Young girls whose betrothals[9] had been arranged discarded old diaries in the hole. There were also those who were inaugurating[10] new love affairs and threw into the hole old photographs of themselves taken with former sweethearts. The police felt comforted as they used the hole to get rid of accumulations of expertly done counterfeit[11] bills. Criminals breathed easier after throwing material evidence into the hole.

Whatever one wished to discard, the hole accepted it all. The hole cleansed the city of its filth; the sea and sky seemed to have become a bit clearer than before.

Aiming at the heavens, new buildings went on being constructed one after the other.

One day, atop the high steel frame of a new building under construction, a workman was taking a break. Above his head he heard a voice shout:

"He‑y, come on ou‑t!"

---

[7] **corpses** (KAWRPS-ihz) *n. pl.* dead bodies of human beings

[8] **vagrants** (VAY-gruhnts) *n. pl.* persons who wander from place to place and usually have no means of support; tramps

[9] **betrothals** (bih-TROH-thuhlz) *n. pl.* engagements

[10] **inaugurating** (ih-NAW-gyuh-rayt-ihng) *v.* beginning; starting

[11] **counterfeit** (KOWN-tuhr-fiht) *adj.* phony

But, in the sky to which he lifted his gaze there was nothing at all. A clear blue sky merely spread over all. He thought it must be his imagination. Then, as he resumed his former position, from the direction where the voice had come, a small pebble skimmed by him and fell on past.

The man, however, was gazing in idle reverie[12] at the city's skyline growing ever more beautiful, and he failed to notice.

---

[12] **reverie** (REHV-uh-ree) *n.* daydreaming

POSTREADING

Critical Thinking

1. What is Shin'ichi Hoshi's attitude toward the villagers' use of the hole?

2. Why would a Japanese writer be particularly concerned about environmental pollution and waste disposal?

3. What decisions have you made that may affect the environment? What effect do you think your choices will make?

Writing Your Response to "He-y, Come on Ou-t!"

In your journal, write about your reaction to the ending of the story. What did you think would happen? Were you surprised by the ending? Why or why not?

Going Back Into the Text: Author's Craft

A **surprise ending** is a conclusion that has an unforeseen twist. Although an ending might be unexpected, good writers give you clues to prepare you for what will happen. One clue is feeling that the hole goes through the center of the Earth. Surprise endings in science fiction are meant to shock you and make you think about what is happening and what you are doing.

1. What are some other clues to the ending?

2. Why does this ending have such an impact?

3. Why do you think that Hoshi wrote a surprise ending in this story?

Reviewing the Region

1. Choose an author or character from this chapter who had to overcome great adversity. Give examples that show how the author's or character's struggle was related to the culture in which it took place.

2. Write a brief explanation of how one of the selections in this chapter demonstrates the beliefs and values of the country in which it was written.

3. Which selection in this chapter appealed to you most? Explain the reasons for your choice.

4 South and Southeast Asia

In India, two great epic poems, the *Mahabharata* and the *Ramayana*, are the major works of ancient literature. These poems and many other ancient tales which explore the history of the region and attempt to explain Hindu ideals began as part of an oral tradition. As traders and adventurers moved from place to place, these stories were translated and spread throughout the world. They were later written down.

In this chapter, you will read a folktale called "Savitri." This folktale is among the tales of another epic poem of India, the *Rig Veda*, which also was first told orally.

As time passed, writers produced great literature in many languages. The three poems in this chapter were originally written in the Tamil language.

During the period of colonialism in India, from the 1800s through the mid-1900s, the British introduced new forms of literature, such as the novel and the autobiography. These forms were then adopted by writers in other countries in Asia. In this chapter, you will read an excerpt of an autobiography written by a survivor of the Vietnam War. Her cultural heritage helped her find peace after the decades of war in her country.

India's most famous writers of recent times often focus on contemporary problems, such as the struggle of the poor in overcrowded cities and in small villages. In this chapter, you will read a story about city life and the struggle to balance family and work.

Many of the people in South and Southeast Asia, however, do not live in cities. You will read a short story in this chapter about villagers in Malaysia who depend on farming and hunting for their livelihood.

As you read the selections in this chapter, you will find a strong attachment that the authors show to their native country or culture. Think about the differences and the similarities between the attachments that you find.

Shuja-ud-daulla, the ruler of Oudh, gave this painting to an English lord in 1767. The painting is a miniature on a page in an album. It is typical of Moghul art in India. *Victoria and Albert Museum, London.*

Savitri

Reading the Myth in a Cultural Context

India is the largest country in South Asia in terms of area. It is a land of varied physical features, climates, religions, and cultures. Some of the world's oldest civilizations began here.

Archaeologists have found evidence that a civilization flourished along the Indus River as early as 2500 B.C. Little is known of this culture. About 1500 B.C., Aryan peoples from central Asia invaded. Historians believe that the Aryans were the first people to tame horses, making their conquest easy. Their influence spread throughout northern India, and Aryan culture dominated the region for 1,000 years. This period is known as the Vedic Age.

Aryan beliefs are contained in a collection of myths known as the *Veda*. Composed sometime after 1500 B.C., the Veda is the world's oldest known group of religious writings. At first, Vedic tales were passed on through the oral tradition. Later written down, the Veda is the scripture of the Hindu religion. With about 650 million practitioners worldwide, Hinduism is one of the world's great religions.

Hindu mythology refers to a number of gods. In addition, there are many other supernatural beings. Yama, the lord of the dead, is one. According to tradition, Yama is the first human who died. He now rules a kingdom of light below the earth. This is a place of rejoicing for those who have achieved salvation by living a good life. However, no living person is allowed to pass the gates of Yama's realm.

Hinduism teaches that there are three paths to salvation. The path of devotion requires daily worship of a personal god and sacrifice. Those who follow the path of knowledge practice study and meditation. Hindus who choose the path of duty do what is right without regard to personal gain.

"Savitri" is believed to be one of the oldest Vedic myths. The tale was passed from generation to generation because of its simple beauty and the wisdom of its theme. As you will see, the message is still embraced by modern Hinduism and other religions.

Focusing on the Selection

As you read "Savitri," think about life then and now. What is really important in this world? What things, which may have apparent value, are really only "illusion," as Savitri would say? What kind of achievements bring the most personal satisfaction? Think about what people believed in the Vedic Age. Do these values still apply in our modern world?

Savitri

retold by *J. F. Bierlein*

In ancient India there was a beautiful, pious,[1] and uncommonly wise princess named Savitri. As she grew into a woman, her father, King Ashvapati, despaired[2] that she would never marry and produce an heir. For Savitri was more interested in philosophical questions than in any of the young princes who visited her as suitors.[3] Her interest was not in wealth, jewels, or power, but in spiritual things. At that time kings usually chose husbands for their daughters, but Savitri was so wise that the king decided to allow her to choose her own husband.

To her father's surprise Savitri asked to choose her husband from among the holy men, not the wealthy princes. Her father was at first very shocked. But then Savitri explained that her choice would be a holy man of princely rank. Ashvapati was so relieved that his daughter at last was interested in a husband that he readily gave his consent.

Savitri donned the costume of a holy hermit, a sadhu, and traveled throughout the land. Everywhere that she went people were moved by her beauty of face and soul, her charity, piety,[4] and great wisdom. Indeed, she was absent so long that her father was growing worried about her. But the reports of Savitri's good deeds poured in from throughout the realm. Even the holy hermits were impressed by her wisdom for one so young.

When Savitri finally returned to her father's palace, she gave alms[5] to the poor gathered at the gate. There was much excitement in the palace as

---

[1] **pious** (PEYE-uhs) *adj.* earnestly religious
[2] **despaired** (dihs-PAIRD) *v.* lost hope
[3] **suitors** (SOO-terz) *n. pl.* men who present themselves as possible marriage partners
[4] **piety** (PEYE-ih-tee) *n.* virtue
[5] **alms** (ahmz) *n.* charitable gifts of money

Ashvapati and his adviser, the sage Narada, went to greet her at the gate. This was contrary to custom; the king never met any visitor at the gate.

Savitri announced that she had chosen a husband. There was a king who was completely blind and who had lost his kingdom, having been deposed by an evil usurper[6] who took advantage of the king's blindness. This king had a son named Satyavant ("Truth-seeker") who had gone to live among the sadhus until the throne was restored. Savitri explained that only Satyavant, who had lived as a holy hermit, could rule wisely and understand the plight[7] of the poor. Having lived a life of poverty, Satyavant alone could see through the illusions and judge the people fairly. But even as she spoke of Satyavant, Narada grew sad. The sage turned to her and said, "My child, all that you say is true, but you cannot marry him. It is ordained[8] that Satyavant will die within a year of your wedding."

King Ashvapati, hitherto thrilled that Savitri was about to marry, was distraught.[9] Satyavant certainly sounded like a perfect son-in-law, but he could not bear to see his beloved daughter widowed so young. Moreover, Satyavant might die before Savitri could produce an heir. With a deep sigh, Ashvapati told Savitri that she must not marry her chosen prince.

But Savitri was wise and persuaded her father to give his blessing; it was better to be married for love even if just for one year. Whether or not Satyavant was to die, she was in love with him and no other. Savitri said that she was prepared for whatever the gods had ordained. Ashvapati granted her wish.

Ashvapati had just begun to plan a royal wedding with great feasts, but Savitri insisted that she marry in the style of the holy hermits, not of wealthy rulers. Luxury, she pointed out, was only an illusion. Again, Ashvapati granted her request.

Woman Leaving the Night Palace is a miniature from the period of Moghul rule in India.

---

[6] **usurper** (yoo-SERP-uhr) *n.* a person who seizes control without legal authority

[7] **plight** (PLEYET) *n.* a difficult situation or condition

[8] **ordained** (awr-DAYND) *v.* arranged or decided beforehand by an authority

[9] **distraught** (dihs-TRAWT) *adj.* upset

Savitri went out into the forest among the sadhus and there she and Satyavant were married, clad in the robes of simple hermits. She shared her husband's contemplative[10] life on the edge of the great forest, the deepest, darkest forest in the world. She never told Satyavant of his foretold death. As she gave alms to the poor, people would say, "May you never know widowhood," and the tears would stream down Savitri's face. As the first year of their marriage drew to a close, Savitri prayed to the gods to give her the strength to protect her husband.

On the very eve of their first anniversary, Satyavant asked Savitri to accompany him into the deep forest to cut wood. As they walked into the ever-thickening woods, the animals knew of Satyavant's imminent[11] death, and fled. The little birds sang their best songs, thinking that this might be the last sound Satyavant heard. They proceeded farther and farther into the forest, where it was so thick that one could not see the sunlight. They walked on, Satyavant with his ax over his shoulder and Savitri at his side.

Then Satyavant began to chop down a great tree. Suddenly he dropped his ax and turned white. He was in horrible pain and he told Savitri that it felt as if his head were being pierced by a thousand needles [a cerebral hemorrhage?].[12] Darkness clouded his eyes and he fell to the ground barely breathing.

At that moment Savitri heard the footsteps of a stranger approaching. This stranger had dark blue skin and red eyes—he was no stranger; it was Yama, the lord of the dead. Nonetheless Savitri asked the "stranger" to identify himself. "You know who I am," said Yama. "You also know why I am here." Yama took his cord and wrenched the soul of Satyavant from the body. As Yama turned around to take the soul to his kingdom, Savitri fell on the ground in his path.

Yama told her that it was useless; Satyavant's time had come as the gods had ordained. But Savitri pleaded with him, and Yama asked her politely to get out of his way. Then Savitri rose to her feet and began to follow Yama to the Underworld.

Yama told her to turn back; this was the land of the dead, not the living. It was now Savitri's duty to be a good wife and see to it that the funeral rites[13] were properly performed, not to detain Yama from his mission. Yama, who is often thought of as heartless and cruel, can be compassionate. Often he will take the souls of very sick people to free them from their suffering. The lord of the dead was touched by Savitri's insistence.

---

[10] **contemplative** (kahn-TEHM-pluh-tihv) *adj.* devoted to thoughtful observation or meditation
[11] **imminent** (IHM-uh-nuhnt) *adj.* about to occur
[12] **cerebral hemorrhage** a stroke
[13] **rites** *n. pl.* ceremonies or other solemn or formal procedures

Yama said, "Your love for your husband is very great and so is your courage; I will grant you one wish." Savitri replied, "Restore the kingdom to Satyavant's father." Yama told her, "It is done. Now return to the living, Savitri."

But Savitri would not turn back. She was so close to the gates of Yama's kingdom that the sky was now black and she could hear the snarling of the four-headed dog that guards the gate to the dead. No mortal[14] had ever come this close to the land of Yama.

"Please turn back now!" ordered Yama. "No living mortal can ever enter my kingdom!" Savitri told Yama that she would not leave her husband for any reason. Yama begged her once more to turn back, but she refused. Yama then said that no man had ever entered his kingdom; Savitri, always wise, responded that she was no man, but a woman. Yama was now as impressed by her wisdom as by her courage, and he offered her a second wish. "Restore the life of my husband." Yama granted this wish, saying, "It is already done — now go back and you will find Satyavant, not dead but sleeping."

Before Savitri turned back, Yama told her, "Just one more thing — my blessing goes with you always. You have learned the wisdom of the gods. No woman could ever have followed me alive to the very door of my kingdom if the gods were not on her side. Your wish and more will be granted you, for you know that love is stronger than death; love is the power that Yama cannot defy. Return to where you left Satyavant and live well."

She walked back to the glade where Satyavant lay, not dead, but sleeping as Yama had promised. She kissed him and his eyes opened. He told Savitri that he had a strange dream wherein Yama had carried his soul away, but Savitri's love had rescued it. Savitri laughed and told him to forget this silly dream. It was not until many years later that she told him that this story was no dream; it had actually happened.

As they left the deep forest, messengers came to Satyavant with wonderful news: His father was restored to the throne. In fact, the old king had regained his sight as soon as he sat on his rightful throne! The young couple ran to the palace and Satyavant's father was delighted to see his son for the first time in years, and to lay eyes on his beautiful daughter-in-law. Something inside the heart of the old king told him that Savitri had brought this reversal of fortune to pass.

Satyavant and Savitri passed many more years in the forest, living a simple life as hermits, raising their children in poverty, humility, honesty, and wisdom. Later, when Satyavant's father died at a goodly age, Satyavant

---

[14] **mortal** (MAWR-tuhl) *n.* a human being, as a creature who must die

and Savitri ruled the land of both Satyavant's father and Savitri's father, Ashvapati, with equity.[15]

When it was time to die, Yama greeted them as old friends and told them that their souls were only with him for a visit, as they were to go to the highest heaven. When they left this earth, they had over one hundred descendants.

---

[15] **equity** (EKH-wih-tee) *n.* fairness; justice

POSTREADING

Critical Thinking

1. How do the reactions of other characters to Savitri show that wisdom can bring about change for the better?

2. How do you think Savitri's character illustrates the goals of a Hindu who follows the path of duty toward salvation?

3. Which of Savitri's several admirable traits do you admire most? Why?

Writing Your Response to "Savitri"

In your journal, write about someone you know who demonstrates one or more of the qualities you admired in Savitri. Which trait(s) of the heroine does this person possess to an extraordinary degree? What are some of the ways in which he or she has shown this quality?

Going Back Into the Text: Author's Craft

The **theme** is the main or central idea in a literary work. The theme may be stated or implied. In nonfiction, the theme is usually stated. Often, it appears as a topic sentence near the beginning of the piece.

In fiction, theme is almost always implied, or expressed indirectly. The author uses elements of fiction (e.g., character and plot) to provide the readers with information. Readers then draw their own conclusions about the author's message. The theme may not be clear until the story's end.

One exception to this rule is the fable. A fable is a short tale in which animals speak and act like humans. The theme or moral of the fable is stated at the end in a phrase or sentence.

With a partner, talk about the implied theme of "Savitri." Think about the way the author uses the elements of fiction to communicate a message. Then draw your own conclusions about the meaning of the myth. The following questions can guide your discussion:

1. How does the author use Savitri's character and plot events to help readers understand the theme?

2. How does Savitri's life illustrate the paths to salvation that are part of Hindu teachings?

3. If you wanted to add a stated theme in the form of a one-sentence moral, like those at the end of fables, what would you write?

This World Lives Because/
Children/Tirumāl

Reading the Poems in a Cultural Context

One of the ways that a people keep their traditions alive is through literature. The poems you are about to read are from the Tamil literature of southern India. Tamil is a language spoken in India by people called Dravidians. The Dravidians were among the earliest people to live in India. They developed an advanced civilization in about 2500 B.C. in the area that is now Pakistan and western India. A thousand years later, when the Aryans invaded this region, the Dravidians moved south. Today, their descendants live mostly in the southeastern Indian state called Tamil Nadu. Madras is an important city in this region.

The Tamil poems are classical both because they are ancient and because they have withstood the test of time. One scholar calls them "the most important native source of historical and cultural information for this period in Tamil South India." About 2,000 of these poems, written by some 500 poets, are in existence today.

Many of the poems have themes of love and compassion. An example is the poem "Children." Other poems are about war, kings, and death. Still others offer praises to Hindu gods. "Tirumāl" is part of a hymn to the god Vishnu.

Although the poems have existed for several millenia, they have not always been available to the Tamil people. During the 1700s Hindu scholars banned the study of the classical Tamil anthologies for being secular and irreligious. It wasn't until the late 19th century that a Tamil scholar learned of these works and made them available again. Thanks to him, a great poetic tradition still reaches across time from an ancient civilization to a modern one.

Focusing on the Selections

As you read the Tamil poems, look for the ways that the poets represent their subjects. What symbols do they use to describe things? How do these symbols add power to the Tamil poems?

This World Lives Because

Iḷam Peruvaḷuti
translated by A. K. Ramanujan

This world lives
because

> some men
> do not eat alone,
> not even when they get
> the sweet ambrosia[1] of the gods;

> they've no anger in them,
> they fear evils other men fear
> but never sleep over them;

> give their lives for honor,
> will not touch a gift of whole worlds
> if tainted;[2]

> there's no faintness in their hearts
> and they do not strive
> for themselves.

Because such men are,
this world is.

---

[1] **ambrosia** (ahm-BROH-zhuh) *n.* the food of the gods
[2] **tainted** (TAYNT-uhd) *adj.* spoiled or corrupted by something undesirable

Children

Pāṇṭiyaṉ Aṟivuṭai Nampi
translated by *A. K. Ramanujan*

Even when a man has earned much
of whatever can be earned,
shared it with many,
even when he is master of great estates,

if he does not have
children
      who patter on their little feet,
      stretch tiny hands,
      scatter, touch,
      grub with mouths
      and grab with fingers,
      smear rice and ghee[1]
      all over their bodies,
      and overcome reason with love,

all his days
have come to nothing.

---

[1] **ghee** (gee) *n.* butter from which the milk fat has been removed

Tirumāl

Kaṭuvaṉ Iḷaveyiṉaṉār
translated by A. K. Ramanujan

In fire, you are the heat.
      In flowers, you are the scent.
Among stones, you are the diamond.

In words, you are truth.
      Among virtues, you are love.
In a warrior's wrath, you are the strength.

In the Vedas,[1] you are the secret.
      Of the elements, you are the first.

In the scorching sun, you are the light.
      In the moonlight, you are the softness.

Everything, you are everything,
the sense, the substance, of everything.

This miniature depicts the Hindu God Vishnu and his wife Lakshmi. Vishnu is one of the main gods of Hinduism and is believed to descend to the earth to spread comfort and guidance. Vishnu and his wife are riding on Sesha, the Serpent of Eternity. *Albert Museum, London.*

---

[1] **Vedas** (VAYD-uhz) *n. pl.* the collection of Hindu sacred writings of hymns and prayers

POSTREADING

Critical Thinking

1. In "This World Lives Because," how does the poet reveal his feelings about certain people?

2. What generalization might you make about the Tamil civilization after reading "Children"?

3. Can you think of someone who fits the description in "This World Lives Because"? What is an example of how this person lives up to the words of the poem?

Writing Your Response to "This World Lives Because," "Children," "Tirumāl"

In your journal, write about your response to one of the poems. What overall feeling did it give you? What lines were the most meaningful to you? How did they help connect you with the Tamil traditions of the past?

Going Back Into the Text: Author's Craft

Sometimes writers use **symbols** to reveal a theme or central message in their work. A symbol is anything that represents something else. For example, colors are often used as symbols. What do the colors in the American flag stand for?

As you review these poems, look for symbols. Use the following questions as guidelines to help you:

1. In "Tirumāl," what symbols does the poet use to describe Vishnu?

2. How do the symbols in "Tirumāl" reveal the depth of the poet's feelings?

3. In the poem "Children," what do you think children stand for in the poet's mind?

MAKING CULTURAL CONNECTIONS

ASIA, AUSTRALIA, AND THE PACIFIC ISLANDS

Every region of the world has monuments. Monuments can be buildings, works of art, natural features, or historic structures. Think about the monuments in your community or state. They say something about your culture in the same way that the monuments in the photos on these pages tell about the cultures to which they belong. Use the photos on these pages to find clues to the cultures of this unit.

Pictured here is the temple Angkor Wat in Cambodia. This Hindu temple is the largest religious building in the world. Its highest point rises 200 feet (61 m) and it is surrounded by a moat that is 2.5 miles (4 km) in circumference. It is made entirely of stone.

Ayers Rock is located in Australia's Great Western Plateau. This reddish rock is 1,000 feet high (305 m) and 6 miles (9.75 km) around. It is the largest rock in the world.

Notice the Communist flag flying high over Tiananmen Square in Beijing, China. You may recall that on May 13, 1989, a group of students gathered in Tiananmen Square to protest for democracy. Hundreds of protesters were killed when soldiers and riot police opened fire on them.

LINKING
Literature, History, and Culture

What do the photos on this page and the selections in this unit tell you about the cultures of Asia, Australia, and the Pacific?

▶ The temple Angkor Wat reflects the importance of Hinduism in this region. What do the myth "Savitri" and the poem "Tirumāl" tell you about the beliefs of the Hindu religion?

▶ Caves at the base of Ayers Rock are considered sacred by several aboriginal groups. What do the selections in Chapter 5 tell you about the native groups' respect for nature?

▶ Tiananmen Square has become a symbol of political repression. How do the poems by Ch'iu Chin and the excerpt from Harry Wu's autobiography talk about this theme?

The Tiger

Reading the Story in a Cultural Context

Singapore, the home of S. Rajaratnam, is an island city-state in Southeast Asia. It is a major banking and trade center. More than 90 percent of this country's people live in an urban environment.

A narrow body of water separates Singapore from the Malay Peninsula, the setting for this story. Unlike Singapore, much of Malaysia is rural. Mountains cover its interior. On either side of the mountains are rain forests that stretch outward to within 20 miles of the coast. These dense tropical woodlands cover three-quarters of Malaysia's land area.

Two-thirds of Malaysians live in *kampongs*, small, isolated villages, that dot the countryside. These people are subsistence farmers. That means they depend on the crops they grow and the animals they raise for survival. The surrounding forests are home to a stunning array of wildlife. The Malaysians live in a delicate balance with nature including animals that share their environment. Among these is the tiger.

The tiger is the largest of the "big cats." It averages 7 feet in length and can weigh more than 600 pounds. With its massive body and long, powerful teeth, this awesome hunter can bring down animals twice its size. Unlike lions, which live in prides (groups of lions), the tiger is a solitary animal. It hunts alone.

For eons, tigers ruled the wild from Siberia in the north to Malaysia in the south. Tales of "man-eaters" terrified villagers, but tigers almost never attacked people. As long as game was plentiful in the forest, tigers usually avoided humans. The rare exceptions were almost invariably old cats, too weak with age, to hunt faster or stronger prey.

Today, tigers are now an endangered species. Their population has declined by 95 percent in this century. Deforestation, caused by the spread of human settlements and over harvesting of trees, has destroyed much of their habitat. Even more dangerous to their survival are poachers. These illegal hunters sell tiger skins for huge sums. Unless people protect it, the tiger may soon be extinct.

Nevertheless, the word *tiger* still strikes fear in villagers. S. Rajaratnam uses this dread to weave a subtle tale about a chance encounter between a woman and a tiger. He suggests that bonds exist in nature that are stronger than human reasoning.

Focusing on the Selection

As you read "The Tiger," think about the different emotions Fatima feels before, during, and after her encounter with the tiger. Think too about the tiger as a character. How do Fatima's feelings change? What changes does she see in the tiger? How does her attitude differ from that of the other villagers? Why does she feel the way she does about the tiger? What motivates the villagers?

The Tiger

◆◆◆

S. Rajaratnam

Fatima felt the cool yellow water of the river, a sheet of polished gold in the sunglow. The water flowed slowly around her as she clung to the bank. Then she moved further along until she stood waist deep. The wet sarong[1] clung to her brown figure, the plump body of a pregnant woman. Her face was round, with the high cheekbones of the Malays.2 A delicate sadness in the black eyes gave her the expression of one brooding over some private vision within her.

With a quick toss of her head, she unloosened her black, glossy hair. She let the wind whisper gently through it. From where she stood she could neither see nor hear the village. In front of her stretched an unbroken expanse of lalang[3] grass and tall trees. The stillness of the evening was disturbed at times by the cry of a lonely water bird. Now and then a rat dived with a gentle splash into the river. Other timid, nervous animals could be heard in the tall grass. The air was full of the scent of wild flowers and mud and grass. A feeling of loneliness and wonder came over Fatima. It was as though she had stumbled into a world still in the dawn of creation. The earth seemed a huge swamp in which wandered ancient and ugly monsters.

So, when she heard the low, rumbling growl of the tiger, it only added to her dream world. But suddenly came a dull angry roar. Fatima knew that it was not a creature of her imagination but the real thing.

The tiger was framed by the lalang and low to the ground. Fatima stared at its huge head and shoulders. It was not more than 20 yards from her. The sun gave a wicked glint to its watchful yellow eyes. Its ears were

---

[1] **sarong** (suh-RAWNG) *n.* a simple wraparound dress or skirt
[2] **Malays** (muh-LAYZ) *n. pl.* people of the Malay Peninsula in Southeast Asia
[3] **lalang** (LAH-lahng) *n.* a kind of very tall, thick grass

This painting by Henri Rousseau is called *Tropical Storm with a Tiger*. Imagine Fatima bathing in a river, startled by a tiger such as this one.

drawn back warningly. It turned its head and snarled. Around its red tongue, the yellow teeth looked like tree stumps.

Fatima was frozen into helpless fear by the glaring eyes of the tiger. The sudden stillness that fell around her made her mind numb. She dared not move. She dared not take her eyes from the watching animal. Yet the tiger, too, was still, as though it had been made motionless by the unexpected meeting with a human being.

Fatima and the animal watched one another. She was frightened; it was suspicious. Its growls continued, but they became less angry each time. It showed no signs of really wanting to attack her. Instead, after a while the animal took less of an interest in her. Its huge paws stretched out in front. Now and then the claws dug into the damp grass. Except when she moved, the animal's attention seemed to be nowhere in particular. The glare in its eyes had changed into a sullen and sometimes bored expression. Fatima noticed the surprising changes of mood in the animal's eyes.

By now the dusk had crept in from over the hills. Gone was the colorful scene of a short time before. Gray shadows drifted off into darkness. A faint mist from the river had spread itself over the land. The distant hoot of an owl marked the movement of day into night.

Now Fatima had only a quiet fear of the tiger. She felt tiredness creep over her. She shivered with the cold. She grew desperate, as the tiger showed no signs of going away. Her hands wandered over her stomach. She was a being of two lives, she realized. She *had* to escape. She just *had* to! Her eyes could still make out the shadowy form of the tiger in the falling light.

Fatima had studied the animal very carefully. She could tell when it was going to turn its eyes away from her. She waited, her body tense in the water with a fearful strength. Then with a desperate movement she dived underwater. She scraped the bottom of the river as she swam toward the opposite bank, in the direction of the village. She came to the surface only when she felt that her lungs would burst for air. She felt lost in the middle of the river. When she heard the faraway growl, a fear that she had not felt even close to the tiger seized her.

She swam wildly toward the shore. Finally she saw the twinkling oil lamps of the village.

The village was in panic by the time Fatima's mother had spread an exaggerated version of the story her daughter had told her. The women gathered the children into their arms. They called out to the men to do something about the tiger. The men rushed around, worried about their cattle and goats. The old men chewed betel nuts and demanded to know what the fuss was all about.

More tired than she had ever been, Fatima lay on a straw mat. The village headman and a crowd came to question her as to the location of the tiger. Fatima's mother started to give an exciting, noisy tale of her daughter's meeting with the "hairy one." The headman grew impatient. He commanded the old lady to hold her peace for a while. Then he turned to question Fatima. She was impatient as she answered his questions. For some reason, unlike the people around her, she didn't want the tiger hunted and killed. The headman noted the reluctance in her voice. He frowned.

"Allah!" exclaimed the old lady, wishing to be the center of interest once more. "It was Allah who snatched my daughter away from the jaws of the 'hairy one.'"

She threw up her skinny brown hands, as though to thank Allah. The headman shrugged his shoulders.

"Perhaps it was," he said, "but the next time, Allah will not be as kind. The tiger is perhaps by now drunk with the scent of human flesh. It is not a pleasant thing to have near our village. The beast must be hunted down and destroyed without delay."

He looked at the faces of the men, silent and nervous. They knew the dangers of tracking down the tiger in the night. The thick, shadowy lalang grass gave the beast protection. It could strike quickly and silently.

"Well?" said the headman.

The men gazed at the floor in silence. The headman's face twitched. He was about to call them cowards when Mamood, a younger man, came in.

"What is this I hear?" Mamood asked eagerly. His face was on fire with excitement. He carried a gun on his shoulder. "The women told me that a tiger attacked our Fatima. Is it true?"

The headman told him the facts. Mamood listened, fingering his new double-barreled gun. He was all for hunting the tiger at once. He loved hunting. And the fact that it was a tiger made him all the more eager.

"Now," Mamood said when the headman had finished, "who will come and help kill the tiger? I shall drag home the body of that beast before sunrise. But only if you help me."

The men hesitated, but before long a dozen offered to help. They knew Mamood was a good shot.

"Good!" exclaimed Mamood, running his fingers along the gun barrel. "I knew I could count on you."

Then he and the men left.

"Believe me, daughter," said Fatima's mother, "Mamood is a wild tiger himself." She locked the door after the men.

Fatima rose up from her mat. She looked out of the narrow window. The moon cast a gentle light over everything it touched. She could see the moon through the tall coconut trees. Men moved about in the moonlight, preparing for the hunt. They called out to one another. Fatima stared at them sadly.

Then the men left. Now there were only the gray trees and the whisper of the worried wind. Straining her ears, she heard the far-off sound of the river.

Somewhere out there, she thought, was the tiger. She had wondered about the animal the whole evening. She hoped that it was far out of the men's reach.

"O Allah!" cried her mother, pounding some nuts in a wooden bowl. "Tonight is the night for death. Think of those men out there. A tiger is as clever as a hundred foxes."

"They should have left the tiger alone," said Fatima. She still looked out the window.

"That's a crazy thing to say," said the woman. "Somebody has to kill the tiger before it kills me. That's sense."

"Perhaps it would have just gone away."

"A tiger that comes near a village does not just go away," snapped the old woman. "It stays around till it gets what it wants. They are usually killers that come near a village."

"But this one didn't look like a killer," argued Fatima.

The old woman snorted, but said nothing.

"The tiger was not more than 20 yards from me," said Fatima. "It could have jumped on me easily. But it didn't. Why? Can you explain that? It kept watching me, it's true. But then I was watching it too. At first its eyes glared at me, but later they were gentle and bored. There was nothing really fierce about it. . . ."

"Now you are talking crazy," said her mother, fiercely pounding the nuts. "The way your father used to. Heaven forgive me that I should talk so of your dead father, but he was a crazy man sometimes."

Fatima scowled out of the window and listened. There was a silence over the village. Her hands, swollen and red, were knotted tightly together as she strained to hear some sound. The pound, pound of her heart echoed the noise her mother made with the wooden bowl. Then a sharp pain shot through her. Her hands went to her stomach.

"What is it, Fatima?" said her mother, looking up.

"Nothing," answered Fatima between pressed lips.

"Come away from that draft and lie down," said her mother.

Fatima went on standing by the window. She felt the pain rise and fall. She closed her eyes and pictured the tiger. It crouched in the lalang, its eyes now red and glaring, now bored and gentle.

Then she heard the distant crack of a rifle. Another shot followed. Fatima quivered as if the shots had been aimed at her. Then came the roar of the tiger—not the growl she had heard that evening, but full of pain and anger. For a few seconds the cry of the animal seemed to fill up her heart and ears. Her face was tight with pain. Her body glistened with sweat. A moan broke between her shut lips.

"Allah! Allah!" cried out the old woman. "You look ill. What is it? Come and lie down. Is it . . .?"

"I've got the pains, mother," gasped Fatima.

The old woman led the girl toward the mat. She made her lie down.

"Oi, oi, it's a fine time to have a baby!" cried her mother, a little frightened. "You lie down here while I get some hot water to drink. I'll have to wait till the men return before I go for the midwife."

Fatima lay on the mat, her eyes shut tight. Her mother boiled the water and muttered.

"Listen," said the old woman. "The men are returning. I can hear their voices."

The air suddenly was filled with the excited voices of men and women outside.

The old lady opened the door cautiously. She called out to someone.

"Hurrah for Mamood, auntie!" called a youth rushing in. "He's shot the tiger. It's a big animal. No wonder it put up a good fight. And then what do you think happened?"

Fatima looked at the youth with interest. The old lady turned her tiny wrinkled head impatiently toward the boy.

"Well, what happened?"

"They said," explained the youth, "that after they had killed the animal they heard noises. Then by the light of their lamps they saw three of the tiniest tiger cubs. Their eyes were hardly open. Mamood says that they would not be more than a few hours old. No wonder the beast fought so hard."

Fatima moaned in pain. The sweat glistened like yellow pearls on her forehead.

"Mother!" she cried.

The old woman pushed the astonished youth toward the door.

"Get the midwife, boy," she shouted. "Quick! Go! The midwife."

The youth stared, gasped, and then ran for the midwife.

POSTREADING

Critical Thinking

1. How do you think the details in the author's opening description create an unreal, fantastic atmosphere for Fatima's unusual encounter?

2. How is the selection related to a difficult environmental concern faced by Malaysians today?

3. If you were a villager, whose side would you take in the debate about the tiger, that of Fatima or the old woman?

Writing Your Response to "The Tiger"

In your journal, write about an animal that made a lasting impression on you (e.g., a pet, an animal in a zoo or circus). How did the animal act? What feelings did you have toward the animal? How did the animal change you?

Going Back Into the Text: Author's Craft

As events occur in a story, excitement grows. We become involved with the characters. What will happen to them? How will the conflict be resolved? Our uncertainty creates tension. This is especially true if we sympathize with certain characters. This feeling of anxiety is called **suspense**.

Authors use atmosphere to build suspense. They relieve the tension in one of two ways. They may fulfill our expectations. We expect Fatima to escape from the tiger. Suspense builds as we learn how. Authors may also shatter our expectations by a surprise or *plot twist*. The tiger's behavior puzzles us until we learn why she behaves the way she does.

With a partner, talk about the ways the author builds and relieves suspense in "The Tiger." Think of what you anticipated while reading. Then decide when the author fulfills your expectations and when he surprises you. The following questions can guide your discussion:

1. How did Fatima's escape from near-drowning in the river meet your expectations or surprise you?

2. Why was the outcome of the tiger hunt what you expected or a surprise?

3. Looking back, how do you think the author prepares us for the surprising revelation that the tiger is guarding cubs?

PREREADING

Forty-Five a Month

Reading the Story in a Cultural Context

Where do writers get their material? For many novelists and short-story writers, the answer is simple: they find material in their everyday lives. In other words, characters, plots, and settings take root in writers' observations and then take life in writers' imaginations.

It is in this way that the writer R. K. Narayan explores middle-class life in India. Narayan, perhaps the most famous novelist and short-story writer in India, lives in Mysore in the nation's southern part.

Narayan's observations of people began in his childhood when he was raised by his grandmother. Almost everyday, people would visit her to seek advice on marriage or to have their horoscopes read. Narayan's grandmother also taught him Tamil (an Indian language) and shared with him her knowledge of Indian tales and poetry.

While writing his first novel, *Swami and Friends*, Narayan created a fictional town called Malgudi. Like Mysore, Malgudi is in southern India. The characters in the novel include street vendors, holy men, students, teachers, financial experts, and office clerks. Their lives are touched by both the tragic and comic events that Narayan believes characterize human behavior. Many of his characters struggle to hold on to their cultural traditions in a confusing modern world.

In 1982, Narayan published a book of short stories called *Malgudi Days*. The story "Forty-Five a Month" is from that collection. Although this story centers on the relationships within an Indian family, it also deals with the traditional obedience of middle-class workers in India. In the story, the main character struggles with his obedience to his employer and the need to spend time with his family. This problem is a universal one in contemporary life.

Focusing on the Selection

As you read "Forty-Five a Month," review the elements of the story's plot. Why do you think R. K. Narayan tells the first part of the story from Shanta's point of view and the rest of the story from her father's point of view? How does this highlight the conflict?

Forty-Five a Month

R. K. Narayan

Shanta could not stay in her class any longer. She had done clay-modelling, music, drill, a bit of alphabets and numbers and was now cutting coloured paper. She would have to cut till the bell rang and the teacher said, "Now you may all go home," or "Put away the scissors and take up your alphabets—" Shanta was impatient to know the time. She asked her friend sitting next to her, "Is it five now?"

"Maybe," she replied.

"Or is it six?"

"I don't think so," her friend replied, "because night comes at six."

"Do you think it is five?"

"Yes."

"Oh, I must go. My father will be back at home now. He has asked me to be ready at five. He is taking me to the cinema this evening. I must go home." She threw down her scissors and ran up to the teacher. "Madam, I must go home."

"Why, Shanta Bai?"

"Because it is five o'clock now."

"Who told you it was five?"

"Kamala."

"It is not five now. It is—do you see the clock there? Tell me what the time is. I taught you to read the clock the other day." Shanta stood gazing at the clock in the hall, counted the figures laboriously[1] and declared, "It is nine o'clock."

The teacher called the other girls and said, "Who will tell me the time from that clock?" Several of them concurred[2] with Shanta and said it was

---

[1] **laboriously** (luh-BAWR-ee-uhs-lee) *adv.* with great effort
[2] **concurred** (kuhn-KERD) *v.* agreed

nine o'clock, till the teacher said, "You are seeing only the long hand. See the short one, where is it?"

"Two and a half."

"So what is the time?"

"Two and a half."

"It is two forty-five, understand? Now you may all go to your seats—" Shanta returned to the teacher in about ten minutes and asked, "Is it five, madam, because I have to be ready at five. Otherwise my father will be very angry with me. He asked me to return home early."

"At what time?"

"Now." The teacher gave her permission to leave, and Shanta picked up her books and dashed out of the class with a cry of joy. She ran home, threw her books on the floor and shouted, "Mother, Mother," and Mother came running from the next house, where she had gone to chat with her friends.

Mother asked, "Why are you back so early?"

"Has Father come home?" Shanta asked. She would not take her coffee or tiffin[3] but insisted on being dressed first. She opened the trunk and insisted on wearing the thinnest frock[4] and knickers,[5] while her mother wanted to dress her in a long skirt and thick coat for the evening. Shanta picked out a gorgeous ribbon from a cardboard soap box in which she kept pencils, ribbons and chalk bits. There was a heated argument between mother and daughter over the dress, and finally Mother had to give in. Shanta put on her favourite pink frock, braided her hair and flaunted[6] a green ribbon on her pigtail. She powdered her face and pressed a vermilion[7] mark on her forehead. She said, "Now Father will say what a nice girl I am because I'm ready. Aren't you also coming, Mother?"

"Not today."

Shanta stood at the little gate looking down the street.

Mother said, "Father will come only after five; don't stand in the sun. It is only four o'clock."

The sun was disappearing behind the house on the opposite row, and Shanta knew that presently it would be dark. She ran in to her mother and asked, "Why hasn't Father come home yet, Mother?"

"How can I know? He is perhaps held up in the office."

Shanta made a wry[8] face. "I don't like these people in the office. They are bad people—"

---

[3] **tiffin** (TIHF-uhn) *n.* a midday snack

[4] **frock** *n.* a dress

[5] **knickers** *n. pl.* loose-fitting short pants gathered at the knee

[6] **flaunted** (FLAWNT-ihd) *v.* showed off

[7] **vermilion** (vuhr-MIHL-yuhn) *adj.* bright red

[8] **wry** (reye) *adj.* twisted to one side

She went back to the gate and stood looking out. Her mother shouted from inside, "Come in, Shanta. It is getting dark, don't stand there." But Shanta would not go in. She stood at the gate and a wild idea came into her head. Why should she not go to the office and call out Father and then go to the cinema? She wondered where his office might be. She had no notion. She had seen her father take the turn at the end of the street every day. If one went there, perhaps one went automatically to Father's office. She threw a glance about to see if Mother was anywhere and moved down the street.

It was twilight. Everyone going about looked gigantic, walls of houses appeared very high and cycles and carriages looked as though they would bear down on her. She walked on the very edge of the road. Soon the lamps were twinkling, and the passers-by looked like shadows. She had taken two turns and did not know where she was. She sat down on the edge of the road biting her nails. She wondered how she was to reach home. A servant employed in the next house was passing along, and she picked herself up and stood before him.

"Oh, what are you doing here all alone?" he asked. She replied, "I don't know. I came here. Will you take me to our house?" She followed him and was soon back in her house.

Venkat Rao, Shanta's father, was about to start for his office that morning when a *jutka*[9] passed along the street distributing cinema handbills. Shanta dashed to the street and picked up a handbill. She held it up and asked, "Father, will you take me to the cinema today?" He felt unhappy at the question. Here was the child growing up without having any of the amenities[10] and the simple pleasures of life. He had hardly taken her twice to the cinema. He had no time for the child. While children of her age in other houses had all the dolls, dresses and outings that they wanted, this child was growing up all alone and like a barbarian[11] more or less. He felt furious with his office. For forty rupees[12] a month they seemed to have purchased him outright.

He reproached himself for neglecting his wife and child—even the wife could have her own circle of friends and so on: she was after all a grown-up, but what about the child? What a drab, colourless existence was hers! Every day they kept him at the office till seven or eight in the evening, and when he came home the child was asleep. Even on Sundays they wanted him at the office. Why did they think he had no personal life, a life of his own? They gave him hardly any time to take the child to the park or the pictures. He was

---

[9] *jutka* *n.* a two-wheeled horse-drawn carriage
[10] **amenities** (uh-MEHN-ih-teez) *n. pl.* comforts: conveniences
[11] **barbarian** (bahr-BAIR-ee-uhn) *n.* a crude or uncivilized person
[12] **rupees** (ROO-peez) *n. pl.* Indian units of money

going to show them that they weren't to toy with him. Yes, he was prepared even to quarrel with his manager if necessary.

He said with resolve,[13] "I will take you to the cinema this evening. Be ready at five."

"Really! Mother!" Shanta shouted. Mother came out of the kitchen.

"Father is taking me to a cinema in the evening."

Shanta's mother smiled cynically.[14] "Don't make false promises to the child—" Venkat Rao glared at her. "Don't talk nonsense. You think you are the only person who keeps promises—"

He told Shanta, "Be ready at five, and I will come and take you positively. If you are not ready, I will be very angry with you."

He walked to his office full of resolve. He would do his normal work and get out at five. If they started any old tricks of theirs, he was going to tell the boss, "Here is my resignation.[15] My child's happiness is more important to me than these horrible papers of yours."

All day the usual stream of papers flowed onto his table and off it. He scrutinized,[16] signed and drafted. He was corrected, admonished and insulted. He had a break of only five minutes in the afternoon for his coffee.

When the office clock struck five and the other clerks were leaving, he went up to the manager and said, "May I go, sir?" The manager looked up from his paper. "You!" It was unthinkable that the cash and account section should be closing at five. "How can you go?"

"I have some urgent private business, sir," he said, smothering the lines he had been rehearsing since the morning: "Herewith my resignation." He visualized Shanta standing at the door, dressed and palpitating with eagerness.

"There shouldn't be anything more urgent than the office work; go back to your seat. You know how many hours I work?" asked the manager. The manager came to the office three hours before opening time and stayed nearly three hours

This is a photo of an Indian man with his daughter. As in "Forty-Five a Month," many Indians struggle to spend time with their families because of their jobs.

---

[13] **resolve** (rih-ZALV) *n.* firmness of purpose; determination

[14] **cynically** (SIHN-ih-klee) *adv.* with doubt; with a sneer

[15] **resignation** (rehz-ihg-NAY-shuhn) *n.* a written statement giving notice that one quits a job

[16] **scrutinized** (SKROOT-uhn-eyezd) *v.* examined in detail with careful attention

after closing, even on Sundays. The clerks commented among themselves, "His wife must be whipping him whenever he is seen at home; that is why the old owl seems so fond of his office."

"Did you trace the source of that ten-eight difference?" asked the manager.

"I shall have to examine two hundred vouchers.[17] I thought we might do it tomorrow."

"No, no, this won't do. You must rectify[18] it immediately."

Venkat Rao mumbled, "Yes, sir," and slunk back to his seat. The clock showed 5:30. Now it meant two hours of excruciating[19] search among vouchers. All the rest of the office had gone. Only he and another clerk in his section were working, and of course, the manager was there. Venkat Rao was furious. His mind was made up. He wasn't a slave who had sold himself for forty rupees outright. He could make that money easily; and if he couldn't, it would be more honourable to die of starvation.

He took a sheet of paper and wrote: "Herewith my resignation. If you people think you have bought me body and soul for forty rupees, you are mistaken. I think it would be far better for me and my family to die of starvation than slave for this petty forty rupees on which you have kept me for years and years. I suppose you have not the slightest notion of giving me an increment.[20] You give yourselves heavy slices frequently, and I don't see why you shouldn't think of us occasionally. In any case it doesn't interest me now, since this is my resignation. If I and my family perish of starvation, may our ghosts come and haunt you all your life—" He folded the letter, put it in an envelope, sealed the flap and addressed it to the manager. He left his seat and stood before the manager. The manager mechanically received the letter and put it on his pad.

"Venkat Rao," said the manager, "I'm sure you will be glad to hear this news. Our officer discussed the question of increments today, and I've recommended you for an increment of five rupees. Orders are not yet passed, so keep this to yourself for the present." Venkat Rao put out his hand, snatched the envelope from the pad and hastily slipped it in his pocket.

"What is that letter?"

"I have applied for a little casual leave, sir, but I think ..."

"You can't get any leave for at least a fortnight to come."

"Yes, sir. I realize that. That is why I am withdrawing my application, sir."

"Very well. Have you traced that mistake?"

---

[17] **vouchers** (VOW-chuhrz) *n. pl.* receipts

[18] **rectify** (REHK-tuh-feye) *v.* correct

[19] **excruciating** (ehk-SKROO-shee-ay-tihng) *adj.* very intense or concentrated

[20] **increment** (IHN-kruh-muhnt) *n.* an increase in salary; a raise

"I'm scrutinizing the vouchers, sir. I will find it out within an hour. . . ."

It was nine o'clock when he went home. Shanta was already asleep. Her mother said, "She wouldn't even change her frock, thinking that any moment you might be coming and taking her out. She hardly ate any food; and wouldn't lie down for fear of crumpling her dress. . . ."

Venkat Rao's heart bled when he saw his child sleeping in her pink frock, hair combed and face powdered, dressed and ready to be taken out. "Why should I not take her to the night show?" He shook her gently and called, "Shanta, Shanta." Shanta kicked her legs and cried, irritated at being disturbed. Mother whispered, "Don't wake her," and patted her back to sleep.

Venkat Rao watched the child for a moment. "I don't know if it is going to be possible for me to take her out at all—you see, they are giving me an increment—" he wailed.

POSTREADING

Critical Thinking

1. How does this story show that the author treats his characters sympathetically?

2. What aspects of life in India contribute to the conflict in this story?

3. How do you react when someone breaks a promise to you?

Writing Your Response to "Forty-Five a Month"

In your journal, record your reaction to the actions of Venkat Rao. How else do you think he could have acted? What advice would you like to give him?

Going Back Into the Text: Author's Craft

A **plot** is what happens in a story. In other words, it is the sequence of events. A plot includes both the story's characters and a central conflict—a struggle between opposing forces. Events in the story introduce the central conflict, which increases as the plot develops. The plot reaches a high point of interest called a climax. Often, the climax is followed by a resolution or ending to the central conflict.

As you analyze the plot in this story, use the following questions as guidelines:

1. Which character struggles with the central conflict in this story? What is the conflict?

2. What events lead to the conflict in the story? How does the conflict increase?

3. What event marks the climax? What resolution, if any, occurs at the end?

PREREADING

from *When Heaven and Earth Changed Places*

Reading the Selection in a Cultural Context

Perhaps you have visited or seen pictures of the Vietnam Veterans' Memorial in Washington, D.C. This monument honors the American soldiers who died in the Vietnam War. The war, fought in Southeast Asia during the 1960s and '70s, was one of the most controversial conflicts in United States history.

At that time, many Americans worried that communism was a threat to a democratic way of life. Because South Vietnam was in danger of being overrun by Communists from the North, the United States got involved, first with advisors, and only later with military force. While many Americans supported this involvement, others were against it.

When the war was finally over, much of Vietnam had been destroyed. Cities were bombed, homes burned, and rice fields ruined. Thousands of Vietnamese fled their country. Large numbers came to the United States to start new lives.

The Vietnam War has been over for many years now. Slowly, the wounds have healed. Books, movies, and magazine articles have told about people's experiences and explained their feelings. In 1989, a book called *When Heaven and Earth Changed Places* was published. This book, by a Vietnamese woman named Le Ly Hayslip, tells of her journey from war to peace.

Le Ly Hayslip came to the United States during the war and eventually became a citizen. Before that, she lived in a village called Ky La in central Vietnam. Like the other peasants, she was taught by the Viet Cong that the Americans were there to take over the country while the Viet Cong would bring "Communist happiness." As she explains, "The cadre leaders encouraged our natural prejudices (fear of outsiders and love of our ancestors) with stirring songs and tender stories about Uncle Ho [Ho Chi Minh] in which the Communist leader and our ancient heroes seemed to inhabit one congenial world." In order to achieve a future of harmony and independence however, Ho wanted total war. Thus it was that Le Ly Hayslip, like many others, aided the Communists against the American soldiers.

In 1986, Hayslip went back to Vietnam to find her lost family, village, and people. *When Heaven and Earth Changed Places* is the story of what she remembers and what she found. It is her explanation of what the war meant to people like herself. But most of all, the book is written as a sign of peace and goodwill. It is dedicated to all who fought for their country and to those who did not fight, but "suffered, wept, raged, bled, and died just the same."

Focusing on the Selection

As you read the selection, look for details that describe the setting. What can you learn about Vietnam from this account?

from *When Heaven and Earth Changed Places*

◆◆◆

Le Ly Hayslip

When the planting was over, we would sit back and turn our attention to the other tasks and rewards of village life: from making clothes and mending tools to finding spouses[1] for eligible children and honoring our ancestors in a variety of rituals.[2]

On the fourteenth of each month (measured on our lunar calendar) and on the thirtieth and thirty-first of the month (*Ram mung mot*—when the moon is full) we brought fruit, flour, and the special paper objects such as money, miniature furniture and clothes—all manufactured for religious purposes—into the house and burned them at our family altar. My father would then bow and pray for the safety of our property and our lives. His main concern was for our health, which he addressed specifically if one of us was sick, but he never ended a prayer without a heartfelt request for the war to stop.

But planting was only part of village life. Like daylight and darkness, wakefulness and sleep, the labors and rituals of harvest defined the other half of our existence.

According to legend, human problems with rice didn't end with the forgetful beetle. When god saw that the mix-up in magic sacks had caused so much trouble on earth, he commanded the rice to "present itself for cooking" by rolling up to each home in a ball. Of course, the rice obeyed god and rolled into the first house it was supposed to serve. But the housewife, unprepared for such a sight, became frightened and hit it with a broom,

---

[1] **spouses** (SPOWS-ehz) *n. pl.* husbands or wives
[2] **rituals** (RIHCH-oo-uhlz) *n. pl.* ceremonies used by a religion

scattering the rice ball into a thousand pieces. This so angered the rice that it went back outside and shouted, "See if I come back to let you cook me! Now you'll have to come out to the fields and bring me in if you want your supper!"

That was the closest any Vietnamese ever came to a free bowl of rice.

Beginning in March, and again in August, we would bring the mature rice in from the fields and process it for use during the rest of the year. In March, when the ground was dry, we cut the rice very close to the soil—*cat lua*—to keep the plant alive. In August, when the ground was wet, we cut the plant halfway up—*cat gat*—which made the job much easier.

The separation of stalk and rice was done outside in a special smooth area beside our house. Because the rice was freshly cut, it had to dry in the sun for several days. At this stage, we called it *phoi lua*—not-yet rice. The actual separation was done by our water buffalo, which walked in lazy circles over a heap of cuttings until the rice fell easily from the stalks. We gathered the stalks, tied them in bundles, and used them to fix roofs or to kindle our fires. The good, light-colored rice, called *lua chet*, was separated from the bad, dark-colored rice—*lua lep*—and taken home for further processing.

The very best rice, of course, we gave back to Mother Earth. This seed rice was called *lua giong* and we put it into great jars which we filled with water. The wet rice was then packed under a haystack to keep warm. The nutrients, moisture, and heat helped the rice seeds to sprout, and after three days (during which we watered and fertilized the seedbed like a garden), we recovered

(top) Vietnamese villagers carrying freshly harvested rice. Does this rice look anything like the rice you are accustomed to eating? (left) Woman sifting rice. (right) Villagers using a machine to harvest rice from the field.

the jars and cast the fertile *geo ma* seeds into the ground we had prepared. But this was rice we would enjoy another day. The preparation of rice to eat now was our highest priority.

When the *lua chet* was dry, we stored a portion in the main part of our house, which we called *nha tren*, or top house, because my father slept there and it held our ancestral shrine. This rice was kept in bins behind a bamboo curtain which was also a hiding place for valuables, weapons and supplies, and little kids like me when soldiers came to the village.

In the back part of the house, called *nha duoi*, or lower house (because the mother and children slept there), we had an area of open floor where we would eventually conclude our labor. Once the brown rice grains were out of their shells, we shook them in wide baskets, tossing them slightly into the air so that the wind could carry off the husks. When finished, the rice was now ready to go inside where it became "floor rice" and was pounded in a bowl to track the layer of bran that contained the sweet white kernel. When we swirled the cracked rice in a woven colander,[3] the bran fell through the holes and was collected to feed the pigs. The broken rice that remained with the good kernels was called *tam* rice, and although it was fit to eat, it was not very good and we used it as chicken feed (when the harvest was good) or collected it and shared it with beggars when the harvest was bad.

We always blamed crop failures on ourselves—we had not worked hard enough or, if there was no other explanation, we had failed to adequately honor our ancestors. Our solution was to pray more and sacrifice more and eventually things always got better. Crops ruined by soldiers were another matter. We knew prayer was useless because soldiers were human beings, too, and the god of nature meant for them to work out their own karma[4] just like us.

In any event, the journey from seedling to rice bowl was long and laborious and because each grain was a symbol of life, we never wasted any of it. Good rice was considered god's gemstone[5]—*hot ngoc troi*—and was cared for accordingly on pain of divine punishment. Even today a peasant seeing lightning will crouch under the table and look for lost grains in order to escape the next bolt. And parents must never strike children, no matter how naughty they've been, while the child is eating rice, for that would interrupt the sacred communion between rice-eater and rice-maker. Like my brothers and sisters, I learned quickly the advantages of chewing my dinner slowly.

---

[3] **colander** (KUL-uhn-duhr) *n.* a bowl-shaped kitchen utensil with holes in the bottom, used for draining off liquids from foods

[4] **karma** (KAHR-mah) *n.* fate or destiny, as of the Hindu or Buddhist faith

[5] **gemstone** (JEHM-stohn) *n.* precious stone used in jewelry

POSTREADING

Critical Thinking

1. How does the author's description reveal her feelings about the simple farming life she led in a Vietnamese village? Why does she want readers to understand what this life was like?

2. What cultural customs were part of rice farming in Le Ly Hayslip's village?

3. What traditions or customs do you follow regarding food? Do these involve growing, preparing, blessing, and/or eating the food?

1. One part of the setting in this selection is the writer's house. Why is this important to her story?

2. The rice fields are also part of the setting. Why are these fields important?

3. What time elements are part of the setting in this selection?

4. How does understanding the setting help explain the motivation that Vietnamese peasants had for protecting their land?

Writing Your Response to *When Heaven and Earth Changed Places*

In your journal, describe the part of the selection that gave you the best insight into village life in Vietnam. How does this life compare to your own?

Going Back Into the Text: Author's Craft

The **setting** of a literary work is the time and place when events occur. A writer uses descriptive words and phrases that act upon the senses and bring the setting to life so that readers can experience it.

As you read the selection, use the following questions to help you understand why the setting is important.

Reviewing the Region

1. Conflict is an important part of every story. Choose one of the stories from this chapter and discuss how the conflict in the story reflects the culture in which it was written.

2. Describe how an author's cultural heritage can affect his or her choice of theme, characters, or events. Use examples from the chapter to support your answer.

3. If you could speak with one of the characters in the selections in this chapter, whom would you choose? What would you say to him or her? Explain.

5 Australia and the Pacific Islands

In the islands of the Pacific, myths, stories, and legends were passed down from generation to generation by priests and story-tellers. Unfortunately, European explorers, settlers, and mission-aries did not value these tales, so the telling of them was sometimes forbidden, and some stories were forgotten. However, a few people made an effort to remember and to record the oral literature. As the native people learned to read and write, they recorded their own traditions in their own voices. Many of the stories in this chapter were modeled on these traditional tales of gods and heroes.

In this chapter, you will read two myths that have been passed down for centuries and recorded only recently. The first comes from Tahiti and tells how man and the Earth were created. The second selection is a myth about the formation of one of the two major islands of New Zealand.

Recent times have seen Australian writers rise to prominence. You will read a selection by an Australian Aborigine. His stories show the close relationship that his people have to the land.

Early New Zealand literature was primarily created by writers of European ancestry. Today,

This painting by John Weeks, is called *The Early Settler's Homestead.* Europeans first settled in New Zealand in the early 1800s. Most of them were British hunters attracted by the seals and whales in the South Pacific. *Metropolitan Museum of Art*

Maori writers are emerging. You will read a story in this chapter by Patricia Grace who is a pop-ular Maori writer. Grace often writes about the everyday lives of contemporary Maori people.

As you read the selections in this chapter, think about the similarities between the expe-riences of the native peoples from the Pacific Islands and from other lands, such as South Africa, Canada, or the Caribbean Islands.

Tangaroa, Maker of All Things

Reading the Myth in a Cultural Context

Oceania is the name given to a vast region in the Pacific Ocean. Oceania is mostly water. Scattered about this region are approximately 30,000 islands. Polynesia, a roughly triangular area covering thousands of square miles, is one of the three main divisions of Oceania. The word *Polynesia* means "many islands."

The islands of Polynesia are classified in two ways. Some are volcanic in origin. These high islands are the rugged tops of underwater mountain ranges forced to the surface by violent eruptions. Others are flat coral islands. These low islands were built up over time from the remains of tiny marine animals.

Although the islands spread across enormous distances, there is a common Polynesian cultural heritage. Most anthropologists believe the first inhabitants migrated in stages from Southeast Asia over 20,000 years ago. Important evidence for this is the similarity between Polynesian languages and those of Indonesia.

Shared mythological themes are evident throughout Polynesian culture. One of the most frequent is the image of the universe as a giant shell. When opened, the upper half of the shell forms the heavens; the lower half becomes the earth. The importance of ancestry and being the oldest child among siblings is another.

Because of the great distances involved, it is not surprising that different versions of the same Polynesian myth exist from island to island. One example is the role of the creator. In one version, Areop-enap, the ancient spider, raises the sky. In another, it is Nareau, the first being. In this selection, from the beautiful island of Tahiti, Tangaroa, a god, emerges from his shell to become the "sky-raiser." In some variations of this creation myth, Tangaroa, is the god of oceans and fish, vitally important resources to an island culture.

As you read, think about how details in this creation myth reflect elements unique to a culture that is isolated by vast distances. Also look for shared elements found in creation myths from other parts of the world.

Focusing on the Selection

As you read "Tangaroa, Maker of All Things," think about how you would explain nature and the world to others if you lived in ancient times before scientific knowledge. Why is the Earth located at the center of the universe? Why are the heavens pictured as a dome with the sun, moon, and stars placed on it at an equal height? What kind of order does the maker follow in creating matter on earth? Why is greater emphasis placed on certain creatures? Make some notes in your journal. Compare what you write now with information you learn from reading myths of other cultures.

Tangaroa, Maker of All Things

edited by *Antony Alpers*

For a long time Tangaroa[1] lived within his shell. It was round like an egg and in the lasting darkness it revolved in the void.

There was no sun, there was no moon, there was no land nor mountain, all was moving in the void. There was no man, no fowl nor dog, no living thing; there was no water, salt or fish.

At the end of a great time Tangaroa flicked his shell, and it cracked and fell apart. Then Tangaroa stepped forth and stood upon that shell and called:

"Who is above there? Who is below there?"

No voice replied. He called again:

"Who is in front there? Who is behind there?"

Still no voice answered. Only Tangaroa's voice was heard, there was no other.

Then Tangaroa said, "O rock, crawl here!"

But no rock was to crawl to him.

He therefore said, "O sand, crawl here!"

There was no sand to crawl to him. And Tangaroa became angry because he was not obeyed. He therefore overturned his shell and raised it up to form a dome for the sky, and he named it Rumia, that is, Overturned.

After a time great Tangaroa, wearied from confinement, stepped out from another shell that covered him; and he took this shell for rock and sand.

But his anger was not finished, and so he took his backbone for a mountain range and his ribs for the ridges that ascend. He took his innards for the broad floating clouds and his flesh for fatness of the earth, and his arms and legs for strength of the earth. He took his fingernails and toenails for the scales and shells of fishes in the sea.

---

[1] **Tangaroa** (tang-ah-ROH-uh) *n.* the name of a mythical being

This painting by Paul Gauguin is called *The Three Huts Tahiti*. Gauguin is a Frenchman whose most famous work depicts the people and landscapes of Tahiti, the origin of this legend.

Of his feathers he made trees and shrubs and plants to clothe the land. Of his guts he made lobsters, shrimps, and eels, for the streams and for the sea.

And the blood of Tangaroa became hot, and it floated away to make the redness of the sky, and also rainbows. All that is red is made from Tangaroa's blood.

But the head of Tangaroa remained sacred to himself, and he still lived, the same head upon a body that remained.

Tangaroa was master of everything that is. There was expansion and there was growth.

Tangaroa called forth gods. It was only later that he called forth man, when Tu[2] was with him.

As Tangaroa had shells, so has everything a shell. The sky is a shell, which is endless space, where the gods placed the sun, the moon, the constellations, and the other stars.

The land is a shell to the stones and to water, and to the plants that spring from it. The shell of a man is woman, since it is from her that he comes forth. And a woman's shell is woman, since it is from her that she comes forth.

No one can name the shells of all the things that are in this world.

---

[2] **Tu** (too) *n.* a man's name

POSTREADING

Critical Thinking

1. How does the author let us know that Tahiti, where this version of the Polynesian creation myth originated, is a volcanic island rather than a coral reef?

2. How do you think the animals mentioned in this myth reflect Polynesian culture?

3. What elements in this Polynesian myth do you think are also found in creation myths from other cultures?

Writing Your Response to "Tangaroa, Maker of All Things"

In your journal, write about a question concerning the origins of the earth or the mysteries of nature that fascinates you. What makes this question so intriguing to you? Why is it mysterious? What do you think is the explanation for this phenomenon?

Going Back Into the Text: Author's Craft

Figures of speech describe one thing (the subject) in terms usually applied to another (the image). The image creates a vivid impression of the subject in the reader's mind. A metaphor is a figure of speech. It compares two things that are distinctly different. "All the world's a stage" is a metaphor. The theater image creates a vivid impression of the world as a play in which we all act a part.

The author of "Tangaroa" uses metaphors to describe objects in nature. In one case, the subject of the metaphor is implied rather than stated directly. This occurs when the universe (subject) is compared to a shell (image). The subject, the universe, is implied, not stated.

With a partner, talk about the use of metaphors in "Tangaroa." Think of the impressions created in your mind by the various images. Discuss metaphors you might use to describe events in nature if you were writing a Polynesian myth. The following questions can guide your discussion.

1. Why is a shell a vivid image for the universe? (Think about what a shell is; how it is shaped; what it looks like when the shell is open/closed; what a shell feels like.)

2. What are two other examples of metaphors in the work? What are the subjects? What are the images in each?

3. If you were explaining violent events in nature by comparing them to the Tangaroa's anger, what metaphor would you use for each of the following?

   • thunder
   • lightning
   • a hurricane wind
   • an earthquake

MAKING THEMATIC CONNECTIONS

Places Called Home

Perhaps no feeling is stronger than the love one has for a homeland. Our homelands define who we are and how we view the world around us. Rich with ancestry and tradition, our birthplaces provide us with our heritage. For some, there can be no greater loss than to be separated from home or to see it devastated by war.

Many selections in this book represent the strong sense of nationalism—the love and pride of one's country—that the authors feel. For those who have been separated from their countries because of war, oppression, or other circumstances, their pain and longing are evident.

The poem "Chilean Earth" is a joyous celebration of the author's home. She speaks of the beauty of the land and how it influenced its people. "When Heaven and Earth Changed Places" describes the process of planting and harvesting rice in Vietnam. You learned how the Vietnamese revere this most important

Both the home and the style of dress in this painting are typical of 19th-century China. Think about what makes your home or homeland special to you.

crop and the importance of ritual throughout every step from planting to eating. In "Hearing of the Earthquake in Kyoto," a Japanese poet expresses his fear and sadness after hearing of a series of earthquakes that have wreaked havoc in his hometown on the Kamo banks. In "Warmth of Blood," an imprisoned Arab finds comfort in his memories of his home and his beloved. "The Oath of Athenian Youth" is the pledge said by young men of ancient Greece when they came of age. It reflects a strong sense of duty to their country.

Through lush imagery and rich sensory detail, "Interior" and "The Prebend Gardens" reflect the poet's love for his African homeland and ancestry that is characteristic of Negritude literature. The Caribbean poems "Jamaica Market," "On Leaving," and "The Child's Return" express the poets' sense of loss in being separated from their homelands. Finally, "A Night in the Royal Ontario Museum" tells of the loss of a different kind of home—that of the time in which the author lives. Locked in a museum after closing, the author wanders through representations of different eras of time and yearns for her home in the present.

There is an old saying that goes "Home is where the heart is." This is no more true than in these selections, in which the authors have expressed their heartfelt emotions about their own homes.

ACTIVITY

The selections described above are about places that are probably unfamiliar to you. But because the authors have described their homelands and how they feel about them in such vivid detail, it is easy to picture what these places must be like.

You will find that the word "home" means many different things to many people. For you, it could be the place where your family lives or a place where you used to live, even a place where you've never lived. A home can be a house or a city or a country. Write a poem or essay about the place you call "Home." How would you describe your home? What qualities does it have? How do you feel about your home? You might compare your home to something else. For example, some people have called New York City a mosaic; its people are the many different colored tiles that make up a beautiful picture.

As you write, think about the many different aspects of your home. What kind of buildings does it have? What is the weather like? What kind of plants and animals inhabit it? What kind of special activities is your home known for?

Maui and
the Great Fish

Reading the Story in a Cultural Context

Kiri Te Kanawa is one of the world's foremost opera singers. As a student, she won a scholarship to study music in London. She made her debut there at the Royal Opera House in 1971. Since that time, she has recorded many albums and sung in every major opera house in the world.

Kiri Te Kanawa's singing career requires that she travel most of the year. But with all her success and all her travels, she never forgets the place she was born—New Zealand. To Te Kanawa, this is "the beautiful Land of the Long White Cloud."

Although Kiri Te Kanawa's mother was a Pakeha (white person), her father was a Maori. The Maoris were among the first people to live in New Zealand. They migrated to New Zealand from Polynesia.

As a child, Te Kanawa spent many hours with Maori friends and relatives. One of her favorite memories is of the stories she heard. Her mother told magical bedtime stories, while her Maori relations told the stories of "why and how so many of the places where we played had been given their special names."

Kiri Te Kanawa also loved to go sailing and fishing with her father. She says, "I love the many Maori stories of fishing and boating adventures because they remind me of those wonderful expeditions." The story you are about to read is one of those tales. Kiri Te Kanawa has retold it as part of a book titled *Land of the Long White Cloud*. It is her way of sharing her rich cultural heritage.

In this story you will meet Maui, a favorite Maori god who is known as a trickster. The story tells how Maui catches a great fish, which is the South Island of New Zealand. To this day, the Maori name for the North Island is *Te Ika A Maui* which means "the fish-hook of Maui." According to Maori legend, Maui used the North Island as his hook to catch the South Island, his fish.

Focusing on the Selection

As you read "Maui and the Great Fish," look for the ways that Kiri Te Kanawa has utilized the techniques of the storytellers she heard as a child. One of these techniques is the use of repetition. How does repetition emphasize the meaning of parts of the story?

Maui and the Great Fish

◆◆◆

retold by *Kiri Te Kanawa*

Maui[1] was, they say, half man and half god. He knew many magic spells and had many magic powers that his older brothers didn't know about, or if they did they pretended to ignore.

One day, when he heard his brothers talking about going fishing, Maui decided that he wanted to go too. So, before his brothers had woken up he went down to where the canoe was, carrying his special fishing hook. Hearing his brothers approach he quickly hid under the floorboards of the boat.

The brothers arrived and they were laughing about having managed to escape without Maui. They were looking forward to having a good day's fishing without being bothered by their young brother.

They pushed out from shore and were still laughing when suddenly they heard a noise.

"What was that?" asked one of them.

Then they thought they heard someone talking. They couldn't see anyone; they couldn't see anything except for the water.

"Oh, it must have been a seagull or something screeching in the distance," suggested another of the brothers.

Then they heard the sound again. It was Maui, laughing and saying in a strange voice "I am with you. You haven't tricked me at all."

New Zealand's North Island is more mountainous than the South Island. Can you see why the North Island might be compared to a "fish hook" by the Maoris?

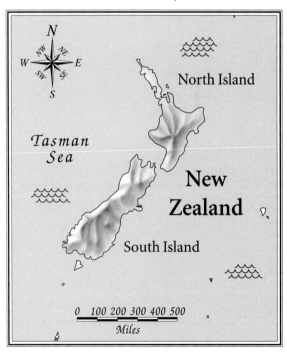

---

[1] **Maui** (MOW-ee) the name of a folk hero; Maui is also the name of the second largest island in Hawaii

The brothers were becoming quite scared now. It sounded like muffled speech but there was no one to be seen.

On they paddled into the deep waters. Again they heard the voice and this time one of the brothers said he thought the noise was coming from under the floorboards so he wrenched up a few. There was Maui, laughing loudly and boasting "I tricked you! I tricked you!"

The brothers were amazed to see Maui there. They decided to turn back immediately. "You are not coming with us," they said. "You're far too young and our father doesn't want you to come with us."

But Maui said, "Look back! Look back to the land! Look how far away it is!"

He had used his magic powers to make the land seem much further away than it really was. The brothers, not realizing that it was a trick, reluctantly agreed to take Maui with them.

They paddled on for a while and then stopped. Just as they were about to throw over the anchor and start their fishing, Maui said, "No. Please don't do that because I know a much better place further out, full of fish—all the fish you could want. Just a little while longer and you'll have all your nets filled in half the time."

The brothers were tempted by this promise of fish and paddled out a little further when Maui stopped them and told them to start fishing. So they threw over their nets which within a few minutes were overflowing. They couldn't believe their luck.

Their boat was lying low in the water with the weight of their catch so the brothers told Maui that they were going to turn back. But Maui said, "No, it's my turn. I haven't had a chance to do my fishing."

"But we have enough!" they replied.

"No! I want to do my fishing," insisted Maui.

With that, he pulled out his special fishing hook made of bone, and asked for some bait. The brothers refused to give him any so Maui rubbed his nose so hard that it began to bleed. Then he smeared the hook with his own blood and threw it over the side.

Suddenly the boat was tossed about, and Maui was thrilled because he was sure he had caught a very big fish. He pulled and pulled. The sea was in a turmoil and Maui's brothers sat in stunned silence, marvelling at Maui's magic strength.

Maui heaved and tugged for what seemed like an age until at last the fish broke the surface. Then Maui and his brothers could see that what he had caught was not a fish but a piece of land, and that his hook was embedded in the doorway of the house of Tonganui, the son of the Sea God.

Maui's brothers couldn't believe their eyes. This beautiful land pulled up from the sea, was smooth and bright, and there were houses on it and burning fires and birds singing. They had never seen anything so marvellous in their whole lives.

Realizing what he had done Maui said, "I must go and make peace with the gods because I think they are very angry with me. Stay here quietly and calmly, until I return."

As soon as Maui had gone the brothers forgot his instructions and began to argue for possession of the land.

"I want this piece," said one.

"No! I claimed it first. It's mine!" shouted another.

Soon the brothers began to slash at the land with their weapons. This angered the gods even more and its smooth surface was gashed and cut. It could never be smoothed out again.

To this day, those cuts and bruises of long ago can still be seen in the valleys and mountains of New Zealand.[2]

---

[2] **New Zealand** (NOO ZEE-luhnd) an island country in the Pacific Ocean

POSTREADING

Critical Thinking

1. How does retelling the story bring Kiri Te Kanawa closer to her Maori homeland and heritage?

2. How does the story explain the creation of the Maori homeland?

3. Maui used his magic power to trick his older brothers. If you had such a power, how would you use it?

Writing Your Response to "Maui and the Great Fish"

In your journal, write about your response to the story. Is there a place that you think is as special as the island that Maui pulls from the sea? What is it like? Why do you think it's marvelous?

Going Back Into the Text: Author's Craft

Writers and storytellers use **repetition** to emphasize meaning, to link ideas, or to create rhythm. This kind of repetition is carefully planned for its effectiveness. A writer might repeat a word, phrase, sentence, or group of sentences.

As you read the story, use these questions to help you identify how repetition is used:

1. In the first paragraph, what is it that repetition emphasizes about Maui?

2. How is repetition used when the brothers hear someone talking?

3. Why do you think Maui repeats the words, "I tricked you! I tricked you!"?

Family Council

Reading the Story in a Cultural Context

The first people who lived on the continent of Australia arrived about 40,000 years ago. They probably came from Southeast Asia. Later immigrants called the natives Aborigines. Today many Aborigines call themselves "Koori." The Aborigines spread across Australia, developing a civilization that was isloated from the rest of the world.

Aborigines lived as hunter-gatherers, wandering along the sea coasts and river valleys. They needed few material possessions. Family groups hunted for small animals and searched for berries, nuts, and eggs. The different groups spoke as many as 250 different languages. Many Aborigines continue to live with the same traditions as their ancestors.

Although customs differed among the groups, they all felt a deep religious bond with nature. "We see all things natural as part of us. All things on Earth we see as part human," explains a present-day Aborigine. Their rich oral tradition has preserved their religious beliefs. According to Aboriginal traditions, long ago in "Dreamtime," their ancestors roamed the Earth. As they rambled, they created mountains, valleys, and rivers, as well as plants and animals. These and other stories were told and retold around camp fires. Aborigine artists painted the stories on rocks and carved them on stones. Dancers told the stories in movement and music.

Until recently, many Australians looked down on Aborigines. Their rich oral traditions were ignored. However, Aborigines adapted their ancient stories and artistic traditions to modern life. In the 1960s, Koori writers drew the attention of the Australian literary world. Today, many Koori poems, plays, and novels are written in English and protest the mistreatment of the native peoples. Other native literature serves as a rallying cry to bring the Aborigines together. Still other literature preserves and honors the Koori heritage.

The personal narrative that you will read here is written by the Aborigine writer Oodgeroo. The story explores Koori traditions about family relationships and hints at the value Aborigines give to nature. It is significant that the title of the book that this story comes from is *Dreamtime*.

Focusing on the Selection

As you read "Family Council," think about how a personal narrative can give you insight into how other people live and think. Be aware of what you learn about Aborigine culture and family life. What do Aborigines value? How are Koori families similar to or different from yours?

Family Council

◆◆◆

Oodgeroo

The family was holding one of its many council meetings. This time the grievance committee[1] was airing its views. My two sisters and brothers were complaining that I did not pull my weight[2] when it came to bringing home the food supplies from the hunt. They could all boast of a high tally of birds and animals they had brought home for the family larder.[3] Although I always went hunting with them, I never did any good with my slingshot and bandicoot[4] traps. They said I spent too much time dreaming, or gathering flowers, or looking for discarded feathers, or drawing trees and animals and birds in the sand. That never made any sense to them, because the water always came and washed away my efforts with the receding tide. If I wasn't doing these things, then they complained that I'd go tramping off through the bush.[5]

They were right. I never did take home any birds or animals for the larder. However, I did try to make up for my bad hunting record in other ways.

My eldest brother was allowed to make the first complaint against me. "She shouldn't be allowed to eat the food we bring home," he said. "She goes barging into the swamps and clumps of bushes just when I get a line on an extra-choice fat bird—and then I miss it because my stupid sister has warned it of our presence."

My second brother said darkly, "I think she gets up early and beats us to the bandicoot traps to let the creatures out."

---

[1] **grievance committee** (GREE-vuhns kuh-MIHT-ee) a group of people formed to discuss complaints
[2] **pull ... weight** do one's full share of the work
[3] **larder** (LAHR-duhr) *n.* supply of food; a place where food is stored
[4] **bandicoot** (BAN-dih-koot) *n.* a ratlike Australian animal with a long snout
[5] **bush** (bush) *n.* wild country

My elder sister chipped in now. "She won't even help to carry home the bandicoots or birds when we do catch them."

My younger sister was not to be left out. "She deliberately puts Spitfire into her bandicoot trap to chase away the bandicoots. That cat of hers is wild—just like her! None of us can get anywhere near Spitfire except for her. She has it trained to frighten us away."

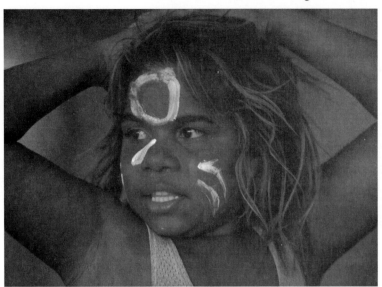

An Aboriginal girl with her face painted.

When my father finally asked me to speak, I didn't have much to say. All I could answer was that although it was true I didn't catch any game, it was quite untrue that I ever deliberately barged in to chase it away. Sometimes I just forgot about the need to keep still and quiet. And though I had a habit of getting up earlier than the others, I never released the bandicoots out of the traps. As for my younger sister, she was talking through her hat.[6] I always set my bandicoot trap in just the same way as everyone else, but each time I went to see if I'd caught a bandicoot in it, I always found my cat in the trap instead. And it was, in fact, Spitfire that my brother had seen me releasing from the trap one morning, not a bandicoot! I had nothing to say to answer my elder sister's complaint that I would not carry the dead birds and animals home. I simply told my father straight out that I didn't like to do that.

Father was our arbitration judge.[7] The rules were simple. Either we agreed with his decision, or we unanimously[8] opposed it and appealed for another hearing. Having listened to the complaints and my defense, it was now his job to overrule the plaintiffs,[9] if he could. I certainly hadn't been much help to him.

He turned to my brothers and sisters. "Who catches the most fish, and goes fishing most often of all of you?" They had to admit that I was the best fisherman in the family.

---

[6] **talking through her hat** talking foolishly

[7] **arbitration judge** (ahr-bih-TRAY-shuhn juj) a person chosen to settle an argument or complaint

[8] **unanimously** (yoo-NAN-uh-muhs-lee) *adv.* in complete agreement

[9] **plaintiffs** (PLAYN-tihfs) *n. pl.* the persons who brought charges against someone

"And who is best at crab spotting and catching?" my father went on.

Again they admitted that it was me.

"And the shellfish — how often is this gathered, and who spends the most time filling the bags with it?"

Yes, they agreed that I did.

"So," said my father, "your sister has earned her place at the table. Even a fisherman must eat in order to fish."

There were never any more complaints against me after this. The others accepted the fact that they would have to put up with my bad hunting, and that I would never change. So I went on fishing, looking for crabs, and gathering shellfish — and I went on collecting fallen feathers, ferns and flowers while my brothers and sisters worked hard to bring home the rest of the game.

POSTREADING

Critical Thinking

1. What does Oodgeroo tell you about how Aborigines resolve conflict?

2. How do the narrator's actions reflect Aborigine traditions and values?

3. Compare the way a typical American family resolves conflict with that of the Aborigine family.

Writing Your Response to "Family Council"

What event, character, or description from the selection did you find especially striking or intriguing? In your journal, explain why this aspect of the story struck you. How does it relate to your life?

Going Back Into the Text: Author's Craft

A **personal narrative** is an autobiographical incident or an account of an event in a person's life written by that person. Personal narratives are written from the first-person point of view, using the pronouns *I* and *me*. While a personal narrative may not be an objective account of what happened, it often offers vivid descriptions of events and people that only an eyewitness or a participant can provide.

As you review this personal narrative, use these questions as guidelines:

1. Who is telling about the events in this narrative?

2. What details could only a participant in the event know?

3. Why did the writer choose to tell about this incident? What was her purpose?

Butterflies

Reading the Story in a Cultural Context

The original New Zealanders were Polynesian tribes called the Maori. About 800 years ago, these seafaring people paddled 100-foot-long ocean canoes. The Maori called the two islands that make up New Zealand "the land of the long white cloud." Once there, the Maori settled in villages and farmed. They held religious ceremonies in *marae*, or gathering places. There, Maori songs, poems, and dances celebrated important occasions.

Like Australia, New Zealand was invaded by British settlers who fought the Maori for their land. The British government tried to wipe out Maori culture, language, and customs. Much of their land was taken illegally by colonists, in violation of treaties between the Maori and Great Britain. By the 1870s, the Maori population was reduced from 250,00 to 50,000.

Today, the Maori form a minority of less than a half million. Many are of mixed ancestry. Yet in the 1990s, they have made a vigorous effort to force the government to return land taken from them and to restore their rights.

A revival in Maori culture has also been taking place in recent years. While early New Zealand literature was primarily created by writers of European ancestry, today Maori writers are emerging. The world has begun to acknowledge writers of Maori descent such as Witi Ihimaera, Kiri Te Kanawa (also an opera

star), and Keri Hulme. These Polynesian writers frequently present aspects of Maori culture and expose European prejudice toward other peoples and their beliefs.

Patricia Grace is a Maori and the author of "Butterflies". She often writes about traditional tribal values, wisdom, and family love, called *aroha* in the Maori language. Grace was born in Wellington in 1937 and grew up in the city. She chose to write in English because she was aware that her city background did not provide her complete fluency in the Maori language. Her stories often focus on humanity and cultural pride by presenting strong character portraits. Perhaps because she is the mother of seven, many of her narratives present reflections on childhood.

"Butterflies" is typical of Grace's writing. It points out the wisdom of grandparents, whose understanding of cultural differences help a child through a difficult experience.

Focusing on the Selection

As you read "Butterflies," think about the setting, or where the story takes place. What does the setting add to the story? How does the setting help you focus on the themes of family relations and the wisdom of the Maori culture? How does the setting help make such ordinary events come alive?

Butterflies

◆◆◆

Patricia Grace

A Maori girl of
New Zealand.

The grandmother plaited[1] her granddaughter's hair and then
she said, "Get your lunch. Put it in your bag. Get your apple.
You come straight back after school, straight home here. Listen
to the teacher," she said. "Do what she say."

Her grandfather was out on the step. He walked down the
path with her and out on to the footpath. He said to a neighbour, "Our granddaughter goes to school. She lives with us now."

"She's fine," the neighbour said. "She's terrific with her two
plaits in her hair."

"And clever," the grandfather said. "Writes every day in her
book."

"She's fine," the neighbour said.

The grandfather waited with his granddaughter by the crossing and then
he said, "Go to school. Listen to the teacher. Do what she say."

When the granddaughter came home from school her grandfather was
hoeing round the cabbages. Her grandmother was picking beans. They
stopped their work.

"You bring your book home?" the grandmother asked.

"Yes."

"You write your story?"

"Yes."

"What's your story?"

"About the butterflies."

"Get your book, then. Read your story."

---

[1] **plaited** (PLAY-ted) *v.* braided

The granddaughter took her book from her schoolbag and opened it.

"I killed all the butterflies," she read. "This is me and this is all the butterflies."

"And your teacher like your story, did she?"

"I don't know."

"What your teacher say?"

"She said butterflies are beautiful creatures. They hatch out and fly in the sun. The butterflies visit all the pretty flowers, she said. They lay their eggs and then they die. You don't kill butterflies, that's what she said."

The grandmother and grandfather were quiet for a long time, and their granddaughter, holding the book, stood quite still in the warm garden.

"Because you see," the grandfather said, "your teacher, she buy all her cabbages from the supermarket and that's why."

POSTREADING

Critical Thinking

1. How does Patricia Grace create a sense of reality in this story?

2. How does this story show the Maori value of *aroha*?

3. What qualities do you associate with grandparents? Why? How do the grandparents in the story compare to your image?

Writing Your Response to "Butterflies"

In your journal, write about a description or idea from the story that is especially meaningful to you. Discuss why it is memorable.

Going Back Into the Text: Author's Craft

The **setting** of a literary work is the time and place of the action. Setting serves a number of possible functions. It may simply provide background for the action or it may be an important element in the plot or central conflict. It may help to create a certain *mood* or emotion.

1. Describe the setting of "Butterflies."

2. Why is understanding the setting of "Butterflies" crucial to understanding the point of the story?

Reviewing the Region

1. Review the two myths in this chapter. Discuss the ways in which the myths reflect a specific culture's view of the creation of the world.

2. Choose a selection from this chapter and discuss the ways in which family life affects the characters' personal development.

3. Have you ever felt that others did not understand your point of view? Choose a character from one of the stories in this chapter and relate the character's difficulty to your own experience.

FOCUSING THE UNIT

COOPERATIVE/COLLABORATIVE LEARNING

With three of your classmates, make a "Cultural Scrapbook" of Asia, Australia, and the Pacific. Each member of the group should select different countries to research. Using newspapers and magazines, collect pictures of people and places from the country or region you have selected. You can cut out the pictures and glue them on sheets of plain paper. Create a cover from construction paper and bind the book.

Instead, you may wish to make a video "Cultural Scrapbook" by filming the pictures.

Below is part of a sample narration that one group of students used to accompany their "Cultural Scrapbook."

Student 1: Today we are going to take you on a tour of a fascinating culture. Without leaving your seat, you will meet the people of East Asia, South and Southeast Asia, Australia, and the Pacific. So sit back and enjoy our video, "Faces of the East."

Student 2: Our tour starts with Japan, a nation of about 125 million people. Located on an archipelago off the east coast of Asia, Japan consists of four main islands: Honshu, Hokkaido, Kyushu, and Shikoku.

Student 3: Next we go to India, one of the oldest civilizations in the world. It is also a country of great diversity. More than 16 major languages are spoken in India.

Writing Process

Literature can serve as a source of information about many subjects. Look back over the journal entries you made for this unit. From the different chapters in this unit, select two or more selections that you particulary liked. Write an expository essay to explain how one of the selections taught you something important. Your audience might be students in your class, the members of a service organization such as the Boy or Girl Scouts, or your teacher. First, describe what you learned from the readings. Then add details from the selections to make your point. Refer to the handbook at the back of the book for help with the writing process. Use the model essay as a guideline.

Problem Solving

How can we make the world a better place? This is the problem many of the writers in Unit 2 confront in their short stories, poems, and folktales. These writers describe values by which people should live. Choose two or more of the authors included in the unit and explain the values they endorse to deal with the problems of their time, place, and culture. Do you think their value systems would benefit modern American culture? Why or why not? In the form of a debate, newspaper editorial, advice column, or speech, express your reactions to the author's responses to the problem of leading a moral life. You can work alone, with a partner, or in a small group.

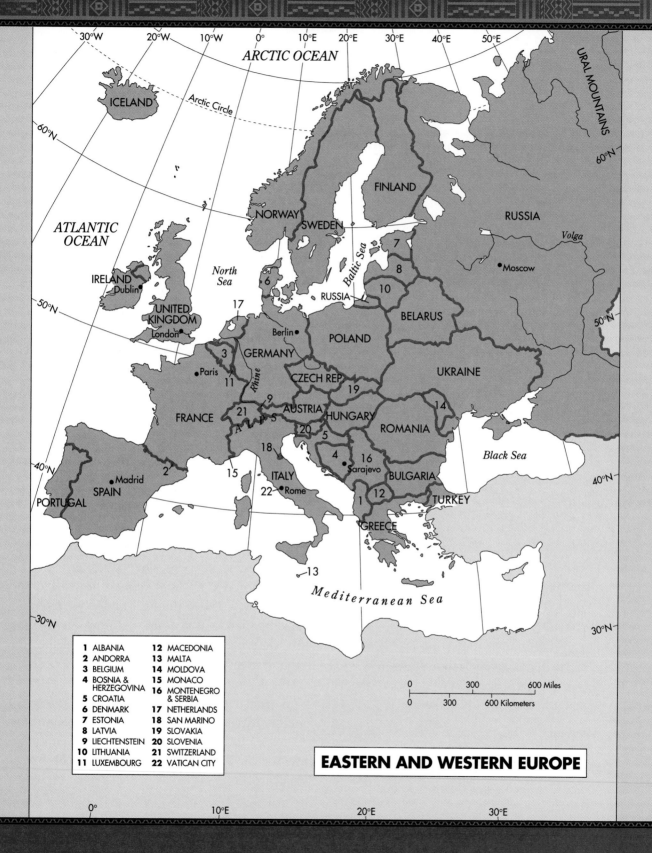

EASTERN AND WESTERN EUROPE

1	ALBANIA	**12**	MACEDONIA
2	ANDORRA	**13**	MALTA
3	BELGIUM	**14**	MOLDOVA
4	BOSNIA & HERZEGOVINA	**15**	MONACO
5	CROATIA	**16**	MONTENEGRO & SERBIA
6	DENMARK	**17**	NETHERLANDS
7	ESTONIA	**18**	SAN MARINO
8	LATVIA	**19**	SLOVAKIA
9	LIECHTENSTEIN	**20**	SLOVENIA
10	LITHUANIA	**21**	SWITZERLAND
11	LUXEMBOURG	**22**	VATICAN CITY

UNIT 3
Eastern and Western Europe

You emperors, kings, dukes, and knights, and all other people [who want to] know the diversity of the races of mankind, as well as of kingdoms . . . and regions of all parts of the East, read through this book, and you will find in it the greatest and most marvelous characteristics of the peoples of Armenia, Persia, India, and Tartary, as they are . . . described in the present work by Marco Polo.

These are the first words from the diary of Marco Polo. Born in 1254, Polo was one of the first Europeans to travel to the Far East. His journal tells of the wonders of China, where he traveled in the 1270s, the beginning of the period that is known as the Renaissance.

The Renaissance, which means "rebirth," began in Italy and spread throughout Europe during the 14th and 15th centuries. The Renaissance grew out of a renewed interest in the cultures of ancient Greece and Rome.

The ancient Greeks had developed one of the first civilizations in Europe. Their civilization was at its height between 400 and 600 B.C. It provided a foundation for government, art, literature, theater, science, and philosophy in Europe.

The Roman Empire ruled many of the lands surrounding the Mediterranean Sea from 27 B.C. to A.D. 395. Under Roman rule, trade flourished and much of Europe was united under a common system of law. After centuries of rule, the Roman Empire declined because of invading warriors and internal rivalries. The eastern portion of the Roman Empire survived for another thousand years as the Byzantine Empire, centered in present-day Turkey.

Greek and Roman civilizations were rediscovered during the Renaissance when art flourished, and learning advanced. Writers such as William Shakespeare and Miguel de Cervantes composed their famous works during this period. Europeans also sent out voyagers and explorers to conquer foreign civilizations and to develop trade routes. This age of exploration began with Marco Polo and lasted for nearly three centuries.

Throughout the Renaissance, a scientific revolution also took place. Scholars such as Nicolaus Copernicus, Galileo Galilei, and Sir Isaac Newton made advances in the sciences and math. Their discoveries in physics and astronomy and their new ideas such as the theory of gravity, sparked the beginning of modern science.

The advances in science led to the Industrial Revolution which raised the standard of living throughout much of Europe and made the United Kingdom the first great industrial nation in the world. Not long after, political revolutions occurred throughout Europe. One of the bloodiest was the French Revolution of 1789, in which the peasants rebelled against the nobility and established a new, more democractic form of government.

Time Line

Literature titles are placed on the time line to reflect the historical time or event that relates to the selection, not to reflect the publication dates of the selections.

300s
Germanic groups conquer Roman Empire

1000s
Christians split into Roman Catholic and Eastern Orthodox religions

27 B.C. - A.D. 395
Rule of Roman Empire

| 500 B.C. | 100 | A.D. 300 | 500 | 1000 |

450 B.C.
Athens is a direct democracy.
The Oath of Athenian Youth

1095
The First Crusade begins. Crusades continue for hundreds of years.

A similar rebellion of the masses took place in Eastern Europe more than 100 years later. The people of Russia rebelled against the Russian czar in 1917 and formed a new government to replace him. Shortly after, a revolutionary group known as the Bolsheviks overthrew that government. The Bolsheviks, later known as the Communists, formed yet another government. The statement on the day of their successful revolution summarizes their demands.

> *The Provisional Government is deposed. . . . The cause for which the people were fighting: immediate proposal of a democratic peace, abolition of landlord property-rights over the land, labor control over production, [and] creation of a Soviet Government.* ***LONG LIVE THE REVOLUTION OF WORKMEN, SOLDIERS, AND PEASANTS!***

Thus was formed the Communist Party, which would form the Union of Soviet Socialist Republics (USSR) and rule it for 70 years.

In western Europe during the end of the 19th century, many countries had scrambled to establish colonies in Africa and Asia that could meet their demands for natural resources. As the race for colonies and competition for trade increased, hostility among anxious and powerful European nations grew. Wars over territories and borders grew to world proportions. By 1917, the countries of Europe had been devastated by World War I.

Peace treaties made after the war left Germany crippled and angry. By 1939, another war was brewing in Europe. The Prime Minister of England made the following statement, when it became evident that a second war could not be avoided.

> *This is a sad day for all of us, and to none is it sadder than to me. . . . I trust I may live to see the day when Hitlerism has been destroyed and a liberated Europe has been re-established.*

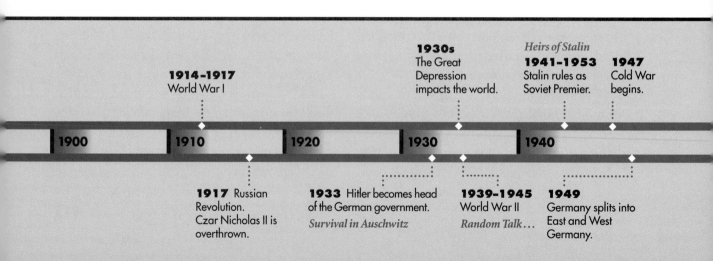

1930s
The Great Depression impacts the world.

Heirs of Stalin
1941-1953
Stalin rules as Soviet Premier.

1947
Cold War begins.

1914-1917
World War I

| 1900 | 1910 | 1920 | 1930 | 1940 |

1917 Russian Revolution. Czar Nicholas II is overthrown.

1933 Hitler becomes head of the German government.
Survival in Auschwitz

1939-1945 World War II
Random Talk . . .

1949 Germany splits into East and West Germany.

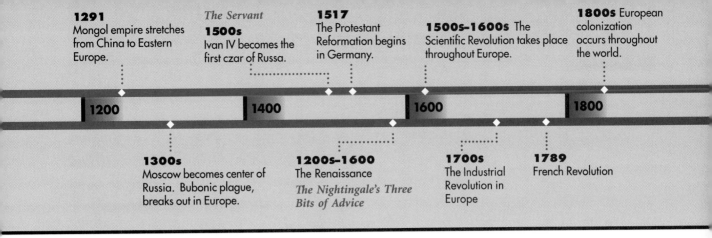

1291
Mongol empire stretches from China to Eastern Europe.

The Servant
1500s
Ivan IV becomes the first czar of Russa.

1517
The Protestant Reformation begins in Germany.

1500s–1600s The Scientific Revolution takes place throughout Europe.

1800s European colonization occurs throughout the world.

1200

1400

1600

1800

1300s
Moscow becomes center of Russia. Bubonic plague, breaks out in Europe.

1200s–1600
The Renaissance
The Nightingale's Three Bits of Advice

1700s
The Industrial Revolution in Europe

1789
French Revolution

Hitlerism was destroyed but its cost was high. Millions of soldiers died fighting the war. In addition, millions of Jews and members of other minorities were killed in death camps.

A liberated Europe was established but the power of the Western European nations had been broken. Slowly, the nations of Europe gave up their colonies. The United States and the Soviet Union emerged as the most powerful nations in the world.

Over the next four decades, the Cold War would involve many of the countries of the world. During this period, the United States and the Soviet Union opposed each other without actually fighting. They engaged in an arms race, building ever more powerful weapons. Then, when wars broke out throughout Asia and the Americas, the Soviets supported one side and the United States and Western Europe supported the other. Eventually, economic and political upheavals within the Soviet Union ended the Cold War.

In 1991, the Soviet Union broke apart and the republics declared their independence. The Commonwealth of Independent States was formed in December of that year.

The nations of Europe attempted to recover from the turmoil of the Cold War by setting up the Common Market, later renamed the European Community (EC). The EC united European countries and brought their economies and governments closer together. Eventually, the EC organization benefited European industries, trade, and standard of living.

Although most of Europe has enjoyed peace in the late 20th century, trouble spots remain. Some nations have experienced ethnic strife. Civil wars have split the former Yugoslavia and threaten to undermine peace talks in Northern Ireland. Still, these struggles differ from the struggles of the past. Today, groups of nations meet to try to settle disputes. Most countries recognize the benefits of keeping the peace—both within and outside of their borders.

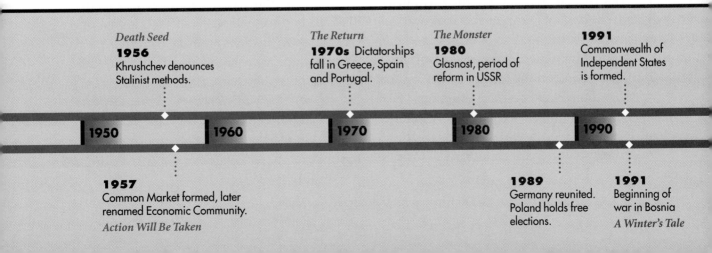

Death Seed
1956
Khrushchev denounces Stalinist methods.

The Return
1970s Dictatorships fall in Greece, Spain and Portugal.

The Monster
1980
Glasnost, period of reform in USSR

1991
Commonwealth of Independent States is formed.

1950

1960

1970

1980

1990

1957
Common Market formed, later renamed Economic Community.
Action Will Be Taken

1989
Germany reunited. Poland holds free elections.

1991
Beginning of war in Bosnia
A Winter's Tale

CHAPTER

6 Eastern Europe

Eastern European literature first appeared around the 800s and 900s. Most of the works from this period were religious hymns and writings of saints.

Around the 1600s, the Western world began to affect Eastern European literature. Under Peter the Great, Western works were translated into Russian.

During the 1800s, Russian literature experienced a "golden age" of its own. Russian writers produced masterpieces that were praised all over the world. This chapter begins with a story from this era. It deals with the ordinary life of a peasant. Another story in this chapter is based on a legend from this era. In this story, a rabbi helps relieve the poverty and sickness of the people in his town in Poland.

Throughout the 1800s, the czar of Russia often censored writers for fear that they would criticize the government. However, clever writers wove criticism into their stories to avoid censorship. This technique was developed further after the Russian Revolution in 1917.

Writers were granted limited freedom when Khrushchev gained power in the 1950s. Three poems in this chapter address the turmoil of this era. The Eastern European literary world did not experience real freedom of expression until the 1980s brought the fall of the Iron Curtain.

Today, people in the former Soviet Union cope with a turbulent political situation. They have more freedom, but also struggle with food shortages, crowded housing, and high taxes. These daily struggles are the subject of today's

This painting by Kasimir Malevich is called *To the Harvest.* Another work by Malevich appears on page A11 of *The Art of Tapestries.* Notice that the subject matter in both paintings is farming. The climate in the former Soviet Union makes farming a constant effort.

Russian literature. You will read a satire of these living conditions in this chapter.

Elsewhere in Eastern Europe, war in the Balkans has inspired writers to call for action. This chapter includes an essay by a journalist from Croatia who has gained the world's attention through her reports of the war.

As you read this chapter, remember the fear of censorship that each author dealt with. Think about what messages are disguised in each selection.

The Servant

Reading the Story in a Cultural Context

From the latter part of the nineteenth century to the early part of the 20th century, many European writers concentrated on portraying characters in situations that reflected the realities of life. Their stories reflected the social problems of the day and dealt with the lives of ordinary people, such as factory workers, shopkeepers, and servants.

Some of the greatest masters of realistic fiction were Russian. S. T. Semyonov wrote novels that dealt with the famine and disease brought on by the Russian Civil War of 1918 to 1920, which ended with the rise of a Marxist society. The Communist dictatorship wanted to control economic activity. All men under fifty were drafted for labor or for the armed services. Women took the place of men in factories and on construction projects. To feed the people in the cities and the army, soldiers seized food from the peasants. As a result, many people went hungry.

"The Servant" reflects the uncertainties of life faced by many Russian peasants. In the story, Gerasim, a peasant, is desperate to find work at a time when it was extremely difficult to find employment. He seeks the help of a friend, Yegor Danilych, who is a coachman to a wealthy merchant. The friend convinces his employer to hire Gerasim. But to do so, the employer must get rid of an elderly servant. Gerasim is faced with a difficult choice. He can take the job and escape his desperate position or he can turn down the job and save an old couple from poverty.

Through the choices made by Gerasim, Yegor Danilych, and the employer, Semyonov reveals the desperation of the working class. However, Semyonov also demonstrates the boundlessness of human compassion in the face of suffering.

Focusing on the Selection

As you read "The Servant," pay attention to the details about Russian life it conveys. What is the economic situation of the peasant class? What is the relationship between servants and their employers? How does the employer show compassion? How does Gerasim show compassion? How does Yegor Danilych show both compassion and a lack of compassion?

The Servant

$\blacklozenge$ $\blacksquare$ $\blacklozenge$

S. T. Semyonov

I

Gerasim returned to Moscow just at a time when it was hardest to find work, a short while before Christmas, when a man sticks even to a poor job in the expectation of a present. For three weeks the peasant lad had been going about in vain seeking a position.

He stayed with relatives and friends from his village, and although he had not yet suffered great want, it disheartened[1] him that he, a strong young man, should go without work.

Gerasim had lived in Moscow from early boyhood. When still a mere child, he had gone to work in a brewery[2] as bottle-washer, and later as a lower servant in a house. In the last two years he had been in a merchant's employ, and would still have held that position, had he not been summoned back to his village for military duty. However, he had not been drafted. It seemed dull to him in the village, he was not used to the country life, so he decided he would rather count the stones in Moscow than stay there.

Every minute it was getting to be more and more irksome for him to be tramping the streets in idleness. Not a stone did he leave unturned in his efforts to secure any sort of work. He plagued[3] all of his acquaintances, he even held up people on the street and asked them if they knew of a situation—all in vain.

---

[1] **disheartened** (dihs-HAHR-tuhnd) *v.* discouraged
[2] **brewery** (BROO-uh-ree) *n.* a place where beer is manufactured
[3] **plagued** (playgd) *v.* pestered or annoyed

Finally Gerasim could no longer bear being a burden on his people. Some of them were annoyed by his coming to them; and others had suffered unpleasantness from their masters on his account. He was altogether at a loss what to do. Sometimes he could go a whole day without eating.

II

One day Gerasim betook himself to a friend from his village, who lived at the extreme outer edge of Moscow, near Sokolnik. The man was coachman to a merchant by the name of Sharov, in whose service he had been for many years. He had ingratiated[4] himself with his master, so that Sharov trusted him absolutely and gave every sign of holding him in high favour. It was the man's glib[5] tongue, chiefly, that had gained him his master's confidence. He told on all the servants, and Sharov valued him for it.

Gerasim approached and greeted him. The coachman gave his guest a proper reception, served him with tea and something to eat, and asked him how he was doing.

"Very badly, Yegor Danilych," said Gerasim, "I've been without a job for weeks."

"Didn't you ask your old employer to take you back?"

"I did."

"He wouldn't take you again?"

"The position was filled already."

"That's it. That's the way you young fellows are. You serve your employers so-so, and when you leave your jobs, you usually have muddled up the way back to them. You ought to serve your masters so that they will think a lot of you, and when you come again, they will not refuse you, but rather dismiss the man who has taken your place."

"How can a man do that? In these days there aren't any employers like that, and we aren't exactly angels, either."

"What's the use of wasting words? I just want to tell you about myself. If for some reason or other I should ever have to leave this place and go home, not only would Mr. Sharov, if I came back, take me on again without a word, but he would be glad to, too."

Gerasim sat there downcast.[6] He saw his friend was boasting, and it occurred to him to gratify[7] him.

---

[4] **ingratiated** (ihn-GRAY-shee-ayt-ihd) *v.* worked (oneself) into another's good graces
[5] **glib** (glihb) *adj.* smooth speaking but insincere
[6] **downcast** (DOWN-kast) *adj.* depressed; sad
[7] **gratify** (GRAT-uh-feye) *v.* give what is desired; satisfy

"I know it," he said. "But it's hard to find men like you, Yegor Danilych. If you were a poor worker, your master would not have kept you twelve years."

Yegor smiled. He liked the praise.

"That's it," he said. "If you were to live and serve as I do, you wouldn't be out of work for months and months."

Gerasim made no reply.

Yegor was summoned to his master.

"Wait a moment," he said to Gerasim. "I'll be right back."

"Very well."

III

Yegor came back and reported that inside of half an hour he would have to have the horses harnessed, ready to drive his master to town. He lighted his pipe and took several turns in the room. Then he came to a halt in front of Gerasim.

"Listen, my boy," he said, "if you want, I'll ask my master to take you as a servant here."

"Does he need a man?"

"We have one, but he's not much good. He's getting old, and it's very hard for him to do the work. It's lucky for us that the neighbourhood isn't a lively one and the police don't make a fuss about things being kept just so, else the old man couldn't manage to keep the place clean enough for them."

"Oh, if you can, then please do say a word for me, Yegor Danilych. I'll pray for you all my life. I can't stand being without work any longer."

"All right, I'll speak for you. Come again to-morrow, and in the meantime take this ten-kopek[8] piece. It may come in handy."

"Thanks, Yegor Danilych. Then you *will* try for me? Please do me the favour."

"All right. I'll try for you."

Gerasim left, and Yegor harnessed up his horses. Then he put on his coachman's habit, and drove up to the front door. Mr. Sharov stepped out of the house, seated himself in the sleigh, and the horses galloped off. He attended to his business in town and returned home. Yegor, observing that his master was in a good humour, said to him:

"Yegor Fiodorych, I have a favour to ask you."

---

[8] **kopek** (KOH-pehk) *n.* a unit of money in Russia

"What is it?"

"There's a young man from my village here, a good boy. He's without a job."

"Well?"

"Wouldn't you take him?"

"What do I want him for?"

"Use him as man of all work round the place."

"How about Polikarpych?"

"What good is he? It's about time you dismissed him."

"That wouldn't be fair. He has been with me so many years. I can't let him go just so, without any cause."

"Supposing he *has* worked for you for years. He didn't work for nothing. He got paid for it. He's certainly saved up a few dollars for his old age."

"Saved up! How could he? From what? He's not alone in the world. He has a wife to support, and she has to eat and drink also."

"His wife earns money, too, at day's work as charwoman."[9]

"A lot she could have made! Enough for *kvas*."[10]

"Why should you care about Polikarpych and his wife? To tell you the truth, he's a very poor servant. Why should you throw your money away on him? He never shovels the snow away on time, or does anything right. And when it comes his turn to be night watchman, he slips away at least ten times a night. It's too cold for him. You'll see, some day, because of him, you will have trouble with the police. The quarterly inspector will descend on us, and it won't be so agreeable for you to be responsible for Polikarpych."

"Still, it's pretty rough. He's been with me fifteen years. And to treat him that way in his old age—it would be a sin."

"A sin! Why, what harm would you be doing him? He won't starve. He'll go to the almshouse.[11] It will be better for him, too, to be quiet in his old age."

Sharov reflected.

"All right," he said finally. "Bring your friend here. I'll see what I can do."

"Do take him, sir. I'm so sorry for him. He's a good boy, and he's been without work for such a long time. I know he'll do his work well and serve you faithfully. On account of having to report for military duty, he lost his last position. If it hadn't been for that, his master would never have let him go."

---

[9] **charwoman** (CHAHR-wuhm-uhn) *n.* a woman employed to do cleaning
[10] **kvas** (kuh-VAHS) *n.* a light alcoholic beverage
[11] **almshouse** (AHLMZ-hows) *n.* house for the poor

IV

The next evening Gerasim came again and asked:

"Well, could you do anything for me?"

"Something, I believe. First let's have some tea. Then we'll go see my master."

Even tea had no allurements[12] for Gerasim. He was eager for a decision; but under the compulsion[13] of politeness to his host, he gulped down two glasses of tea, and then they betook themselves to Sharov.

Sharov asked Gerasim where he had lived before and what work he could do. Then he told him he was prepared to engage him as a man of all work, and he should come back the next day ready to take the place.

Gerasim was fairly stunned by the great stroke of fortune. So overwhelming was his joy that his legs would scarcely carry him. He went to the coachman's room, and Yegor said to him:

"Well, my lad, see to it that you do your work right, so that I shan't have to be ashamed of you. You know what masters are like. If you go wrong once, they'll be at you forever after with their fault-finding, and never give you peace."

"Don't worry about that, Yegor Danilych."

"Well—well."

Gerasim took leave, crossing the yard to go out by the gate. Polikarpych's rooms gave on the yard, and a broad beam of light from the window fell across Gerasim's way. He was curious to get a glimpse of his future home, but the panes were

Russian artist Ilya Repin painted this interior of a bourgeois Russian home in the early 20th century. Sharov's house may have looked like this one.

---

[12] **allurements** (uh-LOOR-muhnts) *n. pl.* strong attractions
[13] **compulsion** (kuhm-PUL-shuhn) *n.* an influence or urge

all frosted over, and it was impossible to peep through. However, he could hear what the people inside were saying.

"What will we do now?" was said in a woman's voice.

"I don't know, I don't know," a man, undoubtedly Polikarpych, replied. "Go begging, I suppose."

"That's all we can do. There's nothing else left," said the woman. "Oh, we poor people, what a miserable life we lead. We work and work from early morning till late at night, day after day, and when we get old, then it's 'Away with you!'"

"What can we do? Our master is not one of us. It wouldn't be worth the while to say much to him about it. He cares only for his own advantage."

"All the masters are so mean. They don't think of any one but themselves. It doesn't occur to them that we work for them honestly and faithfully for years, and use up our best strength in their service. They're afraid to keep us a year longer, even though we've got all the strength we need to do their work. If we weren't strong enough, we'd go of our own accord."[14]

"The master's not so much to blame as his coachman. Yegor Danilych wants to get a good position for his friend."

"Yes, he's a serpent.[15] He knows how to wag his tongue. You wait, you foul-mouthed beast, I'll get even with you. I'll go straight to the master and tell him how the fellow deceives him, how he steals the hay and fodder.[16] I'll put it down in writing, and he can convince himself how the fellow lies about us all."

"Don't, old woman. Don't sin."

"Sin? Isn't what I said all true? I know to a dot what I'm saying, and I mean to tell it straight out to the master. He should see with his own eyes. Why not? What can we do now anyhow? Where shall we go? He's ruined us, ruined us."

The old woman burst out sobbing.

Gerasim heard all that, and it stabbed him like a dagger. He realized what misfortune he would be bringing the old people, and it made him sick at heart. He stood there a long while, saddened, lost in thought, then he turned and went back into the coachman's room.

"Ah, you forgot something?"

"No, Yegor Danilych." Gerasim stammered out, "I've come—listen—I want to thank you ever and ever so much—for the way you received me—and—and all the trouble you took for me—but—I can't take the place."

---

[14] **of our own accord** without assistance; by ourselves
[15] **serpent** (SER-puhnt) *n.* a sly or dangerous person; like a snake
[16] **fodder** (FAHD-uhr) *n.* food for horses or cattle

"What! What does that mean?"

"Nothing. I don't want the place. I will look for another one for myself."

Yegor flew into a rage.

"Did you mean to make a fool of me, did you, you idiot? You come here so meek—'Try for me, do try for me'—and then you refuse to take the place. You rascal, you have disgraced me!"

Gerasim found nothing to say in reply. He reddened, and lowered his eyes. Yegor turned his back scornfully and said nothing more.

Then Gerasim quietly picked up his cap and left the coachman's room. He crossed the yard rapidly, went out by the gate, and hurried off down the street. He felt happy and lighthearted.

POSTREADING

Critical Thinking

1. How does S. T. Semyonov reveal his attitude toward the coachman, Yegor Danilych?

2. What does this story tell you about the economic situation of the working class in Russia?

3. How has reading this selection helped you understand what it means to sacrifice something?

Writing Your Response to "The Servant"

In your journal, write about your response to the story. Think of a time you wanted something very badly. What would have changed your mind about getting what you wanted?

Going Back Into the Text: Author's Craft

Even though "The Servant" is a work of fiction, it is set within a particular **historical context**. Semyonov uses the political culture and economic conditions of Russia during the 1920s as a backdrop for the story. It is this historical context that motivates the characters to behave in a certain way.

With a partner, review the story and decide what it says about early-20th-century Russia. Use the following questions as guidelines in your discussion.

1. What historical information about Russia does the author give?

2. What do you think motivated Yegor to behave as he did?

3. What other stories do you know that are set within a historical context?

PREREADING

If Not Still Higher

Reading the Story in a Cultural Context

Isaac Loeb Peretz wrote in both Hebrew and Yiddish. He is best known for his short stories, though he also wrote plays, poetry, and essays. Peretz grew up in Poland with a strict Orthodox Jewish education. One of his neighbors recognized his extraordinary intelligence in interpreting the Talmud, the book of Jewish law, and gave young Isaac the key to his library. Thus, at the age of fifteen, Peretz began to read books in French, German, Polish, and English, all of which he taught himself with the aid of dictionaries. His writing reflects his Jewish upbringing and studies. His best work is about the Eastern European mystical lore that is found in Jewish, or Hasidic, monologues, romances, and folktales. His collection of sketches, *Travel Pictures*, depicted life in a Jewish *shtetl*, or town, particularly the poverty and starvation found there. He also wrote allegories, stories that use symbols to convey their meanings. Peretz's allegories dealt with the social concerns of his time, especially those that affected Jewish life throughout the world. His broad interests, which included history, science, social welfare, and Jewish national survival, all appear in his writing.

"If Not Still Higher" is Peretz's most popular Hasidic tale. The story comes from a legend about a rabbi who disguised himself as a peasant and brought firewood to a sickly old widow.

In the story, the rabbi disappears every Friday morning, just before the Sabbath, the day of rest and worship that all Jews observe. The rabbi's followers have convinced themselves that he must go to heaven, where he prays for them. Curious about the rabbi's true whereabouts, a Lithuanian villager determines to follow him.

Focusing on the Selection

As you read "If Not Still Higher," think about the message that the author is trying to convey. Why do you think the Rabbi disguised himself? How does the Rabbi show compassion? How does the way in which the author tells the story contribute to its effect?

If Not Still Higher

━━━━━ ◆ ◆ ◆ ━━━━━

Isaac Loeb Peretz

And the Rabbi of Nemirov,[1] early every Friday morning, disappears. He melts into thin air! He is not to be found anywhere, either in the synagogue[2] or worshiping somewhere. And he most certainly is not at home. His door stands open. People go in and out as they please; no one ever steals anything from the rabbi. But there is not a soul in the house.

Where can the rabbi be?

Where should he be, if not in heaven? Yes, the townsfolk decide, surely the rabbi takes weekly trips to heaven. In heaven, that's where he is.

Is it likely that a rabbi should have no affairs on hand with the Holy Days so near?

The rabbi's followers need a livelihood,[3] peace, health, successful matchmakings.[4] They wish to be good and pious,[5] and their sins are great. Satan with his thousand eyes spies out the world from one end to the other. He sees and accuses and tells tales. Who shall help if not the rabbi? So think the people of Nemirov.

Once, however, there comes a Lithuanian.[6] And he laughs at the idea of the rabbi's going to heaven. He points out a special bit of the Gemara[7] and hopes it is plain enough. It says that even Moses could not ascend into heaven, but remained suspended 30 inches below it. And who, I ask you, is going to argue with a Lithuanian?

---

[1] **Nemirov** (neh-MEER-awv) *n.* a small town in Poland

[2] **synagogue** (SIHN-uh-gahg) *n.* Jewish house of worship

[3] **livelihood** (LEYEV-lee-hood) *n.* support; way of making a living

[4] **matchmakings** (MACH-mayk-ihngs) *n. pl.* arranging of marriages

[5] **pious** (PEYE-us) *adj.* holy; very religious

[6] **Lithuanian** (lih-thuh-WAY-nee-uhn) *n.* a person from the country of Lithuania

[7] **Gemara** (guh-MAR-uh) *n.* part of the Talmud, a book of Jewish law and custom

What becomes of the rabbi?

"I don't know, and I don't care," says the Lithuanian one Thursday night. And all the while he is determined to find out.

That very same evening, soon after prayers, the Lithuanian steals into the rabbi's room, lays himself down under the rabbi's bed and lies low.

He intends to stay there all night to find out where the rabbi goes and what he does.

Another in his place would have dozed and slept the time away. Not so the Lithuanian.

Day has not broken when he hears the call to prayer.

The rabbi has been awake for some time. The Lithuanian has heard him sighing and groaning for a whole hour. Whoever has heard the groaning of the Rabbi of Nemirov knows what sorrow, what distress of mind, was in every groan. The soul that heard would be dissolved in grief. But the heart of a Lithuanian is of cast iron. The Lithuanian hears and lies still. The rabbi lies still too. The rabbi—long life to him!—lies *upon* the bed, and the Lithuanian *under* the bed.

He confesses afterwards, the Lithuanian, that when he was alone with the rabbi, terror took hold of him. He grew cold all over. An excellent joke, to be left alone with the rabbi before dawn!

But the Lithuanian is dogged.[8] He quivers and shakes like a fish, but he does not budge.

At last the rabbi—long life to him!—rises.

First he does what is proper for a Jew. Then he goes to the wardrobe and takes out a bundle. This contains the dress of a peasant. There are linen trousers, high boots, a long coat, a wide felt hat, and a long, broad leather belt studded[9] with brass nails. The rabbi puts them on.

Out of the pocket of the coat dangles the end of a thick cord, a peasant's cord.

On his way out the rabbi steps into the kitchen, stoops, takes a hatchet, puts it into his belt, and leaves the house. The Lithuanian, who has been watching all this, trembles. But he follows the rabbi out.

A fearful Holy-Day hush broods[10] over the dark streets. It is broken frequently by a cry of supplication[11] or the moan of some sick person behind a window.

The rabbi keeps to the street side and walks in the shadow of the houses.

---

[8] **dogged** (DAW-gihd) *adj.* determined
[9] **studded** (STUD-ihd) *adj.* ornamented; decorated
[10] **broods** (broodz) *v.* hangs over like a dark cloud
[11] **supplication** (sup-luh-KAY-shun) *n.* prayerful and humble request

He glides from one house to the other, the Lithuanian after him. And the Lithuanian hears the sound of his own heartbeat mingle with the heavy footfall of the rabbi. But he follows on, and together they emerge from the town.

Behind the town stands a little wood. The rabbi—long life to him!—enters it. He walks on 30 or 40 paces, and then he stops beside a small tree. And the Lithuanian, with amazement, sees the rabbi take his hatchet and strike the tree. He sees the rabbi strike blow after blow. He hears the tree creak and snap. Then the little tree falls, and the rabbi splits it up into small logs. Then he makes a bundle, binds it round with the cord, throws it on his shoulder, replaces the hatchet in his belt, leaves the wood, and goes back into the town.

In one of the back streets he stops beside a poor, tumbledown little house and taps at the window.

"Who is there?" cries a frightened voice from within.

"I," answers the rabbi in a peasant accent.

"Who is 'I'?" inquires the voice further. And the rabbi answers again in a peasant speech.

"This is Vassil[12] speaking."

"Which Vassil? And what do you want, Vassil?"

"I have wood to sell," says the sham peasant. "Very cheap. Next to nothing."

And without further ado he goes in. The Lithuanian steals in behind him, and sees, in the gray light, a poor room with poor, broken furniture.

The Jewish artist Marc Chagall often depicted Jewish shtetl life in his paintings. In *Above Vitebsk* he portrays a rabbi floating above the shtetl.

In the bed lies a sick woman huddled up in rags, who says bitterly, "Wood to sell. And where am I, a poor widow, to get the money to buy it? Even God does not send such gifts."

"I will give you six groschen[13] worth on credit."

"And how am I ever to repay you?" groans the poor woman.

"Foolish creature!" The rabbi scolds her. "See here. You are a poor sick woman, and I am willing to trust you with the little bundle of wood. I believe that in time you will repay. And you, you

---

[12] **Vassil** (va-SEEL) *n.* a common first name for a man in Poland
[13] **groschen** (GROH-shuhn) *n.* a small Polish coin

have such a great, mighty God, and you do not trust Him! Not even to the amount of a miserable six groschen for a little bundle of wood!"

"And who is to light the stove?" moans the widow. "Do I look like getting up to do it? And my son away at work!"

"I will light the stove for you," says the rabbi.

And he lays the wood in the stove. Then he waits and watches the wood crackle merrily. Finally, when the fire is burning perfectly, he closes the stove door.

The Lithuanian, who sees all of this, remains with the rabbi as one of his most devoted followers.

And later, when anyone tells how the rabbi, early on Friday mornings, raises himself and flies up to heaven, the Lithuanian, instead of laughing, adds quietly, "If not still higher."

POSTREADING

Critical Thinking

1. How does Isaac Loeb Peretz reveal his attitude toward the rabbi?

2. What aspects of Jewish belief are portrayed in the story?

3. Has someone ever secretly done a favor for you? What did the person do and how did it make you feel? Is there someone for whom you would like to do a favor? Tell what you would do for the person and why.

Writing Your Response to "If Not Still Higher"

In your journal, write about the part of the story that affected you most strongly. Why is it meaningful to you? Does it relate to an experience or person in your own life? If so, explain how.

Going Back Into the Text: Author's Craft

The way in which an author tells a story is called **style**. This includes a writer's choice of words, sentence structure, use of figurative language, rhythms, and even the tense. For instance, in "If Not Still Higher," Peretz chooses to tell the story in the present tense. The action appears to be happening as the reader reads the story, not some time in the past. Peretz expresses much using few words. In fact, he was strongly against using any unnecessary words in telling a story.

As you review the author's style in the story, use these questions as guidelines.

1. How would you describe the author's style in this story?

2. Why do you think the author chose to write the story in the present tense?

3. Can you think of a story with a very different style than this one? How might this story be different if told in that style?

PREREADING

And When Summer Comes to an End...

Please Give This Seat to an Elderly or Disabled Person

Reading the Poems in a Cultural Context

Nina Cassian grew up in a city in Transylvania populated by Romanians, Germans, Hungarians, and Jews. In her view, this multicultural background helped build in her a respect for people of all backgrounds and religions. When she was eleven, her family moved to Bucharest. Her father could not find work and her family lived in poor conditions. She was fortunate, however, to attend a private school on charity. When the Fascists took control of Romania, she was expelled and required to attend a high school for Jewish girls. It was there that she became a Communist. She believed that Communism would solve all of society's problems. Later in her life, she would realize her mistake.

Following World War II, Cassian published her first book of poetry, *On the Scale of One to One*. Her often surreal poems, filled with rich, metaphorical language, angered the authorities, who branded her as an enemy of the people. She tried to tone down her style and use only easy-to-understand words, but her lyrical language nevertheless shone through in her writing. Finally, she gave up writing altogether and turned to composing music, where she could not be accused of challenging the government. After the death of Stalin, in 1953, she was allowed to write again.

In 1985, she came to the United States to teach a course in creative writing. She had every intention of returning to her homeland. However, while she was in this country, Soviet police discovered writings of Cassian's that were highly critical of the government. The authorities emptied and sealed up the house Cassian had left behind in Bucharest and banned all her writing. They even removed her work from all anthologies, histories, and textbooks.

Both of the poems you will read strongly evoke Cassian's sense of loss and of being out of place. You will see that "And When Summer Comes to an End..." depicts the changing seasons. However, the poem is also about getting older and losing one's place in society.

"Please Give This Seat to an Elderly or Disabled Person" also reflects the author's feelings about old age. In this poem, she is literally out of place, forced to stand during a journey while others refuse to give up their seats. In addition to her age, the poet's "disabilities" further distance her from her fellow passengers.

Focusing on the Selections

As you read the poems, think about the attitudes the poet expresses about change and rejection. What emotions do the poems convey? How does the language reinforce the poet's feelings of being out of place? Think about the effect that is created by the different lengths of the lines.

And When Summer Comes to an End . . .

Nina Cassian

And when summer comes to an end
it's like the world coming to an end.
Wilderness and terror—everywhere!

Days shrink
till all dignity's gone.
Wet slabs of cloth
drape our bodies
dejected coats
And when we shiver, stumbling
into the holes of Winter Street
on the corner of Decline . . .

What's the good of living
with the idea of Spring
—dangerous as any Utopia?[1]

20th-century Russian painter Natalia
Goncharova titled this piece *Self Portrait
with Yellow Lilies.*

Please Give This Seat to an Elderly or Disabled Person

Nina Cassian

I stood during the entire journey:
nobody offered me a seat
although I was at least a hundred years older than anyone else on board,
although the signs of at least three major afflictions
were visible on me:
Pride, Loneliness, and Art.

---

[1] **Utopia** (yoo-TOH-pee-uh) *n.* a perfect society

POSTREADING

Critical Thinking

1. What aspects of Nina Cassian's personal history are conveyed in each poem?

2. How do you think the poet's cultural and historical background influenced her work?

3. How do each of the seasons affect you? Have you ever been ignored when you needed help? Think about how your ideas and feelings are similar to those expressed in the poems.

Writing Your Response to "And When Summer Comes to an End" and "Please Give This Seat to an Elderly or Disabled Person"

In your journal, write your reactions to the poems. What phrases or images made the strongest impression on you? How do these poems relate to your own life?

Going Back Into the Text: Author's Craft

Both "And When Summer Comes to an End" and "Please Give This Seat to an Elderly or Disabled Person" are written in **free verse**. Free verse is poetry that does not have a regular rhythmical pattern, or meter. Metrical poetry, on the other hand, has a regular pattern of stresses and line lengths and a predictable rhythm. In free verse, the poet uses whatever rhythms are appropriate to what he or she is saying. Often, free verse is written in the rhythms of everyday speech.

The poet makes up his or her own rules about how long each line should be and where to break the lines. Line length may be determined by the thoughts the poet wants to express or how the poem will look on the page. The line length and word placement tell the reader how to read the poem and where to pause. The poet may emphasize certain ideas by breaking the lines in unusual places.

As you review the poet's use of free verse, use these questions as guidelines:

1. How do these poems demonstrate the use of free verse?

2. How do the length and placement of lines in each poem help to convey the poet's meaning?

3. How do free verse techniques help to make these poems effective? How might they be different if they were written as metrical poetry?

MODEL LESSON

Random Talk . . . ,
The Heirs of Stalin,
Refugees

Responding to Literature

Notice the sidenotes in the margins of "The Heirs of Stalin." These notes reflect one student's reading of the poem by Yevgeny Yevtushenko. The student recognizes the terror that Stalin inspired and the speaker's fear that, even though Stalin is dead, his followers might rise again. Compare this student's observations with your own.

Reading the Poems in a Cultural Context

The following three poems reflect the political oppression that these poets suffered. For two of the authors, the persecution resulted in their deaths. Raisa Blokh's poem "Random Talk . . ." was written while she was imprisoned in one of Hitler's concentration camps. The poem tells about the pain of remembering her former life in the Soviet Union and her realization that she will never again experience her homeland. She died in the concentration camp in 1943.

In his poem, "The Heirs of Stalin," Yevgeny Yevtushenko imagines that the dictator Stalin is only pretending to be dead. He fears that Stalin's followers will carry on his reign of terror and persecution, and he warns Russians to beware of the re-emergence of Stalinism.

Yevtushenko, who is the former Soviet Union's most famous contemporary poet, graduated from Moscow's Gorky Literary Institute in 1952. Shortly after, premier Nikita Khrushchev publicly denounced the former Communist leader Joseph Stalin. Yevtushenko later became a prominent spokesperson for Russian youth and for the new regime's commitment to more liberal policies.

Ilya Krichevsky also wrote of political oppression. His poem "Refugees" eerily foretells his own fate. Krichevsky, a twenty-two-year-old unknown poet, was one of three people killed during the August 1991 attempt by the Russian military to overthrow Mikhail Gorbachev. Along with Yevtushenko, Krichevsky joined other Russians in forming a living ring around the Parliament of Russia to defend it from the approaching tanks. Krichevsky's poem details the bloody conflict of the opposing sides.

Focusing on the Selections

As you read these poems, think about what the authors are trying to communicate to their readers. What does Blokh want the reader to feel about life in a concentration camp? Why does Yevtushenko portray Stalin as only pretending to be dead? How does Krichevsky's foretelling of the dissidents' fates contribute to the poem's message?

Random Talk . . .

Raisa Blokh
translated by *Nina Kossman*

Random talk has blown in
Dear unnecessary words:
The Summer Garden, Fontanka, and Neva.[1]
Where are you flying to, words of passage?
Other people's cities roar here.
Other people's rivers plash.[2]
You're not to be taken, hidden, chased away.
But I must live—not simply reminisce.[3]
So as not to feel pain again.
I will never go again over the snow to the river,
Hiding my cheeks in the Penza kerchief,
My mittened hand in Mother's hand.
This was; it was and is no more.
What is gone, was swept away by the blizzard.
That's why there is so much emptiness and light.

The idealism and festivity portrayed in this painting *The Parade of the Red Army* is typical of Soviet art after the Russian Revolution of 1917.

---

[1] **Summer . . . Neva** (NEE-vuh) *n.* a central garden, a central road, and a river in St. Petersburg Russia

[2] **plash** *v.* splash

[3] **reminisce** (rem-uh-NIHS) *v.* remember and tell of past experiences

The Heirs of Stalin

Yevgeny Yevtushenko
translated by *George Reavey*

Mute was the marble.
                  Mutely glimmered the glass.
Mute stood the sentries,[1]
                  bronzed by the breeze.
But thin wisps of breath
                  seeped from the coffin
when they bore him
                  out the mausoleum[2] doors.
Slowly the coffin floated by,
                  grazing the fixed bayonets.
He was also mute—
           he also!
                  but awesome and mute.
Grimly clenching
           his embalmed fists,
he watched through a crack inside,
                  just pretending to be dead.
He wanted to fix each pallbearer[3]
                  in his memory:
young recruits from Ryazan and Kursk,[4]
in order somehow later
                  to collect strength for a sortie,[5]

The first few lines of this poem are unsettling. I sense danger.

I think the speaker is trying to express that Stalin was almost superhuman in his ability to inspire fear in his people. He is cold and hard like glass and marble, but his memory is as alive as ever.

---

[1] **sentries** (SEHN-treez) *n. pl.* soldiers posted at some spot; guards
[2] **mausoleum** (maw-suh-LEE-uhm) *n.* a large and stately tomb
[3] **pallbearer** (PAWL-bair-uhr) *n.* one of the persons who carries the coffin at a funeral
[4] **Ryazan** (ree-uh-ZAN) . . . **Kursk** (kersk) *n.* cities in former Soviet Russia
[5] **sortie** (SAWR-tee) *n.* an armed attack made from a place surrounded by enemy forces

and rise from the earth
                              and get
                                       to them,
                                                the unthinking.
He has worked out a scheme.
                              He's merely curled up for a nap.
And I appeal
              to our government with a plea:
to double
              and treble[6] the guard at this slab,
so that Stalin[7] will not rise again,
                              and with Stalin—the past.
We sowed crops honestly.
                              Honestly we smelted[8] metal,
and honestly we marched,
                              in ranks as soldiers.
But he feared us.
                    Believing in a great goal, he forgot
that the means must be worthy
                              of the goal's greatness.
He was farsighted.
              Wily[9] in the ways of combat,
he left behind him
              many heirs[10] on this globe.
It seems to me
              a telephone was installed in the coffin.
To someone once again
                    Stalin is sending his instructions.
To where does the cable yet go
                              from that coffin?

I think the poet is speaking figuratively. He is frightened that Stalinism, or a political regime like that of Stalin, will come to power again.

I wonder what kind of means Stalin used. I will check my history textbook.

---

[6] **treble** (TREHB-ul) v. triple

[7] **Stalin** (STAH-lihn) n. Joseph Stalin, a Soviet dictator; as head of the government and the Communist Party, Stalin was known for his widespread use of terrorism

[8] **smelted** (SMEHLT-ihd) v. melted down or fused

[9] **wily** (WEYE-lee) adv. calculating

[10] **heirs** (AIRZ) n. pl. persons who inherit

No, Stalin did not die.
                        He thinks death can be fixed.
We removed
                him
                        from the mausoleum.
But how do we remove Stalin
                        from Stalin's heirs?
Some of his heirs
                tend roses in retirement,
but secretly consider
                        their retirement temporary.
Others
        from platforms rail against Stalin,
but,
    at night,
                yearn for the old days.
It is no wonder Stalin's heirs,
                        with reason today,
visibly suffer heart attacks.
                        They, the former henchmen,[11]
hate a time
            when prison camps are empty,
and auditoriums, where people listen to poetry,
                        are overfilled.
My motherland commands me not to be calm.
Even if they say to me: "Be assured . . ."—
                        I am unable.
While the heirs of Stalin
                are still alive on this earth,
it will seem to me
                that Stalin still lives in the mausoleum.

I think that the heirs to which he refers are the people who worked for Stalin. They could also include people who support the principles of Stalinism.

The speaker distrusts the silence of Stalin's former supporters, just as he distrusts death's power over Stalin.

---

[11] **henchmen** (HEHNCH-mehn) *n. pl.* loyal and trusted followers who obey unquestioningly the orders of their leader

Refugees

Ilya Krichevsky
translated by *Albert C. Todd*

On and on we go over steppes,[1]
forests, swamps, and grasslands,
still yet a long, long way to go,
still yet many who will die in ditches.
. . . .
Fate is harsh: you there will go to the end,
                                    you will not,
you will tell grandchildren all of it,
you will die as the dawn barely breaks,
blinded by a pistol's fire.
But ours is to go on, and on, tearing calluses,
not eating, not sleeping, not drinking,
through forests, hills, and deaths—
                        in an open field!
To live is what we want, we want to live!

---

[1] **steppes** (stehps) *n. pl.* vast, grassy plains, as found in southeastern Europe and Siberia

POSTREADING

Critical Thinking

1. What do Blokh, Yevtushenko, and Krichevsky tell you about their feelings toward their homeland?

2. How do you think the personal and historical backgrounds of these poets influenced their writing?

3. Have you ever felt victimized because of your beliefs? If so, explain how. If not, how might you respond to such an experience?

Writing Your Response to "Random Talk . . . ," "The Heirs of Stalin," and "Refugees"

In your journal, write about a feeling, idea, or image in one of the poems that is especially meaningful to you. Why is it special? In what ways does it relate to your own life?

Going Back Into the Text: Author's Craft

A poet's goal in writing is more than simply to convey a theme, to describe a subject or to play with language. A poet's main intention is to communicate with the reader. This is known as the **author's purpose**. To understand the author's purpose, you must first understand the poem's central idea and experience its emotional impact.

Each of these poems was written in response to a historical or political predicament in which the author found himself or herself. All of the poets tried to communicate their emotional responses to their plight.

As you review the author's purpose in each of the poems, use these questions as guidelines:

1. What is the author's purpose in each poem?

2. How did each of the poets try to accomplish his or her purpose?

3. Did the poets succeed in their purposes? Explain why or why not.

MAKING CULTURAL CONNECTIONS

EUROPE

Every region of the world has monuments. Monuments can be buildings, works of art, natural features, or historic structures. Think about the monuments in your community or state. They say something about your culture in the same way that the monuments in the photos on these pages tell about the cultures to which they belong. Use the photos on these pages to find clues about the cultures in this unit.

Pictured here is Catherine the Great's Winter Palace in St. Petersburg, Russia. Catherine, like other czars before her, used this palace as a winter residence. As many as 100,000 peasants lost their lives during its construction.

The ruins of the Colosseum stand in Rome, Italy, which was the seat of the Roman Empire. Romans gathered in the Colosseum to watch games and sporting events, such as chariot races and sword fights. The Colosseum was so well built that the arena could be flooded for mock naval battles without leaking!

Warsaw, Poland, like many European cities, is a blend of new and old. Many new, modern buildings have been built side by side with old buildings. Here is the old town square in Warsaw.

LINKING
Literature, History, and Culture

What do the photos on this page and the selections in this unit tell you about the cultures of Europe?

▶ Many peasants died while building the Winter Palace. What do "The Servant" and "The Heirs of Stalin" say about the lives of ordinary people under repressive governments?

▶ Many cultures build areas where people can meet and tell stories. What do the stories "If Not Still Higher" and "The Nightingale's Three Bits of Advice" tell you about the writers' cultures?

▶ The people of Rome live with the ruins of past civilizations. How do you think the people of cities such as Sarajevo, as shown in "A Winter's Tale," live with the ruins of the past?

PREREADING

The Bicycle

Reading the Poem in a Cultural Context

Jerzy Harasymowicz's poetry is deeply rooted in his native landscape of the Carpathian mountains and the city of Cracow in Poland. His poems have an almost surreal—that is, fantastic or dreamlike—quality to them. He often incorporates elements of fairy tales. He is considered by some to be a "primitive" poet, intertwining nature-related myths into his poetry. However, his technique is very much a modern one. He usually writes poetry without meter or rhyme and uses many metaphors. His poems have a strong sense of imagery and gentle humor that make them quite popular with readers.

"The Bicycle" is typical of Harasymowicz's poetry. In this fantastical poem, an ordinary bicycle is left behind by some tourists. The bicycle joins a herd of mountain goats where it becomes their leader. As the poem follows the bicycle's adventures, the author evokes the natural landscape and animals of his homeland. By bringing the bicycle to life and giving it the qualities and behaviors of a goat, the author creates a mix of imagery that is quite unexpected. In so doing, he tells a story that is surreal, humorous, and, in the end, moving.

Focusing on the Selection

As you read "The Bicycle," pay attention to both the fantasy and the realism in the poem. What in the poem is real? What is fantasy? How do the realistic elements make the reader accept the fantasy?

The Bicycle

Jerzy Harasymowicz

once
forgotten by tourists
a bicycle joined
a herd
of mountain goats

with its splendidly turned
silver horns
it became
their leader

with its bell
it warned them
of danger

with them
it partook[1]

in romps
on the snow covered
glade

the bicycle
gazed[2] from above
on people walking;
with the goats

it fought
over a goat,
with a bearded buck

it reared up at eagles
enraged
on its back wheel

it was happy
though it never
nibbled at grass

or drank
from a stream

Think about the hidden messages in this poem. What does the bicycle
represent for the author?

---

[1] **partook** (pahr-TUK) *v.* took part, participated
[2] **gazed** (gayzd) *v.* looked intently; stared as in wonder
or expectancy

until once
a poacher
shot it

tempted
by the silver trophy
of its horns

and then
above the Tatras[3] was seen
against the sparkling
January sky

the angel of death erect
slowly
riding to heaven
holding the bicycle's
dead horns.

---

[3] **Tatras** *n.* a mountain range between Czechoslovakia and Poland

POSTREADING

Critical Thinking

1. How does Jerzy Harasymowicz reveal his feelings toward the bicycle?

2. What does Harasymowicz tell you about the landscape of his country?

3. Can you think of other objects that might come to life? What form do you think they would take? What do you think might happen?

Writing Your Response to "The Bicycle"

In your journal, write about your response to the poem. What images made a particular impression on you? Tell what it was about the images that caught your attention.

Going Back Into the Text: Author's Craft

"The Bicycle" combines elements of **fantasy** and **realism**. Fantasy is highly imaginative writing that contains elements not found in real life. Realism, on the other hand, presents details of actual life. "The Bicycle" tells a fanciful story of a bicycle that joins a herd of mountain goats and becomes one of them, while still retaining its form as a bicycle. While the bicycle's experiences are pure fantasy, the description of the goatherd's behavior is accurate. Together, these elements help create a poem that mixes life as it is with unusual possibilities.

Fantasy can be used both to entertain readers and to make a more serious statement. For example, a reader may be amused by the descriptions of the bicycle acting like a goat. But when a poacher shoots the bicycle, the poem becomes more serious and may make the reader consider the effects of shooting an innocent animal.

Use the questions below to review the elements of fantasy in the poem.

1. What parts of the poem are pure fantasy?

2. What parts have realistic details?

3. What do you think is the author's intent?

The Monster

Reading the Story in a Cultural Context

Women in the former Soviet Union work in the same professions as men and receive equal pay for equal work. However, while most men usually have to worry only about keeping their jobs, women often bear an extra burden. They must stand in long lines for scarce food, lug home bags of groceries, do the dishes, clean the house, do the laundry, and take care of the children.

Even with all their domestic responsibilities, most women are still able to cope. In many families, the wife and not the husband is considered the head of the household.

Nina Katerli was born in Leningrad in 1934 and lives there to this day. As with many other Soviet women writers, Katerli has another profession. She graduated from the Lensoviet Technological Institute and worked as an engineer. Her work has greatly influenced her writing. Her stories, which are often written as fantasies or in the style of fairy tales, often have technological elements.

In "The Monster," Katerli writes a humorous story of a household of three women whose lives are controlled by a hideous monster. The story explores the changing attitudes the women have to the monster as it gradually loses its power.

The monster can be looked at in two ways. Some readers may see the monster as representing old age and the frustration people feel as they grow older and are not able to do the things they once did. Aunt Angelina pities the deteriorating monster. She tries to make him believe that he still has his powers. She behaves like a dutiful daughter who cannot accept that her parents are becoming old and sick.

On the other hand, the story can also be read as a comment on the collapse of communism in the Soviet empire. Like the monster, the Communist government was once feared. Now, both the monster and the government have lost the power to control people.

Focusing on the Selection

As you read "The Monster," think about what the monster represents. How is the monster like old age? How is it like a terrifying government? What does the loss of power mean?

The Monster

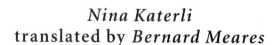

Nina Katerli
translated by *Bernard Meares*

"If only things were the way they used to be," said Aunt Angelina, and wiped her eyes.

"The way they used to be? Thanks very much! That's all I need. The way they used to be." Anna Lvovna could be seen choking back her tears and sniffling. "All my life I've lived in this apartment and cooked soup on a single burner in my own room, and I scarcely use any gas at all. And until very recently I had to go to the public baths, even though we have a bathtub right here. I was afraid to go to the toilet too often, not to mention the way my personal life . . ."

"No, if only things were the way they used to be," Aunt Angelina repeated obstinately. "I simply can't look at him the way he is now."

I myself had gotten used to the Monster, and even as a child had not been very much afraid of him. I was born after he moved into our apartment, so for me there was nothing unusual about coming across a shaggy creature with a single crimson[1] eye in the middle of its forehead and a long scaly tail, whether in the hall near the bathroom or in the kitchen. But why go in for descriptions? One monster's very much like another, and ours was no more monstrous than the next.

They say that before I was born the other tenants in our apartment had filed an application with some agency, requesting that the Monster be evicted and housed someplace else, even that he be given an apartment all to himself. But the application was rejected on the grounds that if all monsters were given individual housing, there would be nothing left for

---

[1] **crimson** (KRIHM-zuhn) *adj.* vivid purplish red

large families. The argument ran that there were too many monsters and too few apartments, and when our application was turned down, the reason given was: "Yours is not the most serious case: There has not been a single fatality or instance of grievous[2] bodily harm."

The fact that Anna Lvovna's husband had been turned into an aluminum saucepan for a whole month did not constitute grievous bodily harm, apparently. They say that as soon as her husband had returned to normal after having had borscht[3] boiled in him and meat stewed in him for a month, he immediately abandoned her. Anna Lvovna was left on her own and since then has never forgiven the Monster for ruining her life.

I don't know how the story would have ended—Anna Lvovna, they say, was threatening to drop a burned out light bulb in the Monster's feeding dish—but at that very time the Monster set off to work as an exhibit in a long traveling exposition organized by the museum of ethnography[4] and anthropology.[5]

In time, the tale about Anna Lvovna's husband came to be forgotten, but as the Monster grew older, he began to turn nasty, and gave us no peace at all.

You'd go into the bathroom and the sink and bathtub would be full of frogs and newts;[6] or suddenly all the refrigerators would

Housing in the former Soviet Union is arranged by the government. Often, several unrelated families share one apartment because housing is scarce. If the people sharing an apartment don't get along, it is very difficult to make a change.

---

[2] **grievous** (GREE-vuhs) *adj.* extremely serious

[3] **borscht** (bawrsht) *n.* a Russian soup containing beets

[4] **ethnography** (ehth-NAHG-ruh-fee) *n.* the systematic recording of human cultures

[5] **anthropology** (an-thruh-PAHL-uh-jee) *n.* the scientific study of the origins and physical, social, and cultural development and behavior of human beings

[6] **newts** (noots) *n. pl.* salamanders or lizardlike animals

begin to howl horribly and heat up, the milk inside them would boil and the meat would roast; or else poor Anna Lvovna's nose would erupt in a boil[7] of amazing size that changed color with each passing day. One day it would be blue, the next day lilac, and the day after that a poisonous green color.

It should be mentioned that Aunt Angelina and the Monster were on somewhat more equable[8] terms. If she found a tortoise in her cupboard instead of bread, she would exclaim with pleasure, "Look a reptile! I'll take it straight to the kindergarten for their pet corner!"

I now realize that when I was little the Monster simply couldn't stand me because I annoyed him so much. Everything I did annoyed him: I clattered up and down the hall and I laughed too loudly and I loved peeking into his room at him. So he kept giving me tonsillitis. Not serious cases, but the kind that if you so much as laugh you lose your voice, and if you run you get sent to bed.

When I grew up, the Monster did me great harm for a time; whenever anyone called me up, he would always get to the phone before the others and hiss, "She's not in. She's gone out with someone else."

I live alone now. My parents are no longer alive, I have never had a family of my own, and Aunt Angelina, with whom I share the apartment, takes care of me after a fashion, but as for the Monster . . . At least he's stopped tormenting me. Of course, if I come back late from the theater or from visiting friends, I'm bound to trip over the cat in the hall even though we've never had a cat. Or I'll tear my new dress on barbed wire. But that's nothing—mere trivialities.[9] And recently even that kind of thing has stopped happening. Something's gone wrong with the Monster. You wouldn't recognize him: his eye has turned from red to a kind of dirty ginger color and his fur has gone gray; to put it in a nutshell, our Monster is getting old. He's stopped going to work and sits for days on end in his room, just hissing occasionally and sometimes sighing. And it was only today that Aunt Angelina said she'd prefer things the way they used to be because it broke her heart to look at the Monster, and she didn't have the energy to sweep up his scales after him.

"About those dreadful scales I totally agree with you, Angelina Nikolayevna," declared Anna Lvovna. "It's disgraceful! He must be made to do an additional week of cleaning duty. Nobody should have to wipe his dirt up after him!"

---

[7] **boil** *n.* a painful, pus-filled swelling of the skin and the tissue beneath it

[8] **equable** (EHK-wuh-buhl) *adj.* even

[9] **trivialities** (trihv-ee-AL-uh-teez) *n. pl.* things that are of little importance

At this point the conversation came to a sudden halt because the Monster's door squeaked loudly, and a minute later there he was in the kitchen.

"Picking on me behind my back, eh?" he asked, and his eye reddened slightly. "Well, now I'm going to make you all freeze. You've never felt such cold!"

And the Monster began to blow so hard that his cheeks turned blue and his head started to tremble.

He blew and blew and suddenly I noticed Aunt Angelina shivering and jumping in place and knocking her legs against each other and rubbing her nose as if it had been frostbitten.

"It's so cold, oh, it's freezing!" she moaned dolefully,[10] for some reason winking at me. Then she suddenly screeched, "What are you standing around like that for? Keep moving! Keep moving! Or else you'll catch your death of cold! Hands on your waist! Bend your knees! One, two, three!"

I wasn't that cold; in fact, I was even rather warm, all the more so because we were in the kitchen and all the gas burners were lit. But Aunt Angelina was winking and shouting so that I, too, put my hands on my hips and started doing knee bends.

"There you go! There you go!" shouted the Monster gleefully. "Now you're going to dance for me!"

I scarcely had time to think before Aunt Angelina grabbed me by the hand and began leaping about in a frenzied[11] dance. I followed her lead.

"This is a nuthouse!" declared Anna Lvovna angrily and left the kitchen.

The Monster stared after her with a frightened look, then turned to Aunt Angelina as she danced and asked quietly, "Why isn't she dancing? Why did she go away?"

"She's stiff with cold!" shouted Aunt Angelina, gasping for breath but continuing to dance. "Can't you see?"

But the Monster had already forgotten what he had been asking. Dragging his tail and leaving a trail of scales across the floor, he went over to his refrigerator and opened the door.

"Where's my bone?" he said in perplexity.[12] "I remember it was here yesterday. I bought it at the store!"

"Your bone? There it is, you made soup out of it this morning, don't you remember?" shouted Aunt Angelina, stamping away, but at the same

---

[10] **dolefully** (DOHL-fuhl-lee) *adv.* very sadly
[11] **frenzied** (FREHN-zeed) *adj.* filled with wild excitement
[12] **perplexity** (puhr-PLEHK-sih-tee) *n.* confusion; puzzlement

time managing to pass the Monster her own white enamel saucepan with soup in it.

"I did? Oh . . ." and the Monster looked uncertainly into the saucepan, "I never had a pot like this."

"But it really is your pot, I just cleaned it up a bit, that's all."

"Aaargh!" he roared, "You dare touch my pot? I forbid you to! For that both of you will . . . you will both . . . turn to stone for thirty-five minutes!"

Aunt Angelina suddenly froze the way children do when they play Statues. As fate would have it, my nose started itching and I was about to rub it with my hand when she inconspicuously[13] but painfully jabbed me in the side, so I froze, too.

The Monster glared at us triumphantly, then grabbed the boiled chicken out of Aunt Angelina's saucepan and ate it whole.

"A delicious bone!" he rumbled, licking his lips, and then took pity on us.

"You can go now," he said dismissively,[14] and strode imperiously[15] out of the kitchen, slurping soup from the top of the saucepan.

"Why did you give him your entire dinner?" I asked, when the door closed behind the Monster. "And where is his bone, anyway?"

"He didn't have a bone!" said Aunt Angelina, "He hasn't been to the store for a week."

"Then what's he looking for?"

"God knows! Maybe he forgot. Or maybe he's just being that way to show us that everything's all right. But he doesn't have any money, not a single kopeck,[16] and he's going hungry."

"What about his pension?"

"He doesn't have a pension! He's an exhibition object, and . . . he's been written off, dropped from the show." Aunt Angelina lowered her voice. "It's as if he doesn't exist. And now I'm afraid about his room. I'm afraid he'll be evicted. Just make sure you don't tell Anna Lvovna."

"I won't breathe a word," I said, also in a whisper.

Aunt Angelina and I began taking turns buying bones and chopped meat from the butcher and leaving them in the Monster's refrigerator. On one occasion she left two apples and a small carton of kefir.[17]

---

[13] **inconspicuously** (ihn-kuhn-SPIHK-yoo-uhs-lee) *adv.* not noticeably

[14] **dismissively** (dihs-MIHS-ihv-lee) *adv.* directing someone to leave

[15] **imperiously** (ihm-PEER-ee-uhs-lee) *adv.* with overbearing self-importance

[16] **kopeck** (KOH-pehk) *n.* a coin worth 1/100 of a ruble, a unit of money of the former Soviet Union

[17] **kefir** (keh-FER) *n.* a beverage of fermented cow's milk

"All this meat's very bad for him! It can ruin his digestion," she said. "I wanted to buy him a big bottle of kefir but he always immediately bolts any food he has, so I bought a carton instead."

"He's bound to throw out the apples," I said.

"We'll see. Maybe he won't realize. Lately his eyesight's been getting poor," and at that moment Aunt Angelina looked around at the door; Anna Lvovna was just coming into the kitchen.

"It makes me laugh just to look at the two of you," she declared. "All this undercover charity—do you think I'm blind? Such pretense—what a show! And for whom! If he was human, it would be one thing, but he's not, he's just vermin."[18]

"You should feel sorry for him; after all, he's old," I said.

"My dear, pity's not a feeling you should brag about, pity's humiliating. And in this case," she said as she put her coffeepot on the stove, "in this case, pity doesn't enter into it. It was one thing when he was making himself useful in his . . . in his freak show; we could put up with him then, but not now. Animals should live in the wild."

The Monster had crept into the kitchen so softly that we didn't even know he was there. He now stood in the doorway and his eye was as ruddy[19] as it had been in the first flush of youth.

"So, I'm an animal, am I?" he said slowly and slumped onto a stool. "I'll show you."

His breathing was heavy and irregular, the sparse gray fur on his head and neck stood on end.

"I'll show you. . . . Your . . . legs . . . will . . . give way . . . beneath you! . . . Yeah! . . . You will . . . all . . . fall . . . on the floor . . . and then . . . One, two, three . . . All fall down!"

Aunt Angelina and I collapsed simultaneously.[20] Anna Lvovna remained standing, leaning against the edge of the stove, and grinned, staring the Monster straight in the eye.

"And you?" said the Monster. "What about you? This doesn't mean you, I suppose? Fall down, I tell you!"

"Give me one good reason why I should," she said, scowling.

"Because I've put a spell on you, that's why."

"Oh, you slay me," said Anna Lvovna, going right up to him. "What have we here, a magician? All you know how to do is leave your scales all

---

[18] **vermin** (VER-mihn) *n.* an insect or rodent that is destructive or annoying

[19] **ruddy** (RUD-ee) *adj.* having a healthy pink or reddish color

[20] **simultaneously** (seye-muhl-TAY-nee-ahs-lee) *adv.* at the same time

over the floor and help yourself to everyone else's food! You're just trash and you're due for the dump! Just garbage. You've been written off!"

"Written off?" repeated the Monster in a whisper. "Who's been written off? Me? Written off? Not true, not true! I can do anything! Look at them! They fell down!"

"Ha! Ha! Ha!" Anna Lvovna burst out laughing. "They're just pretending. They're sorry for you, see. You've been written off. You've lost your job. I've been to the museum myself and I've seen the directive with my own eyes."

"No!" The Monster leapt up from the stool and rushed from the door to the stove, thrashing his mangy[21] tail across the floor. "I'll show you. I'll turn you into a rat! A rat! Now!"

"Ha! Ha! Ha!" was Anna Lvovna's only reply, and suddenly she stamped on the Monster's tail with all her might.

The Monster screamed. One after another great tears streamed from his eye, which immediately turned pale blue and dimmed. Aunt Angelina and I jumped up from the floor.

"You ought to be ashamed of yourself! Let him go! An old man. Don't be so cruel to him!"

"A rat! A rat!" hissed the Monster, forgetting himself, and he poked Anna Lvovna in the shoulder with a dark and crooked finger. "One! Two! Three!"

"Ha! Ha! Ha!" sniggered Anna Lvovna.

But now Aunt Angelina and I began to shout. "A rat! A rat!" we screamed. "You're a rotten rat! Vermin! One! Two! Three!"

Suddenly Anna Lvovna was gone.

She had just been laughing in our faces, her shoulders shaking in her white blouse, when suddenly she was no more. She had totally disappeared, as if she had never existed.

The kitchen suddenly fell silent. Something live jabbed against my foot and immediately leapt away to the wall. I screeched and jumped onto the stool.

A large gray rat shot across the kitchen and scuttled under Anna Lvovna's table. The Monster was whimpering softly, his face turned toward the wall.

"See," said Aunt Angelina, "you did it. Don't cry. Now let's go and have some soup."

---

[21] **mangy** (MAYN-jee) *adj.* shabby

"It's you who did it, not me. And it's true, you know; I have been written off. There has been a directive."[22]

"What do we care about directives," said Aunt Angelina, carefully stroking the Monster's fur. "Don't you be afraid of anybody. And if anybody touches you I'll give him . . . I'll give him ants."

"And so will I," I said. "Okay?"

The Monster didn't reply. Slumped against the wall, he dozed off, shutting his eye and wrapping his thin hairless tail around his legs.

---

[22] **directive** (dih-REHK-tihv) *n.* an order or instruction

POSTREADING

Critical Thinking

1. What does this story reveal about Nina Katerli's attitude toward communism or old age?

2. In what ways does the story reflect the culture in which it was written?

3. Have you ever gone along with someone or a group even though you felt they were wrong? If so, why? If not, why not?

Writing Your Response to "The Monster"

In your journal, write about one character in the story. Which character is most like you? Why? If you were in the same situation as the human characters, what might you do?

Going Back Into the Text: Author's Craft

Metaphor is a figure of speech that uses imagery to describe something by saying it is something else. Writers often use metaphor to help readers better understand ideas and feelings. Metaphors are not intended to be taken literally. Instead, they are used to add color to writing by comparing and contrasting unlike things. For example, a cowardly person might be called a chicken, or a person with great beauty could be called a rose.

Sometimes, as in this story, metaphor is used to convey a larger theme or idea. With a partner, review this story to see how Katerli uses the monster as a metaphor. These questions can serve as guidelines.

1. What do you think the monster represents?

2. How do the physical characteristics and actions of the monster serve to reinforce the metaphor?

3. What other metaphor could Katerli have used in place of the monster?

PREREADING

A Winter's Tale

Reading the Essay in a Cultural Context

Before you read this selection, check a map and locate the region in Eastern Europe known as the Balkans. Certain countries of the Balkans—Croatia, Bosnia-Herzegovina—are the focus of this writer's concern.

Slavenka Drakulić grew up in Sarajevo. This city was once part of Yugoslavia, but in 1991, when Yugoslavia broke apart, Sarajevo became part of the new nation of Bosnia. It also became a city of conflict as ancient feuds among the people of the Balkans erupted into a long and ugly war. It was a war that many people in the United States did not understand. By the time the war had broken out, Slavenka Drakulić had grown up and become a writer.

In 1992, Drakulić published a book called *The Balkan Express*. This book is a collection of "half-stories, half-essays." Many of these first appeared in magazines and newspapers in the United States and in other countries. Says Drakulić, "This is not the book about the war as we see it every day on our television screens or read about it in the newspapers. *The Balkan Express* picks up where the news stops . . . because the war is happening not only at the front, but everywhere and to us all."

For Drakuli´c, the war is "like a monster, a mythical creature coming from somewhere far away." At first she tries to convince herself that it will not affect her life, but then the monster closes in on her and she begins to "breathe in death." The essays and stories that she includes in *The Balkan Express* are her attempts to communicate to the world through analysis and personal stories the way war changes people from within. "A Winter's Tale" is from this book.

Focusing on the Selection

As you read "A Winter's Tale," think about the comparisons that the writer makes between life in the West and life in a war-torn land. How does Slavenka Drakulić make her readers see the war from within?

A Winter's Tale

$\blacklozenge\;\blacklozenge\;\blacklozenge$

Slavenka Drakulić

A mulberry tree in my yard is covered with ice, its tiny twigs forming a fine lace on my window. Snow in Vienna still has its innocent white color. Christmas is in the air.

I am sitting at my table, reading newspapers that I bought at the train station. This morning, I am reading an article in the Bosnian[1] daily *Oslobodjenje* about food rations in Sarajevo:[2] 150 grams of bread daily per person, 6.5 grams of potatoes, 6 grams of rice. And as I read these numbers, I become aware of the slice of bread I am holding in my hand. I look at it, as if I see it for the first time: How much is 150 grams? Could it be just one slice, like the one I am now reluctantly chewing? Or is 150 grams two, or maybe three, slices? And if so, what can one do with that? I am almost tempted to get up and put the piece of bread on a scale, but then I give up. The exercise would be pointless. How could 150 grams ever be enough?

Then I remember that I wanted to cook potatoes for lunch today— only as a side dish, of course. But as I fix my gaze on the text, 6.5 grams of potatoes is no longer abstract[3]—it is absurd. It can't be even a single potato; as I imagine a plate with it in front of me, not a single one. In *7,000 Days in Siberia*, his memoir of life in Stalin's gulag,[4] Karlo Stajner wrote: "'We got 600 grams of bread, tea and nine grams of sugar today." I put the newspaper down and look at my table. There is butter, milk, jam, one egg and a cup of coffee. I like to drink strong espresso[5] in the morning. This

---

[1] **Bosnian** (BAHZ-nee-uhn) *adj.* of Bosnia, a region in the former Yugoslavia
[2] **Sarajevo** (SAHR-uh-yeh-voh) *n.* city in the former Yugoslavia and the former capital of Bosnia
[3] **abstract** (AB-strakt) *adj.* something that is not concrete
[4] **gulag** (GOO-lahg) *n.* a labor camp of the former Soviet Union
[5] **espresso** (eh-SPREHS-oh) *n.* a strong coffee brewed by forcing steam through finely ground, darkly roasted coffee beans

morning, however, my espresso tastes different. I know that I am not in Sarajevo, but today, looking at snow falling and thinking about bread, somehow I am there. Or, at least, I feel that I am not completely present here.

When I was a child, we used to get packages from our relatives in America. They would send us beautifully smelling soaps and cocoa, pink chewing gum, silk stockings, razor blades, delicious chocolates and cans of instant coffee. I used to wonder what life would look like in a country of such richness. But then I did not wish to be an American. Now I wish just that. Or to be a Swede, perhaps an Austrian, a citizen of any country where there is no war, where people decorate their Christmas trees, have a family dinner and give nice little presents to each other. But I am from the bloodstained Balkans. And even if Croatia[6] is not quite "there" (which is, at least, what we Croats[7] would like to believe), millions of fine threads link me: language, home, relatives, friends, news. The difference between me and any Viennese citizen is that I can't forget all that.

I am also a writer. Not long ago, I wrote about the coming of winter in Bosnia, about a need to do something to stop the carnage.[8] But reading about rations[9] in Sarajevo only makes me aware of my own failure: it is impossible for me to write about the second winter of dying, hunger and cold, for whatever I write is not going to change a thing. Besides, write for

These Bosnian refugees have been evacuated from their homes because fighting has put them in danger. They will stay in gymnasiums like this indefinitely.

---

[6] **Croatia** (kroh-AY-shuh) *n.* a region in the former Yugoslavia
[7] **Croats** (KROH-ahts) *n. pl.* people from Croatia
[8] **carnage** (KAHR-nihj) *n.* great and bloody slaughter
[9] **rations** (RASH-uhnz) *n. pl.* food issued or available to members of a group

whom? For the politicians? For them, the case is more or less closed. For the international news media? For them, everything has already happened. What story could rival all that has taken place: concentration camps, the suffering of children, the bombing of the Mostar bridge? The world has seen it all before, meticulously[10] documented by countless TV cameras and described by millions of words. The world has even seen live transmissions of death, like the one recently on "Nightline," when two people in Mostar died in front of the TV cameras, one of them a child. What more can one see?

No one is innocent regarding what is going on in this war. Everyone knows—we all do. Very few people can say that their work has made a difference. On the contrary, there is a growing business centered around Sarajevo and Bosnia, and, sadly, the limelight[11] is too often on the participants, not the public. There are lots of books, theatrical productions, documentaries. Bernard Henri-Levy, a French philosopher, made the film *Sarajevo*. Susan Sontag staged Beckett's *Waiting for Godot*. Jenny Holzer printed the cover of *Suddeutsche Zeitung* magazine with blood donated by refugee[12] women. I don't doubt their good intentions. All I say is that if attention and understanding alone could save Sarajevo, then it would have been saved long ago.

As I sit at my table on a quiet, ordinary winter day, I feel helpless for the first time. My words—any words—have no real meaning. I am sick and tired of them. Finally, all we have achieved with words is to establish Sarajevo as a metaphor[13] for tragedy. So what? Are people there going to suffer less of cold because of our good intentions? Will it help them survive, if they get 150 grams of bread? I doubt it, and this doubt, like an acid, is eating me from the inside. I can write about the war as long as I believe in the power of communication and in my own moral right to do it. But today, thinking of bread and potatoes, I feel I do not believe in that power any longer. I somehow have used all my words, given to me as a writer, to make people understand pain, fear and suffering. With the coming winter in Bosnia, I am afraid that my words would just melt away, like this first snow falling over Vienna.

Zagreb[14]
January 1992

---

[10] **meticulously** (muh-TIHK-yuh-luhs-lee) *adv.* very carefully and precisely
[11] **limelight** (LEYEM-leyet) *n.* the center of public attention
[12] **refugee** (rehf-yoo-JEE) *n.* person who flees his or her country to escape oppression or persecution
[13] **metaphor** (MEHT-uh-fawr) *n.* a figure of speech in which two unlike things are compared
[14] **Zagreb** (ZAH-grehb) *n.* the capital of Croatia

POSTREADING

Critical Thinking

1. How does Slavenka Drakulić feel about the war in Bosnia?

2. Why is it hard to break the "threads" that link the writer to her homeland?

3. Have you ever felt powerless about something that mattered greatly to you? How did you try and resolve your feelings and the situation?

Writing Your Response to "A Winter's Tale"

In her despair, Slavenka Drakulić writes: "Very few people can say that their work has made a difference." In your journal, record your response to these words. Do you want to make a difference? What do you want to do? How will you do it?

Going Back Into the Text: Author's Craft

One way that a writer can make things clear for readers is with **comparisons**. A comparison shows how things are similar or how they differ. Usually a comparison starts with something that is familiar to the reader and then shows how this relates to something new or unfamiliar.

As you read this selection, use the following questions to help you identify the comparisons:

1. How does Slavenka Drakulić compare Vienna in winter with a winter in Sarajevo?

2. What comparisons does Drakulić make between her breakfast and the rations in Bosnia?

3. Why does she compare her feelings about her homeland as a child and at the time of writing?

Reviewing the Region

1. Choose two authors from this chapter. Compare and contrast their attitudes toward the culture in which they are writing.

2. Poetry is often a powerful means of expressing cultural values and beliefs. Choose a poem from this chapter and give examples of the ways in which the author reveals his or her beliefs.

3. In many of the selections in this chapters, the narrators or characters find themselves in situations over which they have no control. Have you ever found yourself in such a situation? Compare your response to that of a narrator or character from the chapter.

7 Western Europe

Since the time of the ancient empires, literature has been a prominent aspect of European life. Ancient Greece produced great writers, such as Homer, who wrote such classic tales as *The Iliad* and *The Odyssey.* They are still among the most popular works of literature today. This chapter begins with the oath of loyalty taken by young men at the height of Greek civilization.

From the Renaissance, with its emphasis on the ancients, sprang the Enlightenment, which focused on the individual and reason. A selection in this chapter comes from the French Enlightenment.

Nationalism also plays a strong role in Europe's literary history. Jakob and Wilhelm Grimm of Germany roamed the German countryside collecting folktales for their well-known book, *Grimm's Fairy Tales.* In this chapter, you will find a tale from Ireland that preserves Irish folk history in the same way the tales that Grimm collected did in Germany.

Turmoil in Europe at the start of the 20th century had a great impact on literature. You will read an excerpt

from the life story of a survivor of Hitler's death camps of World War II. Three poems also reflect the chaotic political situation created by both world wars.

Contemporary European literature dealt with the everyday lives and struggles of the working class. You will read two stories that characterize life in Germany and Spain.

As you read the selections in this chapter, listen to the different voices. How do these stories help you understand the countries in which they were written?

This decorative "mosaic" is made of painted tiles cemented together. It was made in the third century A.D. by a Roman artist in present-day France. The people in the mosaic are harvesting grapes, which are still a common crop in France and Italy.

The Oath of Athenian Youth

Reading the Selection in a Cultural Context

Democracy was born in the civilization of ancient Greece. Citizenship was important to the people of Athens, Greece. All Athenians participated in making the laws, and every citizen was allowed to vote. Of course, not everyone had the good fortune to be granted citizenship. Women and foreigners could never become citizens, nor could slaves.

The Athenians placed the highest importance on education. Freeborn boys (those who were not born into slavery) began their education at age six and continued until age fourteen or sixteen. At school they learned reading, writing, and arithmetic, as well as music and gymnastics—much the same curriculum we have today. Girls were educated at home by their mothers or nurses. While they did learn to read and write, they were taught mostly domestic skills, such as weaving, embroidering, and music.

At age sixteen, when they had completed their formal studies, boys turned their attention to physical exercises that would prepare them for war. At age eighteen, they became soldiers and received training for two years in the duties of a citizen and a soldier. They lived and ate together, wore uniforms, and were supervised day and night. For the first year, they had to undergo strenuous drills and attend lectures on literature, music, and geometry.

When they reached age nineteen, the Athenian youths were entrusted with protecting the city against attack from invaders, as well as riots by its citizens. Before they were entrusted with this duty, however, they each had to take the oath that you are about to read. The oath was taken during an elaborate and solemn ceremony.

"The Oath of Athenian Youth" details both the actions that had to be taken and those that had to be avoided to become a good citizen of Athens.

Focusing on the Selection

As you read "The Oath of Athenian Youth," think about the qualities of citizenship that this pledge evokes. What do you think the author wanted to accomplish with the oath? Why do you think the Athenian youths had to make a pledge?

The Oath of Athenian Youth

Anonymous

We will never bring disgrace to this, our community, by any act of dishonesty or cowardice.

We will fight for the ideals and sacred things of the community, both alone and with many.

We will revere and obey the community's laws, and will do our best to incite[1] a like reverence and respect in those above us who might try to annul[2] them or set them at naught.[3] We will try always to improve the public's sense of civic duty.

Thus, in all these ways, we will transmit this community, not only not less, but greater, better, and more beautiful than it was transmitted to us.

This marble sculpture from 450–425 B.C. represents the classical and idealized model of a Greek youth.

---

[1] **incite** (in-SEYET) *v.* arouse
[2] **annul** (uh-NUL) *v.* reduce to nothing
[3] **naught** (nawt) *n.* nothingness

POSTREADING

Critical Thinking

1. How does the writer of this oath reveal his feelings about his country?

2. What kind of a society does this oath reflect?

3. Do you think young adults in today's society should pledge an oath to their country? If so, what should be in the oath? If not, why not?

Writing Your Response to "The Oath of Athenian Youth"

Write about your reactions to this oath in your journal. What do you think are the most important pledges in this oath? Do you think this oath is still valid today? Explain why you think as you do.

Going Back Into the Text: Author's Craft

All authors write to communicate something to their readers. This is known as **author's purpose**. For instance, a writer may want to make readers laugh or move them to tears. A writer may write to inform, to enlighten, or to persuade readers to take action. "The Oath of Athenian Youth" asks those who recite it to make some specific pledges and contributions to the community.

As you review the author's purpose in "The Oath of Athenian Youth," use these questions as guidelines:

1. Why do you think this oath was written?

2. What did the Athenian youths promise to do? What did they promise not to do?

3. Do you think the writer of this oath succeeded in his purpose? Explain why you think the way you do.

The Nightingale's Three Bits of Advice

Reading the Story in a Cultural Context

French folktales have a long history, dating at least as far back as the mid-16th century. In those days, country folk told stories about their daily lives. Then, in the late 17th century, the French replaced their folktales with fantasies made up by literary writers. In 1697, however, a collection of folktales published by Charles Perrault brought back the traditional tale, which has come to represent French folklore ever since.

Henri Pourrat began collecting folktales when he was a boy, and continued for nearly fifty years. He was a native of Auvergne, a beautiful rural region situated in the middle of France. By gathering the folklore of his community, he hoped to capture and preserve the culture of the French people.

In 1905, Pourrat suffered from tuberculosis, a disease which had already caused the death of his brother. While he recovered, his delicate health required him to lead a quiet, restrained life. He turned to writing poems and stories as well as gathering folktales and folksongs. In time, he became one of the major regional writers of 20th-century France. That meant that instead of migrating to Paris and writing about the city like many of his contemporaries, he remained at home and wrote of the people and their lives in his own region. In his writing and retelling of folktales, from the lives of ordinary peasants, Pourrat recorded a kind of universal nature of mankind.

"The Nightingale's Three Bits of Advice" is a very short tale with a universal theme. In fact, this is a tale that has been told in one form or another throughout the world. In the story, a villager captures a nightingale. The bird convinces him that he will gain three pieces of advice that he will find useful. The nightingale gives the man his advice and he is set free. But the nightingale decides to test the man to see if he really took the advice. One by one, the villager discards the wise bird's pieces of advice until he realizes that he is a fool.

Focusing on the Selection

As you read "The Nightingale's Three Bits of Advice," observe how the nightingale sets up what will happen. How does the nightingale prove his cleverness? How does the bird show the man to be a fool?

The Nightingale's Three Bits of Advice

Henri Pourrat
translated by *Royall Tyler*

There was once a villager who, seeing winter now over with all its cold and snow, and spring at last coming back to the fields, set out his traps to catch small birds. People normally do that in the dead of the year, in the snow. By now, the thorn hedges were in leaf, and daffodils were blooming in the meadows around the mill. But he was lucky. He managed to catch a nightingale.

He was going to stifle the nightingale under his thumb when it spoke to him.

"Man," said the nightingale, "what will you gain by killing me? Weigh me and see. I won't fill your belly. On the contrary, let me fly free, and you'll gain three pieces of advice which will serve you wonderfully well, if only you can get them into your head."

"Nightingale, I swear I'll let you go if your advice is as good as you say."

"Then listen," said the nightingale. "One, don't go after what's beyond your reach. Two, don't cry over what's hopelessly lost. Three, don't go madly believing things that defy[1] belief."

The villager listened with mouth agape. He hesitated a moment, then opened his hand. The nightingale flew at top speed to perch on a pine tree a dozen paces off.

"Man, oh man, what a fool you are! You let me go, and here I have a treasure in my breast: a pearl bigger than a goose egg, in fact bigger than your fist!"

---

[1] **defy** (dih-FEYE) *v.* go beyond

The villager was beside himself. All he could think of was the pearl he'd held in his hand and then let go again. Such a huge pearl! How could he get it back? If he picked up a stone, the nightingale would be out of range with a few flicks of its wings. It made him so sick to think he'd lost an enormous fortune that he suddenly went as yellow as a crabapple. Even the whites of his eyes were yellow.

Head high, but in a strangled voice, he tried to talk the nightingale round.

"Come, little nightingale of the woods, come, my wild nightingale, my friend, come and perch on my fingers! I'll take you home in great honor. You'll find there everything nightingales love, and it'll all be yours. I've a special present for you, too—one worth more to you than I can tell."

"Man, poor man," answered the nightingale from the top of the tree, "you're sillier than a stove-in[2] basket. What have you done with my three pieces of advice? You've let them run straight out of your head like water! I'm beyond your reach, and you're still after me. I'm lost to you and you're miserable about it. And finally, it defies belief that I should have in my breast a pearl three times bigger than my body, and you're determined to believe it. A lot of good my advice has done you!"

With that, the nightingale fluttered up toward the clouds. The villager just stood there in his clogs, thoroughly ashamed of himself.

This painting from the 15th century is from *Book of the Property of Things.* It is called "The Property of Animals" and illustrates the attributes of real and legendary animals.

---

[2] **stove-in** (stowv-ihn) *adj.* smashed inward

POSTREADING

Critical Thinking

1. What values and beliefs does this story express?

2. What human characteristics are illustrated in the story? What characteristics does the nightingale have?

3. How does the message in the story apply to you or someone you know? Give examples from your own experience.

Writing Your Response to "The Nightingale's Three Bits of Advice"

What interests you most about the characters, dialogue, or events of this folktale? In your journal, write about what stands out most vividly for you in this story. What, if anything, in the story relates to your own life?

Going Back Into the Text: Author's Craft

Authors often use key words to let readers know the **sequence** of a story. Such words as *first, next,* and *last,* or *before* and *after,* act as clues as to when certain events happen. In "The Nightingale's Three Bits of Advice," the author uses the numbers *one, two,* and *three* to signal the order of events that will take place.

As you review the sequence in the story, use these questions as guidelines:

1. What was the first event in the story?

2. How do the nightingale's three bits of advice signal what will happen in the story?

3. What was the last event in the story?

Paying on the Nail

Reading the Story in a Cultural Context

One of the earliest forms of literature was the folktale. These stories, told orally from generation to generation, were often created to convey a moral, explain customs or traditions, or simply to make the listener laugh. The stories often changed according to who was telling them. Storytellers would add their own details or change characters and settings. Consequently, most folktales have many versions of the same story. Folktales are usually about common folks involved in some sort of struggle or in a problem that must be solved.

The Irish have a great tradition of storytelling. Because Ireland is an agricultural and fishing community, folktales often involve fishermen, farmers, and the craftsmen who cater to them. A common character in the Irish folktale is the trickster, a character who tricks or gets the better of other characters.

"Paying on the Nail" is a folktale that tells of a trickster named Shynail. The character, a horsetrader, gets his name because of his reluctance to trade horses at fairs where there was a market cross. In Irish towns, market crosses were placed around the areas of trading. No trading was allowed to take place outside the crosses. These crosses were also sometimes referred to as "nails." They were great places to strike a bargain. Shynail cheated his customers by appearing to pay in full when he actually did not. Because the market cross was a symbol of honest dealing and the Christian faith, Shynail avoided trading within the designated market areas.

In the story, a farmer who sells a horse to Shynail is determined not to let the trickster get the better of him. He insists that payment for the horse be made "on the nail," or within the market crosses. Shynail agrees. Before they get to the market, however, they stop for a drink of water. Shynail convinces the farmer that his time would be better spent working on his farm instead of pushing on ahead to the market. He suggests that the farmer use the nails of his horse's shoe as a "nail." The farmer agrees, and Shynail pays in full. His first act of honesty, however, allows him to play his biggest form of trickery on his fellow villagers.

Focusing on the Selection

As you read "Paying on the Nail," think about Shynail's methods of trickery. What is the difference between his trick of getting away with paying less and his trick at the end of the story? How did he benefit from each of his tricks? Which of his tricks hurts his fellow villagers? Did either of his tricks help his fellow villagers?

Paying on the Nail

◆◆◆

Padraic O'Farrell

Market crosses were used to define the limits of trading areas in Irish towns. Sometimes called "nails," they were also places where bargains were struck, the cash being paid "on the nail." Traces of one still remain in Clonmel.[1] It is called the "Bargain Stone" by some and "The Pay on the Nail Stone" by others.

Here are some horse dealers in modern Ireland. A good reputation is earned through fairness and honesty even today.

One Tipperary[2] horse dealer always avoided fairs where there was a market cross. His innate[3] superstition made him fear cheating at the symbolic testament to straight dealing. That's how he earned the nickname, Shynail. The cleverest of Munster[4] farmers were deceived by his trickery, achieved by perfecting a sleight-of-hand[5] technique while paying for stock. No matter how a vendor's eyes were glued on Shynail as he counted out the banknotes, he was able to fool the man into thinking he had been paid in full.

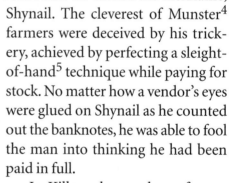

In Killenaule one day, a farmer made a deal with Shynail and when the rogue[6] took out a fist of notes to

---

[1] **Clonmel** (klahn-MEHL) *n.* a municipal borough of Ireland
[2] **Tipperary** (tihp-uh-RAIR-ee) *n.* a county in Ireland
[3] **innate** (ihn-AYT) *adj.* inborn
[4] **Munster** (MUN-stur) *n.* a province in Ireland
[5] **sleight-of-hand** (SLEYET-uv-hand) *adj.* skillfully deceptive
[6] **rogue** (rohg) *n.* a dishonest person

pay, the farmer refused to take any until they went to Clonmel, where payment could be made "on the nail." Shynail demurred,[7] but the farmer sent for two of his fastest horses and bade[8] Shynail to mount one and head for the town while he rode behind on the other; he didn't want the crooked dealer to escape.

In order to give himself time to think, Shynail agreed and off they went. Nearing Fethard, the buyer shouted over his shoulder to the farmer that he wanted a drink of water. They pulled in at a well and Shynail remarked casually that it was hot work riding such a distance for nothing. He pointed out to the farmer how he could be employing himself better back home working on the farm. But the farmer insisted that he should be paid on the nail and nowhere else.

"Then why don't you raise your horse's hoof and I'll put the money on a horse-shoe nail," said Shynail. The farmer thought for a minute and then agreed. He raised one of the animal's hooves and held it between his thighs the way a blacksmith would. Shynail counted out the money and this time he paid the total amount. The farmer was delighted and was full of praise for Shynail and began apologising to him for not trusting him. All the way back to Killenaule, he kept asking Shynail to forgive him, but the rogue replied that all he wanted was a drink because he was very thirsty. So at the end of the journey, the farmer brought Shynail into an inn and bought him some ale. He told the innkeeper and his customers about how Shynail had been wronged and how he had found him to be the straightest dealer in Ireland.

Why did Shynail play straight? The clever man realised that just a few farmers at that time shod[9] their horses. When word spread about the incident that day, many would avail[10] of the opportunity to have their very own nail on which to pay at every fair. After all, when Shynail had responded so favourably, a well-shod horse could pay for itself in no time.

Shynail started up a forge[11] in Killenaule and he made more money from fitting shoes on horses than he could ever have hoped to get by dealing in them.

---

[7] **demurred** (dih-MERD) *v.* objected or hesitated

[8] **bade** (bayd) *v.* ordered

[9] **shod** (shod) *v.* fit with shoes

[10] **avail** (uh-VAYL) *v.* take advantage of; make use of

[11] **forge** (forj) *n.* a blacksmith's shop

POSTREADING

Critical Thinking

1. How does this folktale reveal the character of the horsetrader, Shynail?

2. What does this folktale tell you about how trading was done in an Irish town?

3. What do you think the message is in this folktale? Explain your thoughts.

Writing Your Response to "Paying on the Nail"

In your journal, write your response to this folktale. What is your opinion of Shynail's "trick"? Explain why you think as you do.

Going Back Into the Text: Author's Craft

The **trickster folktale** is a story that centers on a character who gets the better of others. Often, the trickster does it in such a way that those he tricks do not even know it. In some folktales, the trickster is an animal, such as Brer Rabbit, Raven, or the wily fox. A trickster can also be human, such as Shynail.

In many trickster tales, the trickster throws a predictable world into chaos. The trickster is often amoral, meaning he does not recognize good or evil. This serves to reinforce our own morality. Sometimes the trickster himself is tricked. But win or lose, the appeal of the trickster is that his or her cleverness outwits everyone in the end.

With a partner, use the following questions to review why "Paying on the Nail" is a folktale:

1. What is Shynail's problem? How do his character traits allow him to solve his problem?

2. Do you think Shynail got away with his "trick"? Explain why you think the way you do.

3. Invent your own trickster folktale or retell one that you know.

THE ART OF TAPESTRIES

In the next 16 pages, you will see paintings, sculptures, masks, murals, folk art, ceramics, and woodcarvings that express the viewpoints of artists from many different cultures. These works of art illustrate the similarities and differences of the many cultures that make up the population of the world. As you look at each piece, ask yourself: What do I see? What does each work show me about the artist and his or her culture?

When early Egyptians told a story through art, they used drawings which stood for people, places, and things. As they told more and more stories, the figures became more abstract. The figures developed into an alphabet known as hieroglyphics. In this Egyptian wall painting, the artist tells the story of wheat harvesting.

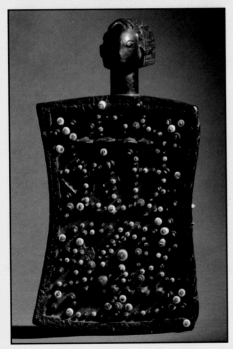

This is a memory board used by a tribe in Zaire called the Luba. It was used as a tool for storytellers in the tribe. Each bead triggers an ancestral story. A memory board is particularly useful since history is passed down orally through the generations.
Museum of African Art, NYC.

This plaque decorated a palace in Benin during the 16th century. At this time, brass and bronze were imported to Africa in exchange for slaves. The metal workers of Benin developed extremely sophisticated sculpting techniques.
British Museum, London.

Day's End. Contemporary Somali painter, Abdim Dr No, portrays women returning to their village after a day of work.
Somalian, Private Collection.

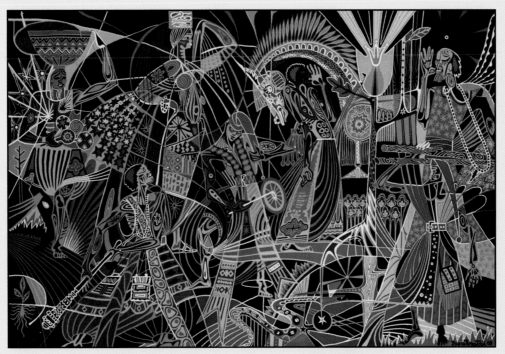

Papa Ibra Tall, a painter and designer from Senegal made a gift of this tapestry to the United Nations in 1970. *Pilgrimage to Touba* depicts a yearly event attended by thousands of Moslems. *Permanent Collection of the United Nations.*

This carved ivory mask was worn on the belt of a 16th century King from Nigeria.

This colored page from a book was painted by the Turkish artist, Lokman, in 1588. It depicts the Turkish sultan, Suleyman the Magnificent, attacking the city of Vienna in 1528. At the time, Turkey was very powerful, controlling much of South-Eastern Europe.
Topkapi Palace Museum, Istanbul, Turkey.

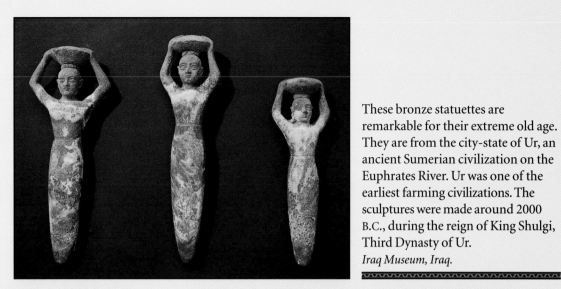

These bronze statuettes are remarkable for their extreme old age. They are from the city-state of Ur, an ancient Sumerian civilization on the Euphrates River. Ur was one of the earliest farming civilizations. The sculptures were made around 2000 B.C., during the reign of King Shulgi, Third Dynasty of Ur.
Iraq Museum, Iraq.

Turkish artist, Mehdi, painted *Men Playing Chess* during the 19th century. Here, he illustrates Middle Eastern cultural traditions. Notice that all three men in this painting are wearing a traditional cap called a "fez".

The Japanese artist, Katsuhika Hokusai, made this wood block print, *Autumn Leaves on the Tsutaya River*, at the end of the 18th century. Hokusai later became an important influence on Impressionist painters in 19th century France, where his prints were immensely popular.

British Museum, London, Great Britain.

This terra-cotta statuette was made in China between the 5th and 6th centuries. It was made in honor of a Chinese cavalry officer who died in battle against invading Mongolian tribes.
Muse Guimet, Paris, France.

This ceramic vase, or celadon, was made by a Korean artist in the 12th century, during the Koyo Period. The word celadon is also the word for the grayish green color of these vases.
Victoria and Albert Museum, London, Great Britain.

Woman Reading a Letter, a wood block print made by the Japanese artist, Utamaro, in the 18th century. The only women who could read at this time were women of the Japanese royal court.

This Indian miniature on paper was painted in the 17th century. It depicts the time of year we call August when the position of the sun is in the constellation Leo. Notice that the woman holding the sun is riding on Leo the lion.

The Pierpont Morgan Library, New York.

This bronze sculpture was made in Southern India in the 11th century and depicts the Hindu god, Siva Nataraja. Siva or Shiva, is the god of destruction and renewal. In this sculpture, as Lord of the Dance, Siva is dancing with his many arms inside a circle to symbolize the constant activity of destroying and renewing everything in the world.

This gouache [gwahsh] painting by Indian artist Shiva Dayal Lal shows an outdoor Indian market where the many colored fruits and grains of India are sold. Gouache is a way of painting with color mixed with gum from trees. The effect is similar to watercolor. *Victoria and Albert Museum, London, Great Britain.*

A Maori warrior is depicted in this sculpture from New Zealand. The artist used the Maori practice of face painting on this statue's face.

This bark painting was created by an Aboriginal artist. Typical aboriginal paintings are limited to the colors yellow, red, white, and black. Such earth colors have spiritual meaning to the native Australians.

The Gathering of the Rye, by Kazemir Malevich, was painted in 1912. It portrays Russian women working in the fields. Malevich was an internationally recognized artist who painted in a geometric style that was influenced by Cubism. *Stedelijk Mus. Amsterdam.*

The style and subject matter of *The Bolshevik* by Boris Kustodiev is typical of the 1920's. Artists at this time were encouraged to idealize the Communist philosophies. The leaders of the Russian Revolution used art such as this as propaganda to inspire the masses. *Galleria Statle Tret'jakov Moskva.*

This painting from the Renaissance was done by Sofonisba Anguissola, a female Italian artist. At this time in history, very few women were artists. The painting is of the artist's three sisters. Look back at page A5 for another game of chess.

Museum Naradove, Poznan, Poland.

Isidro Nonell y Monturiol, a Spanish artist, used Expressionist painting techniques to convey the mood of this 1904 painting, *Misery*.

Museo del Arte moderno, Barcelona, Spain.

The Peasant's Wedding was painted in the Netherlands in 1565. The painter Pieter Brueghel the Elder depicts a memorable scene of peasant life in great detail. During the Renaissance, painters depicted mainly court life and religious subjects. However, Brueghel shows the dignity of the natural informality of peasant life. The long dinner table which juts out towards the viewer on the left was a daring new way to show space in a painting. *Kunsthistoriches Vienna, Austria.*

Jan Vermeer painted *Woman with a Water Jug* in 17th century Holland. Vermeer was a master of painting the effects of light. In this painting, light is pouring through the window on the left and on to the young woman and the still life on the table. The perfectly balanced composition includes a map on the upper right of the picture. The map was to remind the viewer that Holland was a center of learning and exploration. *Metropolitan Museum of Art, NYC.*

The Bus, painted by Frida Kahlo in 1929, shows Mexican commuters. Frida Kahlo was an accomplished artist during an exciting period of art in Mexico. Her circle of artist and writer friends included her husband, the artist, Diego Rivera, whose work you will also encounter in this book.

Fundacion Dolores Olmedo, Mexico City, Mexico.

This carved stone, from the Mayan Civilization of Chiapas, Mexico, was carved in A.D. 725. It depicts a ruler being handed a headdress by his wife before a battle.

National Museum of Anthropology, Mexico City.

Return from the Fair. Brazilian artist Candido Portinari painted this piece in 1940. Portinari is well known for depicting people of African descent in his art.
Museum of the Americas.

Late Autumn was painted in 1937 by Canadian artist, John Hollis Kaufman. It reflects the vast expanse of nature in Canada.
Private Collection.

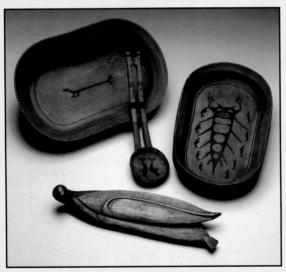

A Native Canadian artist made these wooden serving dishes. They are decorated with images of real and mythological animals.
Washington, D.C., Smithsonian Institution.

This mask from the Tsimshian People of British Columbia, Canada, is said to portray the moon. It may have been used in a ritual or as a decorative object.
Provincial Museum, Victoria, British Columbia, Canada.

Death Seed/Woman, You Are Afraid/
from *My Mother's House*

Reading the Poems in a Cultural Context

Poets often express feelings of conflict in their work. The conflicts can be external, between two people or ideas. They can also be internal, such as opposing feelings in someone's mind. Conflict can also be expressed through images that clash with one another. In the poems you are about to read, there is both an obvious and a subtle conflict.

Ricarda Huch's poem "Death Seed" depicts the traditional symbol of death, the Grim Reaper. In the poem, we see a lush field of grain. A man stands in the field sowing seeds into the field from which he has reaped, or harvested, the grain. The scene appears to be very peaceful and the man appears to be ensuring that grain will continue to grow in the field. However, the poet notices the man's stern face and realizes that she has met Death. In a subtle way, this poem reveals a conflict of images. As the poet sees it, Death does not just take life, but makes sure that new life will take its place.

"Woman, You Are Afraid," by Maria Wine, expresses the conflict the poet feels within herself. She first compares herself to a terrified and defenseless animal in a forest. The forest might be seen as the unknown and the terror that one faces not knowing what lies ahead. The poet then realizes that she herself is the forest and that she does not know herself and is therefore afraid.

Leah Goldberg's poem from *My Mother's House*, expresses its conflict very subtly. The poet does not believe that she resembles her grandmother, who was very beautiful. But as she peers into the mirror that belonged to her grandmother, she is able to see that though she may not have her grandmother's outward beauty, her inner beauty shines through. By the end of the poem, she has resolved her conflict over the distance she feels from her grandmother and is able to feel a connection to her heritage.

Focusing on the Selections

As you read these three poems, pay attention to the conflicts that the poets express. What words and images do each of the poets use to convey their feelings and thoughts? How do the images reveal the conflicts in the poems?

Death Seed

Ricarda Huch

In a field of swaying grain
I saw a man moving.
From his free hand slid seeds
which he sowed again.
Strange to me seemed a reaper
who blessed with new seed the same field.
Then I saw his stern face:
Behold, it was Death I had met.

Woman, You Are Afraid

Maria Wine

Woman, you are afraid of the forest
I see it in your eyes
when you stare into the darkness:
the terrified look of a defenseless creature.
Woman, *you* are a forest
strange and deep: I see
you are afraid of yourself.

Carl Holsoe painted *Woman Seated at a Table by a Window* during this century. Notice how the woman's posture affects the mood of the painting. How different would the mood be if the woman were standing?

from *My Mother's House*

Leah Goldberg
translated by *Robert Alter*

My mother's mother died
in the spring of her days. Her daughter
Would not remember her face. Her portrait inscribed
in my grandfather's heart
Was expunged[1] from the world of images
After his death.

Only her mirror was left in the house.
Through the passage of time it had sunk in its silver frame.
And I, her pale grand-daughter, I who do not resemble her,
Today look into it as into
A lake hiding treasures
Under the water.

Deep down, behind my face,
I see a young woman
With ruddy cheeks, smiling.
A wig on her head,
She fixes
A long earring to her earlobe, threading it
Through the tiny hole in the delicate flesh
Of the ear.

Deep down, behind my face, shines
The bright golden fleck in her eyes.
And the mirror maintains
The family tradition:
That she was very beautiful.

---

[1] **expunged** (ik-SPUNJD) *v.* removed completely

POSTREADING

Critical Thinking

1. What feelings do Huch, Wine, and Goldberg express in their poems?

2. What do the poems say about the personal histories of each poet?

3. How are you like your parents and/or grandparents? How are you different? What makes you afraid?

Writing Your Response to "Death Seed," "Woman, You Are Afraid," and "My Mother's House"

What phrases or images from the poems made the strongest impression on you? Why? How do they relate to you or someone you know? Write your responses in your journal.

Going Back Into the Text: Author's Craft

Writers use sights, sounds, tastes, smells, and textures to create strong images in the reader. This use of sensory experiences is called **imagery**. Often, writers use imagery to express an emotion or idea. For instance, a writer may express feelings of nervousness by saying a butterfly is fluttering in her belly.

Poets can use imagery to create a tone or feeling about their subject. Some images may be strong and powerful. Others may be more subtle. "Death Seed," for instance, portrays the classic image of the Grim Reaper to signify death. Other poems, such as "Woman, You Are Afraid," and "My Mother's House," use images more sparingly and subtly.

Use the following questions as guidelines to review the imagery in each poem:

1. What images can you find in each poem?

2. How does the imagery in these poems help to express the emotions of the poets?

3. Which images do you think are most effective? Why?

PREREADING

from *Survival in Auschwitz*

Reading the Autobiography in a Cultural Context

From the 1930s to the 1940s, Adolf Hitler's Nazi regime killed six million Jews—nearly two thirds of all Jews in Europe. Millions of non-Jews died in the Holocaust as well. Jews were taken from their homes, separated from their families, and forced to work in labor camps. Those that did not die of disease, starvation, or exhaustion were exterminated by means of poison gas, electrocution, or lethal injection.

Although Italy supported Hitler's government, the Italian dictator Benito Mussolini had no plans to persecute Italy's Jews. However, when the two nations joined forces, Mussolini adopted Hitler's views and decided that Italy, too, needed "racial purity." In 1938, the Italian government agreed to a series of "racial laws," making it illegal for Jews to study or teach in public schools, serve in the armed forces, or own land over a certain value. In 1943, the Germans invaded Italy. Jews were rounded up and taken to concentration camps.

While many of the Italians courageously hid their Jewish neighbors or smuggled them out of the country, nearly 7,000 out of 45,200 Italian Jews were captured by the Germans. Most of them died at the hands of the Germans.

Born of Jewish parents in Turin, Italy, Primo Levi did not really practice his religion. But it was his religion, nevertheless, that would change his life forever. Levi was completing a university degree in chemistry at the time the racial laws went into effect. In spite of the ban against Jewish students, he managed to make it through and earn his degree in 1941. When the Germans invaded Italy, Levi joined an underground resistance group working against the Nazis. Shortly after, he was captured by the Germans and sent to a concentration camp in Auschwitz, Poland.

Levi was one of the tiny minority who made it out alive. He would become one of the most famous authors to write about the Nazi Holocaust. His book *The Reawakening* deals in part with the factors that helped him survive. In addition to "good luck," he believes that his training as a mountain climber and his profession as a chemist won him some privileges. He also feels he was helped by his belief in the human spirit and the will to survive and to let the world know of the horrors that occurred. His personal narrative "Survival in Auschwitz," which is excerpted here, tells of his first day in a prison camp.

Focusing on the Selection

As you read the excerpt from "Survival in Auschwitz," think about the conflicts the author recounts. What understanding of human nature does the author reveal? What conflicts do the characters feel toward each other? What conflicts do they feel within themselves?

from *Survival in Auschwitz*

◆◆◆

Primo Levi
translated by *Stuart Woolf*

The journey did not last more than twenty minutes. Then the lorry stopped, and we saw a large door, and above it a sign, brightly illuminated (its memory still strikes me in my dreams): *Arbeit Macht Frei,*[1] work gives freedom.

We climb down, they make us enter an enormous empty room that is poorly heated. We have a terrible thirst. The weak gurgle of the water in the radiators makes us ferocious; we have had nothing to drink for four days. But there is also a tap—and above it a card which says that it is forbidden to drink as the water is dirty. Nonsense. It seems obvious that the card is a joke, "they" know that we are dying of thirst and they put us in a room, and there is a tap, and *Wassertrinken Verboten.*[2] I drink and I incite my companions to do likewise, but I have to spit it out, the water is tepid[3] and sweetish, with the smell of a swamp.

This is hell. Today, in our times, hell must be like this. A huge, empty room: we are tired, standing on our feet, with a tap which drips while we cannot drink the water, and we wait for something which will certainly be terrible, and nothing happens and nothing continues to happen. What can one think about? One cannot think anymore, it is like being already dead. Someone sits down on the ground. The time passes drop by drop.

We are not dead. The door is opened and an SS[4] man enters, smoking. He looks at us slowly and asks, *"Wer kann Deutsch?"*[5] One of us whom I have

---

[1] **Arbeit Macht Frei** (AHR-beyet mahkt freye) a German expression meaning "Work makes you free."

[2] **Wassertrinken Verboten** (VAHS-uhr-trihnk-uhn fer-BOHT-uhn) German for "It is forbidden to drink the water"

[3] **tepid** (TEHP-ihd) *adj.* moderately warm; lukewarm

[4] **SS** stands for Schutztaffel, a Nazi secret police organization

[5] **Wer kann Deutsch?** (ver kahn doich) German for "Who knows German?"

never seen, named Flesch, moves forward; he will be our interpreter. This SS man makes a long calm speech; the interpreter translates. We have to form rows of five, with intervals of two yards between man and man; then we have to undress and make a bundle of the clothes in a special manner, the woolen garments on one side, all the rest on the other; we must take off our shoes but pay great attention that they are not stolen.

Stolen by whom? Why should our shoes be stolen? And what about our documents, the few things we have in our pockets, our watches? We all look at the interpreter, and the interpreter asks the German, and the German smokes and looks him through and through as if he were transparent, as if no one had spoken.

I had never seen old men naked. Mr. Bergmann wore a truss[6] and asked the interpreter if he should take it off, and the interpreter hesitated. But the German understood and spoke seriously to the interpreter pointing to someone. We saw the interpreter swallow and then he said: "The officer says, take off the truss, and you will be given that of Mr. Coen." One could see the words coming bitterly out of Flesch's mouth; this was the German manner of laughing.

Now another German comes and tells us to put the shoes in a certain corner, and we put them there, because now it is all over and we feel outside this world and the only thing is to obey. Someone comes with a broom and sweeps away all the shoes, outside the door in a heap. He is crazy, he is mixing them all together, ninety-six pairs, they will be all mixed up. The outside door opens, a freezing wind enters and we are naked and cover ourselves up with our arms. The wind blows and slams the door; the German reopens it and stands watching with interest how we writhe[7] to hide from the wind, one behind the other. Then he leaves and closes it.

This print is called *Death Embracing a Woman.* It was made by German artist Kaethe Kollwitz in 1921. Germany faced a devastating depression between World Wars I and II.

---

[6] **truss** (truhss) *n.* a support for the abdomen
[7] **writhe** (reyeth) *v.* twist or turn

Now the second act begins. Four men with razors, soapbrushes and clippers burst in; they have trousers and jackets with stripes, with a number sewn on the front; perhaps they are the same sort as those others of this evening (this evening or yesterday evening?); but these are robust[8] and flourishing. We ask many questions but they catch hold of us and in a moment we find ourselves shaved and sheared. What comic faces we have without hair! The four speak a language which does not seem of this world. It is certainly not German, for I understand a little German.

Finally another door is opened: here we are, locked in, naked, sheared and standing, with our feet in water—it is a shower-room. We are alone. Slowly the astonishment dissolves, and we speak, and everyone asks questions and no one answers. If we are naked in a shower-room, it means that we will have a shower. If we have a shower it is because they are not going to kill us yet. But why then do they keep us standing, and give us nothing to drink, while nobody explains anything, and we have no shoes or clothes, but we are all naked with our feet in the water, and we have been traveling five days and cannot even sit down.

And our women?

Mr. Levi asks me if I think that our women are like us at this moment, and where they are, and if we will be able to see them again. I say yes, because he is married and has a daughter, certainly we will see them again. But by now my belief is that all this is a game to mock and sneer at us. Clearly they will kill us, whoever thinks he is going to live is mad, it means that he has swallowed the bait,[9] but I have not; I have understood that it will soon all be over, perhaps in this same room, when they get bored of seeing us naked, dancing from foot to foot and trying every now and again to sit down on the floor. But there are two inches of cold water and we cannot sit down.

We walk up and down without sense, and we talk, everybody talks to everybody else, we make a great noise. The door opens, and a German enters; it is the officer of before. He speaks briefly, the interpreter translates. "The officer says you must be quiet, because this is not a rabbinical school."[10] One sees the words which are not his, the bad words, twist his mouth as they come out, as if he was spitting out a foul taste. We beg him to ask what we are waiting for, how long we will stay here, about our women, everything; but he says no, that he does not want to ask. This Flesch, who is most unwilling to translate into Italian the hard cold German phrases and refuses to turn into German our questions because he knows that it is useless, is a

---

[8] **robust** (ro-BUST) *adj.* strong and healthy
[9] **swallowed the bait** believed too easily; accepted without question or suspicion
[10] **rabbinical school** a school for the training of rabbis, scholars, and teachers of Jewish law

German Jew of about fifty, who has a large scar on his face from a wound received fighting the Italians on the Piave.[11] He is a closed, taciturn[12] man, for whom I feel an instinctive respect as I feel that he has begun to suffer before us.

The German goes and we remain silent, although we are a little ashamed of our silence. It is still night and we wonder if the day will ever come. The door opens again, and someone else dressed in stripes comes in. He is different from the others, older, with glasses, a more civilized face, and much less robust. He speaks to us in Italian.

By now we are tired of being amazed. We seem to be watching some mad play, one of those plays in which the witches, the Holy Spirit and the devil appear. He speaks Italian badly, with a strong foreign accent. He makes a long speech, is very polite, and tries to reply to all our questions.

We are at Monowitz, near Auschwitz, in Upper Silesia,[13] a region inhabited by both Poles and Germans. This camp is a work-camp, in German one says *Arbeitslager*, all the prisoners (there are about ten thousand) work in a factory which produces a type of rubber called Buna, so that the camp itself is called Buna.

We will be given shoes and clothes—no, not our own—other shoes, other clothes, like his. We are naked now because we are waiting for the shower and the disinfection, which will take place immediately after the reveille,[14] because one cannot enter the camp without being disinfected.

Certainly there will be work to do, everyone must work here. But there is work and work: he, for example, acts as a doctor. He is a Hungarian doctor who studied in Italy and he is the dentist of the Lager.[15] He has been in the Lager for four and a half years (not in this one: Buna has only been open for a year and a half), but we can see that he is still quite well, not very thin. Why is he in the Lager? Is he Jewish like us? "No," he says simply, "I am a criminal."

We ask him many questions. He laughs, replies to some and not to others, and it is clear that he avoids certain subjects. He does not speak of the women: he says they are well, that we will see them again soon, but he does not say how or where. Instead he tells us other things, strange and

---

[11] **Piave** (PYAH-vay) *n.* a river in Italy, located between Padua and Venice

[12] **taciturn** (TAS-ih-tern) *adj.* silent by habit; not talkative

[13] **Auschwitz** (OWSH-vihts) ... **Silesia** (sih-LEE-zhuh) *n.* during World War II, Auschwitz was the site of the largest of the German (Nazi) concentration camps; about $2 \frac{1}{2}$ million people were exterminated there

[14] **reveille** (REHV-uh-lee) *n.* the sounding of a bugle early in the morning to awaken persons in a camp

[15] **Lager** (LAHG-uhr) *n.* German for "camp"

crazy things, perhaps he too is playing with us. Perhaps he is mad—one goes mad in the Lager. He says that every Sunday there are concerts and football matches. He says that whoever boxes well can become cook. He says that whoever works well receives prize-coupons with which to buy tobacco and soap. He says that the water is really not drinkable, and that instead a coffee substitute is distributed every day, but generally nobody drinks it as the soup itself is sufficiently watery to quench thirst. We beg him to find us something to drink, but he says that he cannot, that he has come to see us secretly, against SS orders, as we still have to be disinfected, and that he must leave at once; he has come because he has a liking for Italians, and because, he says, he "has a little heart." We ask him if there are other Italians in the camp and he says there are some, a few, he does not know how many; and he at once changes the subject. Meanwhile a bell rang and he immediately hurried off and left us stunned and disconcerted.[16] Some feel refreshed but I do not. I still think that even this dentist, this incomprehensible person, wanted to amuse himself at our expense, and I do not want to believe a word of what he said.

At the sound of the bell, we can hear the still dark camp waking up. Unexpectedly the water gushes out boiling from the showers—five minutes of bliss; but immediately after, four men (perhaps they are the barbers) burst in yelling and shoving and drive us out, wet and steaming, into the adjoining room which is freezing; here other shouting people throw at us unrecognizable rags and thrust into our hands a pair of broken-down boots with wooden soles; we have no time to understand and we already find ourselves in the open, in the blue and icy snow of dawn, barefoot and naked, with all our clothing in our hands, with a hundred yards to run to the next hut. There we are finally allowed to get dressed.

When we finish, everyone remains in his own corner and we do not dare lift our eyes to look at one another. There is nowhere to look in a mirror, but our appearance stands in front of us, reflected in a hundred livid[17] faces, in a hundred miserable and sordid[18] puppets. We are transformed into the phantoms[19] glimpsed yesterday evening.

Then for the first time we became aware that our language lacks words to express this offense, the demolition of a man. In a moment, with almost prophetic intuition, the reality was revealed to us: we had reached the bottom. It is not possible to sink lower than this; no human condition is more

---

[16] **disconcerted** (dis-kuhn-SERT-uhd) *adj.* confused and upset
[17] **livid** (LIHV-ihd) *adj.* deathly pale or white, as from fear
[18] **sordid** (SAWR-dihd) *adj.* dirty
[19] **phantoms** (FAN-tuhmz) *n. pl.* ghosts

miserable than this, nor could it conceivably be so. Nothing belongs to us anymore; they have taken away our clothes, our shoes, even our hair; if we speak, they will not listen to us, and if they listen, they will not understand. They will even take away our name: and if we want to keep it, we will have to find in ourselves the strength to do so, to manage somehow so that behind the name something of us, of us as we were, still remains.

We know that we will have difficulty in being understood, and this is as it should be. But consider what value, what meaning is enclosed even in the smallest of our daily habits, in the hundred possessions which even the poorest beggar owns: a handkerchief, an old letter, the photo of a cherished person. These things are part of us, almost like limbs of our body; nor is it conceivable that we can be deprived of them in our world, for we immediately find others to substitute the old ones, other objects which are ours in their personification and evocation of our memories.

Imagine now a man who is deprived of everyone he loves, and at the same time of his house, his habits, his clothes, in short, of everything he possesses: he will be a hollow man, reduced to suffering and needs, forgetful of dignity and restraint, for he who loses all often easily loses himself. He will be a man whose life or death can be lightly decided with no sense of human affinity,[20] in the most fortunate of cases, on the basis of a pure judgment of utility. It is in this way that one can understand the double sense of the term "extermination camp,"[21] and it is now clear what we seek to express with the phrase: "to lie on the bottom."

Häftling:[22] I have learnt that I am a häftling. My number is 174517; we have been baptized, we will carry the tattoo on our left arm until we die.

The operation was slightly painful and extraordinarily rapid: they placed us all in a row, and one by one, according to the alphabetical order of our names, we filed past a skillful official, armed with a sort of pointed tool with a very short needle. It seems that this is the real, true initiation: only by "showing one's number" can one get bread and soup. Several days passed, and not a few cuffs and punches, before we became used to showing our number promptly enough not to disorder the daily operation of food-distribution; weeks and months were needed to learn its sound in the German language. And for many days, while the habits of freedom still led me to look for the time on my wristwatch, my new name ironically appeared instead, its number tattooed in bluish characters under the skin.

---

[20] **affinity** (uh-FIHN-ih-tee) *n.* liking or natural attraction

[21] **extermination camp** *n.* under the Nazis, an "extermination camp," or concentration camp, served as a forced-labor camp to detain and later to kill Jews, Poles, and others

[22] **Häftling** (HEHFT-lihng) *n.* German for "prisoner"

POSTREADING

Critical Thinking

1. Why do you think Primo Levi felt he should write about his experiences at Auschwitz?

2. What does Levi tell you about the way concentration camp prisoners were treated by the Germans?

3. What possessions do you own that mean a great deal to you? Why are they important to you? How would you feel if they were taken away from you?

Writing Your Response to "Survival in Auschwitz"

In your journal, write your ideas and feelings about the selection. Which part affected you the most? Why did it affect you?

Going Back Into the Text: Author's Craft

In writing a **personal narrative**, an author intends to relate an event or series of events in the order in which they happened. A personal narrative usually takes the form of a story, with characters and dialogue. However, because a personal narrative is nonfiction, the events must be factual and accurately retold by the author.

Even though a personal narrative is factual, the author uses such fiction techniques as plot, dialogue, suspense, and characterization to interest the reader. The writer may also comment on the events. For instance, Levi says of the conditions in which he finds himself, "This is hell."

Use the following questions as guidelines in reviewing the elements of personal narrative in the excerpt from "Survival in Auschwitz."

1. What factual information about the concentration camp does Levi provide?

2. What insight does the author bring to his experience?

3. How could a historian check to make sure that Levi's story is true?

PREREADING

Action Will Be Taken

Reading the Story in a Cultural Context

After World War II, Germany faced the enormous task of rebuilding its industries, which had been heavily damaged during the war. Factories, mines, and transportation networks had to be completely rebuilt. The Germans took advantage of this opportunity, installing the most up-to-date equipment and techniques. Germany's new industries were considered to be among the most efficient in the world.

One of the most influential writers of postwar Germany, Heinrich Böll, received numerous awards, including the Nobel Prize. Much of his writing centered on Germany's attempts to rebuild after the war. In particular, he wrote about the bureaucratic failings he saw around him. Some of his stories made fun of Germany's *Wirtschaftwunder*, or economic miracle, in which the government created useless jobs for its citizens in order to decrease unemployment. For example, in one of Böll's stories, a man has a pointless job of keeping count of the number of people who cross a local bridge.

Böll's novels, short stories, plays, and essays express a strong sense of individuality and social morality. He is considered to be a realist whose humorous writing points out truths about society and human nature. "Action Will Be Taken" demonstrates with great comic detail Böll's attitudes toward bureacracies.

Focusing on the Selection

As you read "Action Will Be Taken," think about the contradiction between what is said and what is done. What attitude toward the workplace does the author reveal? What makes this story funny?

Action Will Be Taken

◆◆◆

Heinrich Böll

Probably one of the strangest interludes in my life was the time I spent as an employee in Alfred Wunsiedel's[1] factory. By nature I am inclined more to pensiveness[2] and inactivity than to work, but now and again prolonged financial difficulties compel me—for pensiveness is no more profitable than inactivity—to take on a so-called job. Finding myself once again at a low ebb of this kind, I put myself in the hands of the employment office and was sent with seven other fellow-sufferers to Wunsiedel's factory, where we were to undergo an aptitude[3] test.

The exterior of the factory was enough to arouse my suspicions: the factory was built entirely of glass brick and my aversion[4] to well-lit buildings and well-lit rooms is as strong as my aversion to work. I became even more suspicious when we were immediately served breakfast in the well-lit, cheerful coffee shop: pretty waitresses brought us eggs, coffee and toast, orange juice was served in tastefully designed jugs, goldfish pressed their bored faces against the sides of pale-green aquariums. The waitresses were so cheerful that they appeared to be bursting with good cheer. Only a strong effort of will—so it seemed to me—restrained them from singing away all day long. They were as crammed with unsung songs as chickens with unlaid eggs.

Right away I realized something that my fellow-sufferers evidently failed to realize: that this breakfast was already part of the test; so I chewed away

---

[1] **Wunsiedel's** (VUN-seed-duhlz) *n.* a family name
[2] **pensiveness** (PEHN-sihv-nehs) *n.* thoughtfulness
[3] **aptitude** (AP-tuh-tood) *n.* a capacity for learning
[4] **aversion** (uh-VER-zhuhn) *n.* dislike

reverently, with the full appreciation of a person who knows he is supplying his body with valuable elements. I did something which normally no power on earth can make me do: I drank orange juice on an empty stomach, left the coffee and egg untouched, as well as most of the toast, got up, and paced up and down in the coffee shop, pregnant[5] with action.

As a result I was the first to be ushered into the room where the questionnaires were spread out on attractive tables. The walls were done in a shade of green that would have summoned the word "delightful" to the lips of interior decoration enthusiasts. The room appeared to be empty, and yet I was so sure of being observed that I behaved as someone pregnant with action behaves when he believes himself unobserved: I ripped my pen impatiently from my pocket, unscrewed the top, sat down at the nearest table and pulled the questionnaire toward me, the way irritable customers snatch at the bill in a restaurant.

Question No. 1: Do you consider it right for a human being to possess only two arms, two legs, eyes, and ears?

Here for the first time I reaped the harvest of my pensive nature and wrote without hesitation: "Even four arms, legs and ears would not be adequate for my driving energy. Human beings are very poorly equipped."

Question No. 2: How many telephones can you handle at one time?

Here again the answer was as easy as simple arithmetic: "When there are only seven telephones," I wrote, "I get impatient; there have to be nine before I feel I am working to capacity."

Question No. 3: How do you spend your free time?

My answer: "I no longer acknowledge the term free time—on my fifteenth birthday I eliminated it from my vocabulary, for in the beginning was the act."

I got the job. Even with nine telephones I really didn't feel I was working to capacity. I shouted into the mouthpieces: "Take immediate action" or: "Do something!—We must have some action—Action will be taken—Action has been taken—Action should be taken." But as a rule—for I felt this was in keeping with the tone of the place—I used the imperative.[6]

Of considerable interest were the noon-hour breaks, when we consumed nutritious foods in an atmosphere of silent good cheer. Wunsiedel's factory was swarming with people who were obsessed with telling you the story of

---

[5] **pregnant** (PREHG-nuhnt) *adj.* full, laden
[6] **imperative** (ihm-PEHR-uht-ihv) *n.* in grammar, the command form of a verb

Action Will Be Taken ◆ **289**

The Businessman, Max Roesberg was painted in 1922 by German artist Otto Dix.

their lives, as indeed vigorous[7] personalities are fond of doing. The story of their lives is more important to them than their lives, you have only to press a button, and immediately it is covered with spewed-out exploits.[8]

Wunsiedel had a right-hand man called Broschek,[9] who had in turn made a name for himself by supporting seven children and a paralyzed wife by working night-shifts in his student days, and successfully carrying on four business agencies, besides which he had passed two examinations with honors in two years. When asked by reporters: "When do you sleep, Mr. Broschek?" he had replied: "It's a crime to sleep!"

Wunsiedel's secretary had supported a paralyzed husband and four children by knitting, at the same time graduating in psychology and German history as well as breeding shepherd dogs, and she had become famous as a night-club singer where she was known as *Vamp Number Seven.*

Wunsiedel himself was one of those people who every morning, as they open their eyes, make up their minds to act. "I must act," they think as they briskly tie their bathrobe belts around them, "I must act," they think as they shave, triumphantly watching their beard hairs being washed away with the lather: these hirsute[10] vestiges[11] are the first daily sacrifices to their driving energy. The more intimate functions also give these people a sense of satisfaction: water swishes, paper is used. Action has been taken. Bread gets eaten, eggs are decapitated.

---

[7] **vigorous** (VIHG-uhr-uhs) *adj.* forceful, lively
[8] **exploits** (EHK-sploits) *n. pl.* acts or deeds
[9] **Broschek** (BROHS-chehk) *n.* a family name
[10] **hirsute** (HER-soot) *adj.* hairy
[11] **vestiges** (VEHS-tih-jehz) *n. pl.* remaining traces

With Wunsiedel, the most trivial activity looked like action: the way he put on his hat, the way—quivering with energy—he buttoned up his overcoat, the kiss he gave his wife, everything was action.

When he arrived at his office he greeted his secretary with a cry of "Let's have some action!" And in ringing tones she would call back: "Action will be taken!" Wunsiedel then went from department to department, calling out his cheerful "Let's have some action!" Everyone would answer: "Action will be taken!" And I would call back to him too, with a radiant smile, when he looked into my office: "Action will be taken!"

Within a week I had increased the number of telephones on my desk to eleven, within two weeks to thirteen, and every morning on the streetcar I enjoyed thinking up new imperatives, or chasing the words *take action* through various tenses and modulations:[12] for two whole days I kept saying the same sentence over and over again because I thought it sounded so marvelous: "Action ought to have been taken"; for another two days it was: "Such action ought not to have been taken."

So I was really beginning to feel I was working to capacity when there actually was some action. One Tuesday morning—I had hardly settled down at my desk—Wunsiedel rushed into my office crying his "Let's have some action!" But an inexplicable something in his face made me hesitate to reply, in a cheerful voice as the rules dictated: "Action will be taken!" I must have paused too long, for Wunsiedel, who seldom raised his voice, shouted at me: "Answer! Answer, you know the rules!" And I answered, under my breath, reluctantly, like a child who is forced to say: I am a naughty child. It was only by a great effort that I managed to bring out the sentence: "Action will be taken," and hardly had I uttered it when there really was some action. Wunsiedel dropped to the floor. As he fell he rolled over onto his side and lay right across the open door way. I knew at once, and I confirmed it when I went slowly around my desk and approached the body on the floor, he was dead.

Shaking my head I stepped over Wunsiedel, walked slowly along the corridor to Broschek's office, and entered without knocking. Broschek was sitting at his desk, a telephone receiver in each hand, between his teeth a ball-point pen with which he was making notes on a writing pad, while with his bare feet he was operating a knitting machine under the desk. In this way he helps to clothe his family. "We've had some action," I said in a low voice.

Broschek spat out the ballpoint pen, put down the two receivers, reluctantly detached his toes from the knitting machine.

---

12 **modulations** (mahj-oo-LAY-shuhnz) *n. pl.* inflections of the tone or pitch of the voice

"What action?" he asked.

"Wunsiedel is dead," I said.

"No," said Broschek.

"Yes," I said, "come and have a look!"

"No," said Broschek, "that's impossible," but he put on his slippers and followed me along the corridor.

"No," he said, when we stood beside Wunsiedel's corpse, "no, no!" I did not contradict him. I carefully turned Wunsiedel over onto his back, closed his eyes, and looked at him pensively.

I felt something like tenderness for him, and realized for the first time that I had never hated him. On his face was that expression which one sees on children who obstinately[13] refuse to give up their faith in Santa Claus, even though the arguments of their playmates sound so convincing.

"No," said Broschek, "no."

"We must take action," I said quietly to Broschek.

"Yes," said Broschek, "we must take action."

Action was taken: Wunsiedel was buried, and I was delegated[14] to carry a wreath of artificial roses behind his coffin, for I am equipped with not only a penchant[15] for pensiveness and inactivity but also a face and figure that go extremely well with dark suits. Apparently as I walked along behind Wunsiedel's coffin carrying the wreath of artificial roses I looked superb. I received an offer from a fashionable firm of funeral directors to join their staff as a professional mourner. "You are a born mourner," said the manager, "your outfit would be provided by the firm. Your face—simply superb!"

I handed in my notice to Broschek, explaining that I had never really felt I was working to capacity there; that, in spite of the thirteen telephones, some of my talents were going to waste. As soon as my first professional appearance as a mourner was over I knew: This is where I belong, this is what I am cut out for.

Pensively I stand behind the coffin in the funeral chapel, holding a simple bouquet, while the organ plays Handel's *Largo*, a piece that does not receive nearly the respect it deserves. The cemetery café is my regular haunt; there I spend the intervals between my professional engagements, although sometimes I walk behind coffins which I have not been engaged

---

[13] **obstinately** (AHB-stuh-niht-lee) *adv.* stubbornly

[14] **delegated** (DEHL-uh-gayt-ihd) *v.* selected as a representative

[15] **penchant** (PEHN-chuhnt) *n.* a liking for something

to follow, I pay for flowers out of my own pocket and join the welfare worker who walks behind the coffin of some homeless person. From time to time I also visit Wunsiedel's grave, for after all I owe it to him that I discovered my true vocation,[16] a vocation in which pensiveness is essential and inactivity my duty.

It was not till much later that I realized I had never bothered to find out what was being produced in Wunsiedel's factory. I expect it was soap.

---

[16] **vocation** (voh-KAY-shuhn) *n.* a profession

POSTREADING

Critical Thinking

1. What does Heinrich Böll tell you about his attitudes toward work?

2. What experiences with work do you think prompted Böll to write this story?

3. What behaviors of others do you find silly or stupid? Explain why you feel the way you do.

Writing Your Response to "Action Will Be Taken"

In your journal, write about your reactions to the story. What passage did you find the most humorous? Explain why it made you laugh.

Going Back Into the Text: Author's Craft

Irony refers to a contrast between what is expected to happen and what really happens. For example, the title of Heinrich Böll's story promises a tale filled with action, but in reality, no one takes any action. Irony can also refer to what is said and what is really meant. For instance, a person whose foot is stepped on by her dancing partner who says, "That's okay, I didn't need that foot anyway!" is probably being ironic. Finally, irony can occur when there is a discrepancy between what appears to be true and what is actually true. For example, a character who appears to be dishonest may turn out to be the most honest character in a story.

With a partner, review "Action Will Be Taken" to see the ways in which irony is used. The following questions can serve as guidelines.

1. How does the narrator shouting his orders to take action into his nine telephones reveal the irony of the situation?

2. What is ironic about the job the narrator takes at the factory?

3. Why is the narrator's job as a professional mourner ironic?

MAKING THEMATIC CONNECTIONS

A House Divided

To be different can often mean to struggle against prejudice or to make sacrifices for your beliefs. Some people find it difficult to accept that others think and look different from themselves. They may feel challenged by new ideas or they may fear what they do not know. They may also find it easy to blame their problems on others.

Many selections in this book examine the conflicts that arise between people who are separated from each other because of their cultural group, religion, age, or customs.

In "Survival in Auschwitz," you read about the author's arrival at a Nazi concentration camp. Taken from his Italian home because of his religion, he is systematically stripped of his identity. "The Toilet" takes place in South Africa, where the policy of apartheid divided people by race. The selection "A Winter's Tale" focuses on Croatia, where a religious war has driven neighbors apart. The authors of these selections feel a sense of sadness and helplessness in the face of conflicts that are destroying their homelands.

This painting called *Visiting in Martinique*, depicts diverse cultures in Martinique after the French colonized the island. The interior of the house has a French flavor but the palm tree in the background and the fruit in the corner create a tropical feel.

Customs can also divide people. "The Old Man's Lazy" tells of a government official's lack of understanding for a native Canadian, whose custom prohibits him from tearing down a fence built by a white neighbor. In "Butterflies," a Maori child and her city teacher experience a cultural misunderstanding about people's connections to the earth. In "Marriage Is a Private Affair," a young Nigerian rebels against his own customs by marrying a woman from outside his father's tribe. In "The Monster" and "Please Give This Seat to an Elderly or Disabled Person," you saw that age can also separate people from one another.

These selections demonstrate that being different is never easy. It often requires overcoming prejudice and injustice, if that is possible. However, by expressing their conflicts in writing, the authors demonstrate how race, religion, tradition, and age divide people and nations all over the world.

ACTIVITY

Sometimes when people are faced with prejudice, it is difficult for them to both find a way to hold on to their beliefs and reduce the tension in a situation. Sometimes it is impossible to find a way out, and people must simply cope with the unfairness that they encounter. In this activity, you will try to help a person who finds himself or herself in just such a difficult situation.

1. Form a group of three or four students.

2. Choose one of the selections mentioned above or another selection in this book that deals with the theme of the struggle against prejudice.

3. Discuss with the other members of your group the prejudice that the main character in the selection faces.

4. List situations in which he or she has encountered this prejudice.

5. Brainstorm for ways that you might help the person either cope with the prejudice, escape it, or work to end the hatred he or she encounters.

6. Write a letter to this character offering your advice for how he or she might deal with the prejudice. You might suggest strategies for attacking the prejudice. If the prejudice is too great to attack, you might suggest ways that the person could cope with the effects of the prejudice.

7. Read your group's letter to the class. Then discuss what you learned about the effects of prejudice and make a class list of the ways you've found to fight it.

PREREADING

The Return

Reading the Story in a Cultural Context

Before 1940, when Carmen Laforet began to be recognized for her writing, Spanish literature was almost entirely the work of men. The freshness of Laforet's writing and her keen insight into contemporary life helped forge a path for other women writers to follow.

Laforet's writing reflects her diverse roots. Her mother was born into a poor peasant Castillian family. Her father came from a family of Basque soldiers and artists.

At 18, Laforet left her home in the Canary Islands to attend the University of Barcelona. The year was 1939, a time of great upheaval in Spain. It was at the university that she saw for herself the destruction that the Spanish Civil War had caused. People were starving and the city was devastated. Laforet often went hungry herself. She poured this experience into her first novel, *Nothing*, which was highly praised by critics.

Like most Spaniards, Laforet was brought up in the Catholic faith, though her family did not practice this religion. However, in 1951, she had a mystical experience that prompted her to become a devout Catholic. As a result, much of her work reflects the theme of Christian charity.

"The Return" weaves in the themes of both Christian charity and the social suffering and hunger in Spain in the 1940s. In the story, a man named Julian waits for his release from an asylum run by Catholic nuns, where he was committed to recover from mental illness. His release is timed so that he may spend Christmas Eve with his wife and children. Julian is anxious about rejoining his family. He is frightened about returning to the life he left behind.

The next day—Christmas Day—Julian takes the train home. While traveling, he remembers the events that led to his mental breakdown. He had been out of work and his wife was forced to scrub floors to buy the meager food they could afford for their many children.

Focusing on the Selection

As you read "The Return," think about Julian's relationship with his family. Why do you think he preferred to stay in the asylum? How does he view his place in his family? What hints are there that Julian's return will not be a happy one?

The Return

◆◆◆

Carmen Laforet

It was a bad idea, thought Julian as he pressed his forehead against the windowpane and felt the wet cold go right through to the bones that stood out so clearly under his transparent skin. It was a bad idea, sending him home for Christmas. Besides, they were sending him home for good; he was completely cured.

Julian was a tall man, encased in a nice black overcoat. He was blond, with prominent eyes and cheekbones that emphasized his thinness. But Julian was looking well these days. His wife marveled how well he looked every time she visited him. There was a time when Julian had been a handful of blue veins, legs like long sticks and big gnarled hands. That was two years ago when they committed him to the institution, which, strangely enough, he was reluctant to leave.

"Very impatient, aren't you? They'll be coming for you soon. The four o'clock train is due very shortly and you'll be able to take the five-thirty back. And tonight you will be home, celebrating Christmas Eve. . . . Julian, please do not forget to take your family to midnight Mass, as an act of grace. . . . If our House weren't so far away . . . It would be pleasant to have all of you here tonight. . . . Your children are very handsome, Julian, especially the youngest; he looks like a Christ Child, or a little Saint John, with his curls and blue eyes. I think he would make a fine acolyte,[1] because he has a very bright face. . . ."

Julian listened to the nun's prattle[2] in adoration. Julian loved Sister María de la Asunción very much, for she was fat and short with a smiling face and cheeks like apples. Waiting in that enormous forbidding visitors'

---

[1] **acolyte** (AK-uh-leyet) *n.* a person who assists a priest in the celebration of Mass
[2] **prattle** (PRAT-uhl) *n.* foolish chatter

room, ready for departure and plunged in thought, he had not heard her footsteps. . . . He had not heard her come in, because the nuns, despite their tiers of skirts and their wimples,[3] have a tread as light and silent as a sailboat. But when he noticed her, his heart jumped with joy. The last joy he would derive from this stage of his life. His eyes filled with tears; he had always been inclined to sentimentality, but now it was almost a disease.

"Sister María de la Asunción . . . I would like to attend midnight Mass here with you this year. I think it would be all right if I stayed here until tomorrow. It would be enough to be with my family on Christmas Day. In a certain sense, you are also my family. I . . . I am very grateful to all of you."

"Don't be foolish; that is impossible. Your wife is waiting for you right now. As soon as you have rejoined your family and are working, you will forget all this; it will be like a dream. . . ."

Then Sister María de la Asunción left too, and Julian felt dejected again, for he did not like leaving the asylum.[4] It was a place of death and despair, but for him it had been a place of refuge,[5] of salvation. . . . And even the last few months, when the authorities felt he had fully recovered, it had been a place of happiness. They had even let him drive! And not just going through the motions. He had driven the Mother Superior[6] herself and Sister María de la Asunción to the city to do some shopping. And Julian knew how brave these women had been, putting themselves like that into the hands of a lunatic . . . or a former lunatic: he had once been considered dangerous. But he did not disappoint them. The car had run perfectly under his expert control. The nuns had not even been shaken by the deep ruts in the road. When they got back, they congratulated him and he had felt himself blushing.

"Julian . . ."

Sister Rosa was standing in front of him, the nun with the round eyes and oval mouth. He did not like Sister Rosa very much; in fact, he did not like her at all. And he could not understand why. At the beginning, he was told, they had been obliged to put him into a strait jacket[7] more than once for having tried to attack her. Sister Rosa always seemed frightened of Julian. Now, suddenly, as he gazed at her, he realized whom she resembled. She resembled poor Herminia, his wife whom he loved so much. Life was

---

[3] **wimples** (WIHM-puhls) *n. pl.* headdresses worn by nuns
[4] **asylum** (uh-SEYE-luhm) *n.* an institution for the care of people who are mentally ill or aged
[5] **refuge** (REHF-yooj) *n.* a place of protection or shelter
[6] **Mother Superior** a woman in charge of a convent or other female religious community
[7] **strait jacket** *n.* a jacketlike garment of strong material used to bind the arms tightly against the body as a means of restraining a violent patient

so full of puzzles. Sister Rosa looked like Herminia, and yet, perhaps because of that, Julian could not abide[8] her.

"Julian, a call for you. Will you come to the phone? Mother asked me to tell you to answer it."

"Mother" was the Mother Superior herself. They all called her that. It was an honor for Julian to answer the telephone.

It was Herminia on the line, asking him in a shaky voice to take the train by himself, if he didn't mind.

"Your mother is not feeling well; no, nothing serious—another of her liver attacks. . . . But I didn't dare leave her alone with the children. I couldn't call you earlier; she was in too much pain and I couldn't go out. . . ."

Julian still held the phone in his hand, but he was no longer thinking about his family. All he could think of was that he would have an opportunity to stay here for the night; that he would help them light the lights before the shrine of the Nativity,[9] he would have a wonderful Christmas Eve dinner and sing carols with the rest of them. It all meant so much to Julian.

"Then I'll probably come tomorrow. Don't be frightened. No, nothing wrong; but since you are not coming, I thought I would help the sisters a bit; they have so much to do at Christmas time. Yes, I'll be there for dinner sure. . . . Yes, I'll be home for Christmas Day."

Sister Rosa was at his side, staring at him with her round eyes and oval mouth. She was the only unpleasantness he was glad to be leaving forever. . . . Julian lowered his eyes and humbly requested an audience with "Mother"; he wanted to ask her a special favor.

The next day, Julian was riding in a train through a gray sleet on his way to the city. In a third-class coach he was wedged in between turkeys, chickens and their owners, all bursting with optimism. All of Julian's property that morning consisted of a battered suitcase and the good black-dyed overcoat that kept him pleasantly warm. As they approached the city, as its smell struck his nostrils and he looked out upon the enormous rows of depressing factories and workmen's flats,[10] Julian began to feel he had had no right to enjoy himself so fully the evening before; he should not have eaten so much of so many choice things; he should not have sung in the voice which, during the war, had helped the other soldiers in the trenches through long hours of boredom and sadness.

Julian felt he should not have spent such a warm, cozy Christmas Eve, because for several years now they had had no such celebrations at home.

---

[8] **abide** (uh-BEYED) *v.* put up with; bear
[9] **Nativity** (nuh-TIHV-ih-tee) *n.* the birth of Christ; a representation of Christ as an infant
[10] **flats** (flatz) *n. pl.* apartments

Poor Herminia had probably managed some shapeless nougats[11] made of sweet-potato paste and painted in gay colors, and the children had spent half an hour chewing on them eagerly after an everyday dinner. At least, that is what had happened the last Christmas Eve he had spent at home. He had been out of work for months. He had always been a good provider, but then came the gasoline shortage and things came to a standstill. Herminia scrubbed stairs. She scrubbed countless stairs every day until the poor thing couldn't talk of anything but stairs and the food she could not buy. At the time Herminia was pregnant again and her appetite was something terrific. She was a thin woman, as tall and blonde as Julian; she was easy-going and wore thick glasses despite her youth. . . . Julian could not swallow his own food as he watched her devour her watery soup and sweet potatoes. Watery soup and sweet potatoes: that was what they ate every day at Julian's house all that winter, morning and evening. Breakfast was only for the children. Herminia looked greedily at the hot bluish milk they drank before going

off to school. . . . Julian, who, according to his family, had always been a glutton,[12] left off eating entirely. . . . But that was much worse for everybody, because his mind started to go and he became aggressive. Then he began imagining that his poor flat was a garage and that the beds crammed into all the rooms were luxurious automobiles. And one day he tried to kill Herminia and his mother, and they had to drag him out in a strait jacket. . . . But all that was part of the past. The relatively recent past. Now he was going back, completely recovered. He had been fine for several months now. But the

The Blind Man's Meal was painted by Pablo Picasso during his "blue period." Picasso's paintings from this period often represent the pain and hardships endured by the poor and unfortunate.

---

[11] **nougats** (NOO-guhts) *n. pl.* candies, usually made from nuts and honey or sugar
[12] **glutton** (GLUT-uhn) *n.* a person who eats too much

nuns had sympathized with him and let him linger on a little while longer, just a little while . . . until the Christmas holidays. Suddenly he realized what a coward he had been, putting it off. The streets leading home were full of brilliantly lighted shop windows. He stopped at a pastry shop and bought a tart. He had some money and spent it on that. He had eaten so many the last few days that it did not tempt him, but his family would not feel that way.

It was not easy, climbing the stairs to his flat, his suitcase in one hand, the sweet in the other. It was very high up and he was eager to see them all, to kiss his mother, the old lady who always smiled and pretended nothing was the matter so long as her pains were not too bad.

There were four doors, formerly green, now nondescript. One of them was his. He knocked.

He was in Herminia's skinny arms; the children were shouting. A pleasant smell wafted in from the kitchen. Something good was cooking.

"Papa, we've got turkey!"

That was the first thing they told him. He looked at his wife. He looked at his mother; she had aged greatly and was very pale from her last illness, but she had a nice new woolen shawl over her shoulders. The little dining room boasted a basket brimful of sweets, gewgaws[13] and ribbons.

"Did you win the lottery?"

"No, Julian, when you went off, some ladies came. . . . From a welfare organization, you know. . . . They took good care of us; they found me work and they are going to get you a job too, in a garage."

In a garage? Of course, a former madman could not be a taxi driver. A mechanic, perhaps. Julian gazed at his mother again and saw her eyes were full of tears. . . . But she was smiling, smiling as always.

Suddenly Julian felt his shoulders sag again under a load of responsibilities and worries. He had come back to the large family standing around him and it was his business to rescue them from the clutches of Charity. They would go hungry again, of course. . . .

"But Julian, aren't you glad? . . . We're all together again, all together at Christmas. . . . And what a Christmas we're going to have! Look!"

And again they pointed to the gift basket, to the children eager and wide-eyed. They were doing it for his benefit as he stood there, a sad, thin man with bulging eyes and a black overcoat. And it was as if he had left childhood behind again that Christmas Day so that he might look once more upon life—with all the cruelty that, beneath those gifts, it would have forever.

---

[13] **gewgaws** (GYOO-gawz) *n. pl.* showy trinkets

POSTREADING

Critical Thinking

1. In this story, what do you think Carmen Laforet is saying about Julian's fears?

2. What are the economic realities that await Julian at home? How do they contribute to his fears?

3. Have you ever dreaded going someplace or seeing someone? How did you feel once you actually got there or spent time with the person?

Writing Your Response to "The Return"

In your journal, write about one or two paragraphs that made an impression on you. Why did this passage affect you? Have you had a similar experience or feeling or did the passage remind you of something that happened to someone you know?

Going Back Into the Text: Author's Craft

Foreshadowing is a technique an author uses to give hints or clues as to what's going to happen in the story. The clues can come in dialogue, description, and the attitudes and reactions of the characters.

For instance, when Julian reflects on his attacks on Sister Rosa when he was first brought to the asylum, he realizes that the nun reminds him of his wife. This passage hints at what might happen when Julian rejoins his wife after leaving the convent.

Foreshadowing often serves two purposes. First, by raising questions in the reader's mind, it builds suspense. The reader then will want to continue to read to find out what happens. Second, foreshadowing can also prepare the reader for what will happen. In this way, the events may surprise the reader, but they won't be unexpected. This makes a story believable.

With a partner, spend some time talking about the foreshadowing in the story. Use the following questions and directives to guide your discussion:

1. What is the double meaning of the title? What does it tell you will happen to Julian?

2. Find more examples of foreshadowing in the story and explain how they hint at what will happen.

3. How does the foreshadowing contribute to the suspense of the story?

Reviewing the Region

1. Choose two selections from this chapter and compare the experiences of the narrators or central characters. Discuss the differences and similarities of the characters and of the obstacles they faced.

2. Every culture has a "system," a way things work in society. The "system" is often illogical or unfair. Choose a selection from this chapter and discuss the ways in which the author comments on "the system."

3. The characters in the selections in this chapter reflect many different attitudes toward life and/or society. Which character reflects your attitudes or experiences most closely? Discuss the ways in which the selection relates to your own life.

FOCUSING THE UNIT

COOPERATIVE/COLLABORATIVE LEARNING

Working with a small group of classmates, select an important social issue expressed in Unit 3. Possibilities include refugees, disabilities, or poverty. Together, hold a panel discussion to explore how the issue is treated in the literature and how it relates to your life and culture. Below is a sample dialogue that one group of students used to start their discussion. You can use this model as a jumping-off point for your panel discussion. At the end of the panel, summarize the main ideas and share them with the class.

Student 1: One of the most important cultural issues of the twentieth century is the Holocaust, the destruction of the European Jews by Nazi Germany. When World War II ended, about six million Jews had died in the death camps. Primo Levi describes what life was like in a Nazi death camp in his book *Survival in Auschwitz.*

Student 2: In 1993, the U.S. Holocaust Memorial Museum opened in Washington, DC. The museum documents the events of the Holocaust from 1933 to 1945.

Student 3: As a Jewish American, the Holocaust had a great impact on my life. My grandfather and great aunt escaped from the Nazis in 1936 and came to America. But many people from my family were not able to escape.

Writing Process

Literature is often a vehicle of protest, an effort to make readers aware of injustice. Reread the journal entries you made for this unit. Select two or more selections where your entry described strong emotions. Write a persuasive essay about a selection's effectiveness as protest literature. Your audience might be your classmates, community members interested in the social issue, or history students. First explain what issue each selection describes. Then add details from the selections to argue which selection is most effective. Refer to the handbook at the back of the book for help with the writing process. Use the model essays as guidelines.

Problem Solving

There are a great many crucial social issues facing the world today. Many of the writers in Unit 3 seem to think that literature is an effective way to improve the world. What do you think? Is literature a good way to solve some of the world's problems? Choose two or more of the authors in Unit 3 and analyze their insights into a particular problem. How does their writing help improve the problem? What role do you see literature playing in making the world a better place? In the form of a news show, poem, debate, newspaper editorial, or speech, express your reactions to the problem and solution. You can work alone, with a partner, or in a small group.

NORTH AND SOUTH AMERICA

ARCTIC OCEAN

Greenland
(Den.)

Alaska
(U.S.)

ROCKY MOUNTAINS

CANADA

*Hudson
Bay*

Vancouver

Quebec

St. Lawrence R.
Ottawa
Toronto

Montreal

Mississippi R.

UNITED STATES
OF AMERICA

Los
Angeles

New York
Washington, D.C.

ATLANTIC   OCEAN

*Gulf of
Mexico*

MEXICO

Mexico
City

BELIZE

BAHAMAS

CUBA

HAITI

DOMINICAN REPUBLIC

Puerto Rico
(U.S.)

JAMAICA

Caribbean Sea

ANTIGUA AND BARBUDA
ST. LUCIA — DOMINICA
BARBADOS

GUATEMALA
EL SALVADOR
HONDURAS
NICARAGUA
COSTA RICA
PANAMA

*Panama
Canal*

GRENADA

ST. VINCENT AND THE GRENADINES
TRINIDAD AND TOBAGO
GUYANA
SURINAME
French Guiana
(Fr.)

VENEZUELA

COLOMBIA

ECUADOR

Amazon R.

*PACIFIC
OCEAN*

PERU

Lima

ANDES

BRAZIL

BOLIVIA

MOUNTAINS

PARAGUAY

Rio de Janeiro

CHILE

Buenos Aires

URUGUAY

ARGENTINA

N
W   E
S

0   500   1,000 Miles

0   500   1,000 Kilometers

80°N
60°N
40°N
20°N
0° Equator
20°S
40°S

20°N
0°
20°S
40°S
40°N

160°W   140°W   120°W   100°W   80°W   60°W   40°W   20°W   0°

UNIT 4

The Americas

Most high and most mighty [Prince]:
      ... I am persuaded that, if Your Highness had been informed of even a few of the excesses which this New World has witnessed, all of them surpassing anything that men hitherto have imagined even in their wildest dreams, before entreating His Majesty to prevent any repetition of the atrocities which go under the name of 'conquests'...

Bartolomé de Las Casas was an eyewitness to Spain's conquests in the New World. He wrote this letter to Spain's Prince Philip. It was a plea to end the mass killing of the Native Americans. The Spanish *conquistadores* traveled throughout the New World in search of gold and other mineral wealth. Many Native Americans that the conquistadors met were enslaved, murdered, or died from European diseases.

The Spanish and the Portuguese established settlements throughout the southern and southwestern regions of the present-day United States and Central and South America.

In 1492, the Spanish, led by Christopher Columbus, landed on Hispaniola, which today is Haiti and the Dominican Republic. After taking what riches they could and gradually killing the Arawaks (the native peoples), Spain continued its destruction on its path to New Spain, or Mexico. In Mexico, the Spanish came upon other Native Americans. There they met the Mayas, Aztecs and many other native peoples. These Native Americans had advanced civilizations long before Europeans arrived in the Western Hemisphere. The Mayas in southern Mexico and Guatemala developed a way of writing using picture symbols. You will read some of their writing in this book. The Aztecs lived in a valley in the central highlands of Mexico. Their capital city was Tenochtitlán (tay-noch-tee-TLAHN), one of the largest cities in the world at that time. The Aztecs were skilled craftspeople, goldsmiths, merchants and warriors. The enslavement of native peoples that began with the conquistadors still continues, in altered forms, even today.

In Cholula, a cultural center on the major Central American trade-route, Hernando Cortés began his most widely reported massacre in which he wiped out almost the entire native population. In his full account to Spain's Prince Philip, De Las Casas described the event:
      ... all the dignitaries of the city and the region came out to welcome the Spaniards . . . and then proceeded to escort them into the city. . . . [T]he Spaniards decided that the moment had come to organize a massacre in order to inspire fear and terror in all the people of the territory.

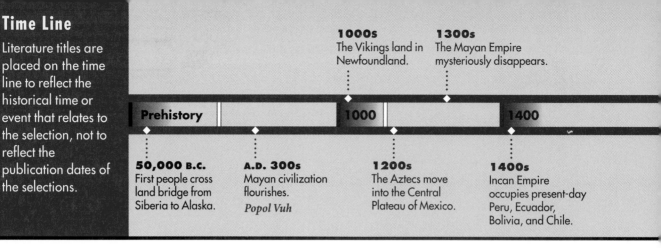

Time Line

Literature titles are placed on the time line to reflect the historical time or event that relates to the selection, not to reflect the publication dates of the selections.

1000s
The Vikings land in Newfoundland.

1300s
The Mayan Empire mysteriously disappears.

Prehistory   1000   1400

50,000 B.C.
First people cross land bridge from Siberia to Alaska.

A.D. 300s
Mayan civilization flourishes.
Popol Vuh

1200s
The Aztecs move into the Central Plateau of Mexico.

1400s
Incan Empire occupies present-day Peru, Ecuador, Bolivia, and Chile.

Native American scribes described Cortés's massacre from a different point of view.

> *. . . and when they had crowded into the temple courtyard, then the Spaniards and their allies blocked the entrances and every exit. There followed a butchery of stabbing, beating, killing of the unsuspecting Cholulans armed with no bows and arrows, protected by no shields . . . with no warning, they were treacherously, deceitfully slain.*

Spain and Portugal controlled most of Latin America from the 1500s to the early 1800s. Great Britain and France also had colonies in the New World. The Europeans not only brought war and slavery to the New World, but also new diseases that caused the death of nearly 90% of Native American civilizations. As a result, a new source of labor was needed for the European farms and plantations. Spanish, Portuguese, French, and British colonists turned to Africans, who had developed a resistance to the European diseases, and forced them to work on their plantations. In many ways the enslavement of Africans was a result of the extermination of Native Americans in the New World. By 1800, as many as 20 million Africans were sold as slaves in the Americas.

In the early 1800s, the ideas of independence from European and North American political philosophies spread throughout Latin America. In 1821, Mexicans won their freedom from Spain after long and bloody battles. Soon after, Simon Bolívar led the fight for freedom in Venezuela, Colombia, Ecuador, and Bolivia. José de San Martín helped to win freedom for Chile and Peru. In 1822, Brazil became free from the control of Portugal. By 1824, most parts of Central and South America were no longer colonies of Spain or Portugal.

During this century, many Latin American governments were not able to meet the chal-

---

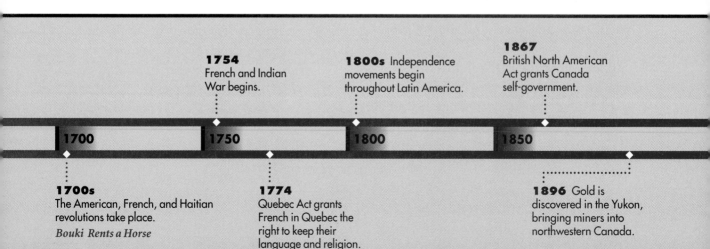

1754
French and Indian War begins.

1800s Independence movements begin throughout Latin America.

1867
British North American Act grants Canada self-government.

1700   1750   1800   1850

1700s
The American, French, and Haitian revolutions take place.
Bouki Rents a Horse

1774
Quebec Act grants French in Quebec the right to keep their language and religion.

1896 Gold is discovered in the Yukon, bringing miners into northwestern Canada.

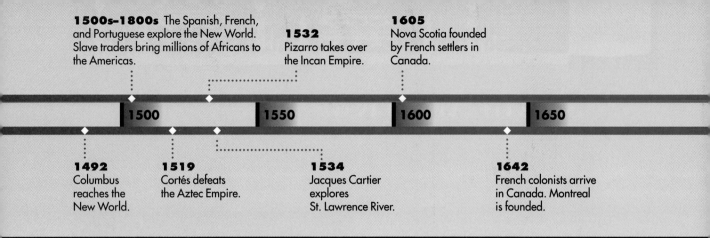

1500s-1800s The Spanish, French, and Portuguese explore the New World. Slave traders bring millions of Africans to the Americas.

1532 Pizarro takes over the Incan Empire.

1605 Nova Scotia founded by French settlers in Canada.

1500   1550   1600   1650

1492 Columbus reaches the New World.

1519 Cortés defeats the Aztec Empire.

1534 Jacques Cartier explores St. Lawrence River.

1642 French colonists arrive in Canada. Montreal is founded.

lenges created by mass movements of peasants into the cities. Nor were they able to solve the problems brought by growing industrialization. By the late 1980s and early 1990s, many of the military governments of Latin America had crumbled and were replaced by civilian governments. While still somewhat unstable, the new, more democratic governments have made great headway throughout Latin America.

CANADA Just as the Aztecs and Mayans of Latin America, the native people living in North America developed distinct cultures and languages. Their cultures reflected the environment in which they lived. As in United States, European settlers and their descendents in Canada moved westward. Their migration destroyed many of the Native American cultures who had lived on the land.

Spanish, French, and British settlers arrived in North America between the 1500s and the 1700s. The first permanent French settlement in Canada was in Nova Scotia in 1605. The French explored several waterways in search of furs and claimed all of the surrounding lands.

But unlike the United States and Latin American countries Canada did not fight a war for freedom from European rule. In 1867, Great Britain peacefully signed the British North American Act which created the independent Dominion of Canada. After 1885, six other provinces joined Canada; the last was Newfoundland in 1949. Canada eventually ended its legal ties to Great Britain with the Constitutional Act of 1982. This act gave Canada complete self-government.

In the last two centuries, Canada has become a stable and active part of the world community. Canada fought in both world wars and has become the home to immigrants seeking freedom from all over the world. Today, Canada and the United States share the longest unguarded border in the world.

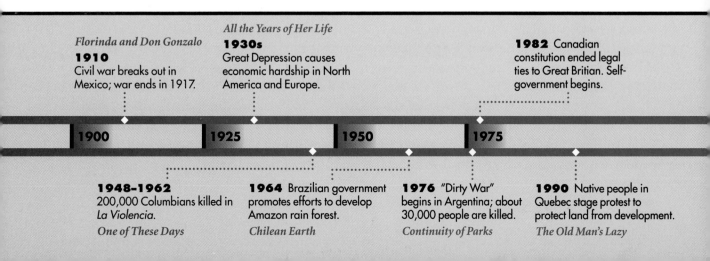

Florinda and Don Gonzalo
1910 Civil war breaks out in Mexico; war ends in 1917.

All the Years of Her Life
1930s Great Depression causes economic hardship in North America and Europe.

1982 Canadian constitution ended legal ties to Great Britian. Self-government begins.

1900   1925   1950   1975

1948-1962 200,000 Columbians killed in *La Violencia.*
One of These Days

1964 Brazilian government promotes efforts to develop Amazon rain forest.
Chilean Earth

1976 "Dirty War" begins in Argentina; about 30,000 people are killed.
Continuity of Parks

1990 Native people in Quebec stage protest to protect land from development.
The Old Man's Lazy

8 Latin America

The Mayan civilization flourished around A.D. 300 in present-day Mexico and Guatemala. They built cities with huge pyramids and other buildings of stone, studied astronomy, and created an accurate calendar. They also created their own number system and developed a way of writing using symbols. This chapter begins with a part of the Mayan Bible, one of the few ancient texts that was not destroyed by Spanish conquistadors when they burned Mayan libraries.

During the colonial period of Latin America, literature had a strong European influence. You will read a favorite Haitian folktale from this period. Since Haiti was influenced by many cultures, you might recognize the plot of other stories from Africa or Europe.

The poems and short stories that follow come from the time after Latin America's independence from European colonists. Even though they were free from European rule, the people still had only a few rights. Often the new nations of Latin America were controlled by small groups of wealthy landowners and military officers. These small groups ruled by economic control or military force. They were often cruel and violent in their use of power. As in many places in the world, the poor, the farmers, and the workers were taken advantage of. However, the rich and diverse cultural heritage of the people of Latin America inspired hope for a better life.

The literature you will read shows the emotional and economic impact of the turbulent Latin American political situations from this time period. You will also see how several writers es-

Andean Family was painted by Héctor Poleo in the 1940s. Poleo is popular for his depiction of common people of Venezuela. He also painted more troubled scenes of the Spanish Civil War. Think about the significance of the weapons in this peaceful scene.

cape these difficult times with humor and magic. In the final poems of this chapter, you will see the love and longing that many Latin Americans feel for their homeland in spite of the difficulties.

Today, Latin American literature has a distinct style. It deals with social and political issues, as well as emotional and personal concerns. You will find that these authors are able to bring to light the issues and concerns of their people and of the world.

PREREADING

from the *Popol Vuh*

Reading the Myth in a Cultural Context

It is believed that part of what is now Guatemala was settled by farmers sometime around 1000 B.C. Over the centuries, the descendants of these people migrated into what is today Guatemala, Honduras, El Salvador, Belize, and Mexico. These people were the Maya, whose advancements continue to amaze scholars.

The Maya had no central capital, no real "empire," as we think of the term today. Mayan cities—which may have been governed by priests or chiefs—controlled the lands around them. Larger cities such as Chichén Itzá, on the Yucatán Peninsula, may have controlled smaller cities in their area.

Most Maya were farmers, and corn was the staple of the Mayan diet. Extended families lived together and trained their children in practical skills. There were no schools.

The Maya believed in many gods—some good, some bad. They offered freshly killed animals, drops of their own blood, and sometimes even human beings to the gods as a sacrifice. The most important religious ceremonies took place in the cities, in temples at the tops of limestone pyramids. There were many religious festivals during the year, when the Maya people worshiped, danced, and feasted. Sometimes these festivals included a game that is similar to modern basketball.

Mayan civilization was at its height from about A.D. 300 to 800. But then something mysterious happened. The people began leaving the area—first they left the cities, and then the farmlands. Was there an epidemic, or a drought, or a rebellion against the chiefs and priests? Scholars are not sure. The Maya of the Yucatán peninsula maintained their society the longest, but the arrival of Spanish *conquistadores* in the 1500s changed their world forever. Today, descendants of the Maya live in Central America, but they are a distinct minority.

The work you are about to read is a piece of Mayan literature. Just like people today, the Maya asked questions like: "Where did we come from?" "Why are we the way we are?" and "What is our purpose in life?" They told stories to answer these questions. Many of these stories survive because the Maya recorded them in hieroglyphic writings.

Perhaps the greatest work of Mayan literature is called the *Popol Vuh*. Its tales take us back to the beginning of the world, as the Maya saw it. Through such myths, the Maya understood that they had a purpose in life—and a responsibility toward each other.

Focusing on the Selection

As you read, think about humanity as a whole. Where do we come from? What is our purpose in life? Maybe you feel uncertain about questions like these, or maybe you are confident in your beliefs. Look at what the Maya believed, and then think about how this ancient story applies to today's world.

from the *Popol Vuh*

◆◆◆

edited by *J.F. Bierlein*

This panel from the Mayan sacred books tells a creation myth with pictures. The Earth Monster, at the bottom of the panel holds the man's foot in her mouth. According to the myth, the Earth Monster couldn't swallow the foot, was unable to sink down to the bottom of the great waters and thus, Earth was created from her floating body.

There were four gods in heaven and each of them sat on his chair, observing the world below. Then the yellow lord suggested that they make a man to enjoy the earth and offer praise to the gods. The other three agreed.

So the yellow god took a lump of yellow clay and made a man from it. But his creation was weak; it dissolved in water and could not stand upright.

Then the red god suggested that they make a man out of wood, and the others agreed. So the red god took a branch from a tree and carved it into a human shape. When they tested it in water, it floated; it stood upright without any problem whatsoever. However, when they tested it with fire, it burned.

The four lords decided to try again. This time the black god suggested making a man out of gold. The gold man was beautiful and shone like the sun. He survived the tests of fire and water, looking even more handsome after these tests. However, the gold man was cold to the touch; he was unable to speak, feel, move, or worship the gods. But they left him on earth anyway.

The fourth god, the colorless lord, decided to make humans out of his own flesh. He cut the fingers off his left hand and they jumped and fell to earth. The four gods could hardly see what the men of flesh looked like as they were so far away. From the seat of the four lords, they looked like busy little ants.

But the men of flesh worshiped the gods and made offerings to them. They filled the hearts of the four lords with joy. One day the men of flesh found the man of gold. When they touched him, he was as cold as a stone.

When they spoke to him, he was silent. But the kindness of the men of flesh warmed the heart of the man of gold and he came to life, offering praise to the gods for the kindness of the men of flesh.

The word of praise from the previously silent creature woke the four gods from their sleep and they looked down on earth in delight. They called the man of gold "rich" and the men of flesh "poor," ordaining that the rich should look after the poor. The rich man will be judged at his death on the basis of how he cared for the poor. From that day onward, no rich man can enter heaven unless he is brought there by a poor man.

POSTREADING

Critical Thinking

1. According to this myth, from where did the first people come?

2. What attitudes does this story suggest were held about those Maya who were poor?

3. The myth also suggests the power of kindness. After reading this tale, what do you think is the most important thing to know about being kind?

Writing Your Response to the *Popol Vuh*

In your journal, make some notes about what you feel is your purpose in life. (You don't have to share your response, so be honest with yourself.) Is your purpose to be one of the "busy little ants," like the men of flesh in this myth? Is it "to enjoy the earth"? What else might it be?

Going Back Into the Text: Author's Craft

This story from the *Popol Vuh* is a **myth**, an ancient tale that helps to explain the unknown. Some myths interpret events in nature—for example, how the sun rises and sets, or why there is winter. Other myths are about people—for example, why there are different races, or how people came to be in the first place. This myth from the *Popol Vuh* explains the origins of humanity.

Myths are so old that no one knows who told a particular myth for the first time. Myths around the world have some common elements, because people everywhere look for answers to many of the same questions. A common characteristic of myths is the presence of the supernatural, usually in the form of one or more gods. Many myths also offer some lesson about life.

With a partner, talk about the elements of myths and this myth, in particular. Use the following questions and directives to guide your discussion:

1. "Where did we come from?" is just one question that this myth addresses. List at least two other questions that you think this part of the *Popol Vuh* attempts to answer.

2. Did the Maya feel that they were similar to the gods they worshiped? Explain your answer.

3. How does this myth compare to other creation stories that you know about?

The Great Prayer

Reading the Poem in a Cultural Context

Alfonso Cortés was one of Nicaragua's greatest poets. In a time of political unrest, he filled his poems with thoughts of spiritual and emotional unrest.

From its early years as an independent nation, Nicaragua has had an unstable government and an uneasy relationship with the United States. Nicaragua was the original choice for a United States-built canal across Central America. As a result, American businesses and governmental leaders took a great interest in Nicaraguan political problems. The canal project was finally moved to Panama because of political turmoil in Nicaragua, but United States Marines continued to occupy Nicaragua from 1912 to 1933 to protect American interests.

Alfonso Cortés's best poetry is not political but emotional and spiritual. His sisters claimed that he went insane in 1927. After that, he created many of his best poems while chained to a wall, writing in tiny letters on small pieces of paper. Nicaraguans still refer to Cortés as *El Poeta Loco* ("The Crazy Poet"), but they respect his achievement as a writer.

Cortés is best known for his metaphysical poetry. In it, he restlessly explores the world that is beyond our senses, the world of our mind and spirit. One such poem is "The Great Prayer." This poem asks us to think about the universe of our mind. The conflict is between the poet and "the void," which is a "place" that exists in his mind. The poem also asks us to consider the power of our dreams. This poem is typical of Cortés's writing—so typical, in fact, that "The Great Prayer" is carved on his tomb.

Focusing on the Selection

As you read "The Great Prayer," think about the world of your mind, your feelings, and your imagination. How would you describe that world to others? How does it affect your life in the real world? Jot down your ideas in your journal. After you have read "The Great Prayer," add to your notes.

The Great Prayer

Alfonso Cortés

Time is hunger, space is cold.
Pray, pray, for only prayer
can quiet the anguish of the void.[1]

Dream is a solitary rock
where the eagle of the soul nests.
Dream, dream away your everyday life.

A South American woman in prayer. Roman Catholicism plays a large role in the lives of many South Americans.

---

[1] **void** (void) *n.* an empty space

POSTREADING

Critical Thinking

1. How does Alfonso Cortés describe the "void" in which he says we live? How does he tell us to deal with that "void"?

2. Do you relate to the meaning of this poem more when life seems confusing or insecure? Why or why not?

3. Reread the final line of "The Great Prayer." Do you agree or disagree with the advice to "dream away your everyday life"? Explain your answer.

Writing Your Response to "The Great Prayer"

As you know, "The Great Prayer" is inscribed on the poet's tomb. In your journal, write a message about life that you would like people to remember. What might you say about how to live? What other advice might you offer?

Going Back Into the Text: Author's Craft

Usually, writers use imagery to help make readers aware of sensory experiences—sights, sounds, tastes, textures, and smells—that are new to them. In "The Great Prayer," however, Cortés uses imagery that appeals to the mind, the imagination, and the spirit.

Cortés achieves his goal through a mix of concrete and abstract imagery. **Concrete imagery** is description that appeals to the senses, whereas **abstract imagery** appeals to the mind. Both types often use comparisons to describe. "The Great Prayer," for example, is filled with abstract ideas—time, space, "the void," dreaming, the soul. Abstract ideas can be hard to describe. Cortés, therefore, uses comparisons to describe them. He compares some abstract ideas to things that we can see or touch (concrete imagery). He compares others to things that we only can imagine (abstract imagery).

With a partner, use the following questions to focus on concrete and abstract imagery in "The Great Prayer."

1. In line 1, how does Cortés describe time and space? How would you label each of those images, and why?

2. "The anguish of the void" (line 3) is an example of abstract imagery. What do you need to think about before you can begin to understand it?

3. Think about the description in lines 4–5. What comparisons can you find there? Are those images concrete or abstract? How are they related?

Bouki Rents a Horse

Reading the Story in a Cultural Context

Haiti occupies the western third of the island of Hispaniola. It was first settled by Spain, but it came under the control of France in 1697. The French called the colony Saint Domingue and imported Africans to work as slaves on sugar cane and spice plantations. More than half a million enslaved Africans worked in the colony by the late 1700s. Through their labor, Saint Domingue became the most prosperous colony in the Caribbean.

In 1791, however, the slaves staged a widespread rebellion. One of their leaders was Toussaint L'Ouverture, who had been born into slavery. When the rebellion was victorious, Toussaint became leader of the new government. After further struggles with France, Saint Domingue became the independent nation of Haiti in 1804.

Today, most Haitians are the descendants of the enslaved Africans who worked the colony's plantations. The majority of them live on tiny farms in the countryside. There, they grow barely enough to feed themselves. Lack of services such as adequate medical care adds to their poverty. It also shortens the average lifespan to about 50 years.

Faced with such difficulties, many Haitians draw strength from traditions that originated in Africa. For example, groups of rural Haitians make planting and harvest a time of *combile*—a blend of labor, singing, and music—as they work from farm to farm. African storytelling traditions have also survived in Haiti. "Bouki Rents a Horse" is a good example. It features a trickster hero, a character who triumphs through deception. His name here is Ti Malice, but he is quite like the African trickster hero known as Anansi the spider. In addition, the African tradition mixes with the realities of life in Haiti. This story, as retold by Harold Courlander, includes such "Haitian" details as the taking of yams to market and the basic unit of Haitian currency, the gourde. It also fulfills a dream of many people who are poor and oppressed—besting someone who takes advantage of them.

Focusing on the Selection

As you read "Bouki Rents a Horse," think about how Bouki's problem finally is solved. Think, too, about the differences among the characters. Why does Ti Malice become even more important than Bouki? How does his solution to Bouki's problem help you understand the people who would tell this story?

Bouki Rents a Horse

retold by *Harold Courlander*

It was time to dig up the yams and take them to market. Bouki went out with his big hoe and dug up a big pile of yams and left them in the sun to dry. While they were drying, he began to consider how he would get them to the city. "I think I will borrow Moussa's donkey," he said at last. "As long as I have the donkey, I might as well dig up some more yams."

So he dug up some more yams, and then he went to Moussa's house for the donkey. But Moussa said, "Bouki, my donkey ran away yesterday, and we haven't found him yet. Why don't you rent a horse from Mr. Toussaint?"

"Toussaint!" Bouki said. "He'll charge more than I can get for the yams! He'll charge me even for *talking* to him!"

But finally Bouki went to Toussaint's house to see if he could rent a horse.

Toussaint said, "This is a good horse. He's too good to carry yams. But you can have him for one day for fifteen gourdes."[1]

Bouki had only five gourdes.

"I'll take the five now," Toussaint said. "You can give me ten more tomorrow when you come for the horse."

Bouki went home. He went to sleep. In the morning when he got up to go to market, Moussa was waiting in front of his house with the donkey.

"Here's the donkey," Moussa said. "He came home in the middle of the night."

Bouki said, "But I already rented Toussaint's horse!"

"Never mind, go tell Toussaint you don't need the horse," Moussa said.

From *The Piece of Fire and Other Haitian Tales.* Copyright © 1964 by Harold Courlander. Reprinted by permission of the Estate of Harold Courlander.
[1]**gourdes** (goordz) *n. pl.* units of money in Haiti

Haitian artist Phonard painted this piece called *Pastoral Scene.* The lively and colorful feel of the piece is common to island art.

"But I already gave him five gourdes," Bouki complained. "I'll never get my money back!"

Just then Ti Malice came along. He listened to the talk. He said, "Take me along to Toussaint's. I'll get your money back for you."

Together Bouki and Ti Malice went to Toussaint's place.

"We've come for the horse," Ti Malice said.

"There he is under the tree," Toussaint said. "But first give me the ten gourdes."

"Not so fast," Ti Malice said. "First we have to see if he's big enough."

"He's big enough," Toussaint said. "He's the biggest horse around here. So give me the ten gourdes."

"First we have to measure him," Ti Malice said. He took a measuring tape from his pocket and stretched it over the horse's back. "Let's see, now," he said to Bouki. "You need about eighteen inches, and you can sit in the middle. I need about fifteen inches, and I can sit here. Madame Malice needs about eighteen inches, and she can sit behind me. Madame Bouki needs about twenty inches, and she can sit in the front."

"Wait!" Toussaint said. "You can't put four people on that horse!"

"Then," Ti Malice said, "Tijean Bouki can go here on the horse's neck. Boukino can sit in his lap, and we can tie Boukinette right here if we're careful."

"Listen!" Toussaint said, starting to sweat. "You must be crazy. A horse can't carry so many people!"

"He can try," Ti Malice said.

"You'll kill him!" Toussaint said.

"We can put my children *here*," Ti Malice said, measuring behind the horse's ears, "but they'll have to push together."

"Just a minute!" Toussaint shouted. "You can't have the horse!"

"Oh yes, we can," Ti Malice said, still measuring. "You rented him to us, and today we are going to use him. Bouki, where will we put the baby?"

"Baby?" Bouki said. "Baby?"

"We'll put the baby here," Ti Malice said. "Madame Bouki can hold him. Then over here we can hang the saddlebags to carry the pigs."

"The deal is off!" Toussaint shouted. "This animal isn't a steamship!"

"Now don't try to back out of the deal," Ti Malice said, "or we'll take the matter to the police."

"Here!" Toussaint said. "Here's your five gourdes back!"

"Five!" Ti Malice said. "You rented him to us for *fifteen*, and now you want to give *five* back? What do you take us for?"

"Yes," Bouki said, "what for?"

"But Bouki only *gave* me five!" Toussaint said.

Ti Malice looked the horse over carefully.

"Where will we put Grandmother?" Bouki asked suddenly.

"Here!" Toussaint shouted. "Here!" He pushed fifteen gourdes into Ti Malice's hands. "And get away from my horse!" He jumped on its back and rode away.

Bouki and Ti Malice watched him go. Then they fell on the ground and began to laugh. They laughed so hard that they had to gasp for air.

Suddenly Bouki stopped laughing. He looked worried. He sat up straight.

"What's the matter?" Ti Malice asked.

"I don't think we could have done it," Bouki said.

"Done what?" Ti Malice asked.

"Put Grandmother on the horse," Bouki said.

POSTREADING

Critical Thinking

1. Why do you think a Haitian audience would appreciate this story?

2. What details tell you a little about Haitian families? About class distinctions among Haitians?

3. How do you feel about Ti Malice's solution to Bouki's problem? Why?

Writing Your Response to "Bouki Rents a Horse"

In your journal, write about a time when you had a problem that reminds you of Bouki's problem with Toussaint. Were you able to solve the problem? Were you happy with the solution? What did you learn from the experience?

Going Back Into the Text: Author's Craft

We don't know who first told this story, but it is a memorable tale. A strong part of its appeal is that we seem to understand its characters so well.

Characterization is the way in which a writer—in this case, a storyteller—lets us know what the different people in a story are like. Sometimes a writer will say directly that a character is greedy, frightened, hopeful, and so on. More often, however, a writer will show the character's traits by letting us see how the characters act and what they say to each other.

With a partner, talk about the different characters in "Bouki Rents a Horse." Think of what you know about them and how you know it. The following questions can guide your discussion:

1. You already know that "Bouki Rents a Horse" is a trickster tale. How does the storyteller help us understand that Ti Malice is a trickster?

2. The owner of the horse is named Toussaint. Do you think that he is meant to be like Toussaint L'Ouverture? How does this name add to our understanding of him?

3. How would you describe Bouki? Give two statements that he makes in the story that help characterize him.

The Street

The Room

Reading the Poems in a Cultural Context

Where are you? That question can be answered in several ways. At this moment, you might be in a classroom, or in your bedroom, or at the library, or at a friend's house. You are in a certain city, in a particular country. But being a teenager, a young adult, is also part of "where" you are. And you could answer the question by talking about your emotions, your cultural background, your plans for the future, or your personal beliefs and values.

Many writers have addressed the various meanings of "Where are you?" You are about to read answers by two Mexican poets. Victor Manuel Mendiola has been a student of economics and the codirector of a publishing house, as well as a poet. His poem "The Room," however, suggests that there is something fragile about our attempts to make the "where" of our emotions appear civilized.

Octavio Paz, winner of the 1990 Nobel Prize for Literature, has explored the "where" of a cultural identity for much of his literary career. His poems and essays often consider how present-day Mexicans are the products of their pre-Columbian past. From his travels around the world (including many years as a member of Mexico's diplomatic corps), Paz also came to see the search for identity as a universal condition. The feeling of that search is very strong in "The Street."

Paz has often chosen experimental ways of expressing his ideas. Politically active himself, he has felt that experimenting with language can provide a key to social change: "Poetry is . . . the voice which, in history, is always saying something different." Yet his poetry also appeals to a wide variety of readers. Paz appreciates the personal impact of his work, as well: "If it happens that what you write for yourself becomes something for others as well, especially for a young reader, then you have achieved something."

Where are you? In both of the following selections, the title seems to suggest a physical location. But look a bit deeper. You may be, emotionally, in one of the places about which these poets are writing.

Focusing on the Selections

As you read these two poems, think about emotions that you try to mask in your everyday activities. How well can you hide those emotions? What kinds of situations can bring them to the surface? Do you think that most people feel the way you do, or are your feelings unique?

The Street

Octavio Paz
translated by *Muriel Rukeyser*

A long and silent street.
I walk in blackness and I stumble and fall
and rise, and I walk blind, my feet
stepping on silent stones and dry leaves.
Someone behind me also stepping on stones, leaves:
if I slow down, he slows:
if I run, he runs. I turn: nobody.
Everything dark and doorless.
Turning and turning among these corners
which lead forever to the street
where nobody waits for, nobody follows me,
where I pursue a man who stumbles
and rises and says when he sees me: nobody.

Mexican artist Diego Rivera painted *Frozen Assets* which depicts a prison at night. Why does Rivera refer to the prisoners as "frozen assets"? How does the mood change between the top and bottom of this painting?

The Room

Victor Manuel Mendiola

Dogs are barking
and something inside you—
in the farthest room of the house of you,
in the deaf shadow of a silence
where you watch yourself alone
closing the windows
and listening to
the lost, bewildered dogs
in this cold country that is time,
in this camp of the hours exposed to all weathers—
goes off with the dogs and howls.

POSTREADING

Critical Thinking

1. How do you think Mendiola and Paz want us to feel about the places that they have described?

2. How might the cultural background of these two Mexican writers have influenced these particular poems?

3. Which poem do you think has the greater emotional power? Explain your answer.

Writing Your Response to "The Room" and "The Street"

In your journal, write about a place that seems ordinary, everyday, and unemotional—but that, under the right conditions, could become a place of great emotion. (For example, think about how a school gym could become a place of great joy or how a parking lot could become a frightening place.) What would have to happen to give that place an emotional "charge"? Would everyone recognize the change—or would you, alone, be aware of it?

Going Back Into the Text: Author's Craft

Mood is the main feeling or atmosphere in a literary work or passage. Moods appeal to a reader's emotions; they can include joy, fear, anger, grief, or hope.

There are several ways in which writers create mood in literature. For example, the details of the setting—especially unusual or repeated details—may suggest gloom, happiness, or mystery. Word choices are important, too. For example, saying that the wind *screamed* does more to create a mood than does saying that the wind merely *blew*. Finally, the writer's attitude also affects the mood of a piece of literature. The result is an emotional setting that influences the reader's thinking about the subject of the writing.

With a partner, review "The Room" and "The Street." Analyze the mood that each poem expresses. Use the following questions to help you compare your thoughts.

1. How are the moods of these poems similar? How are they different?

2. Notice how *dogs* is repeated in "The Room" and *street* and *nobody* are repeated in "The Street." How do you think the repeated words strengthen the mood in each poem?

3. Describe the mood in another poem or story that you have enjoyed.

PREREADING

Keeping Quiet
Chilean Earth

Reading the Poems in a Cultural Context

Chile, a long and narrow country on the west coast of South America, is a varied land. It is a place of rain forests and deserts, of volcanoes and glaciers. It also is a land that has been torn by political and social troubles. These and other aspects of life in Chile appear in the writings of Pablo Neruda and Gabriela Mistral, two of Chile's best-known poets.

Pablo Neruda wrote many kinds of poetry over his long writing career. In his early years, he focused on love and nature. Then he wrote intensely sad poems, full of bizarre images. After World War II, he served in Chile's Senate, but in 1948, the government ordered his arrest. Neruda fled the country and wrote a collection of poems of political protest.

Neruda's return to Chile in 1952 marked another change in his writing. His later poems tended to use simpler images, often from everyday life. The thoughts were clearer and more personal, expressing hope and dignity. "Keeping Quiet," which you are about to read, comes from that time in Neruda's career. Neruda won the Nobel Prize for Literature in 1971 "for poetry that, with the action of an elemental force, brings alive a continent's destiny and dreams."

Gabriela Mistral also won a Nobel Prize for Literature, in 1945. In fact, she was the first Latin American writer to be so honored. Mistral grew up in the Elqui Valley of northern Chile. There she was influenced by the beautiful farmlands, the hard-working people, and her grandmother's love for the Bible. While still a teenager, Mistral became a teacher. For the rest of her life—no matter where she traveled or what acclaim she received—Mistral encouraged people to think of her as a humble rural schoolteacher.

Mistral used her poems to offer vivid images of her homeland or thoughts about the importance of faith—and sometimes both. She frequently spoke for Chilean women, children, and others who had little chance to speak publicly for themselves. She wrote with a style that was simple and yet uniquely powerful. "What the soul does for the body so does the poet for her people" was Mistral's view of her work—and the inscription on her tomb.

Focusing on the Selections

As you read these two poems, think about times when you wished that you could take a break from the activities of the world. What activities would you like to put aside for a while? How would you spend your free time? What would the break do for you? Make some notes in your journal, then refer to those notes as you read the poems.

Keeping Quiet

Pablo Neruda

Now we will count to twelve
and we will all keep still.

For once on the face of the earth,
let's not speak in any language;
let's stop for one second,
and not move our arms so much.

It would be an exotic[1] moment
without rush, without engines;
we would all be together
in a sudden strangeness.

Fishermen in the cold sea
would not harm whales
and the man gathering salt
would look at his hurt hands.

Those who prepare green wars,
wars with gas, wars with fire,
victories with no survivors,
would put on clean clothes
and walk about with their brothers
in the shade, doing nothing.

What I want should not be confused
with total inactivity.
Life is what it is about;
I want no truck[2] with death.

---

[1] **exotic** (ig-ZAHT-ihk) *adj.* having the charm of the unfamiliar or unusual
[2] **truck** (truk) *n.* dealings

If we were not so single-minded
about keeping our lives moving,
and for once could do nothing,
perhaps a huge silence
might interrupt this sadness
of never understanding ourselves
and of threatening ourselves with death.
Perhaps the earth can teach us
as when everything seems dead
and later proves to be alive.

Now I'll count up to twelve
and you keep quiet and I will go.

Peasants by Diego Rivera. The painting has an entirely different mood than the one on page 320. People working was one of Rivera's favorite subjects for painting. Rivera helped lead a campaign to have artists decorate the walls of government buildings. His efforts were successful and today the Mexican government has many beautiful buildings.

Chilean Earth

Gabriela Mistral

We dance on Chilean earth
more beautiful than Lia and Raquel:
the earth that kneads[1] men,
their lips and hearts without bitterness.

The land most green with orchards,
the land most blond with grain,
the land most red with grapevines,
how sweetly it brushes our feet!

Its dust molded our cheeks,
its rivers, our laughter,
and it kisses our feet with a melody
that makes any mother sigh.

For the sake of its beauty,
we want to light up fields with song.
It is free,
and for freedom we want
to bathe its face in music.

Tomorrow we will open its rocks;
we will create vineyards and orchards;
tomorrow we will exalt its people.
Today we need only to dance!

---

[1] **kneads** (needz) *v.* massages or presses with the hands

POSTREADING

Critical Thinking

1. Do Neruda and Mistral consider themselves part of the scenes that they describe? How can you tell?

2. What feelings about life does each poem show?

3. Which poem's advice do you think is more practical? Explain your answer.

Writing Your Response to "Keeping Quiet" and "Chilean Earth"

What would happen if the students and teachers at your school followed the advice in one of these poems? In your journal, jot down some possible results. What activities would be left undone for a time? Would people get along better because of the change? What else would happen?

Going Back Into the Text: Author's Craft

Some poems remind us of songs: Even if we cannot think of a melody for the words, we can imagine someone singing them. This is the main characteristic of **lyric poetry**—poetry that is meant to express strong personal feeling rather than tell a story.

The speakers in some lyric poems present their feelings as if they are alone, thinking. In other lyric poems, the speakers talk directly to someone. Both kinds of lyric poems present many imaginative details to express the feeling of a powerful emotion.

Meet with a partner or a small group. Use the following questions to explore and talk about the lyric qualities of "Keeping Quiet" and "Chilean Earth."

1. What emotion do you think is strongest in "Chilean Earth"? Give two details from the poem that you think help make that feeling sound like a song.

2. In "Keeping Quiet," is the emotion the same? How can you tell?

3. Are the two speakers "singing" to themselves, or are they "singing" to someone else? Explain your answer.

PREREADING

Florinda and Don Gonzalo

Responding to Literature

Notice the sidenotes in the margins of this selection. These notes reflect one student's reading of *Florinda and Don Gonzalo*, a one-act play by Luisa Josefina Hernández. The student points out how the values and traditions of two older Mexicans affect their relationship. The student also notices how Hernández uses certain elements of drama, such as dialogue, conflict, character, and setting. Compare this student's observations with your own.

Reading the Play in a Cultural Context

Plays have always been a part of Latin American life. Even some Mayan plays have survived.

Most of the early plays written in Latin America by Europeans were religious dramas. They were meant to help teach the Indians about Christianity. A small number of plays, however, were written for descendants of the Spanish settlers. Much of the playwriting of the 1600s and 1700s imitated the European theater—but some plays were written to reflect the local culture and values.

Latin American theater came into its own after World War I. Experimental theater companies gave many writers a place to express their ideas about what it meant to live in Latin America during a time of revolutionary changes. Despite setbacks caused by political unrest and government censorship, Latin American theater has continued to grow since World War II.

In Latin America today there is a growing interest in experimental theater. This is particularly true in Mexico, where writers such as Luisa Josefina Hernández have won many awards for their plays. *Florinda and Don Gonzalo* is one of many examples of short plays that she has written. In it, she explores the psychology of her characters and helps us see how we are like them.

Focusing on the Selection

As you read *Florinda and Don Gonzalo*, think about the values that these characters have. How clearly do they express their ideas toward one another? How do their words reveal struggles in their lives? Can you sympathize with those struggles? How do you think they should resolve those struggles?

Florinda and Don Gonzalo

◆◆◆

Luisa Josefina Hernández

I think that *Don* is a title of respect, so maybe Don Gonzalo is a wealthy man. This title has a man's name and a woman's name in it; will this play be a love story?

FLORINDA:[1] My name's Florinda and I'm a dressmaker.

DON GONZALO:[2] I'm pleased to meet you, miss. What can I do for you?

FLORINDA: Ah, nothing. Mrs., I'm a widow. You must know that for more than a year I've been living opposite here, in that blue house. I had a quiet moment and I decided to cross over and visit you.

DON GONZALO: Do you want . . . to sit down?

They are both lonely people. Florinda admits it; Don Gonzalo may not admit it, but he shows it by sitting alone every afternoon.

FLORINDA: No, it isn't necessary. The fact is that I said to myself: "Don Gonzalo spends every afternoon seated in the doorway reading. Perhaps a bit of conversation might suit him."

DON GONZALO: I'm grateful to you.

FLORINDA: No. I was dying to speak with you, because I too feel lonely.

DON GONZALO: Don't you have anyone?

---

[1] **Florinda** (FLAWR-een-dah) *n.* a woman's name
[2] **Don Gonzalo** (dohn gohn-ZAH-loh) *n. don* is a title of respect in Spanish; Gonzalo is the man's name

FLORINDA: Two women who help me: one who takes care of the house and the other, a seamstress, who helps with the sewing. But in the afternoon, when they finish working, they go with their families. I certainly don't have a family.

DON GONZALO: I have my brother and his wife, but they have too many things to do to sit down and talk with me. I understand. . . . I'm somewhat of a nuisance.

FLORINDA: Don't say that!

DON GONZALO: I'm not complaining. It's useless to complain of things which have no remedy.[3] I try to bother them as little as possible. I spend all morning in my room and finally at this time, I come near the door. That's always entertaining. One sees the cars, the people . . .

FLORINDA: But you don't see anything! All the time I've been living across the street, I've never noticed you raise your eyes from your book.

DON GONZALO: Perhaps. Sometimes I don't feel any curiosity.

FLORINDA: Wrong. Curiosity is the source of many discoveries.

DON GONZALO: Like which ones, for example?

FLORINDA: All inventions, like the sewing machine. What would I do without it?

DON GONZALO: Do you work a lot?

FLORINDA: Several hours a day. When some holiday draws near I work more, even at night. But it doesn't matter. I earn more than I need to live on.

DON GONZALO: That feeling must be very satisfying. I haven't earned a penny in my life.

[3] **remedy** (REHM-ih-dee) *n.* cure; something that corrects a fault

So Florinda has her own business! Maybe she and Don Gonzalo are even more alike than I thought at first. I wonder how she feels when she says, "I certainly don't have a family."

Don Gonzalo seems very depressed. Maybe never having had to work has left him without a purpose in life, or with a feeling that his life doesn't matter to the world. Sometimes I complain about working hard, but it feels good to accomplish things, too. Don Gonzalo could learn a lot from Florinda!

FLORINDA: But it brings loneliness.

DON GONZALO: Why don't you get married again?

FLORINDA: I've had two suitors,[4] but I don't like them. We widows are difficult to please. We know a great deal about life.

DON GONZALO: I imagine so. Once, I was in love, when I was very young. A friend of the family who used to come every day . . . we would speak of many things. . . . But, what could only be expected, happened.

FLORINDA: And what was that?

Why didn't Don Gonzalo fight to keep this girl? Has the failure of this relationship poisoned him for the rest of his life? I think that Florinda is right — love matters most!

DON GONZALO: Her parents found out and they advised her to marry another fellow. She resisted for some time, but she ended by accepting him and I agreed. What kind of life would she have had at my side?

Will the adjustment of having a new person in her life be difficult for Florinda after her years alone? Think about the difference between love and companionship.

---

[4] **suitors** (SOO-tuhrz) *n. pl.* men who are courting a woman

FLORINDA: If the two of you loved one another, a lifetime of love.

DON GONZALO: You're very romantic . . . Florinda.

FLORINDA: For a widow, yes.

DON GONZALO: Girls want to have a good time, go out, have friends. I'm used to being a burden, but I couldn't have endured being one for my own wife.

FLORINDA: You're very proud, and in order to be happy it's necessary to have humility.

DON GONZALO: Everything is learned too late. There's always time to think; however, to act there's but a moment, only one.

FLORINDA: Don't be a pessimist,[5] Don Gonzalo. Life is long.

DON GONZALO: That's no consolation[6] for me.

FLORINDA: You're so handsome, Don Gonzalo!

DON GONZALO: . . .

FLORINDA: Pardon me if I've bothered you. That wasn't my intention. I wouldn't want you to consider it all as lost and to speak without hope. Life . . . life's miraculous.

DON GONZALO: Do you believe that?

FLORINDA: Yes. Of course one has to do something on his part. Don Gonzalo, . . . I decided to come to see you after thinking it over for many months. The first time that it occurred to me, I thought that I'd never dare. Then, as time passed I began getting used to the idea, so much so that this morning, I now see it as the most natural thing in the world.

Florinda is some character — she certainly says what is on her mind! She says that he is unhappy because he is proud, but proud of what?

Florinda really becomes aggressive here! Why is she so eager for a relationship with him — does she pity him, or does she want someone to take care of? What does he have to offer?

---

[5] **pessimist** (PEHS-uh-mihst) *n.* a person who tends to take the gloomiest view of a situation
[6] **consolation** (kahn-suh-LAY-shuhn) *n.* comfort

Now I understand a little more of what she wants from this relationship. She does want someone to take care of and someone to keep her from feeling lonely. There is a physical attraction, as well.

Don Gonzalo is the more traditional of these two characters. It is Florinda, not Don Gonzalo, who has approached the matter of romance. It is she who is willing to live together rather than marry.

What is it about these characters, or their culture, that has kept them from meeting before now?

DON GONZALO: Among neighbors, a visit doesn't deserve so many doubts.

FLORINDA: A simple visit, no. But it's a question of something in common.

DON GONZALO: What could it be?

FLORINDA: A proposition. I wanted to ask you if you'd like to come to live with me. I'd take care of you, and you on your part would keep me company and we'd have conversations when you desired to speak and when not, I'd resign myself to your handsome presence.

DON GONZALO: Then it's . . . a proposal of marriage?

FLORINDA: Only in case you wanted to see it that way. I'll be satisfied just with your coming to my house.

DON GONZALO: You're . . . very touching. Remember that I can't help you in anything and that on the other hand I'd give a lot of bother.

FLORINDA: I've already told you that I earn more money than I spend and that I've time to spare. Do you accept, Don Gonzalo?

DON GONZALO: Tell me, what made you think of it?

FLORINDA: From looking at you so much. I used to look at you from behind the window blinds and then I began to dream of you and I imagine you so clearly that I almost knew what you were thinking about when you were distracted from your book or when you sighed. Then I opened the window and I sat down there to sew, but you didn't seem to see me and I became very impatient.

DON GONZALO: I did see you.

FLORINDA: Ah!

DON GONZALO: Only . . . how dare I?

FLORINDA: That had also occurred to me. I thought, "If he has seen me, all the more reason for me to go and speak to him."

DON GONZALO: Won't you be sorry?

FLORINDA: I, Don Gonzalo, am very determined.

DON GONZALO: I'd like to ask one thing of you.

FLORINDA: Whatever you wish.

DON GONZALO: That you marry me.

FLORINDA: Thank you very much, Don Gonzalo. I'll be happy to marry you.

DON GONZALO: And, when . . . when are you coming for me?

FLORINDA: Well, now. The truth is that I was coming now to pick you up, and I intended to return home with you.

DON GONZALO: Now? Right now?

FLORINDA: As it's a matter of only crossing the street and that's so easy. . . .

DON GONZALO: And, the wedding?

FLORINDA: We'll arrange it there.

DON GONZALO: And, my family?

FLORINDA: We'll inform them later . . . as it's just across the street.

DON GONZALO: In everything you're a woman of understanding. Let's go.

FLORINDA: Let's go.

DON GONZALO: Be careful in getting off the sidewalk because this wheelchair is getting shakier by the minute.

FLORINDA: Don't worry, Don Gonzalo. Close your eyes and think that the street is a river. I'll let you know when we reach the other shore.

I still think that Don Gonzalo is a rather weak character. In the future, will Florinda still be happy with him if he continues to be weak?

Is he asking her because he really wants this relationship, or because he does not want to violate tradition?

All we know about Don Gonzalo's relatives is that they consider him a nuisance (or so he thinks). Will they think he is crazy and try to protect him from Florinda, or will they be happy to have someone else care for him?

I like this ending. Lots of life's changes are like stepping onto the shore of a new land. I guess that we should be optimistic about their future together.

POSTREADING

Critical Thinking

1. Hernández is known as an experimental writer. What about this play or its ideas might be called experimental?

2. What details in this play suggest that Don Gonzalo is conservative in his values but that Florinda is liberal in hers?

3. The play leaves the audience with many questions to consider. What do you think will happen next, and why?

Writing Your Response to *Florinda and Don Gonzalo*

In your journal, write about a feeling, idea, or question you had while reading this dialogue. How does this scene relate to an experience in your own life or in the life of someone you know?

Going Back Into the Text: Author's Craft

A play contains many of the same elements as a novel or short story. It has a setting—a time, place, and perhaps a set of attitudes in which the story takes place. It has a plot, driven by some sort of conflict, that builds to a moment of climax and then finds a resolution. If it is well written, it has memorable characters.

One of the main elements of a play, however, is its use of **dialogue**, or conversation between characters. While scenery, costumes, and physical movement give insights into characters, it is most often through dialogue that the characters in a play convey their personalities, values, and beliefs to the audience.

With a partner, review *Florinda and Don Gonzalo* to see how Hernández uses the various elements of a play, in particular dialogue. The following questions can serve as guidelines.

1. What aspects of Florinda and Don Gonzalo's characters are revealed through their dialogue?

2. When does the climax of this play occur? How is it resolved?

3. Sometimes, what is left unsaid is as important as what actually is said in dialogue. Do you think that these two characters have left anything unsaid? Explain your answer.

One of These Days

Reading the Story in a Cultural Context

Gabriel García Márquez was born in the Colombian town of Aracataca, on the Caribbean coast, in 1928. The town had been founded 25 years earlier by refugees from Colombia's fierce civil war. During World War I, the merchants in Aracataca became rich by selling bananas. By the time García Márquez was born, however, those days had passed. Aracataca was a poor, struggling town, and thoughts of power and glory were just memories.

García Márquez grew up with those memories. His grandparents told him folktales, legends, and historical tales of prosperity. Their stories fired his imagination. Later, he set many of his own stories in a town, Macondo, that he based upon Aracataca. Furthermore, his writing often includes a mix of history and mythology—the kinds of stories he heard most often as a child. His novels and short stories have so moved readers that García Márquez won the Nobel Prize for Literature in 1982.

"One of These Days," the story that you are about to read, makes readers think about different kinds of power. García Márquez knew several. There was the power of money, which was important in his home town, Aracataca. There was the imaginative power of his grandparents' stories and his own writing. And there was political power. A desire for political power had caused a civil war in Colombia before García Márquez was born. Then, from the late 1940s to the mid-1960s, another power struggle between the two main political parties resulted in *La Violencia* ("The Violence"). During La Violencia some 200,000 Colombians died. The conflict in "One of These Days" is between two characters who have different kinds of power over each other.

Focusing on the Selection

As you read, think about the implied threat in the words *one of these days*. . . . Think, too, about the meaning of power. Who are the powerful people in your life? In what ways would you like to have power? How can powerful people threaten others? When there is a struggle for power, can you always be certain who will win?

One of These Days

$\blacklozenge\blacklozenge\blacklozenge$

Gabriel García Márquez

Monday dawned warm and rainless. Aurelio Escovar,[1] a dentist without a degree, and a very early riser, opened his office at six. He took some false teeth, still mounted in their plaster mold, out of the glass case and put on the table a fistful of instruments which he arranged in size order, as if they were on display. He wore a collarless striped shirt, closed at the neck with a golden stud, and pants held up by suspenders. He was erect and skinny, with a look that rarely corresponded to the situation.

When he had things arranged on the table, he pulled the drill toward the dental chair and sat down to polish the false teeth. He seemed not to be thinking about what he was doing, but worked steadily, pumping the drill with his feet, even when he didn't need it.

After eight he stopped for a while to look at the sky through the window, and he saw two pensive[2] buzzards who were drying themselves in the sun on the ridgepole of the house next door. He went on working with the idea that before lunch it would rain again. The shrill voice of his eleven-year-old son interrupted his concentration.

"Papá."

"What?"

"The Mayor wants to know if you'll pull his tooth."

"Tell him I'm not here."

He was polishing a gold tooth. He held it at arm's length and examined it with his eyes half closed. His son shouted again from the little waiting room.

"He says you are, too, because he can hear you."

The dentist kept examining the tooth. Only when he had put it on the table with the finished work did he say:

---

[1] **Aurelio Escovar** (awr-EE-lyoh EHS-koh-vahr) *n.* a man's name
[2] **pensive** (PEHN-sihv) *adj.* thoughtful

"So much the better."

He operated the drill again. He took several pieces of a bridge out of a cardboard box where he kept the things he still had to do and began to polish the gold.

"Papá."

"What?"

He still hadn't changed his expression.

"He says if you don't take out his tooth, he'll shoot you."

Without hurrying, with an extremely tranquil[3] movement, he stopped pedaling the drill, pushed it away from the chair, and pulled the lower drawer of the table all the way out. There was a revolver. "OK," he said. "Tell him to come and shoot me."

He rolled the chair over opposite the door, his hand resting on the edge of the drawer. The Mayor appeared at the door. He had shaved the left side of his face, but the other side, swollen and in pain, had a five-day-old beard. The dentist saw many nights of desperation in his dull eyes. He closed the drawer with his fingertips and said softly:

"Sit down."

"Good morning," said the Mayor.

"Morning," said the dentist.

While the instruments were boiling, the Mayor leaned his skull on the headrest of the chair and felt better. His breath was icy. It was a poor office: an old wooden chair, the pedal drill, a glass case with ceramic bottles. Opposite the chair was a window with a shoulder-high cloth curtain. When he felt the dentist approach, the Mayor braced his heels and opened his mouth.

Aurelio Escovar turned his head toward the light. After inspecting the infected tooth, he closed the Mayor's jaw with a cautious pressure of his fingers.

"It has to be without anesthesia,"[4] he said.

"Why?"

"Because you have an abscess."[5]

The Mayor looked him in the eye. "All right," he said, and tried to smile. The dentist did not return the smile. He brought the basin of sterilized instruments to the worktable and took them out of the water with a pair of cold tweezers, still without hurrying. Then he pushed the spittoon with the tip of his shoe, and went to wash his hands in the washbasin. He

---

[3] **tranquil** (TRAN-kwihl) *adj.* calm

[4] **anesthesia** (an-ihs-THEE-zhuh) *n.* loss of the feeling of pain as a result of a drug, such as ether, used by doctors

[5] **abscess** (AB-sehs) *n.* a mass of pus formed as a result of an infection

did all this without looking at the Mayor. But the Mayor didn't take his eyes off him.

It was a lower wisdom tooth. The dentist spread his feet and grasped the tooth with the hot forceps. The Mayor seized the arms of the chair, braced his feet with all his strength, and felt an icy void in his kidneys, but didn't make a sound. The dentist moved only his wrist. Without rancor,[6] rather with a bitter tenderness, he said:

This woodcut is called *A Visit to the Dentist.* Can you relate to the mayor's pain?

"Now you'll pay for our twenty dead men."

The Mayor felt the crunch of bones in his jaw, and his eyes filled with tears. But he didn't breathe until he felt the tooth come out. Then he saw it through his tears. It seemed so foreign to his pain that he failed to understand his torture of the five previous nights.

Bent over the spittoon, sweating, panting, he unbuttoned his tunic and reached for the handkerchief in his pants pocket. The dentist gave him a clean cloth.

"Dry your tears," he said.

---

[6] **rancor** (RANG-kuhr) *n.* bitter resentment

The Mayor did. He was trembling. While the dentist washed his hands, he saw the crumbling ceiling and a dusty spider web with spider's eggs and dead insects. The dentist returned, drying his hands. "Go to bed," he said, "and gargle with salt water." The Mayor stood up, said goodbye with a casual military salute, and walked toward the door, stretching his legs, without buttoning up his tunic.

"Send the bill," he said.

"To you or the town?"

The Mayor didn't look at him. He closed the door and said through the screen:

"It's the same . . . thing."

POSTREADING

Critical Thinking

1. What clues does García Márquez offer about what life in this town is like?

2. What might this story be saying about the power of the Colombian government? About the power of the common people of Colombia?

3. If you had been Aurelio Escovar, how would you have treated the Mayor? Why?

Writing Your Response to "One of These Days"

In your journal, copy one statement from the story that is especially meaningful to you. Then write about that statement. Why is it important in the story? How does it relate to your own experiences?

Going Back Into the Text: Author's Craft

In short stories, novels, and plays, **suspense** can be a powerful force. Suspense is a feeling of strong curiosity or uncertainty about the way that events will turn out. It can come from knowing that something important will happen, but not knowing what. It also can come from knowing what will happen, but not knowing when or how. Suspense is strongest when it involves a character that we care about.

In "One of These Days," we care about Aurelio Escovar. We quickly understand that he is not eager to see the Mayor and that the Mayor is not eager to see him. We become curious about why this is so, and we wonder what will happen if they meet. By creating suspense, García Márquez exercises power over us, his readers, even as he makes us think about the meaning of power.

With a partner, talk about the use of suspense in "One of These Days." Use the questions below to guide your discussion:

1. At what point in the story do you first become curious about what will happen?

2. Which of Escovar's words or actions after the Mayor's arrival increase the feeling of tension or suspense?

3. How is the suspense resolved?

MAKING THEMATIC CONNECTIONS

Rise of the People

The selections represented in this theme have all come from countries in which the people have suffered oppression. In response to their loss of freedom and the iron will of their governments, the people in these countries have risked their lives for freedom.

In "A Chip of Glass Ruby," a Moslem Indian woman living in South Africa risks her safety and that of her family not for her own freedom, but to fight the system of apartheid that has oppressed her native neighbors. In "No Way Out," you read about the great risks a Chinese student takes in an attempt to flee the communist rule in his country. You also read about an earlier time in China's history, when the country was under the rule of the Manchu Dynasty. "A Call to Action" and "To the Tune 'The River Is Red'" tell of the

Diego Rivera is one of Mexico's most famous artists. His art often deals with turbulent political issues. This piece is called *Birth of Class Consciousness*. Rivera depicts Mexicans demanding change. What can you tell about social classes from this painting?

oppression of women in the society and the need to struggle with the revolution of the masses. You also read, in "The Heirs of Stalin," about a Russian poet's memory and terror of a brutal dictator. He fears the return of Stalin's oppression of the Russian people. Finally, "One of These Days" shows the struggle between the people and the government that is so vitally important in the revolutions of South America.

The writers represented in these selections explore both the extent to which oppressive governments will go to keep their people under their firm control and the extent to which those oppressed will go to gain their freedom. While the cultures of the countries represented in these selections differ vastly, the basic human need for freedom remains constant—no matter who you are or where you live.

ACTIVITY

Every family, school, and community has a set of rules that everyone must obey—whether they agree with them or not. Why do you think the rules were created? Do you think students should have a say in the rules they must conform to? Name a rule you agree with. Name one you disagree with.

Now is your chance to make your voice heard. Form a committee of four or five students to come up with a new set of rules. Discuss which rules of your school or community you'd abolish and which ones you think should remain. Each of you should explain why you think the way you do.

Come up with a system to decide your new set of rules. Will you take a vote? If so, how many votes will be needed to adopt a new rule or abandon an old one? Will one person make the decisions for the group? If so, who will decide which person it is? Once you have decided on a final set of 10 rules, write them down and rank them in order of importance.

Discuss among yourselves how well you think your group did. Did you all get along or were there some conflicts? How did you resolve your differences? What, if any, changes would you make in the process? Share your findings and new rules with the class.

How has doing this activity helped you see the strengths of a democracy, as well as the strengths of authoritarian rule? Why do you think some countries have adopted an authoritarian government? Why do you think they resist change?

The Book of Sand

Reading the Story in a Cultural Context

Jorge Luis Borges is often called the greatest Latin American writer of the twentieth century and one of its most influential writers worldwide. He was born in Buenos Aires, Argentina, in 1899. His parents encouraged their children to love books, and Borges's greatest childhood friend was the family library. Borges later went to school in Europe, and European writers and their ideas became important to his own literary development.

Borges first saw his writing published in Spain, where he spent some time after graduating from college. Returning to Argentina in 1921, he wrote several collections of essays and poems. He also helped begin many magazines devoted to experimental writing. Borges was quickly proclaimed one of Argentina's most important writers.

His fame, however, did not protect Borges from political changes in his homeland. He did not consider himself a social reformer, but he did criticize the presidency of Juan Perón. In turn, Perón named Borges the national inspector of poultry, a clear insult. After the fall of Perón in 1955, however, Borges received a much better appointment as Director of the Argentine National Library. He also became the professor of English and American literature at the University of Buenos Aires. During this time, Borges was going blind. He continued to write, however, by dictating his stories, essays, and poems into a tape recorder.

Borges's writings are marked by a mix of fantasy and reality. They often explore great philosophical questions such as the nature of reality, the meaning of time, and the power of language. Borges believed that all languages have a common beginning and a common bond. It is not surprising, therefore, that his writing often refers to ideas from around the world.

Borges is sometimes called an "anti-realist." He questions the meaning of reality. He challenges his readers' assumptions about time and space. Many of his works use the labyrinth as a central image, suggesting that life is a cosmic puzzle. In other works, like "The Book of Sand," he raises questions through images relating to libraries. As one critic has written, the most important element of Borges's stories may be that they exercise his readers' own stiff, half-dead imaginative muscles, and force them to stretch far beyond the demands of a closed and traditional scheme.

Focusing on the Selection

As you read "The Book of Sand," think about how you decide what is real and what is not. Use your journal to jot down some ideas about the word *real*. After you have finished reading the story, review and add to your notes. What questions does Borges encourage you to consider?

The Book of Sand

◆ ▣ ◈ ▣ ◆

Jorge Luis Borges

Thy rope of sands ...
— George Herbert

The line is made up of an infinite number of points; the plane of an infinite number of lines; the volume of an infinite number of planes; the hyper-volume of an infinite number of volumes. . . . No, unquestionably this is not—*more geometrico*[1]—the best way of beginning my story. To claim that it is true is nowadays the convention[2] of every made-up story. Mine, however, *is* true.

I live alone in a fourth-floor apartment on Belgrano Street, in Buenos Aires.[3] Late one evening, a few months back, I heard a knock at my door. I opened it and a stranger stood there. He was a tall man, with nondescript features—or perhaps it was my myopia[4] that made them seem that way. Dressed in gray and carrying a gray suitcase in his hand, he had an unassuming look about him. I saw at once that he was a foreigner. At first, he struck me as old; only later did I realize that I had been misled by his thin blond hair, which was, in a Scandinavian sort of way, almost white. During the course of our conversation, which was not to last an hour, I found out that he came from the Orkneys.[5]

---

[1] *geometrico* (gay-oh-MAYT-ree-koh) *adj.* of geometry, a branch of mathematics that deals with simple shapes formed from straight lines or curves

[2] **convention** (kuhn-VEHN-shuhn) *n.* a custom

[3] **Buenos Aires** (BWAY-nuhs EYE-rehs) *n.* the capital and largest city of Argentina

[4] **myopia** (meye-OH-pee-uh) *n.* nearsightedness

[5] **the Orkneys** (AWRK-neez) *n. pl.* islands off the coast of Scotland

I invited him in, pointing to a chair. He paused awhile before speaking. A kind of gloom emanated[6] from him—as it does now from me.

"I sell Bibles," he said.

Somewhat pedantically,[7] I replied, "In this house are several English Bibles, including the first—John Wiclif's. I also have Cipriano de Valera's, Luther's—which, from a literary viewpoint, is the worst—and a Latin copy of the Vulgate.[8] As you see, it's not exactly Bibles I stand in need of."

After a few moments of silence, he said, "I don't only sell Bibles. I can show you a holy book I came across on the outskirts of Bikaner.[9] It may interest you."

He opened the suitcase and laid the book on a table. It was an octavo[10] volume, bound in cloth. There was no doubt that it had passed through many hands. Examining it, I was surprised by its unusual weight. On the spine[11] were the words "Holy Writ"[12] and, below them, "Bombay."

"Nineteenth century, probably," I remarked.

"I don't know," he said. "I've never found out."

I opened the book at random.[13] The script was strange to me. The pages, which were worn and typographically[14] poor, were laid out in double columns, as in a Bible. The text was closely printed, and it was ordered in versicles.[15] In the upper corners of the pages were Arabic numbers.[16] I noticed that one left-hand page bore the number (let us say) 40,514 and the facing right-hand page 999. I turned the leaf;[17] it was numbered with eight digits. It also bore a small illustration, like the kind used in dictionaries—an anchor drawn with pen and ink, as if by a schoolboy's clumsy hand.

It was at this point that the stranger said, "Look at the illustration closely. You'll never see it again."

---

[6] **emanated** (EHM-uh-nayt-uhd) *v.* came forth

[7] **pedantically** (puh-DAN-tihk-lee) *adv.* with a great show of one's knowledge

[8] **Vulgate** (VUL-gayt) *n.* the Bible used in the Roman Catholic Church

[9] **Bikaner** (bihk-uh-NER) *n.* city in India

[10] **octavo** (ahk-TAY-voh) *n.* a book whose size is six inches by nine inches

[11] **spine** *n.* the supporting back portion of a book cover

[12] **Holy Writ** *n.* Bible

[13] **at random** without a definite purpose or method

[14] **typographically** (ty-puh-GRAF-ihk-lee) *adv.* referring to the printing or typing

[15] **versicles** (VER-sih-kuhlz) *n. pl.* short verses

[16] **Arabic numbers** (AR-uh-bik NUM-berz) the figures 1, 2, 3, 4, 5, 6, 7, 8, 9, 0; so-called because they were introduced into western Europe by Arabian scholars

[17] **leaf** *n.* sheet of paper

I noted my place and closed the book. At once, I reopened it. Page by page, in vain, I looked for the illustration of the anchor. "It seems to be a version of Scriptures in some Indian language, is it not?" I said to hide my dismay.

"No," he replied. Then, as if confiding a secret, he lowered his voice. "I acquired the book in a town out on the plain in exchange for a handful of rupees and a Bible. Its owner did not know how to read. I suspect that he saw the Book of Books[18] as a talisman.[19] He was of the lowest caste;[20] nobody but other untouchables[21] could tread his shadow without contamination. He told me his book was called the Book of Sand, because neither the book nor the sand has any beginning or end."

The stranger asked me to find the first page.

I laid my left hand on the cover and, trying to put my thumb on the flyleaf,[22] I opened the book. It was useless. Every time I tried, a number of pages came between the cover and my thumb. It was as if they kept growing from the book.

"Now find the last page."

Again I failed. In a voice that was not mine, I barely managed to stammer, "This can't be."

Still speaking in a low voice, the stranger said, "It can't be, but it *is*. The number of pages in this book is no more or less than infinite. None is the first page, none the last. I don't know why they're numbered in this arbitrary way. Perhaps to suggest that the terms of an infinite series admit any number."

Then, as if he were thinking aloud, he said, "If space is infinite, we may be at any point in space. If time is infinite, we may be at any point in time."

His speculations irritated me. "You are religious, no doubt?" I asked him.

"Yes, I'm a Presbyterian.[23] My conscience is clear. I am reasonably sure of not having cheated the native when I gave him the Word of God[24] in exchange for his devilish book."

---

[18] **Book of Books** Bible

[19] **talisman** (TAL-ihs-muhn) *n.* an object believed to have magic power

[20] **caste** (kast) *n.* one of the social classes or ranks of the Hindu people in India; caste is passed on from generation to generation

[21] **untouchables** *n. pl.* members of the lowest caste of Hindus

[22] **flyleaf** *n.* a blank page at the beginning (or end) of a book

[23] **Presbyterian** (prehz-bih-TEER-ee-uhn) *n.* a member of a Presbyterian church of the Protestant faith

[24] **Word of God** the Bible

I assured him that he had nothing to reproach himself for, and I asked if he were just passing through this part of the world. He replied that he planned to return to his country in a few days. It was then that I learned that he was a Scot from the Orkney Islands. I told him I had a great personal affection for Scotland, through my love of Stevenson[25] and Hume.[26]

"You mean Stevenson and Robbie Burns,"[27] he corrected.

While we spoke, I kept exploring the infinite book. With feigned[28] indifference, I asked, "Do you intend to offer this curiosity to the British Museum?"

"No. I'm offering it to you," he said, and he stipulated[29] a rather high sum for the book.

I answered, in all truthfulness, that such a sum was out of my reach, and I began thinking. After a minute or two, I came up with a scheme.

"I propose a swap," I said. "You got this book for a handful of rupees and a copy of the Bible. I'll offer you the amount of my pension check, which I've just collected, and my black-letter Wiclif Bible. I inherited it from my ancestors."

"A black-letter Wiclif!" he murmured.

I went to my bedroom and brought him the money and the book. He turned the leaves and studied the title page with all the fervor of a true bibliophile.[30]

"It's a deal," he said.

It amazed me that he did not haggle. Only later was I to realize that he had entered my house with his mind made up to sell the book. Without counting the money, he put it away.

Portrait of Giles Lytton Strachey
by Dora Carrington.

---

[25] **Stevenson** Robert Louis Stevenson, a Scottish author
[26] **Hume** David Hume, a Scottish philosopher and historian
[27] **Robbie Burns** Robert Burns, a Scottish poet
[28] **feigned** (faynd) *adj.* pretending; not real
[29] **stipulated** (STIHP-yuh-layt-ihd) *v.* demanded
[30] **bibliophile** (BIHB-lee-uh-feyel) *n.* a lover or collector of books

We talked about India, about Orkney, and about the Norwegian jarls[31] who once ruled it. It was night when the man left. I have not seen him again, nor do I know his name.

I thought of keeping the Book of Sand in the space left on the shelf by the Wiclif, but in the end I decided to hide it behind the volumes of a broken set of *The Thousand and One Nights.* I went to bed and did not sleep. At three or four in the morning, I turned on the light. I got down the impossible book and leafed through its pages. On one of them I saw engraved a mask. The upper corner of the page carried a number, which I no longer recall, elevated to the ninth power.

I showed no one my treasure. To the luck of owning it was added the fear of having it stolen, and then the misgiving that it might not truly be infinite. These two preoccupations intensified my old misanthropy.[32] I had only a few friends left; I now stopped seeing even them. A prisoner of the book, I almost never went out anymore. After studying its frayed spine and covers with a magnifying glass, I rejected the possibility of a contrivance[33] of any sort. The small illustrations, I verified, came two thousand pages apart. I set about listing them alphabetically in a notebook, which I was not long in filling up. Never once was an illustration repeated. At night, in the meager intervals my insomnia granted, I dreamed of the book.

Summer came and went, and I realized that the book was monstrous. What good did it do me to think that I, who looked upon the volume with my eyes, who held it in my hands, was any less monstrous? I felt that the book was a nightmarish object, an obscene thing that affronted[34] and tainted reality itself.

I thought of fire, but I feared that the burning of an infinite book might likewise prove infinite and suffocate the planet with smoke. Somewhere I recalled reading that the best place to hide a leaf is in a forest. Before retirement, I worked on Mexico Street, at the Argentine National Library, which contains nine hundred thousand volumes. I knew that to the right of the entrance a curved staircase leads down into the basement, where books and maps and periodicals are kept. One day I went there and, slipping past a member of the staff and trying not to notice at what height or distance from the door, I lost the Book of Sand on one of the basement's musty shelves.

---

[31] **Norwegian jarls** (nawr-WEE-juhn yahrlz) *n.* noblemen of Norway
[32] **misanthropy** (mihs-AN-thruh-pee) *n.* a hatred or distrust of people
[33] **contrivance** (kuhn-TREYE-vuhns) *n.* a fake
[34] **affronted** (uh-FRUNT-ihd) *v.* insulted

POSTREADING

Critical Thinking

1. What details in this story reflect Borges's own love for literature?

2. Why might a "book of sand" be upsetting to a person's—or a group's—view of life?

3. What do you think of the narrator's method of setting himself free from the book's power? What would you have done with the book?

Writing Your Response to "The Book of Sand"

What event, character, or idea in "The Book of Sand" speaks most directly to you? What part of the story seems to have a connection to your life? In your journal, write about that element of the story you identify with the most.

Going Back Into the Text: Author's Craft

With the narrator's frequent use of the word *infinite*, you know that "The Book of Sand" is exploring some abstract ideas. Like many writers who tackle abstract concepts, Borges uses symbols to help us think about them. A **symbol** is something real and familiar that represents something abstract and less familiar.

Some symbols are very familiar; we use them all the time without thinking about them. For example, we may say that a lion is the symbol of courage or nobility, or that autumn leaves are a symbol of approaching death. Other symbols are less common, but they still present a comparison to what is familiar. Because they are based on familiar things, symbols may have different meanings from one culture to another.

With a partner, use the following questions to focus on symbols in "The Book of Sand" and on the use of symbols in general:

1. Why is sand an appropriate symbol for infinity?

2. You have read that the image of the library is important to much of Borges's writing. How might it be used as a symbol in "The Book of Sand"?

3. If you were creating your own symbols, what familiar thing would you use to represent each of the following?

   - love
   - anger
   - honesty
   - wisdom

PREREADING

Continuity of Parks

Reading the Story in a Cultural Context

In the years since World War II, Argentina has faced many political and economic troubles. In 1946, Juan Perón was elected president. His economic policies increased personal wages but caused the national income to fall. Inflation and government debt rose. Perón changed Argentina's constitution to obtain greater power. He also restricted the press and free speech.

Many people didn't like Perón's rule. One of these people was Julio Cortázar, a translator and teacher. He left Argentina for France. While he was there, he watched as Argentina's economy continued to suffer under a series of presidents. He saw Perón's return to power in 1973. He also watched as the military took over Perón's government just three years later. Under the new military government, protesters were persecuted. Many were jailed without trial, tortured, and killed. And many of them—the *desaparecidos*, or "disappeared ones"—were never found. In Paris, Cortázar regularly protested on their behalf outside the Argentine embassy and supported freedom movements in other parts of Latin America.

In his writing, Cortázar also supported another freedom—literary freedom. His stories blend the realistic and the fantastic. They change setting unexpectedly, and mix elements of comedy and tragedy. Cortázar saw a connection—a "continuity"—between different ways of thinking about reality. He challenged his readers to see it, too. He once wrote that he was trying "to break the habits of readers—not just for the sake of breaking them, but to make the reader free."

"Continuity of Parks" is a good example of Cortázar's experimentation. It is a story within a story, and the stories are related. This unexpected relationship takes the reader by surprise. Which story is more "real"? Read and decide for yourself!

Focusing on the Selection

As you read, think about what you expect to find in a short story. What makes "Continuity of Parks" so different? How do the details make the story come to life? How does the story challenge your imagination?

Continuity of Parks

◆◆◆

Julio Cortázar

He had begun to read the novel a few days before. He had put it down because of some urgent business conferences, opened it again on his way back to the estate by train; he permitted himself a slowly growing interest in the plot, in the characterizations. That afternoon, after writing a letter giving his power of attorney[1] and discussing a matter of joint ownership with the manager of his estate, he returned to the book in the tranquillity of his study which looked out upon the park with its oaks. Sprawled in his favorite armchair, its back toward the door—even the possibility of an intrusion would have irritated him, had he thought of it—he let his left hand caress repeatedly the green velvet upholstery and set to reading the final chapters. He remembered effortlessly the names and his mental image of the characters; the novel spread its glamour over him almost at once. He tasted the almost perverse pleasure of disengaging himself line by line from the things around him, and at the same time feeling his head rest comfortably on the green velvet of the chair with its high back, sensing that the cigarettes rested within reach of his hand, that beyond the great windows the air of afternoon danced under the oak trees in the park. Word by word, licked up by the sordid dilemma[2] of the hero and heroine, letting himself be absorbed to the point where the images settled down and took on color and movement, he was witness to the final encounter in the mountain cabin. The woman arrived first, apprehensive;[3] now the lover came in, his face cut by the backlash of a branch. Admirably,

---

[1] **power of attorney** a written document giving someone legal authority to represent or act for another, as in handling business affairs

[2] **dilemma** (dih-LEHM-uh) *n.* a situation requiring a difficult choice

[3] **apprehensive** (ap-ruh-HEHN-sihv) *adj.* worried, fearful

she stanched[4] the blood with her kisses, but he rebuffed her caresses, he had not come to perform again the ceremonies of a secret passion, protected by a world of dry leaves and furtive paths through the forest. The dagger warmed itself against his chest, and underneath liberty pounded, hidden close. A lustful, panting dialogue raced down the pages like a rivulet[5] of snakes, and one felt it had all been decided from eternity. Even to those caresses about the lover's body, as though wishing to keep him there, to dissuade[6] him from it; they sketched abominably the frame of that other body it was necessary to destroy. Nothing had been forgotten: alibis,[7] unforeseen hazards, possible mistakes. From this hour on, each instant had its use minutely assigned. The cold-blooded, twice-gone-over reexamination of the details was barely broken off so that a hand could caress a cheek. It was beginning to get dark.

Not looking at one another now, rigidly fixed upon the task which awaited them, they separated at the cabin door. She was to follow the trail that led north. On the path leading in the opposite direction, he turned

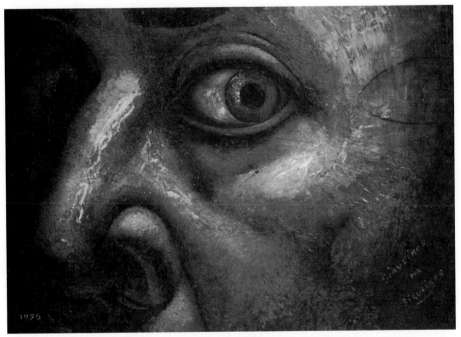

Mexican artist David Sisqueiros was a contemporary of Diego Rivera. He often used disturbing images to grab the attention of his viewers and get his message across. Even his *Self Portrait* has a bold and tormented look.

---

[4] **stanched** (stancht) *v.* stemmed the flow of blood from
[5] **rivulet** (RIV-yuh-liht) *n.* a small stream; brook
[6] **dissuade** (di-SWAYD) *v.* persuade against something
[7] **alibis** (AHL-uh-beyez) *n. pl.* excuses

for a moment to watch her running, her hair loosened and flying. He ran in turn, crouching among the trees and hedges until, in the yellowish fog of dusk, he could distinguish the avenue of trees which led up to the house. The dogs were not supposed to bark, they did not bark. The estate manager would not be there at this hour, and he was not there. He went up the three porch steps and entered. The woman's words reached him over the thudding of blood in his ears: first a blue chamber, then a hall, then a carpeted stairway. At the top, two doors. No one in the first room, no one in the second. The door of the salon, and then, the knife in hand, the light from the great windows, the high back of an armchair covered in green velvet, the head of the man in the chair reading a novel.

POSTREADING

Critical Thinking

1. Think about this statement: *Cortázar uses this story to show that reading can be "dangerous."* Why was it "dangerous" for the man who was reading? How is it dangerous for readers to think about literature in a way that makes them challenge their own assumptions about reality?

2. In what way might this story illustrate the theme of liberation?

3. How do you feel about the mix of fantasy and reality in this story? Explain your answer.

Writing Your Response to "Continuity of Parks"

In your journal, make some notes about the kind of reading you enjoy most. (The source doesn't matter: it could be a certain type of book, story, magazine, or newspaper article.) Try to describe how you feel as you do that kind of reading. Then think about this question: How would it feel to discover that you are the topic of the thing that you're reading?

Going Back Into the Text: Author's Craft

Writing that increases our reading enjoyment often includes many sensory details. **Sensory details** describe how something looks, sounds, feels, tastes, or smells. By using sensory details, writers can bring descriptions to life. These details can also help create a mood that draws us into the writing. In "Continuity of Parks," sensory details draw us into the reader's world—and into the story that he himself is reading.

Think about Cortázar's use of sensory details. The following questions can guide you:8

1. What sensory details does Cortázar use to describe the place the man has chosen to read? What mood do those details create?

2. What sensory details help bring "the final encounter in the mountain cabin" to life?

3. Which part of this short story do you think makes the best use of sensory details? Explain your answer.

Homecoming/The Child's Return/ Jamaica Market/On Leaving/ Zion, Me Wan Go Home

Reading the Poems in a Cultural Context

Look at the map of the Caribbean on page 304. Think about the history of this area. The islands of the Caribbean were home to native people, but were later colonized by many far-off countries, including Spain, France, Portugal, Great Britain, and the Netherlands. Each island of the Caribbean at one time has been a colony of a European country. Some islands remain colonies today. But even in the islands that now are independent nations, there is an influence of a European past.

Another dominant influence in the Caribbean is the *result* of European colonization. Centuries ago, thousands of Africans were enslaved and brought across the Atlantic to work on the islands. Today, descendants of these people make up a large part of the Caribbean population. Their heritage is a major factor in what it means to be "Caribbean."

With its warm weather and natural beauty, the Caribbean today attracts vacationers from around the world. Many of its islands also attract permanent settlers. Immigrants from as far away as India and China have made new lives for themselves in Caribbean nations.

With so much international influence—past and present—it is no surprise that Caribbean literature is a rich and varied mix.

Some of it is heavily influenced by European literary traditions. Much of it reflects African cultures and customs. And much of it combines the two. Some of the strongest Caribbean writing explores modern culture and the nature of the Caribbean identity. In the poems that you are about to read, Jamaican poet Agnes Maxwell-Hall paints a brilliant picture of a common scene in her homeland. The love of homeland is also vividly depicted in the selections written by Dennis Scott (also from Jamaica), Phyllis Allfrey (a journalist and politician from Dominica), and Gertrudis Gomez de Avellaneda (a 19th-century Cuban poet who later lived in Spain but never forgot the home of her youth). The anonymous "Zion, Me Wan Go Home" expresses both a Caribbean love and longing for a far older homeland.

Focusing on the Selections

As you read these poems, think about the sounds and pictures that these various poets create. Make some notes in your journal about them. For example, which words and images seem most vivid? Also notice the unique perspective in each poem. What feelings about the Caribbean, or its people, develop from these poems? What do you think it means to be "Caribbean"?

Homecoming

Dennis Scott

The wind is making countries
in the air, clouds dim,
golden as Eldorado[1] voyages.
                              Those hills
harbour a sea of dreams, they told
us; and as children we were
sad, wanting a rainbow.
                              Now
heart-sailed
from home I name them
Orient, Africa,
New York, London's white
legend; the ports have
a welcoming ring—no end
to their richness, their tumble.
The sirens sing.
                              But

again, again these
hot and coffee streets reclaim
my love. Carts rumble.
The long horn of a higgler's[2] voice
painting the shadows midday
brown, cries about harvest,
and the wind calls back
blue air across the town; it tears
the thin topographies[3] of dream, it blows me
as by old, familiar maps,
to this affectionate short, green
and crumpling hills,

---

[1] **Eldorado** (ehl-duh-RAH-doh) *n.* a legendary city of great wealth in South America; this place was eagerly sought after by early explorers

[2] **higgler's** (HIHG-luhrz) *adj.* of a person who argues so as to bargain over the price of something

[3] **topographies** (tuh-PAHG-ruh-feez) *n. pl.* detailed, natural features of places, as on a map

like paper in the Admiral's fist.
The rain comes down.

There is a kind of tune
we must promise our children,
a shape that the quadrant[4] measures,
no North
to turn them
away from the dissonant[5] cities,
the salt songs,
the hunger of journeys.

It is time to plant
feet in our earth. The heart's metronome[6]
insists on this arc of islands
as home.

Jamaican artist Sidney McLaren painted this piece called *Creative Imagination* in 1977. McLaren was a trained carriage maker and turned to painting only after carriages were replaced by automobiles on the island.

---

[4] **quadrant** (KWAHD-ruhnt) *n.* an instrument with a scale of 90 degrees, used in navigation for measuring altitudes

[5] **dissonant** (DIHS-uh-nuhnt) *adj.* harsh and unpleasant in sound; disagreeable

[6] **metronome** (MEHT-ruh-nohm) *n.* a device, used by musicians to mark time or a steady beat, that makes loud ticking sounds at different speeds

The Child's Return

Phyllis Allfrey

I remember a far tall island
floating in cobalt[1] paint
The thought of it is a childhood dream
torn by a midnight plaint[2]

There are painted ships and rusty ships
that pass the island by,
and one dark day I'll board a boat
when I am ready to die

The timbers will creak and my heart will break
and the sailors will lay my bones
on the stiff rich grass, as sharp as spikes,
by the volcanic stones.

---

[1] **cobalt** (KOH-bawlt) *n.* a dark blue coloring matter made from metallic elements
[2] **plaint** (playnt) *n.* a complaint

Jamaica Market

Agnes Maxwell-Hall

Honey, pepper, leaf-green limes,
Pagan[1] fruit whose names are rhymes,
Mangoes, breadfruit, ginger-roots,
Granadillas,[2] bamboo-shoots,
Cho-cho, ackees,[3] tangerines,
Lemons, purple Congo-beans,
Sugar, okras, kola-nuts,
Citrons, hairy coconuts,
Fish, tobacco, native hats,
Gold bananas, woven mats,
Plantains, wild-thyme, pallid leeks,[4]
Pigeons with their scarlet beaks,
Oranges and saffron yams,
Baskets, ruby guava jams,
Turtles, goat-skins, cinnamon,
Allspice, conch-shells, golden rum.
Black skins, babel[5]—and the sun
That burns all colours into one.

---

[1] **pagan** (PAY-guhn) *adj.* belonging to someone who has little or no religion and who delights
in sensual pleasures
[2] **granadillas** (gran-uh-DEE-uhs) *n. pl.* fruits of passionflowers
[3] **cho-cho** (CHOH-choh) meat snacks, **ackees** (AK-eez) salted fish
[4] **plantains** (PLANT-aynz) *n. pl.* greenish starchy fruit like bananas, **wild-thyme** (weyeld teyem) *n.*
an herb, **leeks** *n. pl.* vegetables related to the onion
[5] **babel** (BAY-buhl) *n.* a confusion of sounds, voices, or languages

On Leaving

Gertrudis Gomez de Avellaneda
translated by *Frederick Sweet*

Sea pearl, western star,
shining Cuba,[1] night hides
your bright sky in its thick veil
as grief clouds my sad brow.

Time to leave. The eager crew,
to wrench me from my earth,
hoists sails, and ready winds
rush from your fiery ground.

Fare well, my happy land, my Eden.[2]
Wherever angry change may force my path
your sweet name will soothe my ear.

Fare well. The huge sail crackles,
the anchor lifts, the anxious ship
cuts the waves and flies in silence.

---

[1] **Cuba** (KYOO-buh) *n.* an island nation in the Caribbean Sea, south of Florida
[2] **Eden** (EED-uhn) *n.* paradise

Zion, Me Wan Go Home

Anonymous

Zion, me wan go home,
Zion, me wan go home,
Oh, oh,
Zion, me wan go home.

Africa, me wan fe go,
Africa, me wan fe go,
Oh, oh,
Africa, me wan fe go.

Take me back to Et'iopia lan,
Take me back to Et'iopia lan,
Oh, oh,
Take me back to Et'iopia lan.

Et'iopia lan me fader's home,
Et'iopia lan me fader's home,
Oh, oh,
Et'iopia lan me fader's home,

Zion, me wan go home,
Zion, me wan go home,
Oh, oh,
Zion, me wan go home.

POSTREADING

Critical Thinking

1. How do you think each poet in this group would complete this statement: *To be Caribbean means* _____ ?

2. Do all the poems suggest the value of loving one's homeland? Explain your answer.

3. Which of these poems did you like the best? Why?

Writing Your Response to "Homecoming," "The Child's Return," "Jamaica Market," "On Leaving," and "Zion, Me Wan Go Home"

In your journal, write about the images, wording, or feeling in one of these poems that you find most meaningful. What makes it so striking? How can you relate it to a situation, a person, or a feeling that you have known?

Going Back Into the Text: Author's Craft

One of the ways in which a poem pleases its readers is through its use of rhythm. **Rhythm** is the pattern of stressed and unstressed syllables in writing. In some poems, the rhythmic pattern repeats fairly regularly. This rhythmic pattern is called *meter*.

There are many different kinds of meter. Anapestic meter, for example, sounds like this: *da da DUM, da da DUM, da da DUM*. Trochaic meter sounds like this: *DUM da, DUM da, DUM da*. At other times, the pattern is far less regular—far more like ordinary conversation.

Still, the rhythm of words and phrases can hold our interest and help us remember a poet's ideas.

With a partner, use the following questions to focus on the use of rhythm in these poems:

1. Of these poems, which one's rhythms are most predictable? Which poem seems the most like everyday conversation? Explain.

2. Dennis Scott and Phyllis Allfrey both use their poems to talk about the idea of returning home. How does their different uses of rhythm help make their poems different?

3. Tap out a rhythm that you find interesting. Then fit words to the rhythm to create a sentence or two about the idea of "home." What do you think of the result?

Reviewing the Region

1. Good writers are able to evoke a "sense of place." Through descriptions of the setting and the actions of the characters, an author can help a reader experience "being there." Choose a selection from the chapter and give examples of the ways in which the author or authors convey a sense of place.

2. How did the selections in this chapter add to your knowledge of this region?

3. Suppose that you suddenly became one of the characters in a short story in this chapter. Would you act exactly as the character does in the story? Why or why not? What might you do differently?

CHAPTER

9 Canada

Among the most powerful group of native peoples in Canada and the area of upstate New York was the Iroquois. They were members of the League of Five Nations, a union of tribes consisting of the Mohawks, Oneidas, Onondagas, Cayugas, and Senecas. The Iroquois remained the most powerful nation throughout the 1600s. As in the United States, European settlers and their descendants in Canada moved westward. Their migration devastated many of the native cultures who had lived on the land. This chapter begins with a poem by a native Canadian of the Turtle Mohawk tribe from Caughnawaga, Quebec. He expresses the conflicts that arise during the struggle between his culture and the culture of Canadians of European descent. Later in the chapter, you will read a poem by Margaret Atwood in which a visit to the Royal Ontario Museum stirs respect for the native cultures that exist in relics of the past.

Like Africa and Latin America, Canadian writing began as colonial literature, written in its two official languages, French and English. Much of modern Canadian literature focuses on the often vast and barren landscape, frontier life, and the wilderness environment. Some of Canada's early colonial literature was written by explorers, traders, priests, and farmers who opened up New France. Since then it has been influenced by many of the same things that affected literature of the United States. For example, one of the stories in this chapter shows the impact of the Great Depression of the 1920s on a Canadian family.

The author of another selection tells a humorous story about a banking disaster. You will also read an excerpt from an autobiography. The author recalls the first episode of her life when she realized the power of words.

While many of Canada's authors have embraced their own distinctive culture, their awareness of both European influence and New World experience gives them both a national and global voice.

This Canadian scene of an Inuit with two birds is actually a stone used for printing. If covered with ink, many prints of the piece could be printed. It is from the Northwest Territories in Canada.

The Old Man's Lazy

Reading the Poem in a Cultural Context

You have learned about the native peoples of Australia and South Africa. These natives have had some of the same experiences as the native peoples who live in Canada. Like the Australian Aborigines and Black South Africans, Native peoples in Canada struggled for both their civil rights and their land against the colonialists who immigrated to their area. Their struggles continue even today.

Native peoples in Canada had a somewhat different experience than Native Americans in the United States after the arrival and settlement of Europeans. The first Europeans to meet these Indians were French fur traders. The two groups generally got along, working and often living together. But in 1763, Great Britain gained control of the region of North America that is now Canada. English settlers soon began to arrive. Great Britain set aside land for various Indian groups but did not (as the United States later would) force the Indians to live on that land.

Still, over the years, tensions grew. Settlers killed millions of buffalo on the Canadian plains. Some Indian lands were threatened by expanding settlement. In the late nineteenth century the *métis* (Canadians of partial Indian ancestry) organized rebellions and demanded the right to live on their lands as they saw fit.

Today, the Canadian Department of Indian Affairs and Northern Development estimates that about 350,000 Indians live in Canada. Most of them live on reserve lands. In addition to voting on regional and national matters, they elect their own reserve leaders. Some Indians work in farming, cattle ranching, and mining; others trap, hunt, and fish for a living. Still others make a life for themselves in Canada's cities.

What does it mean to be Indian in Canada today? That question lies at the heart of the poem by Peter Blue Cloud that you are about to read. "The Old Man's Lazy" reveals one Indian's trust in ancient beliefs and traditions. It shows how some Indians today are torn between their heritage and their desire to fit into the mainstream. It also suggests that prejudice against Indians lives on in the land that they were the first to settle.

Focusing on the Selection

As you read "The Old Man's Lazy," think about what the speaker reveals about his life and values. Think, too, about the conflicts between people and between ideas in the poem. How does the old man feel about the people he describes? What changes has he seen in his world? What things in life does he consider important?

The Old Man's Lazy

Peter Blue Cloud

The Old Man's lazy,
I heard the Indian Agent[1] say,
has no pride, no get up
and go.[2] Well, he came out
here and walked around my
place, that agent. Steps
all thru the milkweed and
curing wormwood; tells me
my place is overgrown
and should be made use
of.

The old split cedar
fence stands at many
angles, and much of it
lies on the ground like
a curving sentence of
stick writing. An old
language, too, black with
age, with different
shades of green of moss
and lichen.[3]
      He always
says he understands us
Indians,
        and why don't
I fix the fence at least;

so I took some fine
hawk feathers fixed
to a miniature woven
shield
      and hung this
from an upright post
near the house.
      He
came by last week
and looked all around
again, eyed the feathers
for a long time.
      He didn't
say anything, and he didn't
smile even, or look within
himself for the hawk.

Maybe sometime I'll
tell him that the fence
isn't mine to begin with,
but was put up by
the white guy who used
to live next door.
      It was
years ago. He built a cabin,
then put up the fence. He
only looked at me once,

---

[1] **Indian Agent** an official representative of the government who is responsible for social work among native peoples

[2] **get up and go** ambition and energy

[3] **lichen** (LEYE-kuhn) *n.* a plant consisting of a fungus and algae that grows on rocks and tree trunks

after his fence was up,
he nodded at me as if
to show that he knew I
was here, I guess.
   It was
a pretty fence, enclosing
that guy, and I felt lucky
to be on the outside
of it.
   Well, that guy
dug holes all over his
place, looking for gold,
and I guess
   he never
found any. I watched
him grow old for over
twenty years, and bitter,[4]
I could feel his anger
all over the place.
   And
that's when I took to
leaving my place to do
a lot of visiting.
   Then
one time I came home
and knew he was gone
for good.

My children would
always ask me why I
didn't move to town
and be closer to them.

Now, they
tell me I'm lucky to be
living way out here.
   And

they bring their children
and come out and visit me,
and I can feel that they
want to live out here
too, but can't
for some reason, do it.

Each day
a different story is
told me by the fence,
the rain and wind and snow,
the sun and moon shadows,
this wonderful earth,
      this Creation.
I tell my grandchildren
many of these stories,
      perhaps
this too is one of them.

A native of Spence Bay, Canada. This Native Canadian and Peter Blue
Cloud probably share many of the same values.

---

[4] **bitter** (BIT-uhr) *adj.* resentful

POSTREADING

Critical Thinking

1. The fence is a central image in this poem. How does Peter Blue Cloud use it to express his speaker's thoughts?

2. What do the old man's words about his children suggest about attitudes of native peoples in modern Canada?

3. Do you think that the Indian Agent is correct in saying that the old man isn't making use of his place? Explain your answer.

Writing Your Response to "The Old Man's Lazy"

The old man speaks because the Indian Agent has criticized him. In your journal, write about some criticism that you have received. What was said to you? How did you react? Do you feel that the person who criticized you was completely wrong, or was there some truth in his or her words? Relate your feelings to those that you find in this poem.

Going Back Into the Text: Author's Craft

"The Old Man's Lazy" is a good example of a poetic form known as **dramatic monologue**. It presents the words or thoughts of one person at an important moment in his or her life (in this case, a moment of criticism from an Indian Agent). It treats us as silent listeners. As the speaker expresses his thoughts, he informs us of the situation that has stirred his thinking. He also reveals his own personality and beliefs. As with most dramatic monologues, "The Old Man's Lazy" leaves us with a detailed picture of the speaker's character.

With a partner, use the following questions to focus on elements of dramatic monologue in "The Old Man's Lazy."

1. What topics does the old man discuss as the poem unfolds? Which topic do you think means the most to him, and why?

2. Think about the mental picture that you had of the speaker after the first few lines. How did that picture change as you listened to what he said about himself?

3. Suppose that this poem was a dramatic monologue told by the Indian Agent. How do you think your ideas about him and about the old man would change? Explain your answer.

PREREADING

All the Years of Her Life

Reading the Story in a Cultural Context

Historic and cultural links exist between Canada and the United States. Both are seen in the writing career of Morley Callaghan.

Callaghan grew up in Toronto. He studied law and spent his summers working for the Toronto *Daily Star*. It was there that he met Ernest Hemingway in the early 1920s. Hemingway helped get Callaghan's writing published. Later, Callaghan spent some time in Paris with Hemingway and a colony of other writers who influenced Callaghan's writing—including F. Scott Fitzgerald, Ezra Pound, and James Joyce.

During the 1920s and 1930s, many of Callaghan's stories were published in magazines. In fact, "All the Years of Her Life," which you are about to read, first appeared in *The New Yorker* in 1935. Like many of his stories from this era, it presents characters whose lives are hard because of the Great Depression. They have financial struggles and they try to make sense of a world that no longer seems secure. In addition, "All the Years of Her Life" uses a type of character that is common in Callaghan's work—a person who makes himself an outcast by committing a crime. (As one reviewer has put it, Callaghan "loves to show how men will act badly if given half a chance.")

"All the Years of Her Life" also explores the relationship between a mother and her son—a relationship that is subtly changed by the events of the story.

Callaghan is sometimes seen as a "journalistic" writer. However, he does more than report the facts about his characters. His stories suggest that moments of spiritual importance can occur unexpectedly, in the middle of everyday events. Callaghan's stories have even been described as "moral parables." Expect to find a moment of awakening—a lesson learned—by someone in "All the Years of Her Life."

Focusing on the Selection

As you read, think about the characters and their hardships. How do you wind up feeling about each of the characters? Which character seems most "real" to you? What can you learn by watching the characters in this story interact?

All the Years of Her Life

Morley Callaghan

They were closing the drugstore, and Alfred Higgins, who had just taken off his white jacket, was putting on his coat and getting ready to go home. The little grey-haired man, Sam Carr, who owned the drugstore, was bending down behind the cash register, and when Alfred Higgins passed him, he looked up and said softly, "Just a moment, Alfred. One moment before you go."

The soft, confident, quiet way in which Sam Carr spoke made Alfred start to button his coat nervously. He felt sure his face was white. Sam Carr usually said "Good night" brusquely,[1] without looking up. In the six months he had been working in the drugstore Alfred had never heard his employer speak softly like that. His heart began to beat so loud it was hard for him to get his breath. "What is it, Mr. Carr?" he asked.

"Maybe you'd be good enough to take a few things out of your pocket and leave them here before you go," Sam Carr said.

"What things? What are you talking about?"

"You've got a compact[2] and a lipstick and at least two tubes of tooth-paste in your pockets, Alfred."

"What do you mean? Do you think I'm crazy?" Alfred blustered. His face got red and he knew he looked fierce with indignation.[3] But Sam Carr, standing by the door with his blue eyes shining bright behind his glasses and his lips moving underneath his grey mustache, only nodded his head a few times, and then Alfred grew very frightened and he didn't know

---

[1] **brusquely** (BRUSK-lee) *adv.* roughly, abruptly, bluntly

[2] **compact** (KAHM-pakt) *n.* a small case containing face powder, a powder puff, and usually a mirror

[3] **indignation** (ihn-dihg-NAY-shuhn) *n.* anger brought on by something unjust, unworthy, or mean

what to say. Slowly he raised his hand and dipped it into his pocket, and with his eyes never meeting Sam Carr's eyes, he took out a blue compact and two tubes of toothpaste and a lipstick, and he laid them one by one on the counter.

"Petty[4] thieving, eh, Alfred?" Sam Carr said. "And maybe you'd be good enough to tell me how long this has been going on."

"This is the first time I ever took anything."

"So now you think you'll tell me a lie, eh? What kind of a sap[5] do I look like, huh? I don't know what goes on in my own store, eh? I tell you you've been doing this pretty steady," Sam Carr said as he went over and stood behind the cash register.

Ever since Alfred had left school he had been getting into trouble wherever he worked. He lived at home with his mother and father, who was a printer. His two older brothers were married and his sister had got married last year, and it would have been all right for his parents now if Alfred had only been able to keep a job.

While Sam Carr smiled and stroked the side of his face very delicately with the tips of his fingers, Alfred began to feel that familiar terror growing in him that had been in him every time he had got into such trouble.

"I liked you," Sam Carr was saying. "I liked you and would have trusted you, and now look what I got to do." While Alfred watched with his alert, frightened blue eyes, Sam Carr drummed with his fingers on the counter. "I don't like to call a cop in point-blank,"[6] he was saying as he looked very worried. "You're a fool, and maybe I should call your father and tell him you're a fool. Maybe I should let them know I'm going to have you locked up."

"My father's not at home. He's a printer. He works nights," Alfred said.

"Who's at home?"

"My mother, I guess."

"Then we'll see what she says." Sam Carr went to the phone and dialed the number. Alfred was not so much ashamed, but there was that deep fright growing in him, and he blurted out arrogantly, like a strong, full-grown man, "Just a minute. You don't need to draw anybody else in. You don't need to tell her." He wanted to sound like a swaggering,[7] big guy who could look after himself, yet the old, childish hope was in him, the longing that someone at home would come and help him. "Yeah, that's right, he's in trouble," Mr. Carr was saying. "Yeah, your boy works for me. You'd better come down in a hurry." When he was finished Mr. Carr went over to

---

[4] **petty** (PEHT-ee) *adj.* small in value
[5] **sap** *n.* slang for a foolish person
[6] **point-blank** (point-blangk) *adv.* without hesitating
[7] **swaggering** (SWAG-uhr-ihng) *adj.* boastful, self-confident

the door and looked out at the street and watched the people passing in the late summer night. "I'll keep my eye out for a cop," was all he said.

Alfred knew how his mother would come rushing in; she would rush in with her eyes blazing, or maybe she would be crying, and she would push him away, when he tried to talk to her, and make him feel her dreadful contempt;[8] yet he longed that she might come before Mr. Carr saw the cop on the beat passing the door.

While they waited—and it seemed a long time—they did not speak, and when at last they heard someone tapping on the closed door, Mr. Carr, turning the latch, said crisply, "Come in, Mrs. Higgins." He looked hard-faced and stern.

Mrs. Higgins must have been going to bed when he telephoned, for her hair was tucked in loosely under her hat, and her hand at her throat

French artist Henri Le Fauconnier painted this portrait. Since 1534, when the French explorer Jacques Cartier landed on the shores of what is now called Quebec, Canada, the two countries have had strong ties.

---

[8] **contempt** (kuhn-TEHMPT) *n.* the feeling that a person is worthless or despised

held her light coat tight across her chest so her dress would not show. She came in, large and plump, with a little smile on her friendly face. Most of the store lights had been turned out and at first she did not see Alfred, who was standing in the shadow at the end of the counter. Yet as soon as she saw him she did not look as Alfred thought she would look; she smiled, her blue eyes never wavered,[9] and with a calmness and dignity that made them forget that her clothes seemed to have been thrown on her, she put out her hand to Mr. Carr and said politely, "I'm Mrs. Higgins. I'm Alfred's mother."

Mr. Carr was a bit embarrassed by her lack of terror and her simplicity, and he hardly knew what to say to her, so she asked, "Is Alfred in trouble?"

"He is. He's been taking things from the store. I caught him red-handed.[10] Little things like compacts and toothpaste and lipsticks. Stuff he can sell easily," the proprietor[11] said.

As she listened Mrs. Higgins looked at Alfred sometimes and nodded her head sadly, and when Sam Carr had finished she said gravely, "Is it so, Alfred?"

"Yes."

"Why have you been doing it?"

"I been spending money, I guess."

"On what?"

"Going around with the guys, I guess," Alfred said.

Mrs. Higgins put out her hand and touched Sam Carr's arm with understanding gentleness, and speaking as though afraid of disturbing him, she said, "If you would only listen to me before doing anything." Her simple earnestness made her shy; her humility[12] made her falter[13] and look away, but in a moment she was smiling gravely again, and she said with a kind of patient dignity, "What did you intend to do, Mr. Carr?"

"I was going to get a cop. That's what I ought to do."

"Yes, I suppose so. It's not for me to say, because he's my son. Yet I sometimes think a little good advice is the best thing for a boy when he's at a certain period in his life."

Alfred couldn't understand his mother's quiet composure,[14] for if they had been at home and someone had suggested that he was going to be arrested, he knew she would be in a rage and would cry out against him. Yet

---

[9] **wavered** (WAY-vuhrd) *v.* moved back and forth, become unsteady

[10] **red-handed** (rehd-HAN-dihd) *adv.* in the very act of a crime or mischief

[11] **proprietor** (pruh-PRY-uh-tuhr) *n.* the owner of a business

[12] **humility** (hyoo-MIHL-ih-tee) *n.* humbleness, modesty

[13] **falter** (FAWL-tuhr) *v.* lose strength or purpose

[14] **composure** (kuhm-POH-zhuhr) *n.* control over one's emotions

now she was standing there with that gentle, pleading smile, saying, "I wonder if you don't think it would be better just to let him come home with me. He looks like a big fellow, doesn't he? It takes some of them a long time to get any sense," and they both stared at Alfred, who shifted away with a bit of light shining for a moment on his thin face and the tiny pimples over his cheekbone.

But even while he was turning away uneasily, Alfred was realizing that Mr. Carr had become aware that his mother was really a fine woman; he knew that Sam Carr was puzzled by his mother, as if he had expected her to come in and plead with him tearfully, and instead he was being made to feel a bit ashamed by her vast tolerance. While there was only the sound of the mother's soft, assured voice in the store, Mr. Carr began to nod his head encouragingly at her. Without being alarmed, while being just large and still and simple and hopeful, she was becoming dominant[15] there in the dimly lit store. "Of course, I don't want to be harsh," Mr. Carr was saying. "I'll tell you what I'll do. I'll just fire him and let it go at that. How's that?" and he got up and shook hands with Mrs. Higgins, bowing low to her in deep respect.

There was such warmth and gratitude in the way she said, "I'll never forget your kindness," that Mr. Carr began to feel warm and genial[16] himself.

"Sorry we had to meet this way," he said. "But, I'm glad I got in touch with you. Just wanted to do the right thing, that's all," he said.

"It's better to meet like this than never, isn't it?" she said. Suddenly they clasped hands as if they liked each other, as if they had known each other a long time. "Good night, sir," she said.

"Good night, Mrs. Higgins. I'm truly sorry," he said.

The mother and son walked along the street together, and the mother was taking a long, firm stride as she looked ahead with her stern face full of worry. Alfred was afraid to speak to her; he was afraid of the silence that was between them too, so he only looked ahead, for the excitement and relief were still pretty strong in him; but in a little while, going along like that in silence made him terribly aware of the strength and the sternness in her; he began to wonder what she was thinking of as she stared ahead so grimly; she seemed to have forgotten that he walked beside her; so when they were passing under the railway bridge and the rumble of the train seemed to break the silence, he said in his old, blustering way, "Thank God it turned out like that. I certainly won't get in a jam like that again."

---

[15] **dominant** (DAHM-uh-nuhnt) *adj.* having the most influence or control
[16] **genial** (JEEN-yuhl) *adj.* cheerful, friendly

"Be quiet. Don't speak to me. You've disgraced me again and again," she said bitterly.

"That's the last time. That's all I'm saying."

"Have the decency[17] to be quiet," she snapped.

When they were at home and his mother took off her coat, Alfred saw that she was really only half-dressed, and she made him feel afraid again when she said, without even looking at him, "You're a bad lot. God forgive you. It's one thing after another and always has been. Why do you stand there stupidly? Go to bed, why don't you?" When he was going, she said, "I'm going to make myself a cup of tea. Mind, now, not a word about tonight to your father."

While Alfred was undressing in his bedroom, he heard his mother moving around the kitchen. She filled the kettle and put it on the stove. She moved a chair. As he listened there was no shame in him, just wonder and a kind of admiration of her strength and repose.[18] He could still see Sam Carr nodding his head encouragingly to her; he could hear her talking simply and earnestly, and as he sat on his bed he felt a pride in her strength. "She certainly was smooth," he thought. "Gee, I'd like to tell her she sounded swell."[19]

At last he got up and went along to the kitchen, and when he was at the door he saw his mother pouring herself a cup of tea. He watched and he didn't move. Her face, as she sat there, was a frightened, broken face utterly unlike the face of a woman who had been so assured a little while ago in the drugstore. When she reached out and lifted the kettle to pour hot water in her cup, her hand trembled and the water splashed on the stove. Leaning back in the chair, she sighed and lifted the cup to her lips, and her lips were groping loosely as if they would never reach the cup. She swallowed the hot tea eagerly, and then she straightened up in relief, though her hand holding the cup still trembled. She looked very old.

It seemed to Alfred that this was the way it had been every time he had been in trouble before, that this trembling had really been in her as she hurried out half-dressed to the drugstore. Now he felt all that his mother had been thinking of as they walked along the street together a little while ago. He watched his mother, and he never spoke, but at that moment his youth seemed to be over; he knew all the years of her life by the way her hand trembled as she raised the cup to her lips. It seemed to him that this was the first time he had ever looked upon his mother.

---

[17] **decency** (DEE-suhn-see) *n.* proper behavior, courtesy

[18] **repose** (rih-POHZ) *n.* quietness, calmness

[19] **swell** *adj.* slang for excellent, fine

POSTREADING

Critical Thinking

1. What do you think that Morley Callaghan is saying about families in this story?

2. How are this culture's views of right and wrong behavior important in the story?

3. Suppose you wanted to act out "All the Years of Her Life." Which part would you play? Whom would you choose for the other parts, and why?

Writing Your Response to "All the Years of Her Life"

In your journal, write about a time when you realized something new about someone you thought you knew (perhaps someone in your family). What event gave you that new understanding? How did it affect your relationship?

Going Back Into the Text: Author's Craft

Authors develop the characters in their stories in different ways, and not all the characters in a particular story are developed in the same way.

Leading characters in short stories are usually round characters. **Round characters** are complex; they have several qualities. We often think of round characters as being "real"—as being a lot like us or people we know.

Flat characters, however, have only one or two basic characteristics. They are meant to be that way, for their job is to help us focus on the main characters of the story.

Think about the way Callaghan develops the character of Mrs. Higgins in this story. Use these questions as guidelines:

1. Does Callaghan present Mrs. Higgins as a round character or a flat character?

2. Which of Mrs. Higgins's qualities seems strongest? What other qualities does she have?

3. How would you describe the character of Alfred Higgins? Of Sam Carr?

MAKING CULTURAL CONNECTIONS

THE AMERICAS

Every region of the world has monuments. Monuments can be buildings, works of art, natural features, or historic structures. Think about the monuments in your community or state. They say something about your culture in the same way that the monuments in the photos on these pages tell about the cultures to which they belong. Use the photos on these pages to find clues to the cultures of this unit.

Banff National Park, in southwest Alberta, Canada, lies on the eastern slopes of the Rocky Mountains. Spanning 2,564 square miles (6,641 square km), Banff is Canada's first national park. Visitors may see hot springs and glaciers, in addition to endangered woodland caribou, elk, bighorn sheep, mountain goats, moose, bears, and wolves.

Civilization in South America thrived long before it was colonized by Europeans. The remains of ancient cities serve as reminders of this past. Pictured here is Macchu Pichu, an ancient Incan city that is located high in the Andes Mountains in Peru.

Mexico City is a huge modern city, with a population of more than 8 million people. Shown here is the Mexican Stock Market Building in Mexico City, which serves as a financial center for the country's growing economy.

LINKING
Literature, History, and Culture

What do the photos on this page and the selections in this unit tell you about the cultures of the Americas?

▶ The remains of ancient civilizations can tell us about people who lived long ago, and about ourselves. What does the speaker observe about the past and about herself in "A Night in the Royal Ontario Museum"?

▶ Monuments can be natural objects, like mountains and lakes. How do the poets of "Chilean Earth" and "Homecoming" think about the natural monuments of their homes?

▶ Throughout the Americas, there are ruins alongside modern structures. Describe the contrasts between traditional and modern values in "Florinda and Don Gonzalo" and "The Old Man's Lazy."

PREREADING

from *Little by Little*

Reading the Autobiography in a Cultural Context

"All the Years of Her Life" (pages 366–373), which you may have just read, is set during the Great Depression of the 1930s. During that time, Jean Little was born in Taiwan (then known as Formosa) to Canadian parents who were both doctors. They soon realized that Jean was born with scarred corneas and other vision problems. Eventually, she was declared legally blind.

The Littles moved back to Canada in 1939, just before the outbreak of World War II. In 1931, Canada had gained its independence from Great Britain, but it was still quite "British" in many ways. Jean Little had to adjust to a variety of changes from the life she had known in the Far East. In her autobiography, *Little by Little*, she describes some of the adjustments. Still, she writes from a child's point of view. In that world, much went on as it always had—getting along with a younger sister, struggling to remember the multiplication tables, complaints about clothing, and so on.

An even greater adjustment came when Little started classes at Victory School in Guelph, Ontario. Before then, special allowances had been made for her eyesight, and she had attended classes for students with vision problems. In fourth grade, however, she was placed in a regular class. Even though both her fourth- and fifth-grade teachers had disabilities as a result of polio, the other students did not accept her differences quickly. Little's desire to be accepted is apparent in the excerpt from *Little by Little* that you are about to read. In it, she shows how humor and imagination help a person meet any challenge.

As an adult, Little worked with disabled children. She began to write novels when she could find no children's stories that presented disabilities in accurate ways. *Mine for Keeps* (1962) was her first novel; since then she has written more than a dozen others. They do not all focus on physical disabilities, but all of them feature someone who, in some way, is "different." Likewise, they all show how it is possible to learn from the challenges that being "different" creates.

Focusing on the Selection

As you read, think about the different kinds of challenges that Jean Little faces. What is her attitude toward her physical problems? What does she do about explaining her lateness to school? What does she do about an older student who bullies her? What can a modern reader learn by reading about her childhood?

from *Little by Little*

━━━━━ ◆◆◆ ━━━━━

Jean Little

I was eating my porridge[1] when Hugh, hurrying too fast, fell down the back stairs. Before Mother could get up, he limped in, sniffling slightly, and displayed a bumped elbow for her inspection. Mother examined it gravely.

"A slight haematoma,"[2] she said in a serious voice. "And an abrasion[3] almost visible to the naked eye. You'll live."

Hugh, who always recovered with the speed of light and who won Mother's admiration with his bravery, chuckled at the impressive words.

"What does that mean?" he asked.

"A little bruise and a scrape I can hardly see."

I glowered at my oatmeal. Why did she have to smile at him like that? He was not so special. I searched my mind for something terrible he had done that I could tell her about.

"Jean, hurry up or you'll be late," Grandma said.

I did not want to go to school. We were going to have another mental arithmetic test, and I still did not know my times tables. If only I could fall down and break my leg . . .

Four-year-old Pat grinned at me.

"Huwwy up, Jean," she parroted. "You'll be late."

I wanted to slap the wide smile off her silly little face. Instead I scooped up a few drops of milk on the tip of my spoon and let fly. The tiny bit of

---

[1] **porridge** (PAWR-ihj) *n.* oatmeal boiled in water or milk until thick, eaten as cereal
[2] **haematoma** (hee-muh-TOH-muh) *n.* a bruise
[3] **abrasion** (uh-BRAY-zhuhn) *n.* a skin scrape

milk splashed her on the nose. I laughed. Before anyone could stop her, Pat grabbed up her mug filled to the brim with milk and sent its entire contents sloshing over me, soaking me to the skin.

The next thing I knew, I was back upstairs changing out of my wet serge[4] dress, cotton petticoat,[5] long brown stockings and underwear into clean dry clothes. Not only was this going to make me really late, but Mother handed me the knitted suit Aunt Gretta had made for my tenth birthday. The ribbed blue skirt was sewn onto a sleeveless cotton vest. Over it went a horizontally striped blue and pink sweater with short sleeves. Nobody else in Miss Marr's class had a homemade knitted suit anything like it.

"I can't wear it," I said in anguished tones.

"It's lovely," my mother said calmly. "Gretta worked hard to make it for you. Don't be ridiculous. Of course you will wear it."

In ten minutes I was gobbling toast and honey, gulping down milk and hating my cheerful little sister who was the cause of all the trouble and who got to stay home and be spoiled by everybody.

When I reached the street, it was ominously[6] quiet. I really was going to be late, and it was all Pat's fault. I ran the first three blocks, but slowed down when I got a stitch in my side. There was still not a single child in sight.

As I passed St. John's School, I could hear the grade four class singing "God Save the King." I sent the small building a look of longing. Mr. Johnston had not had these horrid mental arithmetic tests.

Then I stood stock still. When I got to school, Miss Marr would tell me to put my name on the board to stay after four. I didn't mind staying late—lots of the others got detentions—I wasn't sure what to write, though I had a strong suspicion that you did not write out your whole name. Did you just write your initials? Or one initial and your surname? Or your first name and your last initial?

I had to get it right. The others still called me names when no teacher was near enough to hear. The only game I had ever been invited to play was Crack the Whip, and they always made me go on the end. Then, when the big girl at the front swung everybody around in a long *Crack!*, I ended up flying through the air and landing with a jarring crash on my hands and knees. As I picked myself up, I'd try to look as though I thought crash-landings were fun. Nobody was fooled.

---

[4] **serge** (serj) *n.* a kind of strong cloth, usually of wool, with slanting ridges across it
[5] **petticoat** (PEHT-ee-koht) *n.* a skirt or slip worn as an undergarment
[6] **ominously** (AHM-uh-nuhs-lee) *adv.* in a threatening way; unfavorably

If I wrote my name up there differently than the others did, they would have a new thing to tease me about. I could hear the jeering voices already.

"You're not just cross-eyed, you're so *dumb* you don't even know how to write your name on the board!"

I stood there, thinking hard. How could I save myself? Once in awhile, when a child brought a note from home, he got out of putting his name on the board. Well, my mother would not write me a note.

Perhaps, if your parents were not at home, and some emergency cropped up and you had to deal with it, Miss Marr just might let you sit down without asking for a note. It would have to be a desperate emergency . . .

I began to walk again, taking my time. I had to invent the most convincing lie of my life. Bit by bit, I worked it out. As I imagined how it must have happened, it grew so real that I began to believe it myself. I had every detail ready as I turned the last corner. Then I began to run.

I knew it was essential that I be out of breath when I arrived.

I dashed up the stairs, puffing hard. I opened the door, said a private prayer for help, and entered the grade five classroom. Miss Marr was at her desk. Out of the corner of my eye, I could see monitors collecting the test papers. So far so good.

"Jean," said my teacher, "you're late."

"Yes," I panted, facing her and opening my eyes wide so that I would look innocent and pitiful. "I know. I couldn't help it."

"Why are you late?" she asked.

I took a deep breath.

"Well, I was all ready in plenty of time. But just as I was going out the door, the telephone rang. I knew I should not go back to answer it, but you know my mother and father are both doctors and I was afraid it might be an emergency."

Miss Marr opened her mouth to ask a question, but I rushed on, not giving her time to get a word in edgewise.

"The trouble was, you see, that nobody was home but me. So I took the receiver off the hook and I said, 'Dr. Littles' residence.'"

Everybody was listening now, even the boys who never paid attention. I kept going.

"*MY DAUGHTER IS DYING! MY DAUGHTER IS DYING!*"

I saw my teacher jump as I shrieked the words at the top of my lungs. Her eyes were wide with shock. The class gasped. I did not stop for effect. I could not give the teacher time to interrupt.

"It was a man's voice. He sounded frantic with worry. 'I'm sorry,' I told him, 'my parents are out. If you call back, they should be home in one hour.' 'No! Please, don't hang up,' he begged. 'You must come and save her life. If I wait for your parents, she will surely die.' 'Well, I guess if she is dying, I'd better come. Where do you live?' I asked him. '111 King Street,' he told me."

Miss Marr did not even try to ask a question as I paused to catch my breath. The entire class was sitting spellbound. The silence was absolute. Not a desk seat squeaked. Not a giggle broke the hush.

"I hurried in and got the right medicine from the office and then I ran out the door. I didn't go the long way around by the Norwich Street bridge. I was afraid it would take too long. I went down London Road and across some stepping stones down there. When I got to King Street, there was the house. It was a log cabin with wind whistling through the cracks. And as I came up to it, I saw the door standing open and there were a bunch of people in the doorway and they were all crying. 'What's wrong?' I asked them. 'You are too late,' they sobbed. 'She's dead already.'"

This time, as I snatched a breath, Miss Marr choked back a small sound. She made no attempt to stem the flood of my story. I pressed on.

"'Oh, I am so sorry,' I told them. 'Take me to see her.' So they took me into the cabin and there lay the girl on a trundle bed. Her face was blue and her eyes had rolled up till you could just see white and her teeth were clenched. And her fingers and toes all curled over backwards."

I watched Miss Marr carefully at this point, because I was not absolutely sure what a dead person looked like. The last bit worried me especially. I had heard someone say that when people died, they turned their toes up. That could only mean that their toes curled over backwards, but I was not sure about the fingers.

Miss Marr's face quivered a little and her mouth twitched, but she did not speak. I hurried, eager to finish. It would be a relief to sit down. Even so, in spite of myself, I kept putting in extra bits as they occurred to me.

"'She's not quite dead,' I cried. 'She's just on the point of death. I think I can save her.' I hit her chin and her mouth opened. I poured in the medicine. She fluttered her lashes and turned a normal colour and said weakly, 'Where am I?' I turned and hurried toward the door. But before I could escape, all the weeping people went down on their knees and grabbed hold of my skirt and they said, 'You saved her life! We want to give you a reward. Gold, silver, a bag of emeralds, a horse that will come when you whistle . . . tell us the one thing you want more than anything else in the world and you can have it.'"

I paused for effect this time. I knew no one would break the hush. I wanted my teacher to take in the next bit.

"'The one thing I want more than anything else in the world,' I told them, 'is to be on time for school.' So they let me go and I ran down the hill and across the stepping stones. When I got to the third last stone, though, I slipped and fell in the river and cut my knee. I had to get to shore, go home and bandage my knee and put on dry clothes. Then I hurried here as fast as I could. And that is why I am late."

There was a stunned silence in the classroom. Miss Marr and I stared at each other for a long, long minute. I waited for her to tell me to write my name on the board. Instead, she pointed her finger at my desk. Speaking extremely slowly and wearily, she said, "Take . . . your . . . seat. Just . . . take . . . your . . . seat."

I tried to keep a solemn expression on my face. But it was hard not to grin. I sat down and did not turn my head as a buzz of whispers broke out behind me. I had missed the mental arithmetic test. I had not had to write my name on the board. And I had kept every single person transfixed with my exciting story.

At least three blissful minutes went by before I realized I had no cut on my knee and no bandage, either. Not only that, but I could not remember whether I had told her which knee I was supposed to have cut.

She had believed me. I was sure of that. Yet any second she was going to discover that I had told her a stupendous[7] lie.

I hooked one knee over the other and clasped my hands around the knee on top. I spent the entire morning that way. When I was required to write, I used only one hand. Miss Marr did not ask me a direct question. When recess time came and she said, "Class, stand," I stayed where I was.

Do you think Miss Marr believed Jean's excuse?

"Jean, aren't you going out for recess?" she asked when the others had marched out and there I still sat.

"Oh, Miss Marr," I said in my smallest, most pathetic voice. "I am so tired from saving that girl's life that I have to stay in and have a rest."

Still clutching my knee with both hands, I laid my head down on my desk and shut my eyes.

She did not say a word.

At noon, when she had her back turned, I ran out of the classroom, dashed home, sneaked bandaids from my parents' office and plastered them over both knees, to be on the safe side.

---

[7]**stupendous** (stoo-PEHN-duhs) adj. huge

When I returned to school, Miss Marr smiled and did not ask why both my knees were bandaged.

I sat through the afternoon thinking over what had happened. Did she really guess? The other kids did not seem to have figured out that I had lied. One girl had even smiled at me, as though she might be my friend. Nobody in my class had called me cross-eyed. A boy in grade seven had, though. If only I could shut him up the way I had hushed everybody that morning.

Then I remembered Hugh's knee. That night I asked Mother, "What are the long words for what's wrong with my eyes?"

I was standing beside her chair. She looked up at me.

"Why?" she asked.

"I want to know, that's all. They call me cross-eyed. I want to know the long words, the ones doctors use."

She rhymed off a whole list.

"Say it again. Slowly."

"Strabismus, nystagmus, corneal opacities and eccentric pupils."[8]

I practised.

The next day I was late coming out of school. The same grade-seven boy was waiting for me. He had his first snowball ready.

"Cross-eyed, cross-eyed," he chanted and waited for me to start running so that he could chase me, pelting me with hard-packed snowballs.

I turned on him instead.

"I am not cross-eyed," I said in a strong, clear voice. "I have corneal opacities and eccentric pupils."

I glared at him as I spoke, and my eyes were as crossed as ever. But he was so surprised that he stood there, his mouth gaping open like a fish's.

Then I turned my back and walked away. Perhaps his aim was off because he was so used to firing his missiles at a running target. But the first snowball flew past me harmlessly. The second exploded with a smack against a nearby tree.

I kept walking, chin in the air.

In the last two days, I had learned a lot about the power of words. Snowballs would hit me again and I would run away and cry. I would be late and, eventually, I would even have to write my name on the board.

But I had found out what mere words could do. I would not forget.

---

[8] **pupils** (PYOO-puhlz) *n. pl.* the openings in the center of the irises, which look like black spots

POSTREADING

Critical Thinking

1. As Jean Little recalls this episode from her childhood, how does she show that she is writing from a child's point of view?

2. On her way to school, Little hears a class of children singing. How does the song help provide the setting for this selection?

3. Suppose you could step into this selection at any point and talk to young Jean Little. Which point would you choose? What would you say?

Writing Your Response to *Little by Little*

At the end of this episode, Jean Little has "found out what mere words could do." In your journal, write your feelings about words. What power do words have to teach, persuade, or encourage us? Do you remember learning and then using a new word? When else might you have seen the power of words in your own life?

Going Back Into the Text: Author's Craft

Little by Little is an **autobiography**—a form of nonfiction in which a person tells his or her own life story. Most autobiographies are written in the first person, with the author speaking as "I."

Introducing this autobiography, Jean Little explains, "Although everything that happens in these pages is based on fact, I took my memories and rearranged them, filling in details as I went along. I do not really remember every word that I or others said so long ago. I do, however, know exactly how it felt and what we were likely to have said." Little thus notes that autobiographies are not completely objective, for they present the author's beliefs and perceptions as well as the facts. Still, autobiographies are valuable. They give us insights into the subject's personality and the times in which he or she has lived.

Use the following questions to review the elements of autobiography in this excerpt from *Little by Little*.

1. What do we learn about the Little family through these autobiographical details?

2. Think about the medical details in this excerpt. Which ones do you think are factually accurate? Which ones are colored by a child's point of view?

3. How might this selection be different if it were part of the autobiography of Miss Marr, Jean Little's teacher?

A Night in the Royal Ontario Museum

Reading the Poem in a Cultural Context

Among Canadian writers, Margaret Atwood has been called a "literary standard-bearer." Her writings have done much to stir an interest in writing about what it means to be Canadian.

Atwood was born in Ottawa but grew up in the wilds of northern Quebec. She started writing at the age of five and had her first poem published at the age of nineteen. She went on to teach, write, and work in a publishing house in Toronto.

At that time, there was little "Canadian" literature. Atwood and her friends who were writers were part of a literary "underground." But Atwood wanted to make more Canadians aware of their own literary history. She decided to write what she describes as "the first beginner's guide to Canadian literature." The result was *Survival* (1972), which she has described as "a treatise of sorts on the case for nationalism." The title came from Atwood's main idea—that survival was the central theme in Canadian literature. She also argued that Canadian writers, as a group, should stop letting themselves be shaped by the literature of the United States.

Survival was a controversial book, and it made Atwood famous.

Atwood's novels and collections of poems have often explored Canadian settings and characters. They have examined the idea of survival in a Canadian context. But Atwood also enjoys the beauty of poetry—especially the sound of poetic language. She has said that her poems "usually begin with words or phrases which appeal more because of their sound than their meaning. . . . For me, every poem has a texture of sound which is at least as important to me as the 'argument.'" In "A Night in the Royal Ontario Museum," Margaret Atwood combines sound and argument to create thought-provoking ideas.

Focusing on the Selection

As you read the poem, try to picture the details in your mind. How does the Royal Ontario Museum compare to museums that you have visited? How does the poem get you thinking about history? How does it make you think about survival?

A Night in the Royal Ontario Museum

Margaret Atwood

Who locked me

into this crazed man-made
stone brain
         where the weathered
totempole[1] jabs a blunt
finger at the byzantine[2]
mosaic[3] dome

Under that ornate
golden cranium[4] I wander
among fragments of gods, tarnished
coins, embalmed[5] gestures
chronologically arranged,
looking for the EXIT sign

but in spite of the diagrams
at every corner, labelled
in red: YOU ARE HERE
the labyrinth[6] holds me,

turning me around
the cafeteria, the washrooms,
a spiral through marble
Greece and Rome, the bronze
horses of China

then past the carved masks,
    wood and fur
to where 5 plaster Indians
in a glass case
squat near a dusty fire

and further, confronting me
with a skeleton child, preserved
in the desert air, curled
beside a clay pot and a few beads.

I say I am far
enough,   stop here   please
no more

---

[1] **totempole** (TOH-tuhm POHL) *n.* a post or pole carved and painted with a series of totem symbols, such as birds or bears, used as emblems of a tribe or clan of the northwest coast of North America, and erected in front of their houses

[2] **byzantine** (BIHZ-uhn-teen) *adj.* like a style of architecture developed in the Byzantine Empire, characterized by a circular dome and the use of mosaics

[3] **mosaic** (moh-ZAY-ick) *adj.* of a design made of small pieces of stone, glass, or tile of different colors inlaid on a surface

[4] **cranium** (KRAY-nee-uhm) *n.* something that looks like the part of the skull that encloses the brain; a reference to the dome of the museum

[5] **embalmed** (ehm-BAHMD) *adj.* of a corpse that is treated with a substance to prevent or slow decay

[6] **labyrinth** (LAB-uh-rihnth) *n.* a network of winding, connected passages through which it is difficult to find one's way; a maze

but the perverse museum, corridor
by corridor, an idiot
voice jogged by a pushed
button, repeats its memories

and I am dragged to the mind's
deadend, the roar of the bone-
yard, I am lost
among the mastodons[7]
and beyond: a fossil[8]
shell, then

samples of rocks
and minerals, even the thundering
tusks dwindling to pin-
points in the stellar
fluorescent-lighted
wastes of geology[9]

The Royal Ontario Museum, in Toronto, Canada.

---

[7] **mastodons** (MAS-tuh-dahnz) *n. pl.* extinct animals that resembled the elephant
[8] **fossil** (FAHS-uhl) *adj.* having the remains or traces of a plant or animal that lived long ago
[9] **geology** (jee-AHL-uh-jee) *n.* the scientific study of the earth

POSTREADING

Critical Thinking

1. Survival is an important theme for Margaret Atwood. Do you think that she is talking about survival in this poem? Explain your answer.

2. How do you think a Canadian reader would feel about the history of Canada after reading this poem? Explain your answer.

3. Review the exhibits that the museum visitor names. Which exhibit would you most want to see for yourself? Why?

Writing Your Response to "A Night in the Royal Ontario Museum"

The visitor to the museum seems quite lost. Even the YOU ARE HERE signs are of no help. In your journal, write about feeling either (1) lost in some way (in need of a YOU ARE HERE sign in your life), or (2) sure of your direction (knowing what YOU ARE HERE means in your life). How does your answer help you understand the poem?

Going Back Into the Text: Author's Craft

You may already have noticed that there are no rhymes in this poem. However, sounds are used in other ways. Atwood includes examples of **onomatopoeia**—a word whose sound suggests its meaning. *Roar* (line 39), for example, sounds like a roar. She sometimes uses **alliteration**, beginning words near each other with the same consonant sound. For example, the alliteration of the *d* in "dragged to the mind's/deadend" (lines 38–39) helps us focus on the speaker's feeling.

In this poem, Atwood uses a lot of **assonance**, or repeated vowel sounds. Notice the long *a* sound in "crazed man-made/stone brain" (lines 2–3). The sound links the words and strengthens this description of the museum.

Look for and think about Atwood's use of sounds in this poem. You can use these questions as a guide:

1. Find another example of alliteration and another example of onomatopoeia.

2. In lines 23–25, how does assonance link details in the poem?

3. Find another example of assonance in the poem. Describe its purpose.

My Financial Career

Reading the Essay in a Cultural Context

Although Stephen Leacock was born in England, he and his family moved to an Ontario farm when he was six years old. In college, Leacock received degrees in modern languages and political economy. He later became a college professor, teaching at McGill University, Montreal, for some 35 years.

Leacock was a noted teacher in his field. He also wrote many serious books—works on political science and economics, biographies, histories, and books of literary criticism. However, he is best remembered by Canadians as a popular humorist. Leacock wrote more than 30 books containing humorous stories, essays, and parodies of other writers. Sometimes, as in "My Financial Career," he poked fun at himself. At other times, he took an amused look at the everyday lives of Canadians.

One critic described Leacock's humor as "balanced between cutting satire and sheer absurdity." In "My Financial Career," see how you would describe that humor.

Focusing on the Selection

As you read, think about the situation that Leacock faces and why he feels so nervous. Consider, too, how each event at the bank leads to the next. Why does Leacock consider this embarrassing chain of experiences humorous? Why do you?

My Financial Career

$\blacklozenge$ $\blacklozenge$ $\blacklozenge$

Stephen Leacock

When I go into a bank I get rattled. The clerks rattle me; the wickets[1] rattle me; the sight of the money rattles me; everything rattles me.

The moment I cross the threshold of a bank and attempt to transact business there, I become an irresponsible idiot.

I knew this beforehand, but my salary had been raised to fifty dollars a month and I felt that the bank was the only place for it.

So I shambled in and looked timidly round at the clerks. I had an idea that a person about to open an account must needs consult the manager.

I went up to a wicket marked "Accountant." The accountant was a tall, cool devil. The very sight of him rattled me. My voice was sepulchral.[2]

"Can I see the manager?" I said, and added solemnly, "alone." I don't know why I said "alone."

"Certainly," said the accountant, and fetched him.

The manager was a grave, calm man. I held my fifty-six dollars clutched in a crumpled ball in my pocket.

"Are you the manager?" I said. God knows I didn't doubt it.

"Yes," he said.

"Can I see you," I asked, "alone?" I didn't want to say "alone" again, but without it the thing seemed self-evident.

The manager looked at me in some alarm. He felt that I had an awful secret to reveal.

"Come in here," he said, and led the way to a private room. He turned the key in the lock.

"We are safe from interruption here," he said; "sit down."

---

[1] **wickets** (WIHK-ihts) *n. pl.* grilled or grated windows through which business is conducted
[2] **sepulchral** (suh-PUL-kruhl) *adj.* gloomy

We both sat down and looked at each other. I found no voice to speak.

"You are one of Pinkerton's men, I presume," he said.

He had gathered from my mysterious manner that I was a detective. I knew what he was thinking, and it made me worse.

"No, not from Pinkerton's," I said, seeming to imply that I came from a rival agency.

"To tell the truth," I went on, as if I had been prompted to lie about it, "I am not a detective at all. I have come to open an account. I intend to keep all my money in this bank."

The manager looked relieved but still serious; he concluded now that I was a son of Baron Rothschild or a young Gould.[3]

"A large account, I suppose," he said.

"Fairly large," I whispered. "I propose to deposit fifty-six dollars now and fifty dollars a month regularly."

What other organizations besides banks can you think of that have frustrating and complicated rules?

The manager got up and opened the door. He called to the accountant.

"Mr. Montgomery," he said unkindly loud, "this gentleman is opening an account, he will deposit fifty-six dollars. Good morning."

I rose.

A big iron door stood open at the side of the room.

"Good morning," I said, and stepped into the safe.

"Come out," said the manager coldly, and showed me the other way.

I went up to the accountant's wicket and poked the ball of money at him with a quick convulsive movement as if I were doing a conjuring[4] trick.

My face was ghastly pale.

"Here," I said, "deposit it." The tone of the words seemed to mean, "Let us do this painful thing while the fit is on us."

He took the money and gave it to another clerk.

---

[3] **Baron Rothschild ... Gould** wealthy and famous financiers
[4] **conjuring** (KAHN-juhr-ihng) *adj.* of the process of performing magic

He made me write the sum on a slip and sign my name in a book. I no longer knew what I was doing. The bank swam before my eyes.

"Is it deposited?" I asked in a hollow, vibrating voice.

"It is," said the accountant.

"Then I want to draw a cheque."[5]

My idea was to draw out six dollars of it for present use. Someone gave me a cheque-book through a wicket and someone else began telling me how to write it out. The people in the bank had the impression that I was an invalid[6] millionaire. I wrote something on the cheque and thrust it in at the clerk. He looked at it.

"What! are you drawing it all out again?" he asked in surprise. Then I realized that I had written fifty-six instead of six. I was too far gone to reason now. I had a feeling that it was impossible to explain the thing. All the clerks had stopped writing to look at me.

Reckless with misery, I made a plunge.

"Yes, the whole thing."

"You withdraw your money from the bank?"

"Every cent of it."

"Are you not going to deposit any more?" said the clerk, astonished.

"Never."

An idiot hope struck me that they might think something had insulted me while I was writing the cheque and that I had changed my mind. I made a wretched attempt to look like a man with a fearfully quick temper.

The clerk prepared to pay the money.

"How will you have it?" he said.

"What?"

"How will you have it?"

"Oh"—I caught his meaning and answered without even trying to think—"in fifties."

He gave me a fifty-dollar bill.

"And the six?" he asked dryly.

"In sixes," I said.

He gave it to me and I rushed out.

As the big door swung behind me I caught the echo of a roar of laughter that went up to the ceiling of the bank. Since then I bank no more. I keep my money in cash in my trousers pocket and my savings in silver dollars in a sock.

---

[5] **cheque** (chehk) *n.* British spelling of check; a written order to a bank to pay a certain amount from funds on deposit

[6] **invalid** (IHN-vuh-lihd) *n.* a sick, injured, or disabled person

POSTREADING

Critical Thinking

1. How does Stephen Leacock get us to sympathize with him at the same time that we are laughing at his misadventure?

2. Do you think that most Canadian readers would agree or disagree with Leacock's opinion of banks? Explain your answer.

3. How did reading this essay influence your own ideas about what makes us laugh?

Writing Your Response to "My Financial Career"

In your journal, write about an experience that you were nervous about trying (for example, learning to skate, taking your first driving lesson, or auditioning for a play). What happened when you tried it for the first time? Relate your experience to the experience described in "My Financial Career."

Going Back Into the Text: Author's Craft

Humor is writing that is meant to amuse you—to make you smile or laugh. Humor is often light in tone, and it focuses on unusual circumstances or people. The situations or actions that occur in a humorous story can range from slightly odd to completely ridiculous.

With a partner, talk about the humor in "My Financial Career." These questions can guide your discussion.

1. What seems odd (or even ridiculous) about each of the following details?

    • the description of the accountant

    • the manager's belief about Leacock's identity

    • the way in which Leacock attempts to deposit his savings

    • his attempt to write a check (cheque)

    • Leacock's final decision about where to keep his money

2. "Reckless with misery" is the way Leacock humorously describes himself toward the end of his visit to the bank. Why might that expression be a good description of the humor throughout this essay?

3. In this essay, are we laughing more *with* Leacock or *at* him? Do you think that was what Leacock wanted us to do?

Reviewing the Region

1. An author's message is often revealed by the tone, or mood, of his or her literary work. Choose a selection from this chapter and give examples of the way in which the tone of the work conveys the author's attitudes or beliefs.

2. Some literary works reveal the culture in which they were written more than others. Choose a selection from the chapter that reveals the culture of the author. Explain the ways in which the author accomplishes this.

3. If you had to choose a friend from among the characters in this chapter, whom would you choose? Give reasons for your choice.

FOCUSING THE UNIT

COOPERATIVE/COLLABORATIVE LEARNING

With a small group of classmates, present an art review. Include art from a country in Central America or South America. Each member of your group should select a piece of art from a different artist. Begin by looking at the art in this book. Choose an artist to research. Explain to the class what is significant about the art you have chosen. Where is it from? Why do you like it? Below is part of a sample presentation that one group of students used to review the art from Art of the Tapestries in this book. You may wish to use it as a starting point for your discussion.

Student 1: There is great diversity among the Canadians. About 40% of the population can trace its heritage to England. Nearly 30% of the population has roots in France. The remainder of the population is composed of people of various ethnic origins, including German, Italian, Polish, native peoples, Dutch, and Greek.

Student 2: Native peoples in Canada have a long history of woodcarving and painting. These wooden dishes are finely crafted using primitive tools.

Student 3: Masks and totem poles are another traditional art found among the native peoples in Canada. I like this moon mask because it makes the moon look friendly. People who live close to nature must rely on the moon for survival.

Writing Process

Reread your journal entries for this unit. Look carefully at your writing to find where you related a story to a personal experience. From the two chapters in this unit, choose two or more selections that you could relate to especially well.

The personal essay is a form of writing that reveals a person's feelings, beliefs, or experiences. After choosing a selection from this unit that relates to a personal experience you've had, write a personal essay on the meaning of this experience in your life. Your audience might be a close friend, parent, or relative. Start your essay by describing your experience. Next, explain how this experience was important to you. List the new insights that you gained as a result of this experience. Refer to the handbook at the back of the book for help with the writing process. Use the model essay as a guideline.

Problem Solving

Now that you've read selections from this unit, reread the Unit Opener. Like the United States, Canada and Latin America are made up of many diverse cultures. Think about how diversity creates conflict in your world and in the regions you have just read about. Choose two or more of the authors included in this unit and analyze their insights into this problem. What are your ideas for a solution to the problem? In the form of a skit, dance, musical arrangement, art composition, news story, debate, or poem, express your thoughts and feelings about the problem and propose a solution. You may wish to work alone, with a partner, or in a small group.

CHINUA ACHEBE (1930–) is best known for his novel *Things Fall Apart*. Achebe, who was born in Ogidi, Nigeria, was nominated for the Booker Prize, a prestigious English book award, in 1987 for *Ant Hills of the Savannah*.

YEHUDA AMICHAI (1924–) was born in Germany but moved to Israel as a boy. Among Amichai's works, the poetry collections *Amen, Songs of Jerusalem and Myself, Poems*, and *Time* have been translated into English, as was the novel *Not of This Time, Not of This Place*.

MARGARET ATWOOD (1939–), who was born in Ottawa, grew up in the bush country of northern Quebec and Ontario. Atwood has lived in many parts of Canada, as well as in France, Italy, and England. This award-winning author has published many volumes of poetry, nonfiction, and fiction, including the novels *Surfacing, Lady Oracle*, and *Life Before Man*. She lives in Toronto.

KOFI AWOONOR (George Awoonor-Williams, 1935–) was born in Wheta, Ghana. He has maintained strong ties to the countryside, that he has returned to again and again in his writing. *This Earth, My Brother* (1971) and *The Breast of the Earth* (1975) are still widely read and quoted, and ensure Awoonor's place in the African oral-poetic tradition.

RAISA BLOKH (1901–1943) was passionate about her Soviet homeland. This love contrasts with the pain Blokh suffered in the German concentration camp where she died. These feelings combined to produce her simple and subtle writing style. Her work was finally published in the Soviet Union in 1988, forty-six years after her death.

PETER BLUE CLOUD was born into the Turtle Clan of the Mohawk tribe in Kahnawake, Quebec, and his birth date has been cited by different sources as 1927, 1933, and 1935. He is known as a poet, carpenter, wood carver, drum maker, editor, and author of short stories. After his experience in the aboriginal takeover of Alcatraz State Prison in 1969, he published the poem "Alcatraz," followed by his first book, *Alcatraz is not an Island* (1972). He is now considered one of the Elders of aboriginal poets, and currently lives in Nevada, California.

HEINRICH THEODOR BÖLL (1917–1985) Nobel Prize winner for his book *Group Portrait with Lady*, was born in Cologne, Germany. An outspoken opponent of the Nazis, Böll was drafted into the army and forced to serve. After the war, he discovered that most of his earlier work had been destroyed. He began again by writing of the difficulties of living in postwar Germany in "Die Botschaft (Breaking the News)" and the novella *Der Zug war punktlich (The Train Was on Time)*.

JORGE LUIS BORGES (1899–1986) was born in Buenos Aires and educated in Europe. He published many collections of poems, essays, and short stories. Borges received numerous awards and honors, both in the English and Spanish-speaking worlds; among them, the International Publishers' Prize (shared with Samuel Beckett in 1961), Mexico's Alfonso Reyes Prize (1973), and the Cervantes Prize (shared with Gerardo Diego in 1980). He served as Director of the Argentine National Library from 1955 until 1973.

NINA CASSIAN (Renee Annie Stefanescu, 1924–) was born in Galati, Romania, whose diverse population gave her a multicultural view of the world. Cassian's first book, *On the Scale of One to One*, was attacked by authorities, forcing her to attempt to change her style. She later rejected this charge and emigrated to the United States in 1985. She was granted political asylum here in 1987, and she continues to write and translate here in this country.

CH'IU CHIN (1879–1907) was a poet and political revolutionary in China. Having left her family and children to study in Japan, she returned to China to teach, founding a women's newspaper in Shanghai. Chin was arrested by the Manchu government in 1907, and died accused of treason because of her "revolutionary" poetry.

JULIO CORTÁZAR (1914–1984) left his native country of Argentina in the 1950s to preserve his "intellectual independence" from the Perón regime. His experiments with the novel and the short story allowed him to "break the habits of readers" by playing with reality and time. Cortázar's novel, *Hopscotch* (1963), is about a person trying to shake off the restrictions of time, language, and convention by looking for heaven in the ultimate hope of a hopscotch game.

MAHMOUD DARWISH (1941–) a Palestinian poet and journalist who was born in Galilee, writes in the Arabic tradition of allusion and metaphor. He paints a vivid picture of people caught up in the struggle to maintain their identity in a land that is no longer their own. Darwish now lives in exile in Cairo, Egypt.

SLAVENKA DRAKULIC is one of the leading feminist writers to emerge in Eastern Europe. In her first non-fiction book published in English, *How We Survived Communism and Even Laughed*, Drakulic explores the ways in which government authority affected daily activities, especially women's lives. She also discusses the strong Western influences on Yugoslavian women.

LEAH GOLDBERG (1911–1970) was born in Lithuania. After studying Semitic Languages in Bonn, Germany, she emigrated to Israel in 1935. There, Goldberg took up work as a journalist, translator, and university teacher. She was influential in the development of modern Hebrew culture through her poetry and children's literature, which are still widely read today.

NADINE GORDIMER (1923–) was born to Jewish immigrant parents in the South African mining town of Springs. She won the 1991 Nobel Prize for Literature for her narratives, which explore the changing responses to apartheid in her native country. Gordimer now lives in Johannesburg.

PATRICIA GRACE (1937–) is a New Zealand writer of short stories, novels, and children's books. Her Maori heritage, which strongly influences her writing, can be seen through her characters, who are often children. Grace attempts, in her works, to integrate the love of family, the traditions, and the values of her people with the ways of white European society.

VIRGINIA HAMILTON (1936–) is best known for her novel *M. C. Higgins, the Great,* for which she won the Newberry Medal and a National Book Award in the United States. This novel, like Hamilton's other novels for young adults, centers on the life and emerging self-awareness of an African American teenager.

JERZY HARASYMOWICZ (1933–) was born in Palawy, Poland. This poet, who draws on his native landscape and the city of Cracow for inspiration, mixes fairy-tale-like description with modern verse forms and gentle humor. Harasymowicz has published several books of poetry and has founded two poetic groups.

LE LY HAYSLIP (1949–) grew up in Vietnam and learned about survival at a very young age. To avoid the war, she married an American civilian who worked in Vietnam and came to the United States. She wrote the story of her life in two books, *When Heaven and Earth Changed Places* and *Child of War, Woman of Peace*, which were made into a movie by Oliver Stone. Hayslip now works to aid the poor, handicapped, and displaced children of Vietnam.

SHIN'ICHI HOSHI (1926–) is a Japanese writer who has published nearly 1000 short stories. Among Hoshi's works are the speculative fiction story "Bokkuchan" (1958), and a collection of linked stories, *Koe no Ami* (*Network of the Voice*, 1970), which is about a telephone system invasion.

YUSUF IDRIS (1927–1991), who was born in Egypt, became a writer because he thought he could tell stories better than those he read when he was a child. A master of the short story, Idris's work has been translated into many languages. He was a columnist for *Al-Ahram*, a Cairo newspaper, in the later years of his life.

ISMAIL FAHD ISMAIL (1940–), who is a novelist and short story writer, has also worked in the fields of business, psychology, administration, drama, and cinematography. Ismail's many books include the short story collections *The Dark Spot* (1965) and *Cages and the Common Language* (1975). He now runs a cinematographic products company in his native Kuwait.

NINA KATERLI (1934–) was born in Leningrad and graduated from the Lensoviet Technological Institute as an engineer. Her first short story was published in 1973 in the journal *Kostyor*. Katerli's short story collections, which have been translated into many languages, include *The Window* (1981) and *Colored Postcards* (1986). She still lives in the city of her birth, present-day St. Petersburg.

EPHRAIM KISHON was born in Budapest, Hungary, and emigrated to Israel in 1949. He is considered to be the national humorist of Israel. Kishon is an award-winning writer, playwright, filmmaker, and journalist, winning an Oscar nomination in 1964 for his film *Sallah*, the Israeli Nordau Prize for Literature, and the Sokolov Prize for outstanding journalistic achievement. He now lives in Tel Aviv, Israel, with his family.

ILYA KRICHEVSKY (1963–1991) was an emerging poet in the former Soviet Union. His poetry had attracted the interest of poetry journals, and Krichevsky was scheduled for a discussion in the fall when he lost his life defending Mikhail Gorbachev during the attempted coup of 1991. He was born in Moscow.

CARMEN LAFORET (1921–), who was born in Barcelona, Spain, spent her early life in the Canarie Islands. As a child, Laforet was surrounded by art and artists, and art figures strongly in her writing. She also frequently writes about young people who are looking for their place in the world. Her first and best-known novel, *Nada (Nothing)*, received the Nadal Prize in 1944.

CAMARA LAYE (?–1980) the son of the village goldsmith, was born in French Guinea. He wrote *The Dark Child*, his autobiography, while studying engineering in France. In this book, Laye discusses his boyhood in the village of Koroussa, a place he saw as mysterious and powerful. His story of choosing between the traditions of his people and the lure of success in a wider world—between the past and the future—is considered an African classic.

STEPHEN BUTLER LEACOCK (1869–1944) is probably the most popular humorist in Canada.

His family moved from England to Ontario when he was six. Leacock studied modern languages and economics in Toronto, later teaching at McGill University in Montreal. He wrote many scholarly books, but is best known for his humorous works such as *Literary Lapses* (1910), *Sunshine Sketches of a Little Town* (1912), and *Arcadian Adventures with the Idle Rich* (1914).

PRIMO LEVI (1919–1987), an Italian Jew, survived World War II as a resistance fighter and inmate of Auschwitz. He later wrote about these experiences in *Survival in Auschwitz* (1947) and *The Reawakening* (1963). In 1977, he retired from his position as a manager of a Turin chemical factory to devote himself to writing. Although he wrote on many subjects, he always returned to explore his Holocaust experiences.

JEAN LITTLE was born in Taiwan, grew up in Ontario, and was trained as a teacher of disabled children. Her books for children explore issues associated with being different, and emphasize that almost any problem can be overcome. Little writes with the aid of a talking computer and travels with her seeing eye dog, Ritz. She was awarded the Vicky Metcalf Award in 1974.

GABRIEL GARCÍA MÁRQUEZ (1928–) won the Nobel Prize for literature in 1982. Born in the Caribbean coastal town of Arcataca, Colombia, he was raised by his grandparents, whose retelling of the traditional folktales of the region inspired his unique style of "magical realism." Márquez says of his grandmother's tales that ". . . Caribbean reality resembles the wildest imagination." *One Hundred Years of Solitude* (1967) is his best-known novel.

VICTOR MANUEL MENDIOLA (1954–) is a Mexican poet and publisher. He originally majored in economics at the Universidad Nacionál Autonoma de Mexico, and is now the codirector of Ediciones El Tucan de Virginia. Mendrola's volumes of poetry include *Poemas* (1980), *Sonetos a las cosas* (1982), *Triga* (1983), and *Nubes* (1987).

GCINA MHLOPE (c. 1960–) was born in South Africa and began her writing career as a journalist.

Now well known as an award-winning actress, poet, and writer, Mhlope's talent for and promotion of the art of storytelling is expressed in her many one-woman performances.

GABRIELA MISTRAL (Lucila Godoy y Alcayaga, 1889–1957) was born in Chile. Her poetry embodies a rebellious spirit, while explaining the themes of romantic, religious, charitable, and maternal love. Her 1938 poetry collection *Tala (Felling of Trees)* is considered her best work. A strong advocate of women's and children's issues, Mistral was invited by the Mexican Government in the 1920s to overhaul the country's school system.

MIYAMOTO MUSASHI (1584–1645), who was a samurai warrior of legendary fame, was known to the Japanese as *Kensei* or "sword-saint." *A Book of Five Rings (Go Rin No Sho)* was a reflection on his philosophy of "the way of the sword." It was not a manual, but a meditation, influenced by Zen, Shinto, and Confucian philosophy and practice. It was written in a cave in Kyushu a few weeks before his death.

R.K. NARAYAN won the National Prize of the Indian Literary Academy, India's highest literary honor, for his novel *The Guide* (1958). Born in Madras and educated in Mysore, he is now among the most successful English-language novelists.

PABLO NERUDA (Ricardo Eliecer Neftali Reyes y Basoalto, 1904–1973) won the Nobel Prize for Literature in 1971 for his evocative, symbolic poetry. Born in southern Chile, he created his pseudonym to avoid the disapproval of his railway-worker father, and later adopted the name. He became a career diplomat and was stationed in Spain and Mexico. Neruda became a Communist after the Spanish Civil War. His criticism of the Chilean government forced him to emigrate to Argentina in 1948.

AZIZ NESIN (1915–) is considered a controversial writer in Turkey. His humorous style cuts across social boundaries, often defying official policy and convention. His career is marked by a love-hate relationship with the Turkish authorities, requiring the use of many pen names. Orphaned himself as a young boy, Aziz later founded the Nesin Trust for orphans.

DJIBRIL TAMSIR NIANE (1932–) was born in Conakry, Guinea, and was educated in Senegal and France. He returned to Conakry as a history teacher, headmaster, and professor. Niane has become involved in drama. His fiction and scholarly writings concern the history of Africa and African heroes, such as *Chaka*, a play about the great Zulu king, and *An Epic of Old Mali*.

PADRAIC O'FARRELL is a journalist for a number of Irish newspapers and periodicals, writing poetry, columns, features, and theater pieces with trademark humor. O'Farrell's nineteen books include *How the Irish Speak English* and *Gems of Irish Wisdom*. He lives with his family in Mullingar, Ireland.

OCTAVIO PAZ (1914–) was born in Mexico City and was an important figure in the new generation of Mexican writers that began to develop in the late 1930s. He became a diplomat for his native country, and in 1962 was appointed ambassador to India. Paz resigned this post in 1968 and later founded *Plural* (1971-1976) and *Vuelta* (since 1976), two journals for the arts and politics. He won the Cervantes Award, the most prestigious prize in the Spanish-speaking world, in 1981, and received the Nobel Prize in Literature in 1990.

ISAAC LOEB PERETZ (1852–1915) was born in Poland and received a strict orthodox Hebrew education. He wrote in Hebrew and Yiddish, and is best known for his short stories, including "Bontsha the Silent" and "If Not Higher." Peretz's success as a lawyer, his Hasidic roots, and his concerns for social reform, poverty, and education influenced his writing.

HENRI POURRAT (1887–1959) was born in Ambert, France. His writing grew out of the long hours of rest and frequent walks in his beloved Auvergne region, in which Pourrat recovered from a childhood bout with tuberculosis. His fascination with French folktales led him to collect the tales into *Le Tresor des Contes (The Treasury of Tales)*. Humor infuses his writing, reflecting the traditions of the region he regarded as the true heart of French mythology and folk culture.

RUMI (Jelaluddin Balkhi, 1207–1273) was born in Balkh, Afghanistan, which was at that time part of the Persian empire. His family fled to Konya, Turkey, to escape from the advancing Mongols. In Turkey, Rumi took up the position of dervish sheikh at his father's death. His friendship with Shams of Tabriz resulted in his eventually achieving a high regard among Persian poets. *Mathnawi* and *The Works of Shams of Tabriz* (so named in friendship) are examples of his enduring work.

SERGEY ALEXANDROVICH SEMYONOV (1893–1943) was a novelist in the former Soviet Union. His early writing dealt with the tragedies and difficulties during the civil war that led to the creation of the Soviet Union. *Hunger*, his first novel, was published in 1922 and set the tone for his later work, which reflected his concern for the fragility of the family.

LEOPOLD SEDAR SENGHOR (1906–   ) was born in Joal, in the Sine-Saloum region of western Africa, and was educated in France. He later served as president of the Republic of Senegal from 1960 to 1981. Senghor's work deals with the clash of his rich ancestral heritage, with its ties to land and native spirituality, and an imposed European culture. He is the only black intellectual elected to the French Academy.

ALI AL-SHARQAWI (1947–) is a poet and a veterinary scientist from Bahrain. His style combines modern complex techniques with a dedication to justice and freedom. Al-Sharqawi's collections of poetry include *Thunder in the Season of Drought* (1975), *Palm Tree of the Heart* (1981), *and Psalm 23 for the Singers' Nectar* (1985).

KIRI TE KANAWA (1944–   ) was born in Gisborne, on New Zealand's North Island, and moved as a young girl to Auckland. A world-renowned soprano, she was already an accomplished and popular singer in 1966, when she went to England to study at the London Opera Center. Te Kanawa occasionally performs jazz, musical theater, and popular music, as well as the spiritual and church music she learned as a child. Her Maori heritage is reflected in the tales from her youth.

MARIA WINE (1912–) was born in Sweden and published her first book of poetry in 1943. With more than 16 volumes of poetry and prose to her credit, Wine is an important creative force in Sweden.

HARRY WU (1937–), born in Shanghai, dedicated himself to exposing human rights abuses of the laogai, China's forced labor prison camps. He spent 19 years as a political prisoner in the laogai and was released in 1979. He is now the Executive Director of the Laogai Research Foundation in Milipitas, CA. Wu continues to document the abuses committed by the Chinese government.

YEVGENY (ALEXANDROVICH) YEVTUSHENKO (1933–) was born in Siberia, in Russia, and began to write poetry as a boy. Educated in Moscow, he became the most popular and outspoken poet in the former Soviet Union. Poems such as *Stantzia Zima* (*Winter Station*, 1956) and *Babi Yar* (1968) helped Yevtushenko to gain wide popularity with a younger generation, the disapproval of the established order, and international fame that allowed him to live part-time in England, even under a strict Communist regime. He is now a distinguished professor at Queens College/CUNY in New York City.

Pronunciation Key

Accent is the force or stress given to some works or syllables in speech. In this book, accent is indicated by the use of uppercase letters. Words of one syllable are always shown as accented. Thus, if the word *hand* were pronounced, the pronunciation would be printed (hand). In words of more than one syllable, the syllable that gets the main accent is printed in uppercase letters. The other syllable or syllables are printed in lowercase letters. If the word *handbag* were pronounced, the pronunciation would be printed (HAND-bag). The phonetic respellings are based on the pronunciations given in *Webster's New World Dictionary*.

This glossary defines important terms used in this book. The page on which a term first appears is given in parentheses at the end of the definition.

Vowel Sound	Symbol	Respelling
a as in *hat*	a	HAT
a as in *day, date, paid*	ay	DAY, DAYT, PAYD
vowels as in *far, on*	ah	FAHR, AHN
vowels as in *dare, air*	ai	DAIR, AIR
vowels as in *saw, call, pour*	aw	SAW, KAWL, PAWR
e as in *pet, debt*	eh	PEHT, DEHT
e as in *seat, chief*; **y** as in *beauty*	ee	SEET, CHEEF, BYOO-tee
e in a syllable that ends with a vowel *(Spanish)*	eh	MEH
e in a syllable that ends with a consonant *(Spanish)*	ee	koh-MER
vowels as in *learn, fur, sir*	er	LERN, FER, SER
i as in *sit, bitter*; **ee** as in *been*	ih	SIHT, BIHT-uhr, BIHN
i as in *mile*; **y** as in *defy*; **ei** as in *height*	eye	MEYEL, dee-FEYE, HEYET
i as in *Latina (Spanish)*	ee	lah-TEE-na
o as in *go*	oh	GOH
vowels as in *boil, toy*	oi	BOIL, TOI
vowels as in *foot, could*	oo	FOOT, KOOD
vowels as in *boot, rule, suit*	oo	BOOT, ROOL, SOOT
vowels as in *how, out, bough*	ow	HOW, OWT, BOW
vowels as in *up, come*	u	UP, KUM
vowels as in *use, use, few*	yoo	YOOZ, YOOS, FYOO
vowels as in *guapo (Spanish)*	wa	GWAH-poh
vowels as in *buena (Spanish)*	weh	BWEH-nah
vowels in unaccented syllables *(schwas) again, upon, sanity*	uh	uh-GEHN, uh-PAHN, SAN-uh-tee

Consonant Sound	Symbol	Respelling
ch as in *choose, reach*	ch	CHOOZ, REECH
g as in *go, dig*	g	GOH, DIHG
g before **e** or **i**, as in *gitana (Spanish)*	g	hee-TAH-nah
gh as in *rough, laugh*	f	RUF, LAF
h as in *who, whole*	h	HOO, HOHL
h as in *haga (Spanish)*	(silent)	AH-gah
j as in *jar*; **dg** as in *fudge*; **g** as in *gem*	j	JAHR, FUJ, JEHM
j as in *hota (Spanish)*	h	HOH-tah
k as in *king*; **c** as in *come*; **ch** as in *Christmas*	k	KIHNG, KUM, KRIHS-muhs
ll as in *llama (Spanish)*	y	YAH-mah
ñ as in *niña (Spanish)*	ny	NEE-nyeh
ph as in *telephone*	f	TEHL-uh-fohn
rr as in *carreta (Spanish)*	rr	kah-RREH-tah
s as in *treasure*; **g** as in *bourgeois*	zh	TREH-zhuhr, boor-ZHWAH
s as in *this, sir*	s	THIS, SER
sh as in *ship*	sh	SHIHP
th as in *thin*	th	THIHN
th as in *this*	th	THIHS
wh as in *white*	wh	WHEYET
x as in *fix, axle*	ks	FIHKS, AK-suhl
x as in *exist*	gz	ihg-ZIHST
z as in *zero*; **s** as in *chasm*	z	ZEE-roh, KAZ-uhm

A

abacus (AB-uh-kuhs) *n.* a device for counting and computing that consists of parallel rods with sliding beads

abalone (ab-uh-LOH-nee) *n.* a soft-bodied sea animal whose shell has a brightly colored lining

abide (uh-BEYED) *v.* put up with; bear

abode (uh-BOHD) *n.* a home

abrasion (uh-BRAY-zhuhn) *n.* a skin scrape

abscess (AB-sehs) *n.* a mass of pus formed as a result of an infection

abstract (AB-strakt) *adj.* difficult to understand

ackees (AK-eez) salted fish

acolyte (AK-uh-leyet) *n.* a person who assists a priest in the celebration of Mass

adjured (uh-JOORD) *v.* urged earnestly

adversary (AD-vuhr-sehr-ee) *n.* an opponent or enemy

affably (AF-eh-blee) *adv.* in a friendly manner

affinity (uh-FIHN-ih-tee) *n.* liking or natural attraction

affront (uh-FRUNT) *n.* insult

affronted (uh-FRUNT-ihd) *v.* insulted

Alexander the Great *pr. n.* king of Macedonia from 336–323 B.C.; conqueror of Greek city-states and of the Persian empire from Asia Minor and Egypt to India

alibis (AHL-uh-beyez) *n. pl.* excuses

Allah (AL-uh) *n.* the Moslem name for God

allegations (al-uh-GAY-shuhnz) *n. pl.* accusations made without proof

allurements (uh-LOOR-muhnts) *n. pl.* strong attractions

alms (ahlmz) *n.* charitable gifts of money

almshouse (AHLMZ-hows) *n.* a poorhouse

alternative (awl-TER-nuh-tihv) *n.* choice

Amazon (AM-uh-zahn) *n.* mythological race of female warriors; a tall, strong female

ambrosia (ahm-BROH-zhuh) *n.* the food of the gods

amenities (uh-MEHN-ih-teez) *n. pl.* comforts; conveniences

anesthesia (an-ihs-THEE-zhuh) *n.* loss of the feeling of pain as a result of a drug, such as ether, used by doctors

animated (AN-uh-may-tihd) *adj.* lively

annul (uh-NUL) *v.* reduce to nothing

anonymous (uh-NON-uh-muhs) *adj.* unnamed; of unknown source

anthropology (an-thruh-PAHL-uh-jee) *n.* the scientific study of the origins and physical, social, and cultural development and behavior of human beings

apprehensive (ap-ruh-HEHN-sihv) *adj.* worried, fearful

apprehensively (ap-ree-HEHN-sihv-lee) *adv.* nervously

apprentices (uh-PREHN-tihs-ehz) *n. pl.* persons who are learning a trade or craft

appropriated (uh-PROH-pree-ayt-ihd) *v.* took possession of without permission

aptitude (AP-tuh-tyood) *n.* a capacity for learning

Arabic numbers (AR-uh-bik NUM-berz) the figures 1, 2, 3, 4, 5, 6, 7, 8, 9, 0; so-called because they were introduced into western Europe by Arabian scholars

Arbeit Macht Frei (AHR-beyet mahkt freye) a German expression meaning "Work makes you free."

arbitration judge (ahr-bih-TRAY-shuhn juj) a person chosen to settle an argument or complaint

archaeology (awr-kee-AHL-uh-jee) *n.* the scientific study of the remains of the people, customs, and life of ancient times, such as buildings, tools, and pottery

archery (AHR-chuh-ree) *n.* the skill of shooting with a bow and arrow

aside (uh-SEYED) *n.* a line spoken by a character in a play that the other actors are not supposed to hear

askance (uh-SKANS) *adv.* with a sidelong glance; with distrust

asylum (uh-SEYE-luhm) *n.* a hospital for the helpless or insane

at random without a definite purpose or method

atrocities (uh-TRAW-sih-tees) *n. pl.* tragedies

Auckland (AW-klohnd) *n.* a port city in New Zealand

Auschwitz (OWSH-vits) *n.* during World War II, Auschwitz was the site of the largest of the German (Nazi) concentration camps; about $2\frac{1}{2}$ million people were exterminated there

avail (uh-VAYL) *v.* take advantage of; make use of

aversion (uh-VER-zhun) *n.* dislike

B

babel (BAY-buhl) *n.* a confusion of sounds, voices, or languages

bade (bayd) *v.* ordered

bandicoot (BAN-dih-koot) *n.* a ratlike Australian animal with a long snout

banish (BAN-ihsh) *v.* drive away; cast out

baobab (BAY-oh-bab) *n.* an African tree with a thick trunk and large, hard-shelled, hanging fruit

barbarian (bahr-BAIR-ee-uhn) *n.* a crude or uncivilized person

bari (BAR-ee) *n.* fool

Baron Rothschild . . . Gould *pr. n.* wealthy and famous financiers

basso profundo (BAY-soh proh-FUN-doh) *n.* a deep, heavy voice, as that of a male singer

baubles (BAW-buhlz) *n. pl.* showy pieces of jewelry of little value

beast of burden *n.* an animal, such as a donkey, used to carry loads

beeline *n.* the fastest and most direct course

benefactor (BEHN-uh-fak-tuhr) *n.* a person who gives financial or other aid to another

bequeathed (bih-KWEETHD) *v.* passed on or handed down

beret (buh-RAY) *n.* a soft, round, flat hat of wool or felt

beseech (bih-SEECH) *v.* ask earnestly

betrothals (bih-TROH-thuhlz) *n. pl.* engagements

bewildered (bih-WIHL-duhrd) *adj.* confused

bibliophile (BIHB-lee-uh-feyel) *n.* a lover or collector of books

Bikaner (bihk-uh-NER) *n.* city in India

bitter *adj.* resentful

blandly (BLAND-lee) *adv.* pleasantly; gently

blasphemous (BLAS-fuh-muhs) *adj.* speaking about God or sacred things with disrespect

blithely (BLEYETH-lee) *adv.* in a carefree manner; cheerfully

boil *n.* a painful, pus-filled swelling of the skin and the tissue beneath it

Book of Books *n.* Bible

boot *n.* British for *car trunk*

borscht (BAWRSHT) *n.* a Russian soup made from beets

Bosnian (BAHZ-nee-uhn) *adj.* of Bosnia, a region in the former Yugoslavia

bourgeois (boor-ZHWAH) *adj.* middle class

boutiques (boo-TEEKS) *n. pl.* small shops that specialize in stylish clothes

brewery (BROO-uh-ree) *n.* a place where beer is manufactured

broods (broodz) *v.* hangs over like a dark cloud

brusquely (BRUSK-lee) *adv.* roughly, abruptly, bluntly

Buddha (BOO-duh) *n.* the title of Siddhartha Gautama, the Indian philosopher and founder of the religion Buddhism

Buenos Aires (BWAY-nuhs AHR-eez) *n.* the capital and largest city of Argentina

buff *n.* a person who has great interest in, and some knowledge of, a subject

Robbie Burns Robert Burns, a Scottish poet

bush *n.* wild country

byzantine (BIHZ-uhn-teen) *adj.* like a style of architecture developed in the Byzantine Empire, characterized by a circular dome and the use of mosaics

C

cadres (KAD-reez) *n. pl.* small groups of dedicated people

Cairo (KEYE-roh) *n.* the capital of Egypt and the largest city in Africa

Calabar (KAL-uh-bahr) *n.* port city in Nigeria

calabashes (KAL-uh-bash-uhz) *n. pl.* large, gourd-like fruit with a tough shell

caravan (KAR-uh-van) *n.* a group of people traveling together for safety

carcass (KAHR-kuhs) *n.* the dead body of an animal

caribou (KAIR-uh-boo) *n.* an Arctic deer

carnage (KAHR-nihj) *n.* great and bloody slaughter

cartouche (kar-TOOSH) *n.* a scroll-like ornament

cassia (KASH-uh) *n.* kind of tropical tree

caste (kast) *n.* one of the social classes or ranks of the Hindu people in India; caste is passed on from generation to generation

catatonic state (kat-eh-TAHN-ik stayt) a dazed condition

caviar (KAV-ee-ahr) *n.* the eggs of a sturgeon or other large fish

cerebral hemorrhage (suh-REE-bruhl HEHM-rihg) *n.* a stroke

chamberlains (CHAYM-buhr-lihnz) *n.* the king's managers of the household

chameleon (kuh-MEEL-yuhn) *n.* a small lizard that changes color

chaos (KAY-ahs) *n.* great disorder or confusion

charwoman (CHAHR-woom-uhn) *n.* a woman employed to do cleaning

cheque (chehk) *n.* British spelling of *check*; a written order to a bank to pay a certain amount from funds on deposit

cho-cho (CHOH-choh) meat snacks

civil service *n.* public service branch of the government

Clonmel (klahn-MEHL) *n.* a municipal borough of Ireland

cobalt (KOH-bawlt) *n.* a dark blue-coloring matter made from metallic elements

coefficient (coh-ih-FIHSH-uhnt) *n.* factor or level

cohorts (KOH-hawrts) *n. pl.* associates or companions

colander (KUL-uhn-duhr) *n.* a bowl-shaped kitchen utensil with holes in the bottom, used for draining off liquids from foods

collaborate (kuh-LAB-uh-rayt) *v.* cooperate; work together

commencement (kuh-MEHNS-muhnt) *n.* a beginning; start

commendation (kah-mehn-DAY-shuhn) *n.* high praise

commiserate (kuh-MIHZ-uh-rayt) *v.* sympathize

compact (KAHM-pakt) *n.* a small case containing face powder, a powder puff, and usually a mirror

composing (kuhm-POH-zing) *v.* calming

composure (kuhm-POH-zhuhr) *n.* control over one's emotions

compulsion (kuhm-PUL-shuhn) *n.* an influence or urge

comrades (KAHM-radz) *n. pl.* fellow members or workers

concession (kuhn-SEHSH-uhn) *n.* a business which is allowed to operate in a certain place

concessionaires (kuhn-sehsh-uh-NAIRZ) *n. pl.* persons who operate businesses in certain places

concurred (kuhn-KERD) *v.* agreed

condiments (KON-duh-muhnts) *n. pl.* sauces or spices used as seasonings for food

condolence (kuhn-DOH-luhns) *n.* expression of sympathy

conjuring (KAHN-juhr-ihng) *adj.* of the process of performing magic

consolation (kahn-suh-LAY-shuhn) *n.* comfort

contemplative (kahn-TEHM-pluh-tihv) *adj.* devoted to thoughtful observation or meditation

contempt (kuhn-TEHMPT) *n.* the feeling that a person is worthless or despised

contrary (KAHN-trehr-ee) *adj.* willful or stubborn

contrivance (kuhn-TREYE-vuhns) *n.* a fake

convention (kuhn-VEHN-shuhn) *n.* a custom

conveyed (kuhn-VAYD) *v.* transported

convulsive (kuhn-VUL-sihv) *adj.* having the nature of a spasm

cordial (KAWR-juhl) *n.* a sweetened fruit drink

corpses (KAWRPS-ihz) *n. pl.* dead bodies of human beings

cosmopolitan (kahz-muh-PAHL-uh-tuhn) *adj.* composed of many people from many parts of the world

counterfeit (KOUN-tuhr-fiht) *adj.* phony

counterrevolutionary (KOWN-ter-ehv-oh-LOO-shun-air-ee) *n.* a person who does not support the reform movement, or revolution

cower (KOW-uhr) *v.* crouch or draw back

cranium (KRAY-nee-uhm) *n.* something that looks like the part of the skull that encloses the brain

cream cans *n.pl.* heavy containers to carry cream

crimson (KRIHM-zuhn) *adj.* vivid purplish red

crinkle-paper Congress rosettes *n.pl.* handmade paper flowers worn as a form of protest

Croatia (kroh-AY-shee-uh) *n.* a region in the former Yugoslavia

Croats (KROH-ahts) *n.* people from Croatia

cubism (KYOO-bihs-uhm) *n.* movement of art in which the subject is abstractly represented with cubes.

crucified (KROO-suh-fyd) *v.* destroyed by criticism

Cuba (KYOO-buh) *n.* an island nation in the Caribbean Sea, south of Florida

cursory (KER-suh-ree) *adj.* hasty

cushka (KOOSH-kuh) *n.* a chief

cynically (SIHN-ih-klee) *adv.* with doubt; with a sneer

D

dainty (DAYN-tee) *adj.* graceful or delicate

darns *n. pl.* stitches or patches

debarred (dee-BAHRD) *v.* excluded

deceased's (dih-SEESTS) *adj.* belonging to the dead person

decency (DEE-suhn-see) *n.* proper behavior, courtesy

decreed (dih-KREED) *v.* ordered by (divine) law

deference (DEHF-uhr-uhns) *n.* courteous respect

defy (dih-FEYE) *v.* go beyond

degradation (dehg-ruh-DAY-shuhn) *n.* low status; shame

delegated (DEHL-uh-gayt-ihd) *v.* selected as a representative

demurred (dih-MERD) *v.* objected or hesitated

derisively (dih-REYE-sihv-lee) *adv.* mockingly; with ridicule

Derzhavin (der-ZHAHV-uhn) . . . **Gavrila Romanovich** *n.* Gavrila Romanovich Derzhavin, a Russian poet

desolate (DEHS-uh-liht) *adj.* lonely and sad

desolation (de-suh-LAY-shuhn) *n.* lonely and deserted condition

despaired (dih-SPAIRD) *v.* lost all hope

despondency (dehs-PAHN-dehn-see) *n.* depair

dextrously (DEHK-struhs-lee) *adv.* skillfully

diabolical (dy-uh-BAHL-ih-kuhl) *adj.* extremely wicked

dilemma (dih-LEHM-uh) *n.* a situation requiring a difficult choice

din *n.* continuous loud noise

dinghy (DIHNG-ee) *n.* a small rowboat

dipsomaniac (diph-suh-MAY-nee-ak) *n.* a person who craves alcoholic liquors

directive (dih-REHK-tihv) *n.* an order or instruction

dirge (derj) *n.* funeral song

disarmed (dihs-AHRMD) *v.* removed anger or suspicion from

discern (dih-SERN) *v.* to understand clearly

disconcerted (dis-kun-SERT-uhd) *adj.* confused and upset

disconcertingly (dihs-kuhn-SERT-ihng-lee) *adv.* in a manner that confuses and disturbs

discreetly (di-SKREET-lee) *adv.* modestly; shyly

disheartened (dihs-HAHR-tuhnd) *adj.* discouraged

dismay (dihs-MAY) *n.* sudden loss of confidence

dismissively (dihs-MIHS-ihv-lee) *adv.* directing someone to leave

disposed (dih-SPOHZD) *v.* inclined to act in a certain manner

disputed (dih-SPYOOT-ihd) *v.* argued about; debated

dissonant (DIHS-uh-nuhnt) *adj.* harsh and unpleasant in sound; disagreeable

dissuade (di-SWAYD) *v.* persuade against something

dissuasion (dih-SWAY-zhun) *n.* advising against

distraught (dihs-TRAWT) *adj.* upset

doeks (derks) *n. pl.* head scarves

dogged (DAW-gihd) *adj.* determined

dolefully (DOHL-fuhl-lee) *adv.* very sadly

domestic worker *n.* a servant in a household

dominant (DAHM-uh-nuhnt) *adj.* having the most influence or control

Don Gonzalo (dahn gohn-ZAH-loh) *n.* don is a title of respect in Spanish; Gonzalo is the man's name

downcast (DOWN-kast) *adj.* depressed; sad

dowry (DOW-ree) *n.* money or property brought by a bride to her husband

draught (draft) *n.* a dose of liquid (medicine)

Duero (DWEHR-oh) *n.* a river in Spain and Portugal

duplicator (DOO-plih-kay-tuhr) *n.* a copy machine

E

ecstacy (EK-stuh-see) *n.* a state of great joy

ecstatic (ehk-STAT-ihk) *adj.* showing great joy

Eden (EED-uhn) *n.* paradise

efface (ih-FAYS) *v.* remove by rubbing out; erase

Eldorado (ehl-duh-RAH-doh) *n.* a legendary city of great wealth in South America; this place was eagerly sought after by early explorers

elixirs (ih-LIHK-suhrz) *n. pl.* sweetened drinks consisting of alcohol, water, and medicines that are used for cures

elope (ih-LOHP) *v.* run away with a lover to get married without the consent of parents

eloquence (EHL-uh-kwuhns) *n.* fluent, expressive, and persuasive speaking

emanated (EHM-uh-nayt-uhd) *v.* came forth

embalmed (ehm-BAHMD) *adj.* as of a corpse that is treated with substance to prevent or slow decay

embezzlement (ehm-BEHZ-uhl-muhnt) *n.* theft of money or property

emigrate (EHM-ih-grayt) *v.* leave a native country to settle in another

entrails (EHN-traylz) *pl. n.* the internal organs of the body, especially the intestines

entranced (ehn-TRANSD) *adj.* dreamy

entreat (ehn-TREET) *v.* beg

entreaties (ehn-TREE-tees) *n. pl.* requests

equable (EHK-wuh-buhl) *adj.* even

equity (EKH-wih-tee) *n.* fairness; justice

espresso (eh-SPREHS-oh) *n.* a strong coffee brewed by forcing steam through finely ground, darkly roasted coffee beans

estranged (ih-STRAYNJD) *v.* showing no interest; becoming withdrawn

eternal (ih-TER-nuhl) *adj.* seemingly endless, everlasting

ethnography (ehth-NAHG-ruh-fee) *n.* the systematic recording of human cultures

exalted (ig-ZAHL-tihd) *adj.* having high rank

excrutiating (ehk-SKROO-shee-ay-tihng) *adj.* very intense or concentrated

exemplary (ihg-ZEHM-pleh-ree) *adj.* deserving to be imitated; outstanding

exotic (ig-ZAHT-ihk) *adj.* having the charm of the unfamiliar or unusual

expansive (ihk-SPAN-sihv) *adj.* showing one's feelings freely and openly

exploits (EHK-sploits) *n. pl.* acts or deeds

expressionism (Èhks-PREH-shuhn-ihs-uhm) *n.* movement in art in which subjects are distorted to show an inner experience

expunged (ik-SPUNJD) *v.* removed completely

extermination camp *n.* under the Nazis, an "extermination camp," or concentration camp, served as a forced-labor camp to detain and later to kill Jews, Poles, and others

Extremadura (ehks-struh-muh-DUR-uh) *n.* a region in Spain

F

fabrication (fab-ruh-KAY-shuhn) *n.* a false story

falter (FAWL-tuhr) *v.* lose strength or purpose

fazed (fayzd) *v.* bothered; worried

feigned (faynd) *adj.* pretending; not real

fell *n.* a high, barren field

flats *n. pl.* apartments; an area of level, low-lying ground

flaunted (FLAWNT-ihd) *v.* showed off

flotsam and jetsam *n.* odds and ends

flyleaf *n.* a blank page at the beginning (or end) of a book

fodder (FAHD-uhr) *n.* food for horses or cattle

forge (forj) *n.* a blacksmith's shop

forges (FOR-jihs) *n. pl.* furnaces for heating metal

fossil (FAHS-uhl) *adj.* having the remains or traces of a plant or animal that lived long ago

foster (FAHS-tuhr) *v.* care for

fraudulent (FRAW-dyoo-lunht) *adj.* fake

frenzied (FREHN-zeed) *adj.* filled with wild excitement

frock *n.* a dress

furtively (FUHR-tihv-lee) *adv.* secretly

futile (FYOO-tihl) *adj.* useless

G

Gallup poll (gal-uhp pohl) *n.* a public opinion survey

gazed *v.* looked intently; stared as in wonder or expectancy

gazelle (guh-ZEHL) *n.* a slender, swift-running horned antelope of Africa

Gemara (guh-MAR-uh) *n.* part of the Talmud, a book of Jewish law and custom

gemstone (JEHM-stohn) *n.* precious stone used in jewelry

gendarmerie (jahn-DAHRM-uh-ree) *n.* police force

genial (JEEN-yuhl) *adj.* cheerful, friendly

geology (jee-AHL-uh-jee) *n.* the scientific study of the earth

geometrico (jee-oh-MAYT-ree-koh) *adj.* of geometry, a branch of mathematics that deals with simple shapes formed from straight lines or curves

germinates (JER-muh-nayts) *v.* causes to begin to grow; sprouts

get a line on *v.* locate or aim at

get up and go *n.* ambition and energy

gewgaws (GYOO-gawz) *n. pl.* showy trinkets

ghee (gee) *n.* butter from which the milk fat has been removed

gilded (GIHLD-ihd) *adj.* covered with a thin layer of gold

glib (glihb) *adj.* smooth but insincere speaking

glutton (GLUT-uhn) *n.* a person who eats too much

gnougous (guh-NOO-goos) *n.* a food plant

gourdes (goordz) *n. pl.* units of money in Haiti

gourmet (goor-MAY) *n.* a person who likes and knows fine food and drink

granadillas (gran-uh-DEE-uhs) *n. pl.* fruits of passionflowers

grange (graynj) *n.* farm

gratify (GRAT-uh-feye) *v.* give what is desired; satisfy

grievance committee (GREE-vuhns kuh-MIHT-ee) *n.* a group of people formed to discuss complaints

grievous (GREE-vuhs) *adj.* extremely serious

griot (GREE-oh) *n.* an African oral historian

groschen (GROH-shuhn) *n.* a small Polish coin

Group Areas *n. pl.* in South Africa, areas decreed by congress to segregate people racially into neighborhoods

Guadalaviar (gwahd-uhl-uh-VYAHR) *n.* a river in Spain

gulag (GOO-lahg) *n.* a labor camp of the former U.S.S.R.

H

haematoma (hee-muh-TOH-muh) *n.* a bruise

Häftling *n.* German for *prisoner*

halberd (HAL-buhrd) *n.* a weapon with a long curved blade, used by women to defend their homes

hawker's coat *n.* garb worn by peddlers in South African market place

hawker (HAWK-uhr) *n.* a street peddler

hearths (hahrths) *n. pl.* floors of fireplaces

Hedonistic (heed-uhn-IHS-tihk) *adj.* of the pursuit of pleasure

heirs (AIRZ) *n. pl.* persons who inherit

henchmen (HEHNCH-mehn) *n. pl.* loyal and trusted followers who obey unquestioningly the orders of their leader

Heng-chou (HEHNG-choo) *n.* a place in China

heroines (HEHR-oh-ihnz) *n. pl.* female heroes

hieroglyphics (heye-uhr-uh-GLIHF-ihks) *n. pl.* a system of writing, used in ancient Egypt, in which symbols or pictures represent words or sounds

higgler's (HIHG-luhrz) *adj.* of a person who argues so as to bargain over the price of something

hill-ogre (hihl OH-guhr) *n.* in folklore, a man-eating giant who lives in the hills

hirsute (HER-soot) *adj.* hairy

holey (HOH-lee) *adj.* having holes

Holy Writ (HOH-lee riht) *n.* Bible

homily (HAHM-uh-lee) *n.* sermon; sermonlike speech

hua-chiao (HWAH-jee-aw) *n.* a chair which is carried

Hume (hyoom) *pr. n.* David Hume, a Scottish philosopher and historian

humiliated (hyoo-MIHL-ee-ayt-ihd) *v.* disgraced

humility (hyoo-MIHL-ih-tee) *n.* humbleness, modesty

hymn (hihm) *n.* a song of joy, praise, or thanksgiving

I

Ibo (EE-boh) *n.* an African people in Nigeria

Ichi (EE-chee) *n.* a martial arts system

illusions (ih-LOO-zhuhnz) *n. pl.* mistaken notions or beliefs

immaterial (ihm-uh-TEER-ee-uhl) *adj.* of no importance or relationship to the subject

immemorial (ihm-uh-MAWR-ee-uhl) *adj.* reaching beyond the limits of memory or recorded history

imminent (IHM-uh-nuhnt) *adj.* about to occur

immortal (ih-MAWR-tuhl) *adj.* not subject to death; living forever

impending (ihm-PEHND-ihng) *adj.* likely to happen soon

imperative (ihm-PEHR-uht-ihv) *n.* in grammar, the command form of a verb

imperceptibly (ihm-puhr-SEHP-tuh-blee) *adv.* gradually

imperiously (ihm-PEER-ee-uhs-lee) *adv.* with overbearing self-importance

implore (ihm-PLAWR) *v.* ask urgently; beg

import (IHM-pawrt) *n.* meaning or importance

impressionist (ihm-PREH-shuhn-ihst) a school in which the artist paints the suggestion of a scene.

in a trice *adj.* in a brief space of time; soon

inaudible (ihn-AW-duh-buhl) *adj.* incapable of being heard

inaugurating (ih-NAW-gyuh-rayt-ihng) *v.* beginning; starting

incite (in-SEYET) *v.* arouse

incitement (ihn-SEYET-muhnt) *n.* act of stirring up

inconspicuously (ihn-kuhn-SPIHK-yoo-uhs-lee) *adv.* not noticeably

increment (IHN-kruh-muhnt) *n.* an increase in salary; a raise

indelible (ihn-DEHL-uh-buhl) *adj.* permanent

Indian Agent in Canada an official representative of the government who is responsible for social work among native peoples

indignation (ihn-dihg-NAY-shuhn) *n.* anger brought on by something unjust, unworthy, or mean

"indoor" techniques studies practiced indoors with a great deal of formality and rituals

inexplicable (ihn-EHK-splih-kuh-buhl) *adj.* not capable of being explained

infirmity (ihn-FER-mih-tee) *n.* a disease or disorder that causes bodily weakness

ingratiated (ihn-GRAY-shee-ayt-ihd) *v.* worked (oneself) into another's good graces

initiation (ih-nihsh-ee-AY-shuhn) *n.* a ceremony or ritual with which a new member is admitted

innate (ihn-AYT) *adj.* inborn

innuendo (ihn-yoo-EHN-doh) *n.* a subtle, often spiteful reference to someone not named

inquisitive (ihn-KWIHZ-ih-tihv) *adj.* curious; prying

interrogation (ihn-terhr-uh-GAY-shuhn) *n.* intense, often cruel questioning

intriguer (ihn-TREEG-uhr) *n.* a person who plots or schemes secretly

intuitive (ihn-TOO-ih-tihv) *adj.* based on instinct

invalid (IHN-vuh-lihd) *n.* a sick, injured, or disabled person

invincible (ihn-VIHN-suh-buhl) *adj.* too strong or powerful to be defeated

invoice (IHN-vois) *n.* a list of goods shipped

irony (EYE-ruh-nee) *n.* a wry, mocking way of using words to suggest the opposite of what is meant

'Isa (EE-suh) Jesus, considered by Moslems to be a great prophet

J

jeopardize (JEHP-uhr-deyez) *v.* risk

jersey (JER-zee) *n.* a pullover sweater

jinnee (JIHN-ee) *n.* a spirit who appears in human or animal form to do good or evil

Johannesburg (joh-HAN-ihs-berg) a city in South Africa

Judean (joo-DEE-uhn) *adj.* ancient region in southern Palestine

jurisdiction (joor-ihs-DIHK-shuhn) *n.* range of authority

jutka n. a two-wheeled, horse-drawn carriage

K

Kamo (KAH-moh) *n.* name of a river

karma (KAHR-mah) *n.* fate or destiny, as of the Hindu or Buddhist faith

kefir (keh-FER) *n.* a beverage of fermented cow's milk

kerbing *n.* British for *curbing*

kilometers (KIHL-uh-mee-tuhrz) *n. pl.* units of length equal to 1,000 meters or 0.6214 miles

kneads (needz) *v.* massages or presses with the hands

knickers *n. pl.* loose-fitting short pants gathered at the knee

knocked off *v. informal* stopped work

kopeck (KOH-pehk) *n.* a coin worth 1/100 of a ruble, a unit of money of the former Soviet Union

kvas (kuh-VAHS) *n.* a light alcoholic beverage

L

laboriously (luh-BAWR-ee-uhs-lee) *adv.* with great effort

labyrinth (LAB-uh-rihnth) *n.* a network of winding, connected passages through which it is difficult to find one's way; a maze

Lager (LAHG-uhr) *n.* German for *camp*

lagoons (luh-GOONZ) *n. pl.* bodies of water which are bounded by sandbars or coral reefs

Lagos (LAY-gahs) *n.* the capital of Nigeria

Lai-chou (LEYE-joh) *n.* the name of a town in China

lalang (LAH-lahng) *n.* a kind of very tall, thick grass

lamentations (lam-uhn-TAY-shuhnz) *n. pl.* expressions of sorrow

lamenting (luh-MEHNT-ing) *v.* feeling or expressing great sorrow

languid (LANG-gwihd) *adj.* weak; drooping

larder (LAHR-duhr) *n.* supply of food; a place where food is stored

lassitude (LAS-ih-tood) *n.* feeling of exhaustion or weakness

leaf (leef) *n.* sheet of paper

leeks *n. pl.* vegetables related to the onion

legacy (LEHG-ih-see) *n.* an inheritance

lentils (LEHN-tuhlz) *n. pl.* small, flat, beanlike seeds eaten as a vegetable

leprosy (LEHP-ruh-see) *n.* an infectious bacterial disease that destroys body tissue and can lead to paralysis

li (lee) *n.* Chinese unit of distance, equal to about 1/3 mile

lichen (LEYE-kuhn) *n.* a plant consisting of a fungus and algae that grows on rocks and tree trunks

limelight (LEYEM-leyet) *n.* the center of public attention

lino (LEYE-noh) *n.* British for *linoleum*

Lithuanian (lih-thuh-WAY-nee-uhn) *n.* a person from the country of Lithuania

livelihood (LEYEV-lee-hood) *n.* support; way of making a living

livid (LIHV-ihd) *adj.* deathly pale or white, as from fear

lorry (LAWR-ee) *n.* British for *truck*

M

Malays (muh-LAYZ) *n.* people of the Malay Peninsula in Southeast Asia

malice (MAL-ihs) *n.* ill will

malicious (muh-LIHSH-uhs) *adj.* spiteful

malign (muh-LEYEN) *v.* speak evil of

mangy (MAYN-jee) *adj.* shabby

mastodons (MAS-tuh-dahnz) *n. pl.* extinct animals that resembled the elephant

matchmaker (MACH-may-ker) *n.* someone who arranges marriages

matchmakings (MACH-mayk-ihngs) *n.* arranging of marriages

mates (mayts) *n. pl.* friends; pals

matric (muh-TRIHK) short for matriculation

Maui (MOW-ee) the name of a New Zealand folk hero; Maui is also the name of the second largest island in Hawaii

mausoleum (maw-suh-LEE-uhm) *n.* a large and stately tomb

mauve (mohv) *adj.* a light reddish or grayish purple

meditates (MEHD-ih-tayts) *v.* thinks deeply and quietly

metaphor (MEHT-uh-fawr) *n.* a figure of speech in which two unlike things are compared

meter (MEE-tuhr) *n.* a basic unit of length in the metric system, equal to 39.37 inches

meticulously (muh-TIHK-yuh-luhs-lee) *adv.* very carefully and precisely

metronome (MEHT-ruh-nohm) *n.* a device, used by musicians to mark time or a steady beat, that makes loud ticking sounds at different speeds

Milky Way *n.* the galaxy containing the solar system, seen as a wide band of milky light across the night sky

millet (MIHL-iht) *n.* white seeds of a grassy plant, used as a food grain

misanthropy (mihs-AN-thruh-pee) *n.* a hatred or distrust of people

modulations (mahj-oo-LAY-shuhnz) *n. pl.* inflections of the tone or pitch of the voice

mongrel (MUNG-gruhl) *n.* an animal, especially a dog, of mixed breed

moor (mawr) *n.* a broad stretch of open land, often with swampy areas and patches of low shrubs

Moorish (MOOR-ihsh) *adj.* of the Moors, especially those Moslem people of northern Africa who invaded Spain in the 8th century A.D.

morose (muh-ROHS) *adj.* gloomy

mortal (MAWR-tuhl) *n.* a human being, as a creature who must die

mortar (MAWR-tuhr) *n.* a bowl in which substances are ground with a pestle

mosaic (moh-ZAY-ick) *adj.* of a design made of small pieces of stone, glass, or tile of different colors inlaid on a surface

Moslem (MAHZ-luhm) *adj.* of the religion of Islam and the teachings of Mohammad

Mother Superior a woman in charge of a convent or other female religious community

mourning (MAWR-nihng) *adj.* grieving over a loss

mugwort (MUG-wuhrt) *n.* an herb plant

mukluks (MUHK-luhks) *n. pl.* boots made of seal or reindeer skin

muktuk (MUK-tuhk) *n.* a whale

multitudes (MUL-tih-toodz) *n.* large crowds of people; the masses

munificence (myoo-NIH-fih-suhns) *n.* generosity

Munster (MUN-stur) *n.* a province in Ireland

muse (myooz) *v.* to think deeply

muted (MYOOT-uhd) *adj.* muffled or softer in sound

mutton (MUT-uhn) *n.* the meat of a full-grown sheep

myopia (meye-OH-pee-uh) *n.* nearsightedness

N

nabobs (NAY-bahbz) *n.* provincial governors; persons of great wealth or importance

nascent (NAS-uhnt) *adj.* having recently come into existence

Natal (nuh-TAL) *n.* a province of South Africa

Nativity (nuh-TIHV-ih-tee) *n.* the birth of Christ; a representation of Christ as an infant

naught (nawt) *n.* nothingness

Nehru (NEHR-oo) *n.* statesman and first prime minister of India

Nemirov (nuh-MEER-awv) *n.* a small town in Poland

Neva (NEE-vuh) *n.* river in Russia

New Zealand (noo ZEE-luhnd) an island country in the Pacific Ocean

newts (noots) *n. pl.* salamanders or lizardlike animals

Niani (nee-AH-nee) capital city of Mali

Niger (NEYE-juhr) *n.* a river in Africa, flowing through Mali, Niger, and Nigeria into the Atlantic

Nile (neyel) *n.* the longest river in Africa

nocturnal (nahk-TER-nuhl) *adj.* nighttime

Non-European *adj.* people not of European ancestry; usually a reference to black South Africans

nonchalantly (non-shuh-LAHNT-lee) *adv.* casually unconcerned

Norwegian jarls (nawr-WEE-juhn yahrlz) *n.* noblemen of Norway

nougats (NOO-guhts) *n. pl.* candies, usually made from nuts and honey or sugar

O

oblivion (uh-BLIHV-ee-uhn) *n.* the condition of being completely forgotten

obsession (uhb-SEHSH-uhn) *n.* a thought or emotion that occupies the mind continually

obstinately (AHB-stuh-niht-lee) *adv.* stubbornly

octavo (ahk-TAY-voh) *n.* a book whose size is six inches by nine inches

odes (ohdz) *n. pl.* lyric poems full of noble feelings

of our own accord without assistance; by ourselves

ominous (AW-mih-nuhs) *adj.* threatening

ominously (AHM-uh-nuhs-lee) *adv.* in a threatening way; unfavorably

ordained (awr-DAYND) *v.* arranged or decided beforehand by godly authority

Orkneys (AWRK-neez) *n.* islands in Scotland

orthodox (OR-thuh-dawx) very religious

P

paddy fields *n. pl.* wet lands on which rice is grown

pagan (PAY-guhn) *adj.* belonging to someone who has little or no religion and who delights in sensual pleasures

paid out *v.* slackened, as a rope, and allowed to run out

pallbearer (PAWL-bair-uhr) *n.* one of the persons who carries the coffin at a funeral

palpable (PAL-puh-buhl) *adj.* that which can be touched, felt, or handled

palpitation (pal-pih-TAY-shuhn) *n.* a rapid beating or throbbing

parka (PAHR-kuh) *n.* a warm fur or cloth coat with a hood

partook (pahr-TUK) *v.* took part, participated

partridge (PAHR-trihj) *n.* a plump-bodied bird with brownish feathers, often hunted as game

passes (PAS-uhs) *n. pl.* paperwork required by South African government for black South Africans only

patronize (PAY-truh-nyz) *v.* "talk down" to, be condescending

pedantically (puh-DAN-tihk-uhl-lee) *adv.* with a great show of one's knowledge

pedigree (PEHD-ih-gree) *n.* a record of the ancestors of a purebred animal

penchant (PEHN-chuhnt) *n.* a liking for something

pensive (PEHN-sihv) *adj.* thoughtful

pensiveness (PEHN-sihv-nehs) *n.* thoughtfulness

perfidious (puhr-FIHD-ee-uhs) *adj.* disloyal

perfidy (PER-fih-dee) *n.* lies

perfunctorily (puhr-FUNGK-tuh-ruh-lee) *adv.* in an uninterested manner

perplexity (puhr-PLEHK-sih-tee) *n.* confusion; puzzlement

persevered (puhr-suh-VEERD) *v.* continued; kept trying

persevering (per-suh-VEER-ihng) *adj.* not giving up

Persia (PER-zhuh) *n.* the former name of Iran, an ancient empire in west and southwest Asia

pervasive (per-VAY-siv) *adj.* penetrating

pessimist (PEHS-uh-mihst) *n.* a person who tends to take the gloomiest view of a situation

pestle (PEHS-tuhl) *n.* a tool with a heavy rounded end, used for crushing or mashing substances

petticoat (PEHT-ee-koht) *n.* a skirt or slip worn as an undergarment

petty (PEHT-ee) *adj.* small in value

phantoms (FAN-tuhmz) *n. pl.* ghosts

phosphorescent (fahs-fuhr-REHS-uhnt) *adj.* glowing

Piave (PYAH-vay) *n.* a river in Italy, located between Padua and Venice

piety (PEYE-ih-tee) *n.* virtue

pigments (PIHG-muhnts) *n. pl.* substances used to give color

pious (PEYE-uhs) *adj.* earnestly religious

plagued (playgd) *v.* pestered or annoyed

plaint (playnt) *n.* a complaint

plaintains (PLANT-aynz) *n. pl.* greenish starchy fruit like bananas

plaintiffs (PLAYN-tihfs) *n. pl.* the persons who brought charges against someone

plait (playt) *n.* a braid of hair

plaited (PLAY-ted) *v.* braided

plash *v.* splash

plausible (PLAW-zuh-buhl) *adj.* reasonable

plight (pleyet) *n.* a difficult situation or condition

point-blank *adv.* without hesitating

porridge (PAWR-ihj) *n.* oatmeal boiled in water or milk until thick, eaten as cereal

posh *adj. informal* elegant; showy

post *n.* an appointed position of employment in public office

potion (POH-shuhn) *n.* a drink used as a medicine or poison or to cast a magic spell

power of attorney *n.* a written document giving someone legal authority to represent or act for another, as in handling business affairs

prattle (PRAT-uhl) *n.* foolish chatter

prebend (PREE-behnd) *n.* land owned by the Church of England

predicament (preh-DIK-uh-mehnt) *n.* problem

pregnant (PREHG-nuhnt) *adj.* full, laden

premises (PREHM-ihs-ehz) *n. pl.* house and yard, property

preoccupied (pree-AWK-yoo-peyed) *v.* absorbed

Presbyterian (prehz-bih-TEER-ee-uhn) *n.* a member of a Presbyterian church of the Protestant faith

presumption (prih-ZUMP-shuhn) *n.* speech or conduct that is too bold

Pretoria (prih-TAWR-ee-uh) *n.* administrative capital of the Republic of South Africa

prodigious stature (proh-DIH-juhs STAH-chuhr) enormous height

propagated (PRAHP-uh-gayt-uhd) *v.* made known or accepted

proprietor (pruh-PRY-uh-tuhr) *n.* the owner of a business

prosperity (prah-SPEHR-ih-tee) *n.* economic success

prostrated (PRAS-trayt-ihd) *v.* knelt or lay face down in submission

pull ... weight *v.* do one's full share of the work

pupils (PYOO-puhlz) *n. pl.* the opening in the center of the eye, which looks like a black spot

Pusan (poo-SAHN) a port city in South Korea

Pushkin (POOSH-kihn) *n.* Aleksandr Sergeyevich Pushkin, a well-known Russian poet

Pyramids (PIHR-uh-mihdz) *n. pl.* massive monuments found especially in Egypt, each having rectangular bases and four triangular faces

Q

quadrant (KWAHD-ruhnt) *n.* an instrument with a scale of 90 degrees, used in navigation for measuring altitudes

R

rabbinical school (rah-BIN-ih-kuhl skool) a school for the training of rabbis, scholars, and teachers of Jewish law

radiated (RAY-dee-ay-tuhd) *v.* showed

rancor (RANG-kuhr) *n.* bitter resentment

rand *n. pl.* a former monetary unit of South Africa

rations (RASH-uhnz) *n. pl.* food issued or available to members of a group

rectify (REHK-tuh-feye) *v.* correct

red-handed (rehd-HAN-dihd) *adv.* in the very act of a crime or mischief

refuge (REHF-yooj) *n.* a place of protection or shelter

refugee (rehf-yoo-JEE) *n.* person who flees his or her country to escape oppression or persecution

regaled (rih-GAYLD) *v.* entertained, as with a feast

regency council *n.* a group of people to rule for a child king

rejuvenation (rih-joo-vuh-NAY-shuhn) *n.* the process of restoring youth

remedy (REHM-ih-dee) *n.* cure; something that corrects a fault

reminisce (rem-uh-NIHS) *v.* remember and tell of past experiences

remorse (rih-MAWRS) *n.* bitter regret or guilt

rent *v.* torn apart violently

repose (rih-POHZ) *n.* quietness, calmness

repositories (rih-PAHZ-ih-tor-eez) *n. pl.* vessels

reproach (rih-PROHCH) *n.* blame

repute (rih-PYOOT) *n.* reputation

requite (rih-KWEYET) *v.* repay

resignation (rehz-ihg-NAY-shuhn) *n.* a written statement giving notice that one quits a job

resolutely (reh-so-LOOT-lee) *adv.* with firm purpose

resolve (rih-ZALV) *n.* firmness of purpose; determination

respite (REH-spit) *n.* escape, rest

retreat (rih-TREET) *n.* a safe, peaceful place

Revealed Books *n. pl.* ancient sacred texts

reverie (REHV-uh-ree) *n.* daydream

reveille (REHV-uh-lee) *n.* the sounding of a bugle early in the morning to awaken persons in a camp

rites *n. pl.* a ceremony or other solemn or formal procedure

rituals (RIHCH-oo-uhlz) *n. pl.* ceremonies used in a religion

rivulet (RIV-yuh-liht) *n.* a small stream; brook

riwais *n. pl.* potatoes; spuds

robust (ro-BUST) *adj.* strong and healthy

rogue (rohg) *n.* a dishonest person

roubles (ROO-bihlz) (var. rubles) *n. pl.* units of money in Russia

rounded on *v.* turned against; attacked

ruddy (RUD-ee) *adj.* having a healthy pink or reddish color

runnels (RUN-uhlz) *n. pl.* streamlets

runner *n.* a long, narrow strip of cloth, as for a table

rupees (ROO-peez) *n. pl.* Indian units of money

S

sallow (SAL-oh) *adj.* having a sickly, yellowish color

sap *n.* slang for a foolish person

Sarajevo (sahr-uh-YAY-voh) *n.* city in former Yugoslavia and former capital of Bosnia

sari (SAH-ree) *n.* an outer garment worn by women of India and Pakistan

sarong (suh-RAWNG) *n.* a simple wraparound dress or skirt

savannahs (suh-VAN-uhz) *n. pl.* flat, treeless grasslands of warm regions

scandalous (SKAN-duhl-uhs) *adj.* shameful, bringing disgrace

scathing (SKAY-thihng) *adj.* rude

scrutinized (SKROOT-uhn-eyezd) *v.* examined in detail with careful attention

Second Moon *n.* on the Chinese calendar, a month in spring

seer *n.* a soothsayer

sentries (SEHN-treez) *n. pl.* soldiers posted at some spot; guards

sepulchral (suh-PUL-kruhl) *adj.* gloomy

serge (serj) *n.* a kind of strong cloth, usually of wool, with slanting ridges across it

serpent (SER-puhnt) *n.* a sly or dangerous person; like a snake

Shalom (shah-LOHM) *n.* a Hebrew word meaning *peace*

shekels (SHEHK-uhlz) *n. pl.* ancient Hebrew coins; a unit of money in Israel

shod *v.* fit with shoes

shoeblack (SHOO-blak) *n.* a person who shines shoes

shrine (shreyen) *n.* a site or object that is worshiped

Shu (shoo) *n.* an ancient kingdom in China

sideboard *n.* a piece of dining room furniture containing drawers with shelves

sieges (SEEJ-ihz) *n. pl.* blockades of towns or fortresses by armies

simultaneously (seye-muhl-TAY-nee-ahs-lee) *adv.* at the same time

skited (SKEYET-ehd) *v.* bragged

sleight-of-hand (SLEYET-uv-hand) *adj.* skillfully deceptive

smelted (SMEHLT-ihd) *v.* melted down or fused

soothsayers (SOOTH-say-uhrz) *n. pl.* people who claim to be able to predict the future

sordid (SAWR-dihd) *adj.* dirty and ugly

sortie (SAWR-tee) *n.* an armed attack made from a place surrounded by enemy forces

Sotho (SOH-toh) *n.* a Bantu language of Lesotho in South Africa

sovereigns (SAWV-er-ihns) *n. pl.* kings

Special Branch *n.* certain Branch of police force in South Africa

spectacles (SPEHK-tuh-kuhlz) *pl. n.* eyeglasses

spells *n. pl.* words supposed to have magic powers; magic influences or charms

spine *n.* the supporting back portion of a book cover

spouses (SPOWS-ehz) *n. pl.* husbands or wives

SS *n.* stands for *Schutztaffel*, a Nazi secret police organization

Stalin (STAH-lihn) *n.* Joseph Stalin, a Soviet dictator; as head of the government and the Communist Party, Stalin was known for his widespread use of terrorism

stanched (stanched) *v.* stemmed the flow of blood from

stand on ceremony *v.* be very formal

stay-at-home *n.* a strike

steel *v.* harden

steppes (stehps) *n. pl.* vast, grassy plains, as found in southeastern Europe and Siberia

Stevenson Robert Louis Stevenson, a Scottish author

stipulated (STIHP-yuh-layt-ihd) *v.* demanded

stove-in (STOWV-ihn) *adj.* smashed inward

strait jacket *n.* a jacketlike garment of strong material used to bind the arms tightly against the body as a means of restraining a violent patient

strand *n.* stream

studded (STUD-ihd) *adj.* ornamented; decorated

studious (STOO-dee-uhs) *adj.* devoted to study

stupendous (STOO-pehn-duhs) *adj.* huge

stupor (STOO-puhr) *n.* a daze

subordinates (suh-BAWR-duhn-ihts) *n.* persons of a lower rank

subsonic (suhb-SAW-nihk) *adj.* inaudible

subtly (SUH-tuh-lee) *adv.* quietly

suitors (SYOO-terz) *n.* men who present themselves as possible marriage partners

Sunday week a British expression meaning "a week from Sunday"

sunder (SUN-duhr) *v.* separate; split

supplication (sup-luh-KAY-shun) *n.* prayerful and humble request

surmise (suhr-MEYEZ) *v.* suppose; guess

surveillance (suhr-VAYL-ehns) *n.* the act of watching or supervising closely

swaggering (SWAG-uhr-ihng) *adj.* boastful, self-confident

swallowed the bait believed too easily; accepted without question or suspicion

swell *adj.* slang for excellent, fine

synagogue (SIHN-uh-gawg) *n.* Jewish house of worship

T

taciturn (TAS-ih-tern) *adj.* silent by habit; not talkative

tactically (TAK-tihk-lee) *adv.* wisely planned

tainted (TAYNT-uhd) *adj.* spoiled or corrupted by something undesirable

Taj Mahal (tahzh muh-HAHL) *n.* a famous white marble tomb, or mausoleum, in India

talisman (TAL-ihs-muhn) *n.* an object believed to have magic power

talking through her hat *v.* talking foolishly

Tangaroa (tang-ah-ROH-uh) *n.* the name of a mythical being

taps *n. pl.* faucets

Tatras (TAY-truhs) *n.* a mountain range between Czechoslovakia and Poland

Teng-chou (DEHNG-joh) *n.* the name of a town in China

tepid (TEHP-ihd) *adj.* moderately warm; lukewarm

thatched *adj.* made of plant stalks, such as straw or reeds

tiffin (TIHF-uhn) *n.* a midday snack

Timbuktu (tihm-buhk-TOO) *n.* town in West Africa

Tipperary (tihp-uh-RAIR-ee) *n.* a county in Ireland

togs *n. pl.* set of clothes, such as swim suits

tome (tohm) *n.* a large, heavy book

topographies (tuh-PAHG-ruh-feez) *n. pl.* detailed, natural features of places, as on a map

totem pole (TOH-tuhm POHL) *n.* a post or pole carved and painted with a series of totem symbols, such as birds or bears, used as emblems of a tribe or clan of the northwest coast of North America, and erected in front of their houses

tranquil (TRAN-kwihl) *adj.* calm

Transvaal (trans-VAHL) *n.* a province of South Africa

treacle (TREE-kuhl) *n.* British for *molasses*

treble (TREHB-ul) *adj.* triple

trifles (TREYE-fuhlz) *n. pl.* things of slight importance

trivialities (trihv-ee-AL-uh-teez) *n.* things that are of little importance

trolls *n. pl.* in folklore, evil giants

truck *n.* dealings

truss (truhss) *n.* a support for the abdomen

typhoon (teye-FOON) *n.* a severe tropical hurricane occurring in the western Pacific

typographically (ty-puh-GRAF-ihk-lee) *adv.* referring to the printing or typing

Tyutchev (TYOOT-chehf) *n.* a Russian poet

U

unanimously (yoo-NAN-uh-muhs-lee) *adv.* in complete agreement

unison (YOO-nih-suhn) *n.* agreement

untouchables *n. pl.* (often capitalized) members of the lowest caste of Hindus

untoward (uhn-TAWRD) *adj.* improper

usurper (yoo-SERP-uhr) *n.* a person who seizes control without legal authority

Utopia (yoo-TOH-pee-uh) *n.* a perfect society

V

vagrants (VAY-gruhnts) *n. pl.* persons who wander from place to place and usually have no means of support; tramps

Valencia (vuh-LEHN-see-uh) *n.* a region in Spain

valorous (VAL-uhr-uhs) *adj.* courageous; bold

Vedas (VAYD-uhz) *n. pl.* the collection of Hindu sacred writings of hymns and prayers

vehemently (VEE-uh-muhnt-lee) *adv.* forcefully; earnestly

venerable (VEHN-uhr-uh-buhl) *adj.* worthy of respect because of age

venom (VEHN-uhm) *n.* a poisonous substance

veranda (vuh-RAN-duh) *n.* a roofed porch

vermilion (vuhr-MIHL-yuhn) *adj.* bright red

vermin (VER-mihn) *n.* an insect or rodent that is destructive or annoying

versicles VER-sih-kuhlz) *n. pl.* short verses

vestiges (VEHS-tih-jehz) *n. pl.* remaining traces

vicarious (veye-KAR-ee-uhs) *adj.* experienced by imagined participation

vice versa (VEYE-suh VER-suh) the other way round

vigorous (VIHG-uhr-uhs) *adj.* forceful, lively

vizier (vih-ZER) *n.* in former times, a high official in a Moslem government

vocation (voh-KAY-shuhn) *n.* a profession for which a person is specially suited or trained

void (void) *n.* an empty space

Void (void) *n.* one of the five elements of Buddhism which makes up the cosmos; Nothingness, a Buddhist term for the illusionary nature of worldly things

vouchers (VOW-chuhrz) *n. pl.* receipts

vulgar (VUL-guhr) *n.* the common people

Vulgate (VUL-gayt) *n.* the Bible used in the Roman Catholic Church

W

wardrobe (WAWRD-rohb) *n.* closet or piece of furniture for holding clothes

Wassertrinken Verboten (VAHS-uhr-trihnk-uhn fer-BOHT-uhn) German for *It is forbidden to drink the water*

wavelengths *n. pl.* lines of thought or communication

wavered (WAY-vuhrd) *v.* moved back and forth, become unsteady

Way the Way of strategy

Wer kann Deutsch? (ver kahn doich) German for "Who knows German?"

whither (WIHTH-uhr) *adv.* to what place

wickets (WIHK-ihts) *n. pl.* grilled or grated windows through which business is conducted

wild-thyme (weyeld teyem) *n.* an herb

wily (WEYE-lee) *adv.* calculating

wimples (WIHM-puhls) *n.* headdresses worn by nuns

won (wawn) *n.* Korean monetary unit

Word of God *n.* the Bible

wrath (rawth) *adj.* full of rage

writhe (reyeth) *v.* twist or turn

wry (reye) *adj.* twisted to one side

X

Xhosa (KOH-suh) *n.* a Bantu language spoken in Cape Province in South Africa

Y

ye (yee) *pron.* Old-World term for *you*

Yehovah (yuh-HOH-vuh) the Hebrew name for God

yuan *n.* currency in China

Z

Zagreb (ZAH-grehb) *n.* the capital of Croatia

zealous (ZEHL-uhs) *adj.* fanatically devoted

Zhiguli (zhuh-GOOL-ee) *n.* a name of an automobile

Zulu (ZOO-loo) *n.* the language spoken by the Bantu people of South Africa

When you are asked to write, do you think that you are supposed to produce a perfect stream of words in your first attempt? Few good writers create a finished composition in a single draft, or version. Good writing is often the result of a process, or series of steps, that takes place over a period of time. The steps of the writing process are prewriting, drafting, revising, proofreading, and publishing. The steps follow a logical order. Good writers, however, often return to an earlier stage to adjust or refine some of their ideas. As a writer, you can use the process in a way that is most effective for you.

Prewriting

The process of writing frequently begins long before putting pen to paper or fingers to keyboard. Writers must first decide what they are going to write about, for whom they are writing, and why they are writing. Deciding these three things is the main goal of the prewriting stage. Remember, however, that you can change or adjust any of them as you move through the writing process.

Choosing and Narrowing a Topic. In school, you are often asked to write in response to a specific assignment and occasionally to choose your own topic. In either case, you need to figure out what you already know about your subject and what you must find out. For instance, if your assignment is to write about your ancestors, you might begin by thinking about your family. You may recall a moving story that your grandfather told you about having to leave his homeland. You may realize that you never quite understood the details behind his decision to leave. In this case, you need to find out more about your grandfather's life.

When choosing a topic, it is important to consider the length of the assignment. If your topic seems too large to cover adequately in the space required, narrow it down by focusing on one aspect of your subject. At this point you may find that your original subject is changing.

Determining Audience and Purpose. After you have a topic, you need to identify your audience, or who is going to read what you write. Your audience for most school assignments will be your teacher and your classmates. Your audience might also be friends, family members, the readers of your school newspaper, or a possible employer.

You also must identify your purpose for writing, or the effect you want your writing to have on your readers. Your purpose for writing can vary widely. You may want to inform, amuse, persuade, shock, or incite your readers to action. To achieve your purpose, you must ask yourself what your audience already knows about your topic and how they are likely to feel about it. This information can help you determine how to effectively present your topic to your audience.

Generating Ideas.   Once you know your topic, audience, and purpose for writing, you can begin developing your ideas and gathering information. Your writing ideas may come from your own knowledge and experiences or from outside sources.

Several prewriting strategies can help you develop your writing ideas. Some of these strategies can also help you generate and narrow a topic for a writing assignment. *Making lists* is a good way to help you choose a topic and generate useful ideas. Another prewriting strategy is *freewriting*. This technique involves simply writing down, for a set period of time, whatever comes into your mind about your topic without concern for grammar or structure. *Brainstorming*, which is best done in a group, is another sponta-neous method of associating ideas. In a brainstorming session, group mem-bers share ideas for or about a topic. Brainstorming allows one person's idea to trigger another person's thoughts. *Clustering* is another method of generating ideas that helps you recognize the relationships among details. When you cluster, you write your topic in a circle in the middle of a piece of paper. Then you surround it with related ideas that you connect to the topic with diagonal lines, like the spokes of a wheel.

If you need information about your topic, there are many *outside sources* that you can consult. These resources include textbooks and reference books, newspapers, magazines, computer data banks, and knowledgeable people. Choose the best sources for the type of information you need. What sources might you suggest for a student who is going to write about his grandfather's immigration from the Dominican Republic?

Making a Writing Plan.   After you have developed ideas about your topic, you need to think about how you are going to arrange your material. What order seems to grow naturally out of your ideas? Do you want to tell a story chronologically, or in the order in which events happened? Do you want to organize your arguments in the order of increasing importance? A good strategy for organizing your ideas and information is to make an outline. You can always change your outline, or add or drop an idea at any point. Keep in mind that the writing process is a flexible method, not a lock step series of rules to follow in the same way each time you decide to write.

Drafting and Revising

After you develop and organize your ideas, you are ready to write. However, don't strive to create a polished composition in one version. Use your outline to begin a *first draft* in which you put your thoughts down on paper as completely and freely as you can. Do not stop your writing flow to perfect sentence structure, paragraph organization, spelling, or punctuation. If you think of additional information about your topic or discover a better order of presentation, add your new ideas to your draft.

Revising a Draft. Once you have completed your first draft, the revision stage gives you the opportunity to evaluate and improve your draft. Before you begin revising, it is a good idea to let some time pass and then go back to your draft with a fresh perspective.

Using a checklist of questions such as the following can help you evaluate your draft in a systematic way.

TOPIC, AUDIENCE, PURPOSE

Have I stayed focused on my topic?
Is my writing geared to my audience?
Have I achieved my purpose for writing?
Have I used language appropriate to my topic, audience, and purpose?

CONTENT AND DEVELOPMENT

Have I presented my main ideas clearly?
Have I supported my main ideas with sufficient details, examples, or evidence?
Is my attitude toward my subject consistent?
Are my sources of information reliable and properly identified?

ORGANIZATION

Have I organized my ideas effectively?
Have I used transitions to connect ideas?
Do I have a clear beginning, middle, end?

Peer evaluation is another valuable revising tool. Work with another student or group of students, reading one another's writing and offering responses or suggestions for improvement. Sometimes a reader's comments or questions might reveal that important information is missing, or that the sequence of ideas is confusing. Peer evaluation may help you identify areas in which you need more research or clearer reasoning. Remember, however, that it is you, the writer, who has the final say on any changes in your own work.

Proofreading and Publishing

After you have revised your draft, you are ready to read through it one last time to look for errors in spelling, sentence structure, usage, and the mechanics of capitalization and punctuation. Proofread your work carefully. Errors distract readers from the important ideas you are trying to communicate.

Use a dictionary and a grammar and writing handbook when you proofread. The chart below shows some common editing and proofreading symbols to use as you check your work.

SYMBOL	MEANING	SYMBOL	MEANING
(story)	move text	ٯ	add apostrophe
~~almost~~ e	delete	" "	add quotation marks
∧	insert	¶	begin paragraph
⌒	no space		
⊙	add period	ǂ	lowercase
⌒,	add comma	e̲̲	capitalize

Sharing Your Writing. The final stage in the writing process is *publishing.* Since writing is meant to communicate, the process is not complete until writing is shared with an audience. Below are a few ways you can share your writing with others. Brainstorm with your classmates for other ways to share your writing.

1. Create a class magazine or anthology of student writing.
2. Submit your writing to the school newspaper or yearbook.
3. Send an editorial, or opinion piece, to your local newspaper.
4. Give copies of your writing to anyone you interviewed when gathering information.
5. Enter writing contests.

MODEL ESSAYS

The Expository Essay

Most essays that you are asked to write in school are **expository** in nature. Their purpose is to explain a topic or inform an audience about a subject. The model essay that follows was written in response to the Unit 2 writing assignment on page 215. The essay explains how literature can serve as a guide to history.

Literature as a Window to History

1 Literature can serve as a spotlight on history. 2 It can focus on an event, an individual, or a movement and make the cold, dry facts of history come alive through human experience. 3 The excerpt from Harry Wu's autobiography Bitter Winds is a good example. 4 It is literature that serves as a window to history. 5 Through this autobiography, readers learn not only the facts about Chairman Mao's China, but also experience the feelings of people opposed to the system.

6 This excerpt from Bitter Winds presents the story of Wu's desperate attempt to flee his country. 7 Wu's vivid descriptions establish his reasons for fleeing by showing readers the harshness of China's regime and the tragedy of China's future under communism. 8 For example, Wu points out that instead of modernization, communism "brought famine and economic collapse." 9 To escape, Wu holds a series of secret meetings with three other classmates. They plan to flee to China's neighboring country, Burma. 10 However, since Wu was labeled a rightist, someone who opposed communism, he and his friends were closely watched. 11 Readers learn that the friends knew punishment was certain if their plans to escape were revealed. 12 Eventually, one of his classmates was arrested. 13 This placed Wu under suspicion and eventually in grave danger.

1–2. An introductory topic sentence expresses the thesis, or main idea, of the essay.

3–5. Specific examples are cited to support the thesis.

6–13. The second paragraph gives specific examples that support the thesis.

14–19. The third paragraph gives more facts about the people and events that bring Maoist China to life.

20–21. The last paragraph restates the thesis in greater detail.

22. Essay concludes effectively with a brief summary that includes a personal insight.

14 Next, readers discover the consequences of "counterrevolutionary rightist" thoughts—punishment. *15* Although the Maoists made countless attempts to reform Wu's political thoughts, they could not break his spirit. *16* After a series of meetings and failed attempts to reform him, Wu was expelled from school, arrested, and sent to a harsh reeducation labor camp. *17* The communists had swallowed up all hope of Wu's dream. *18* At the conclusion, the readers learn about quiet courage. *19* Wu is forgotten, but not broken.

20 No Way Out teaches readers about one man's struggle for democracy and freedom from China's communist regime. *21* Through literature like this autobiography, we begin to understand other cultures and their histories, as well as explore the everyday lives of ordinary people living under extraordinary circumstances. *22* We see the human experience because literature brings history alive.

The Personal Essay

One of the best resources that every writer can call upon is personal experience. A **personal essay** focuses on a writer's experience to support or illustrate a main idea. The model essay that follows is a response to the Unit 4 writing assignment on page 393. In the essay, a student has used the story of her mother's accident to show what one can learn from adversity.

Finding Inner Strengths

1 Many people have had difficult times and, through the experience, triumphed over their misfortunes. 2 In the process, they find inner strengths that they did not know they had. 3 Jean Little's story, "Little by Little," tells about overcoming adversity, which is something I know about. 4 When my mother was hit by a car while crossing the street, I discovered a lot about life —— especially about what is important and what isn't.

5 I will never forget the day of the accident. 6 My baby brother and I were home with my grandmother when the police came to tell us my mother had been taken to the hospital. 7 Gram left my brother with a neighbor, and the two of us went to see Mom. 8 I don't think I've ever been as afraid as I was that day. 9 When the doctor came out to talk to us, he said that Mom's neck had been broken. 10 For days we were not sure she would live. 11 Finally, she was out of danger, but the doctors were not sure she would walk again. 12 After months in the hospital, Mom was moved to a rehabilitation center. 13 She began many more months of physical therapy. 14 It was tough, and it was painful.

15 Mom was very brave when we visited her, but I know it hurt her to be separated from us. 16 I told her we missed her, but I never told her how much. 17 It would have made her feel worse. 18 It was hard not having her there to

1–2. The first two sentences relate the personal essay to the assignment and introduce the writer's point, the thesis.

3. Specific selection is cited to reinforce the thesis.

4. Narrows the topic to the writer's personal experience.

5–14. The second paragraph explains the facts and events of the essay.

15–20. The third paragraph elaborates on the writer's inner feelings and gives specific examples that support the thesis.

see me in the school play or to help me with my homework. *19* Sometimes I resented having to do more household chores than I had before. *20* Every time I started to feel sorry for myself, though, I remembered what she was going through.

21 At last Mom came home. *22* She has almost completely recovered, except that she has a slight limp now when she's tired. *23* I learned a lot from Mom's ordeal. *24* Before the accident, I thought I was entitled to have a loving parent who cared about me. Now I know how lucky I am. *25* From watching Mom's struggle, I also learned that determination and hard work can overcome just about any problem.

21–25. Essay concludes by explaining what the writer learned.

The Persuasive Essay

Often you are asked to write an essay that expresses and defends your point of view. The model essay that follows was written in response to the Unit 3 writing assignment on page 303. The essay compares and contrasts two poems that protest political oppression.

Quest for Freedom

1 Yevgeny Yevtushenko's poem "The Heirs of Stalin" and Ilya Krichevsky's "Refugees" both express dislike of totalitarian rule and a longing for freedom. 2 Although one speaker is writing in the former Soviet Union to secure freedom and the other flees his native country to find freedom, the theme of freedom is central to both works. 3 However, I believe that "Refugees" is a more effective protest against oppression than "The Heirs of Stalin."

4 In "The Heirs of Stalin," Yevtushenko describes the misery of living under the Soviet Union's communist regime. 5 Although the poem takes place after Stalin's death, his power still lingers. 6 Yevtushenko pleads with his government to double the guards at his coffin to ensure Stalin will not rise again. 7 But even though Stalin is lying dead in his mausoleum, his followers still live. 8 Yevtushenko expresses fear over the threat to freedom that Stalin's heirs pose. 9 He declares that, "They, the former henchmen, hate a time when prison camps are empty, and auditoriums, where people listen to poetry, are overfilled." 10 At the conclusion, the only hope Yevtushenko sees to secure freedom is to eliminate Stalin's heirs, or else they will forever endanger his liberty.

11 Both Yevtushenko and Krichevsky long for freedom. 12 However, unlike Yevtushenko, who chooses and hopes for freedom, Krichevsky flees to

1. An introductory topic sentence expresses the thesis, or main idea, of the essay.

2–3. Specific examples are cited to support the thesis.

4–10. The second paragraph explains Yevtushenko's poem.

11–17. The third paragraph explains Krichevsky's poem and elaborates on its theme.

seek it. 13 In "Refugees," Krichevsky tells the reader of the risks that are taken in order to flee a totalitarian country. 14 He describes the challenges of wading through his country's swamps and forests and vast, barren lands. 15 He tells us of the constant threat of soldiers' guns that hunt the refugees down. 16 Nothing could break the will of the refugees as they fled toward freedom, even the hours with no food, sleep, or drink. 17 At the end, Krichevsky explains that the refugee is willing to endure these miseries in order to be free to live.

18 While both poems vividly express protest, "Refugees" is the more effective and my favorite. 19 Krichevsky brings the reader through all of the obstacles a refugee must endure, yet never lets the reader forget the goal—survival. 20 "Refugees" is a good example of literature's power to focus attention on oppression and injustice.

18-20. Selection concludes by restating the thesis in greater detail and expressing a personal opinion.

The Descriptive Essay

A **descriptive essay** creates images in the mind of the reader. By using vivid words and figurative language, the writer connects the person, place, or object being described with the experience of the reader. The essay that follows was written in response to the writing assignment on page 113. The essay describes a street scene.

Past and Present Meet in Cairo

1 What am I doing on a street in Cairo? 2 I was just reading about a place like this, and here I am! 3 The street is teeming with people. 4 The explosion of color, sound, and heat is amazing and confusing.

5 Where did all these people come from? 6 Cairo must be bursting at the seams! 7 The people are very different from each other. 8 Some of the men and women are dressed in Western attire; the men wear business suits and the women wear dresses and makeup. 9 Other people are in traditional Moslem garb. 10 Many women are wearing black veils that cover their faces, exposing only their eyes. 11 Clearly there are a variety of lifestyles in this cosmopolitan city.

12 Past and present clash in the street as an ox-cart competes with a luxury automobile for the right of way. 13 Horns blare, people shout, and hundreds of voices speak Arabic in a deafening blast of noise. 14 All of this takes place under a glaring sun, for it is summer and Cairo is like an oven. 15 This is all quite wonderful, but I want to go home!

1–2. Introductory sentences explain the setting.

3–4. Specific examples explain what will be described.

5–11. The second paragraph provides more details.

12–15. The third paragraph completes the description.

ALLITERATION *Alliteration* is the repetition of similar sounds, usually initial consonants, in a group of words. Poets and other writers use alliteration to connect and emphasize ideas and to create rhythmic and musical effects. In "A Night in the Royal Ontario Museum," Margaret Atwood uses alliteration, as illustrated in the line, "dragged to the mind's deadend."

ASSONANCE *Assonance* is when a writer uses repeated vowel sounds. This technique is especially important in poetry, where the spoken word is important. In "A Night in the Royal Ontario Museum," Atwood uses assonance throughout the poem. For example, look and listen to the long "a" sound in "crazed man-made/stone brain."

ALLUSION An *allusion* is a spoken or written reference to a well-known person, place, event, literary work, or work of art. Classical mythology, the Bible, Shakespeare, and world history are frequent sources of allusions in literature. Contemporary writers like Camara Laye sometimes make allusions to current events and to the particular history or experience of the audience they are addressing.

AUTHOR'S PURPOSE The *author's purpose* is the main idea the author wants to convey to the reader. To understand the author's purpose, the reader must first understand the central idea in the story or poem. In "A Call to Action" and "To the Tune 'The River Is Red,'" Ch'iu Chin's purpose is to call attention to the future of her country and what is needed to make that future better.

AUTOBIOGRAPHY An *autobiography* is an account of a person's life written by that person. Because autobiographies are written from the first-person point of view, using the pronouns *I* and *me,* they may not present the most objective account of events. However, they often offer vivid descriptions of events and people that only an eyewitness can provide. "No Way Out" by Harry Wu is an autobiographical account of Wu's failed attempt to escape Communist China.

CAUSE AND EFFECT *Cause and Effect* refers to a relationship between events. One event is said to be the cause of another event or effect. Life is characterized by many cause and effect relationships. In "Owner of the Sky: Olorun the Creator," the fact that the world is too wet *causes* Chameleon to return to the world.

CHARACTER A *character* is a person or animal that plays a role in a literary work. Characters are called *flat* or *round* depending on how they are developed by an author. Flat characters are one-dimensional, having one or two qualities that define and limit them. The characters in myths and fables are often flat. Round characters are more complex, with a mixture of qualities that make them seem more like real people. In "All the Years of Her Life" by Morley Callaghan, Mrs. Higgins is a round (or dynamic) character, while Mr. Carr is a flat character.

COMPARISON *Comparison* is an observation of similarities between two objects or events. In literature, authors use comparison to show similarities between the topics they are writing about. In "A Winter's Tale," Slavenka Drakulić compares her meal in Vienna with the rations of a person in war-torn Sarejevo.

CONFLICT A *conflict* in a literary work is a struggle between opposing forces. Sometimes the struggle is *internal,* meaning it takes place in the mind of a character.

Other conflicts are external. An *external* conflict may be a struggle between characters, between a character and society, or between a character and a force of nature. In "Marriage Is a Private Affair" by Chinua Achebe, Okeke faces a conflict with his son and an internal conflict with himself.

DIALECT A *dialect* is a unique form of a language spoken by the people of a particular region or cultural group. Writers often use dialect in a literary work to convey a realistic sense of character and setting. Dialectical differences appear in vocabulary, pronunciation, and grammar. "Zion, Me Wan Go Home" is a dialect poem from the Caribbean.

DIALOGUE *Dialogue* is conversation between characters in a piece of literature. It is often used to communicate plot details. Instead of telling the reader that a character is funny, the author can show that the character is funny through dialogue. In "Florinda and Don Gonzalo," everything that is revealed about the characters is through dialogue.

DIDACTIC WRITING *Didactic writing* is poetry or literature that teaches factual information or moral lessons. In order for didactic writing to be successful, the reader must be affected by the information or lesson being taught. In "The Marks of the Wise Man, of the Half Wise, and of the Fool," Rumi teaches the qualities that make men wise or unwise.

DRAMA A *drama,* or play, is a literary work written to be performed by actors on a stage. The playwright develops the story through *dialogue,* or the conversations of the characters. *Stage directions* give instructions about props, lighting, costumes, scenery, and the movement and gestures of the actors. Plays can be read and enjoyed as literature, but true drama exists only in performance. "Florinda and Don Gonzalo" is a drama in this book.

DRAMATIC MONOLOGUE A *dramatic monologue* expresses the words and thoughts of one person at an important time in his or her life. The reader is a silent listener in a dramatic monologue. Peter Blue Cloud reveals his thoughts in his dramatic monologue called "The Old Man's Lazy."

EPIC An *epic* is a long tale that tells of a hero's life, and reflects the values of the society where it began. Many epics are part of an oral tradition. "Sundiata" is an epic that is part of the Mali oral tradition.

ESSAY An *essay* is a short piece of nonfiction, usually focused on a single topic. Essays may be written for a variety of purposes and with different tones. The tone is usually determined by the purpose. An essay meant to inform or persuade usually has a more *formal* tone and structure than one meant to amuse or entertain. Personal essays usually focus on the personal experience of the authors. These essays are often *informal* and conversational in tone. A good example of an essay in this book is "A Winter's Tale."

FANTASY *Fantasy* elements in literature stress imaginative possibilities not found in real life. These include nonhuman characters, magical powers, and the suspension of the laws of nature, time, and space. *Realistic details,* on the other hand, make the characters, action, and setting seem true to life. In "The Bicycle" by Jerzy Harasymowicz, the poem blends fantastic elements with realistic elements.

FICTION *Fiction* is prose writing that deals with invented or imaginary events. Short stories like "4 + 1 = 1" are examples of fiction.

FIGURATIVE LANGUAGE *Figurative language* paints a picture in the reader's mind that is different from the meaning of individual words. Metaphors, similes, and personification are examples of figurative language. In "A Lover from Palestine" and "Warmth of Blood," both Darwish and al-Sharqawi use figurative language to make their poems more vivid and powerful.

FIGURE OF SPEECH A *figure of speech* describes one thing in terms usually applied to another. This image creates a vivid picture in the reader's mind. In "Tangaroa, Maker of All Things," the story uses a variety of figures of speech to create many vivid images in the reader's mind.

FOLKTALE A *folktale* is a story about common people that usually teaches a lesson about living in the world. Often folktales involve a clear struggle between good and evil that may be resolved by magic or other supernatural means. Many folktales are composed orally and are passed down from generation to generation by word of mouth. "The Ch'i-lin Purse" is an example of a Chinese folktale.

FORESHADOWING *Foreshadowing* is a technique that authors use to give hints or clues about what is going to happen in the story. These clues can come in a variety of ways. In "The Return," the title foreshadows the fact that Julian's madness may return.

FREE VERSE *Free verse* is poetry without regular rhythm or rhyme. In free verse, poets try to invent a rhythm uniquely suited to their subject. Repetition of words and sentences as well as creative placement of words on the page are common in free verse poems. In "And When Summer Comes to an End . . ." and "Please Give This Seat to an Elderly or Disabled Person," Nina Cassian uses free verse to express her emotions.

HISTORICAL CONTEXT *Historical context* is the particular time period in which a story is written. The historical context helps to explain what motivates characters to act in the ways that they do. Russia in the 1920's is the historical context of "The Servant." This is important because jobs were scarce in Russia at this time.

HUMOR *Humor* is writing that is meant to amuse the reader. Humor is often light in tone, and it focuses on unusual circumstances or people. In "My Financial Career," the narrator's mistakes and confusion at the bank are humorous.

IMAGERY *Imagery* is the use of descriptive words to create a sensory experience for readers, including sights, sounds, tastes, smells, and textures. Imagery contributes to the feeling or tone of a poem. In "Random Talk," "The Heirs of Stalin," and "Refugees," the three poets use imagery to express their feelings about oppression.

IRONY *Irony* refers to a contradiction between what appears to be true and what actually is true. In *verbal irony,* what is said is the opposite of what is really meant, for example, calling a deceptive person "noble." In *dramatic irony,* there is a contrast between what a character knows or expects and what the audience or reader knows. In *situational irony,* an event takes place that contradicts the expectations of the characters and the audience. The surprise ending is an example of situational irony. In "Action Will Be Taken," Heinrich Böll uses irony to convey his attitude about industry.

LYRIC POETRY *Lyric poetry* reminds the reader of a song. When reading a lyric poem, the reader can imagine someone singing it. In addition, lyric poems express strong personal feeling rather than tell a story. "Keeping Quiet" and "Chilean Earth" are two poems that have a songlike quality and also express personal feelings.

METAPHOR A *metaphor* is a figure of speech in which one thing is spoken of as though it were something else. In a metaphor, a comparison is suggested through identification. In "Warmth of Blood," al-Sharqawi uses metaphor when he compares his homeland to a cold jail cell.

MOOD *Mood* is the feeling, or atmosphere, created by a literary work or passage. Writers create mood by their choice of words, images, characters, and setting. In "The Room" and "The Street," the poets create distinct moods to communicate the overall meaning of their poems.

MORAL A *moral* is the lesson taught by a fable. The moral often gives instruction for good conduct. In the "Ch'i-lin Purse," Hsiang-ling is rewarded for an act of kindness she had done years before.

NONFICTION *Nonfiction* is prose writing that presents and explains ideas or that tells about real people, places, events, or objects. Autobiographies, biographies, journalism, like those you'll find in this book, are examples of nonfiction writing.

MOTIVATION The *motivation* in a story is the reason that characters behave in certain ways. Desire, experience, and emotion can affect a character's motivation. In "Till the Candle Blew Out," the motivation of the two boys is to impress Gentle-Flute.

MYTH *Myths* are fictional tales that explain the actions of gods or the causes of natural events. Myths often express the central values of the people who created them. "Popol Vuh" is a creation myth that explains how people were made.

NATIONALISM IN POETRY *Nationalism in poetry* is when a poet expresses pride in his native country. This pride can be political, ethnic, or geographical in nature. Nationalism in African poetry has become a literary movement called *Negritude.* "Interior" is an example of poetry from this movement.

ONOMATOPOEIA *Onomatopoeia* is the use of words that imitate sounds. Examples of such words are *buzz* and *hiss.* "A Night in the Royal Ontario Museum," by Margaret Atwood uses the word *roar,* which imitates a sound.

PERSONAL NARRATIVE A *personal narrative* is an account of an actual event. It usually takes the form of a story with characters and dialogue. However, it must be factual and accurately retold by the author. "Survival in Auschwitz" is a personal narrative of the author's experience in a Nazi concentration camp.

PERSONIFICATION *Personification* is a type of figurative language in which a nonhuman subject is given human qualities. Animals and forces of nature are frequently personified in poetry, folktales, and myths. The Polish poem called "The Bicycle" gives personal qualities to the bicycle.

PLOT The *plot* is the sequence of events in a literary work. In most dramas, novels, and short stories, the plot involves characters in a *central conflict.* The conflict is usually developed by means of a series of complications until it reaches a climax. The *climax* is the point of highest tension when *suspense,* or the reader's curiosity about the outcome, reaches its maximum intensity. The climax is usually followed by the *resolution,* or end, of the conflict. "Forty-Five a Month" is a good example of how a plot is formed in a literary work. Narayan's plot includes a central conflict, climax, suspense, and resolution.

POETRY *Poetry* is one of the three major types, or *genres,* of literature, along with prose (fiction and nonfiction) and drama. Language in poetry is usually more condensed and musical than in prose. Poems are made up of single units called *lines,* which are often grouped together in larger units called *stanzas.* All poems have rhythm, and some have regular rhythm and rhyme patterns. Most poems also contain vivid imagery and figurative language. You will find many examples of poetry in this book.

POINT OF VIEW The *point of view* is the perspective from which a story is told. The person who tells the story is called the *narrator.* In stories using the *first-person point of view,* the narrator is a character in the story and refers to himself or herself as "I." In stories told from the *third-person point of view,* the narrator is outside the story and refers to the characters by name or as "he" or "she." The *limited* third-person narrator sees everything through the eyes of one character. An *omniscient* third-person narrator knows and tells what *all* the characters think and feel. In "Hearing of the Earthquake in Kyoto (1830)," Sanyō uses both the first- and third-person point of view.

REALISM *Realism* is a style of writing in which details of actual life are given by an author. Realistic writing can be powerful because a reader can relate these details to their lives. In "The Bicycle," Harasymowicz uses realistic details like "the snow covered glade" to complement the fantastic elements of the poem.

REPETITION *Repetition* is the use of a sound, word, or group of words more than once to achieve a specific effect. Writers use repetition to emphasize meaning, link ideas, and create rhythm. A *refrain* is a phrase, line, or group of lines that is repeated at regular intervals in a work. In "Maui and the Great Fish," Te Kanawa repeats phrases such as, "I tricked you! I tricked you!" to emphasize the importance of the phrase.

RHYTHM *Rhythm* is the pattern of beats, or stresses, in spoken or written language. Traditional poetry usually has *meter,* a regular rhythmic pattern of stressed and unstressed syllables. Much modern poetry is *free verse,* which has its own irregular rhythms that suit its meaning. In the collection of Caribbean poems, a variety of rhythms are used by the poets to give their poems different spoken qualities.

SATIRE *Satire* is writing that ridicules or pokes fun at individuals, institutions, ideas, or other literature. In "The House on the Border," Nesin uses satire to describe the police department.

SENSORY DETAIL *Sensory details* are words or phrases that help readers imagine the exact events, people, places, things, or ideas that a writer is trying to describe. This helps the reader see, hear, smell, touch or feel the writer's experience. In "The Sea Eats the Land at Home," Awooner uses sensory details in phrases like, "And the mourning shouts of women/Calling on all the gods they worship" to help the reader see this scene.

SETTING The *setting* of a literary work is the time and place of the action. Setting provides a background for the action and is sometimes a crucial element in the plot or conflict. Often the setting creates a mood or atmosphere that helps convey the theme of the work. In "Butterflies" by Patricia Grace, the setting is extremely important because it helps convey the overall meaning of the story.

SEQUENCING Authors often use key words to let readers know the *sequence* of a story. Words like *first, next, later*, help the reader to follow the events of a story. In "The Nightingale's Three Bits of Advice," Pourrat uses sequencing words to help the reader follow the story.

SHORT STORY A *short story* is a brief work of fiction. Short stories usually have a single setting and only a few characters who are involved in a central conflict. You will find many short stories in this book.

SIMILE A *simile* is a figure of speech in which two things are compared using the words *like* or *as*. In "A Lover from Palestine," the author uses the simile "like an orphan" to compare himself to an abandoned child.

SURPRISE ENDINGS A *surprise ending* is the conclusion of a story that has an unforeseen twist. Even though the ending is unexpected, the author usually drops hints throughout the story to prepare the reader for what will happen. In "He-y Come on Ou-t!," Hoshi introduces an ending that should surprise readers.

SUSPENSE *Suspense* is a feeling of strong curiosity or uncertainty about the outcome of events of a story. Suspense is strongest when it involves a character that a reader cares about. In "One of These Days," by Gabriel García Márquez, the reader wonders what will happen when Aurelio Escovar and the Mayor meet.

SYMBOL A *symbol* is a person, place, or object that stands for something beyond itself. In "Children" by Pāṉṟiyaṉ Aṟivuṭai Nampi, the children symbolize all that is good in the world.

THEME The *theme* is the central idea or message about life that a writer conveys in a literary work. A theme may be stated directly. More often, however, writers communicate the theme indirectly, through characterization, plot, and setting. In "Savitri," the main theme is the power of love over death.

TONE The *tone* of a literary work is the writer's attitude toward the subject, the characters, or the reader. The tone might be lighthearted, amusing, reflective, impatient, or angry. Tone is conveyed by the choice of characters and situations and by the choice of language, or *diction*. Many words have *connotations*, or emotional associations for the reader, in addition to their *denotations*, or literal meanings. The connotations of the words a writer chooses affect the tone of a work.

TRICKSTER FOLKTALES A *trickster folktale* is a traditional story that involves a character (the trickster) who gets the better of others. The people the trickster fools do not even know they are being tricked until it is too late. In "Paying on the Nail," Shynail is a horse trader who gets the better of everyone he trades with.

WRITING STYLE A *writer's style* is his or her typical way of writing. Style includes word choice, sentence structure, figurative language, rhythm, and tone. In "If Not Still Higher," Peretz chooses to tell the story in the present tense. This choice is part of Peretz's writing style.

Index of Skills

Index of Artists and Titles

Abbeville Press, Inc., for "The Monster" by Nina Katerli, translated by Bernard Meares. Compilation copyright © 1990 E. I. Kalina and Abbeville Press, Inc. English translation copyright © 1990, Abbeville Press, Inc.

Addison Wesley Longman Ltd. for "Sundiata: An Epic of Old Mali" from *Sundiata: An Epic of Old Mali* by D.T. Niane, translated by G.D. Pickett, copyright © 1965, reprinted by permission of Addison Wesley Longman Ltd.

Antony Alpers, for "Tangaroa, Maker of All Things" by Antony Alpers, from *The World of the Polynesians*. First published in 1970 as *Legends of the South Seas*. Copyright © Antony Alpers, 1970.

Associated University Presses, Inc., for "The House on the Border" by Aziz Nesin from *Contemporary Turkish Literature* edited by Talat Sait Halman. Copyright © 1982, Associated University Presses, Inc.

Estate of Morley Callaghan, for "All the Years of Her Life" by Morley Callaghan.

Peter Blue Cloud, for "The Old Man's Lazy" from *Clans of Many Nations* Copyright © 1995 White Pine Press. Reprinted here with permission of the author.

Cambridge University Press, for "Song for the Sun That Disappeared Behind the Rainclouds" from *Moorish Poetry* by A. J. Arberry. Copyright © 1953, by permission of Cambridge University Press. Reprinted with the permission of Cambridge University Press. Also appeared in *African Poetry* edited by Ulli Beier, published by Cambridge University Press.

Columbia University Press, for "Children," "This World Lives Because," and "Tirumāl" from *Poems of Love and War*, translated by A. K. Ramanujan. Copyright © 1985 by Columbia University Press. Reprinted with permission of the publisher.

Estate of Harold Courlander, for "Bouki Rents a Horse" from *The Piece of Fire and Other Haitian Tales*. Copyright © 1964 by Harold Courlander. Reprinted by permission of the Estate of Harold Courlander.

Doubleday, for excerpt from *When Heaven and Earth Changed Places* by Le Ly Hayslip. Copyright © 1989 by Le Ly Hayslip and Charles Jay Wurts. Used by permission of Doubleday, a division of Bantam Doubleday Dell Publishing Group, Inc.; for "The Heirs of Stalin" by Yevgeny Yevtushenko, "Random Talk…" by Raisa Blokh, and "Refugees" from *20th Century Russian Poetry* by Yevgeny Yevtushenko. Copyright © 1993 by Doubleday, a division of Bantam Doubleday Dell Publishing Group, Inc. Used by permission of Doubleday, a division of Bantam Dell Publishing Group, Inc.

Dutton Signet, for "The Book of Sand" pp. 343–347, from *The Book of Sand* by Jorges Luis Borges, translated by Norman Thomas di Giovanni. Translation Copyright © 1971, 1975, 1976, 1977 by Emece Editores, S.A., and Norman Thomas di Giovanni. Used by permission of Dutton Signet, a division of Penguin USA Inc.

Farrar, Straus & Giroux, Inc. for "The Ch'i-lin Purse" from *The Ch'i-lin Purse: A Collection of Ancient Chinese Stories* by Linda Fang. Copyright © 1995 by Linda Fang, reprinted by permission of Farrar, Straus & Giroux, Inc.

Farrar, Straus & Giroux, Inc. for "The Dark Child" from *The Dark Child* by Camera Laye. Copyright © 1954 and copyright renewed © 1982 by Camera Laye, reprinted by permission of Hill and Wang, a division of Farrar, Straus & Giroux, Inc.

Farrar, Straus & Giroux, Inc. for "Keeping Quiet" from *Extravagaria* by Pablo Neruda. Translation copyright © 1974 by Alastair Reed, reprinted by permission of Farrar, Straus & Giroux, Inc.

Forest Books for "And When Summer Comes to an End…" by Nina Cassian. Copyright © 1988 by Forest Books, reprinted by permission of the publisher.

Reginald Gibbons, for "The Room" by Victor Manuel Mendiola, translated by Reginald Gibbons from *New Writing from Mexico*, copyright © 1992. Reprinted by permission of Reginald Gibbons © 1992.

Grove/Atlantic, Inc., for "Hearing of the Earthquake in Kyoto (1830)" by Rai Sanyō, from *Anthology of Japanese Literature* edited by Donald Keene. Copyright © 1995 by Grove Press, Inc. Used by permission of Grove/Atlantic, Inc.

Harcourt Brace & Company for "Olorun the Creator" from *In the Beginning*, text copyright © 1988 by Virginia Hamilton, reprinted by permission of Harcourt Brace & Company.

HarperCollins Publishers, Inc., for "Once a Great Love" from *Amen* by Yehuda Amichai. Copyright © 1977 by Yehuda

© 1959 by Orion Press, Inc., © 1958 by Giulio Einaudi editore S.P.A. Used by permission of Viking Penguin, a division of Penguin Books USA Inc.

Sinnathamby Rajaratnam for "The Tiger," reprinted by permission of the author.

Random House, Inc. for "The Return" by Carmen Laforet from *Great Spanish Stories* by Angel Flores, editor and translator. Copyright © 1956 by Random House, Inc. Reprinted by permission of Random House, Inc.

Random House, Inc. for "The Servant" from *Best Russian Stories* by Thomas Seltzer. Copyright © 1925 by The Modern Library. Reprinted by permission of Random House, Inc.

Regents of the University of California Press and the University of California Press, for Yusuf Idris' "The Chair Carrier" from *Arabic Short Stories* translated by Denys Johnson-Davies. Copyright © 1983, University of California Press. Reprinted with permission of the Regents of the University of California and the University of California Press.

Shapolsky Publishers, Inc., for "You Can't Fool Menashe" by Ephraim Kishon from *More of the Funniest Man in the World* Copyright © 1989. Reprinted here with permission of Shapolsky Publishers, Inc. 136 West 22nd Street, New York, NY 10011, (212) 633-2022.

Three Continents Press, Inc., for "A Lover from Palestine" by Mahmud Darwish, translated by Abdul Wahals Elmessiri from *Critical Perspectives on Arabic Literature.* Copyright 1980.

University Press of Virginia, for "The Prebend Gardens" by Léopold Sédar Senghor from *The Collected Poetry* edited by Léopold Sédar Senghor ©1990. Reprinted with permission of the University Press of Virginia.

University of Pittsburgh Press, for "Florinda and Don Gonzalo" which originally appeared as part of "Dialogues" by Luisa Josefina Hernández in *Selected Latin American One-Act Plays*, Francesca Colecchia and Julio Matas, eds. and trans. Published in 1973 by the University of Pittsburgh Press. Reprinted by permission of the publisher; for "Homecoming" from *Uncle Time*, by Dennis Scott, © 1973. Reprinted by permission of the University of Pittsburgh Press.

Kathleen Weaver, for "All That You Have Given Me, Africa" by Anoma Kanié, translated by K. Weaver from *Anthologie Negro-Africaine* edited by Lilyan Kesteloot © 1967.

White Pine Press, for "Chilean Earth" by Gabriela Mistral from *A Gabriela Mistral Reader*, translated by Maria Giachetti and published by White Pine Press, Fredonia, NY 14063. Translation copyright © 1993 by Maria Giachetti. Reprinted by permission of the publisher.

Steven White, for "The Great Prayer" by Alfonso Cortés, translated by Steven F. White, ed. and trans., *Poets of Nicaragua: 1918–1979.* Greensboro, North Carolina: Unicorn Press, 1982.

John Wiley & Sons, Inc., for "No Way Out" from *Bitter Winds: A Memoir of My Years in China's Gulag* by Harry Wu and Carolyn Wakeman. Copyright © 1994. Reprinted by permission of John Wiley & Sons, Inc.

Maria Wine for "Woman, You Are Afraid of the Forest" by Maria Wine 1996 (Translated by Nadia Christensen). Reprinted by permission of the author.

W. W. Norton & Company, Inc., for "Please Give This Seat to An Elderly or Disabled Person" by Nina Cassian, translated by Naomi Lazarad, from *Life Sentence: Selected Poems by Nina Cassian*, edited by William Jay Smith. Copyright © 1990 by Nina Cassian. Reprinted by permission of W. W. Norton & Company, Inc.

The Following Selections are in the Public Domain:

"The Marks of the Wise Man" by Rumi; "If Not Still Higher" by Isaac Leib Peretz; "The Oath of Athenian Youth," Anonymous; "Zion Me Wan Go Home," Anonymous; "My Financial Career" by Stephen Leacock.

UNIT ONE CHAPTER ONE
6,   Manu Sassoonian, Art Resource
11,   Granger Collection
21,   Museo Reale Africa Centrale, Art Resource
25,   Struan Robertson, Magnum Photos
28,   Werner Foreman/ Art Resource
32,   Ted Funk, FPG
33 T, Flavia de Faria Castro, FPG
33 B, World Image, FPG
37,   UPI/ Bettmann
45,   Sue Dorfman, Stock Boston
66,   United Nations
74,   Dick Doughty, Impact Visuals

UNIT ONE CHAPTER TWO
79,   Art Resource
81,   Art Resource
89,   Nimatallah/Art Resource
96,   Foto Marburg/ Art Resource
101,   The Jewish Museum, Art Resource
105,   The Jewish Museum, Art Resource
110,   Hillary Marcus, Impact Visuals

UNIT TWO CHAPTER THREE
118,   Scala/ Art Resource
121,   Granger Collection
130,   Art Resource
138,   The Metropolitan Museum of Art, John Stuart Kennedy Fund, 1913 (13.220.2)
141,   Art Resource
144,   FPG
149,   Bill Burke, Impact Visuals
161,   Peter Menzel, Stock Boston

UNIT TWO CHAPTER FOUR
164,   Victoria and Albert Museum/ Art Resource
167,   Free Library of Pennsylvania, Art Resource

174,   Bridgeman, Art Resource
176,   Josef Beck, FPG
177 T, Navaswan, FPG
177 B, Travelpix, FPG
180,   Granger Collection
189,   Wim Van Cappellen, Impact Visuals
194,   Sean Sprague/ Impact Visuals

UNIT TWO CHAPTER FIVE
197,   The Metropolitan Museum of Art, Gift of the Auckland Society of Arts, 1945 (45.159.1)
200,   Superstock
202,   Giraudon, Art Resource
205,   Mapping Specialists
210,   Bill Bachman, Photo Researchers
213,   Bettmann

UNIT THREE CHAPTER SIX
220,   Superstock
226,   Art Resource
232,   Superstock
235,   Art Resource
238,   Art Resource
244,   Telegraph Colour Library, FPG
245T, Travelpix, FPG
245B, M. Corsetti, FPG
247,   Olivia Heussler, Impact Visuals
251,   Giraudon, Art Resource
260,   Teun Voten, Impact Visuals

UNIT THREE CHAPTER SEVEN
263,   Giraudon/ Art Resource
265,   The Metropolitan Museum of Art, Fletcher Fund, 1926 (26.60.2)
269,   Art Resource
272,   Patrick Ward, Stock Boston
276,   Superstock
281,   Art Resource

290,	The Metropolitan Museum of Art, Purchase, Lila Acheson Wallace gift, 1992 (1992.146)
294,	Scala/ Art Resource
300,	The Metropolitan Museum of Art, Gift of Mr. & Mrs. Ira Haupt, 1950 (50.188)

UNIT FOUR CHAPTER EIGHT

308,	American Art Museum
310,	Werner Foreman Gallery, Art Resource
313,	David Maung, Impact Visuals
316,	Art Resource
320,	Art Resource
324,	Art Resource
330,	Janet Delaney, Impact Visuals
338,	Corbis Bettmann
340,	Art resource
346,	Art Resource
351,	The Bettmann Archive
355,	Collection of the Art Museum of the Americas, Organization of American States

UNIT FOUR CHAPTER NINE

361,	John De Visser, Masterfile
364,	Sherman Hines, Masterfile
369,	Giraudon, Art Resource
374,	FPG
375T,	Telegraph Colour Library, FPG
375B,	FPG
381,	Orde Eliason, Impact Visuals
386,	David Michael Davis, FPG
390,	Art Resource

ART INSERT

A1T,	Erich Lessing, Art Resource
A1B,	Courtesy of the Museum for African Art, NY
A2T,	Werner Foreman Archive, British Museum, London, Art Resource
A2B,	Superstock
A3T,	Courtesy of the United Nations
A3B,	Bridgeman Art Gallery
A4	Giraudon, Art Resource
A5T,	Scala, Art Resource
A5B,	SEF, Art Resource
A6	Bridgeman, Art Resource
A7R,	Victoria and Albert Museum, London, Art resource
A7T,	Erich Lessing/Art Resource
A7B,	Scala/Art Resource
A8	The Pierpont Morgan Library, Art Resource
A9T,	Giraudon, Art Resource
A9B,	Victoria and Albert Museum, London, Art Resource
A10T,	SEF, Art Resource
A10B,	The Bettmann Archive
A11T,	Art Resource
A11B,	Scala, Art Resource
A12 T,	Erich Lessing, Art Resource
A13T,	Superstock
A13B,	Superstock
A14T,	Schalkwijk, Art resource
A14 B,	Werner Foreman Archive, Art Resource
A15,	Collection of the Art Museum of the Americas, Organization of American States
A16T,	Superstock
A16BL,	Aldo Tutino, Art Resource
A16BR,	Werner Foreman Archive, Art Resource

ACHEBE, CHINUA. "Marriage Is a Private Affair." In *Girls at War and Other Stories*. William Heinemann, Ltd., 1972.

ALPERS, ANTONY. "Tangaroa, Maker of All Things." In *The World of the Polynesians*. Carry, North Carolina: Oxford University Press, 1987.

ALLFREY, PHYLLIS SHAND. "The Child's Return." In *Penguin Book of Caribbean Verse*. London: Penguin Books Ltd, 1986.

AMICHAI, YEHUDA. "Once a Great Love." In *Amen*. New York: HarperCollins Publishers, 1977. "Late in Life," and "In This Valley." In *Time*. New York: HarperCollins Publishers, 1979.

ATWOOD, MARGARET. "A Night in the Royal Ontario Museum." In *The Animals in That Country*. Ontario, Canada: Oxford University Press Canada, 1968.

DE AVELLANEDA, GERTRUDIS GOMEZ. "On Leaving." In *The Penguin Book of Women Poets*. London, England: Penguin Books Limited, 1980.

AWOONOR, KOFI. "The Sea Eats the Land at Home." In *Modern Poetry From Africa*. edited by G. Moore and Uli Beier. London, England: Penguin Books Limited, 1963.

BEIER, ULLI, translator. "Song for the Sun That Disappeared Behind the Rain Clouds." In *Moorish Poetry* edited by A.J. Arberry. New York: Cambridge University Press, 1953.

BIERLEIN, J.F. "Savitri," and "Popul Vuh." In *Parallel Myths*. New York: Ballantine Books, 1994.

BLOKH, RAISA. "Random Talk." In *20th Century Russian Poetry*. New York: Doubleday, 1993.

BLUE CLOUD, PETER. "The Old Man's Lazy." In *Clans of Many Nations*. White Pine Press, 1995.

BÖLL, HEINRICH. "Action Will Be Taken." In *18 Stories*. Verlag Kiepenheuer und Witsch, 1966.

BORGES, JORGES LUIS. "The Book of Sand." In *The Book of Sand* translated by Norman Thomas di Giovanni. New York: Penguin USA, 1977.

CALLAGHAN, MORLEY. "All the Years of Her Life." In *Six by Twelve: Short Stories by Canadian Writers* edited by John Metcalf. New York: McGraw Hill, 1970.

CASSIAN, NINA. "Please Give This Seat to an Elderly or Disabled Person." In *Life Sentence: Selected Poems by Nina Cassian*. New York: W.W. Norton & Company, Inc., 1990.

CHIN, CH'IU. "To the Tune 'The River Is Red,'" and "A Call to Action." In *Women Poets of China*. New York: New Directions Publishing Corporation, 1973.

CORTÁZAR, JULIO. "Continuity of Parks." In *End of the Game and Other Stories*. New York: Pantheon Books, a division of Random House, Inc., 1967.

CORTÉS, ALFONSO. "The Great Prayer." In *Poets of Nicaragua*. translated by Steven White. Greensboro, North Carolina: Unicorn Press, 1982.

COURLANDER, HAROLD. "Bouki Rents a Horse." In *The Piece of Fire and Other Haitian Tales*. New York: Harcourt Brace & World, 1964.

DARWISH, MAHMUD. "A Lover from Palestine." In *Critical Perspectives on Arabic Literature* edited by Issa J. Boullata. Colorado Springs, CO: Three Continents Press, 1980.

DRAKULIĆ, SLAVENKA. "A Winter's Tale." In *Balkan Express*. New York: HarperCollins Publishers, Inc., 1993.

FANG, LINDA. "The Ch'i-lin Purse." In *The Ch'i-lin Purse: A Collection of Ancient Chinese Stories*. New York: Farrar Straus & Giroux, Inc., 1995.

GOLDBERG, LEAH. "My Grandmother's House." In *The Penguin Book of Women Poets*. Edited by Carol Cosman, Joan Keefe, and Kathleen Weaver. London, England: Penguin Books Limited, 1978.

GORDIMER, NADINE. "A Chip of Glass Ruby." In *Selected Stories*. New York: Viking Penguin, 1961.

GRACE, PATRICIA. "Butterflies." In *Electric City and Other Stories*. Auckland, New Zealand: Penguin Books New Zealand Limited, 1987.

HAMILTON, VIRGINIA. "Owner of the Sky: Olorun the Creator." In *In the Beginning*. New York: Harcourt Brace, 1988.

HAYSLIP, LE LY. *When Heaven and Earth Changed Places*. New York: Doubleday, 1989.

HERNÁNDEZ, LUISA JOSEFINA. "Florinda and Don Gonzalo." In *Selected Latin American One-Act Plays*. Pittsburgh, PA: University of Pittsburgh Press, 1973.

HOSHI, SHIN' ICHI. "He-y, Come On Ou-t!" In *The Best Japanese Science Fiction Stories*. Edited by John L. Apostoloy and Martin H. Greenberg. Tokyo, Japan: Japan Foreign Rights Center, 1978.

HUCH, RICARDA. "Death Seed." In *The Penguin Book of Women Poets*. Edited by Carol Cosman, Joan Keefe, and Kathleen Weaver. London, England: Penguin Books Limited, 1978.

IDRIS, YUSUF. "The Chair Carrier." In *Arabic Short Stories* translated by Denys Johnson-Davies. Berkeley, CA: University of California Press, 1983.

IK, KIM YONG. "Till the Candle Blew Out." In *Love in Winter*. New York: Doubleday, 1968.

ISMAIL, ISMAIL FAHD. "4+1=1." In *The Literature of Modern Arabia*. London, England: Kegan Paul International Limited, 1988.

KANIÉ, ANOMA. "All That You Have Given Me, Africa." In *The Penguin Book of Women Poets*. London, England: Penguin Books Limited, 1980.

KATERLI, NINA. "The Monster." In *Soviet Women Writing*. New York: Abbeville Press, 1990.

KISHON, EPHRAIM. "You Can't Fool Menashe." In *More of the Funniest Man in the World*. New York: Shapolsky Publishers, Inc., 1989.

KRICHEVSKY, ILYA. "Refugees." In *20th Century Russian Poetry*. New York: Doubleday, a division of Bantam Doubleday Dell Publishing Group, Inc., 1993.

LAFORET, CARMEN. "The Return." In *Great Spanish Stories*. Translated by Angel Flores. New York: Random House, Inc., 1956.

LAYE, CAMARA. *The Dark Child*. New York: Farrar Straus & Giroux, 1954.

LEACOCK, STEPHEN. "My Financial Career." In *The Leacock Roundabout*. New York: Dodd Mead & Company, 1972.

LEVI, PRIMO. *Survival in Auschwitz* translated by Steven Wolf. New York: Viking Penguin, 1959.

LITTLE, JEAN. *Little by Little*. Ontario, Canada: Penguin Books Canada Limited, 1987.

MÁRQUEZ, GABRIEL GARCÍA. "One of These Days." In *Collected Stories*. New York: Harper & Row, 1984.

MAXWELL-HALL, AGNES. "Jamaica Market." In *3,000 Years of Black Poetry*. New York: Dodd Mead & Company, 1970.

MENDIOLA, VICTOR MANUEL. "The Room." In *New Writing from Mexico*, translated by Reginald Gibbons. TriQuarterly Books, 1992.

MHLOPE, GCINA. "The Toilet." In *Somehow Tenderness Survives: Stories of Southern Africa*. Edited by Hazel Rochman. New York: HarperCollins Publishers, 1988.

MISTRAL, GABRIELA. "Chilean Earth." In *A Gabriela Mistral Reader*. English translation by Maria Giachetti. Fredonia, New York: White Pine Press, 1993.

MUSASHI, MIYAMOTO. *A Book of Five Rings*. Woodstock, New York: The Overlook Press, 1974.

NARAYAN, R.K. "Forty-Five a Month." In *Malgudi Days*. New York: Penguin USA, 1982.

NIANE, D.T. "Sundiata: An Epic of Old Mali." Translated by G.D. Pickett. Essex, England: Longman Group Limited, 1965.

NUNUKUL, OODGEROO. "Family Council." In *Dreamtime: Aboriginal Stories*. New York: Lothrop, Lee & Shepard Books, a division of William Morrow & Co., Inc., 1972.

NERUDA, PABLO. "Keeping Quiet." In *Extravagaria*. Translated by Alastair Reid. New York: Farrar Straus & Giroux, 1974.

NESIN, AZIZ. "The House on the Border." In *Contemporary Turkish Literature.* East Brunswick, New Jersey: Associated University Presses, Inc., 1982.

O'FARRELL, PADRAIC. "Paying on the Nail." In *Humorous Folktales of Ireland.* Cork City, Ireland: Mercier Press Limited, 1989.

PAZ, OCTAVIO. "The Street." In *Early Poems of Octavio Paz.* Translated by Muriel Rukeyser. New York: New Directions Publishing Corporation, 1973.

PERETZ, ISAAC LOEB. "If Not Still Higher." In *Selected Stories* by Isaac Leib Peretz. New York, Schocken Books, 1974.

POURRAT, HENRI. "The Nightingale's Three Bits of Advice." In *French Folktales.* Translated by Royall Tyler. New York: Random House, Inc., 1989.

RAMANUJAN, A.K., translator. "This World Lives Because," "Children," and "Tirumal." In *Poems of Love and War.* New York: Columbia University Press, 1985.

SANYŌ, RAI. "Hearing of the Earthquake in Kyoto (1830)." In *Anthology of Japanese Literature* edited by Donald Keene. New York: Grove Press, Inc., 1955.

SCOTT, DENNIS. "Homecoming." In *Uncle Time.* Pittsburgh, PA: University of Pittsburgh Press, 1973.

SEMYONOV, S.T. "The Servant." In *Best Russian Stories.* New York: Random House, Inc., 1925.

SENGHOR, LÉOPOLD SÉDAR. "The Prebend Gardens," and "Interior." In *The Collected Poetry.* Charlottesville, Virginia: The University Press of Virginia, 1991.

AL-SHARQAWI, ALI. "Warmth of Blood." In *The Literature of Modern Arabia* edited by Salma Khadra Jayyusi. London, England: Kegan Paul International Limited, 1988.

TE KANAWA, KIRI. "Maui and the Great Fish." In *Land of the Long White Cloud.* New York: Arcade Publishing, Inc., 1989.

WINE, MARIA. "Woman, You Are Afraid." In *The Penguin Book of Women Poets.* London, England: Penguin Books Limited, 1978.

WU, HARRY and CAROL WAKEMAN. "No Way Out." In *Bitter Winds: A Memoir of My Years in China's Gulag.* New York: John Wiley & Sons, Inc., 1994.

YEVTUSHENKO, YEVGENY. "The Heirs of Stalin." In *20th Century Russian Poetry.* New York: Doubleday, 1993.